An Introduction to **FORTRAN IV** Programming

An Introduction to
FORTRAN IV Programming

A General Approach

Second Edition

PAUL W. MURRILL and CECIL L. SMITH

Louisiana State University

(includes appropriate implementation information and error codes for the WATFIV *compiler)*

INTEXT EDUCATIONAL PUBLISHERS
New York

To WHIT

Library of Congress Cataloging in Publication Data

Murrill, Paul W.
    An introduction to FORTRAN IV programming.
    "Includes appropriate implementation information and error codes for the WATFIV compiler."
    Includes index.
    1. FORTRAN (Computer program language) 2. Electronic digital computers—Programming. I. Smith, Cecil L., joint author. II. Title.
QA76.73.F25M88   1975   001.6'424   75-1284
ISBN 0-7002-2469-6

Intext Educational Publishers
666 Fifth Avenue
New York, New York 10019

Manufactured in the United States of America

Contents

Preface
to the Second Edition

The broad and significant acceptance of the First Edition has been, of course, a matter of deep satisfaction to all of those who had a role in its creation. Since its publication, however, there have been many changes both within the computing world and in the manner in which FORTRAN instruction is done. These, plus the experience with the First Edition, have convinced us that there is a need to publish this Second Edition, which we think has the following advantages over the previous edition:

1   Material describing modern developments in computer technology and usage are reflected in the text material. Since time-sharing systems are becoming more popular, discussion of their features is included, especially in Chapters 1 and 3. The instructor will need to supplement the text with material appropriate to any specific time-sharing terminal if one is used, however, since these systems do not have the degree of standardization that is present in conventional card-oriented systems.

2   This text strongly reflects the conviction that students should start to write short, simple programs at a very early stage of their learning experience.

The First Edition was oriented this way and this edition is even more slanted in this direction. Format-free input-output similar to that found in WATFIV is introduced so that the first programs can be written without the trauma of format. Concurrent presentation of format input-output is included, of course, for those systems that require its use. We like to allow students to write three or four programs without format and then to require it thereafter.

3   Material has been included on the WATFIV in-core compiler and its error messages are listed in an appendix. The text is, of course, not dependent on WATFIV; it is present only for student convenience.

4   The number of exercises—which was generous in the First Edition—has been increased and significantly revised.

5   Functions and subordinates were not treated in an especially effective manner in the First Edition; but we think in the current version the exercises themselves have been improved.

6   The treatment of input-output operations has an in-depth coverage in a later chapter (plus, of course, elementary presentations in early chapters), and discussion of handling character data is more useful.

7   Compilers change—one example is the manner in which they handle mixed-mode arithmetic. The First Edition implied that mixed-modes were taboo. Students often quickly learned, however, that the particular compiler they were using could accept mixed-modes, and they would then use such operations without understanding the potential hazards. This Second Edition handles this in a much more direct fashion.

8   The entire text offers a better treatment of such things as compilation, operating systems, computer characteristics, and FORTRAN itself.

We want to express our sincere thanks and appreciation to all those who helped us in this revision—especially to those who have sent us suggestions from colleges and universities throughout the United States. Such assistance, when coupled with the thoughtful advice and aid given to us by our own students and colleagues, make us hope this edition is a significant improvement over the First Edition.

INTRODUCTION TO DIGITAL COMPUTERS

The steam engine and other devices for doing work gave man an extension of his physical capabilities and brought about the Industrial Revolution. In a very similar manner, electronic computers are providing man with tools with which he can process quantities of information and solve problems that otherwise would be impossible to handle. These computers are producing an *informational revolution* that will have more impact on each of our everyday lives than any other aspect of modern technology—even atomic energy. The purpose of this book is to assist you, as a student, in learning to utilize these computers in your day-to-day work.

1-1. DIGITAL-COMPUTER CHARACTERISTICS

Modern electronic computers are of two basic types—digital and analog. The entire content of this book is directed toward understanding and programming digital computers, and no attention is devoted to the study of analog computers or combinations of analog and digital computers (hybrid computers).

Digital computers can be appreciated best by first considering some of their characteristics. Understanding these characteristics will help us to appreciate their usefulness.

1

One of the most prominent characteristics of digital computers is their truly incredible *speed*. Although they only work one step at a time, i.e., *sequentially*, they perform their tasks at rates that are beyond the comprehension of the novice. As an example, some large machines are capable of adding together several hundred thousand 16-digit numbers in less than a second. These tremendous speeds make it possible for the machine to do work in a few minutes that might otherwise require years of time.

Not only is the digital computer capable of working very rapidly, but it also has a perfect *memory*. It has virtually instantaneous "recall" of both data and instructions that are stored inside, and it never forgets or loses the accuracy of the information which it has within its memory.

A digital computer is an extremely *accurate* device. In most machines numbers are handled with seven, eight, or nine significant digits, and twice this accuracy can usually be obtained by the programmer. This means that a machine would have no difficulty multiplying 2782.4362 times 40.127896 and obtaining the product correct to 8 or 16 significant figures.

Coupled with the significant characteristics already listed, the digital computer does its work *automatically*. It can accept instructions from its operator, and then execute these instructions without need for human intervention. This implies that the machine can be given a problem; then while you attend a movie, it will do your work with incredible accuracy and at fantastic speeds. Learning to use such a tool should require no further motivation.

Additional characteristics of the digital computer will be noted later, but for the present it will be more advantageous to see how the machine works.

1-2. HOW THE DIGITAL COMPUTER WORKS

The digital computer is basically a device to accept *data* and a set of instructions as to how to manipulate these data in order to produce a set of answers. The set of instructions is called the *program*, and these are prepared by a *programmer* (you). (See Figure 1-1.) This book is primarily concerned with the preparation of programs. Sometimes

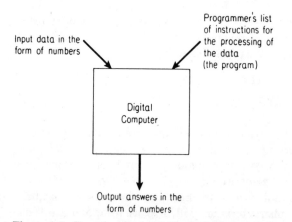

Figure 1-1. Functional role of the digital computer.

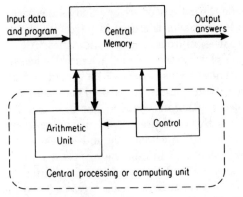

Figure 1-2. Relation of memory unit, arithmetic unit, and control unit (solid arrows represent information flow, dashed arrows represent control signals).

Device	"0" State	"1" State
Current pulse on a wire	No pulse	Pulse
Magnetic field in a magnetic core	Clockwise	Counterclockwise
Switch	Open	Closed

Figure 1-3. Examples of binary devices.

the data may be contained within the program; but more often the data are entered into the computer after the program.

In general, the computer may be thought of as being composed of three main sections: the memory, the central processing unit (CPU), and the input/output processor. The computer *memory* is used for storing data, instructions, intermediate results, and final answers; the *central processing unit* performs all the necessary manipulations of the data; and the *input/output processor* communicates with the outside world. (See Figure 1-2.) Transfer of instructions and data among these units takes very little time—in some machines less than one millionth of a second.

All information and signals in transit inside the computer are handled as electrical signals (usually pulses), and in memory this information is stored in magnetic cores, switches (flip-flops), and/or as magnetized spaces on drums, discs, and tapes. All of these devices are designed to exist in only one of two states which we may associate with the symbols 0 and 1. (See Figure 1-3.) These two states may be considered as *binary digits* or *bits* (a contraction of *"bi*nary dig*its"*) and are used to represent information. Thus the number system employed is basically binary; but it is usually more convenient for instructions and addresses to be "represented" in the octal or hexadecimal number systems. Nonnumeric information (alphabetic and special symbols) in a computer is represented in a binary code, and numbers are represented in one of two ways: In a *binary-coded decimal system* (each digit coded in a fixed number of bits) or the decimal numbers are converted into the *binary number system* (used in most computers primarily designed for scientific work).

1-3. CONTROL AND OPERATION OF THE COMPUTER

While it is not necessary to understand such topics as binary arithmetic, the electronics of digital circuits, or other topics fundamental to the design of digital computers in order to learn to program in FORTRAN, a superficial understanding of the general operation of digital computers will easily reveal the origins of certain rules and conventions incorporated into the FORTRAN language. In reality, FORTRAN reflects basic machine characteristics to a greater extent than most other computer languages.

The general schematic diagram of the computing system in Figure 1-2 is shown in a little more detail in Figure 1-4. As pointed out in the last section, this system is broadly divided into three units: central processing unit, memory, and input/output processor.

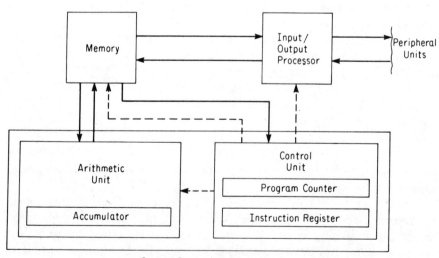

Figure 1-4. Schematic diagram of a simple computer (solid arrows represent information flow; dashed arrows represent control signals).

The central processing unit is further divided into two subunits: the arithmetic unit and the control unit. The *arithmetic unit* is responsible for performing operations such as additions, comparisons, etc., on the information in memory. The *control unit* is responsible for interpreting the instructions sequentially in memory and directing the arithmetic unit and input/output processor to perform the appropriate operations.

The concept of storing both the instructions (i.e., the program) and the data in the same memory unit has been of utmost importance in the development of computing machines. The very earliest computers employed hand-wired programs which made them inconvenient to use. The brilliant mathematician John von Neumann proposed the stored program concept which, coupled with the remarkable advances in electronics technology, led directly to computing machines as we know them today.

Since the central memory plays such an important role in the operation of the computer, a clear view of the organization of this memory is essential. Perhaps the most vivid way of visualizing the memory of the computer is as a set of mailboxes called memory cells, memory locations, or storage locations. This analogy is quite appropriate. In each individual memory cell only one word of information may be stored at any one time. This word of information may be either data (numerical or nonnumerical) or computer instructions. Each memory cell has its own individual address, and it is common to refer to memory cells by their addresses. The word contained in the memory cell appears as a binary number, and by superficial inspection there is no way to identify whether this word is data or whether it is an instruction. The computer must be told explicitly which memory cells contain instructions and which contain data. The control unit of the computer will treat the contents of a memory cell (a word) as though it were an instruction, and the arithmetic unit of the computer will treat the contents of a memory cell as though it were data. Each individual memory cell (or word) contains a fixed, preset number of digits, and that number of digits will limit the amount of significant information that can be stored in that memory cell. The instructions that are used by the computer for the processing of information are constructed so that they deal with memory-cell addresses.

As pointed out in the first section of this book, the digital computer is a sequential machine. Its operation is a sequence of cycles, each of which consists of two phases: a *fetch* phase and an *execute* phase. The fetch phase uses two registers in the control unit: the *program counter* and the *instruction register*. The program counter is often referred to by the more descriptive name of *instruction address register*, and it always contains the address of the next instruction to be executed. At the beginning of the fetch phase, the contents of the location in memory whose address is currently in the program counter is loaded into the instruction register. Therefore, the contents of this memory location will be treated as an instruction. At the completion of the fetch phase the program counter is incremented by one, so that it now points to the next instruction to be retrieved from memory.

At the start of the execution phase, the control unit decodes the instruction and issues specific commands to the various elements of the arithmetic unit. In performing its operations, the arithmetic unit utilizes a register called the accumulator to contain the data on which it is to operate. For example, a typical instruction might be to add the contents of a specific storage location in memory to the current contents of the accumulator. The instruction itself contains the address of the memory location involved and a group of bits (called the *operation code*) whose pattern indicates that addition is to be performed. The control unit relays the address to the memory addressing circuits in order to retrieve the contents of the storage location, and activates the "add" circuit in the arithmetic unit to achieve the desired result.

To illustrate the sequence of operations, suppose we examine the instructions required to add the contents of two storage locations (specifically, at addresses 2749 and 1398) and store the result in a third storage location (specifically, at address 1972). Three instructions are required:

Instruction	Explanation
LW, 2749	"Load Word" copies the contents of the storage location at address 2749 into the accumulator.
AW, 1398	"Add Word" adds the contents of the storage location at address 1398 to the current contents of the accumulator.
STW, 1972	"STore Word" copies the contents of the accumulator into the storage location at address 1972.

In the above explanations, note the use of the word "copies." The instruction LW, 2749 in no way alters the contents of the storage location at address 2749. Similarly, the instruction STW, 1972 does not alter the contents of the accumulator, but does obliterate whatever was previously contained in the storage location at address 1972. Although not specifically mentioned, the instruction AW, 1398 does not alter the contents of the storage location at address 1398. These points can be summarized by the following rule: Read operations on memory are nondestructive; write operations on memory are destructive. FORTRAN follows this rule exactly.

To further illustrate the sequence of operations, suppose the three instructions are stored in the memory locations at addresses 1027, 1028, and 1029. If the program counter initially contains 1027, the sequence of operations is as follows:

1 The contents of the storage location at address 1027 are copied into the instruction register.

2 The program counter is incremented by 1, giving 1028.

3 The contents of the storage location at address 2749 are copied into the accumulator.

4 The contents of the storage location at address 1028 are copied into the instruction register.

5 The program counter is incremented by 1, giving 1029.

6 The contents of the storage location at address 1398 are added to the contents of the accumulator.

7 The contents of the storage location at address 1029 are copied into the instruction register.

8 The program counter is incremented by 1, giving 1030.

9 The contents of the accumulator are copied into the storage location at address 1972.

Many current computers could perform all these operations in less than ten millionths of a second.

Of course, current computers offer far more features than illustrated by the previous example, but their operations are basically straightforward. The examination of these other features is inappropriate for an introductory manual on FORTRAN.

1-4. PROGRAMMING LANGUAGES

In the previous section we discussed how the computer would execute a program: In this section we want to examine the preparation of a program.

Writing a program directly in instructions, as described in the previous section, is said to be programming either in assembly language or in machine language. While this approach is relatively straightforward, it becomes tedious, especially for large programs. In essence the available instructions comprise the computer's language, which we could learn to speak, but would rather not. Of course, the best solution would be for the computer to speak our native language, which for most readers of this book would be English. Unfortunately, this goal has not yet been achieved, although progress is being made.

The current solution is to use an intermediate language that has some of the characteristics in which problems are naturally expressed, but a language that is sufficiently rigorous to permit the computer to perform the translation from the program written in the programming language into the instructions that comprise the computer's natural language. This situation is illustrated in Figure 1-5. The programmer must translate the statement of the problem into statements in the programming language. Using a program known as a *compiler*, the computer translates the statements in the programming language into machine-executable instructions, a process referred to as *compilation*.

Since the statement of problems tends to differ from discipline to discipline, several different programming languages have appeared, each with special characteristics that make one language more attractive to some fields and disciplines than to others. In the business field, COBOL (COMMON BUSINESS ORIENTED LANGUAGE) has dominated, primarily because its features enable large files of data to be manipulated readily. In science areas, FORTRAN (FORMULA TRANSLATOR) has dominated, primarily because algebraic expressions can be readily implemented. However, FORTRAN has enjoyed some use in business circles. The last decade saw the introduction of several new languages, some

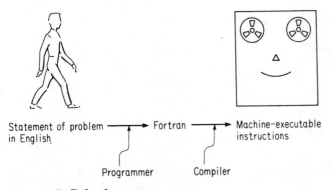

Statement of problem ———▶ Fortran ———▶ Machine-executable
in English   instructions

Programmer   Compiler

Figure 1-5. Role of FORTRAN.

of which are easier to learn than FORTRAN, some of which are more powerful than FORTRAN, and some of which accomplish objectives (text editing, for example) that FORTRAN was never designed to accomplish. Nevertheless, FORTRAN continues to enjoy widespread use, and it will probably continue to do so for the foreseeable future.

Since its introduction in the mid-1950s, FORTRAN has gone through an evolutionary process that has enhanced its utility as a programming language. The last major extension of the language occurred in the early 1960s. At that time, most operational versions of FORTRAN were referred to as FORTRAN II. So many new features were added to the language at that time that the name was changed to FORTRAN IV. Although the FORTRAN available on some current machines is closer to FORTRAN II than FORTRAN IV, the bulk of the manufacturers have implemented FORTRAN IV. Therefore, this text will be devoted almost exclusively to FORTRAN IV.

Although the American National Standards Institute (ANSI) has adopted a standard for the FORTRAN IV language, the implemented versions available on commercial computers normally contain some (usually) minor variations or extensions. In a text such as this, we shall tend to present what we think are the more common implementations. However, at many points these discrepancies force us to use "double-talk" or to insert hedging words such as *generally* or *usually*. Any uncertainties can be clarified by consulting the manuals provided by the computer manufacturer; but these are written for the experienced programmer rather than for the beginner.

A very simple example of a FORTRAN program is shown in Figure 1-6. This program computes the payroll of a business as:

WAGE PAYROLL = (PAY RATE WHICH IS $2.60 PER HOUR) (HOURS WORKED PER PERSON) (NUMBER OF EMPLOYEES)

or

WAGES = (2.60) (HOURS) (PEOPLE)

or

W = (2.60) (H) (P)

In the program in Figure 1-6, the first two statements assign numerical values to variables H and P. The third statement embodies the equation given above with the asterisk (*) denoting multiplication. The fourth statement instructs the computer to

```
1          H=8.0
2          P=6
3          W=2.60*H*P
4          PRINT,'WAGES  =',W
5          STOP
6          END
```
(a) Program

```
WAGES  =        0.1248000E  03
```
(b) Output data

Figure 1-6. Example of a FORTRAN program.

print the characters WAGES = followed by the numerical value of W. The fifth statement, the STOP statement, terminates execution of the program. The END statement informs the compiler that there are no more statements in the program. We shall dwell on the distinction between the STOP and the END statements in more detail in Chapter 3.

In FORTRAN, the statements in the program are executed sequentially, starting with the first statement and continuing until a STOP statement is executed. The output from the program in Figure 1-6 is written in exponential notation with E standing for "10 to the power." That is, the notation .1248000E03 actually means .1248 × 10^3 or 124.80.

1-5. COMPILATION

The statements in the programming language are translated into an equivalent set of machine-executable instructions by programs known as compilers. This must occur prior to the performance of any operation specified within the program, and this act of translation is generally referred to as the *compilation phase*.

Compilers come in two "styles," one of which is referred to as a load-and-go compiler. A *load-and-go* compiler reads the statements in the program, generates the corresponding machine-executable instructions, and places them directly into another area of memory (see Figure 1-7). During this process, the CPU is executing the set of instructions that comprise the compiler. After processing the last statement in the program, and storing the last machine-executable instruction in memory, the compilation phase is completed. An instruction in the load-and-go compiler then directs the CPU to the first instruction in the set of instructions generated from the user's program, and the *execution phase* begins. The CPU executes this set of instructions until all opera-

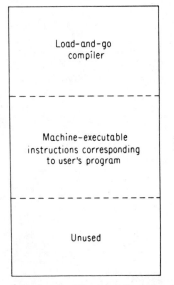

Figure 1-7. Memory allocation for a load-and-go compiler.

tions called for by the user's program have been completed. For any logical termination point in the user's program (such as a STOP statement in FORTRAN), the load-and-go compiler generates instructions that direct the CPU to return to a predetermined location within the compiler itself. When these instructions are executed at the end of the execution phase, the CPU is directed to return to the compiler, thus terminating the execution phase. At this point the user's program has been completed, and the compiler can instruct the computer to proceed to the next program to be run.

Instead of storing the generated instructions directly into memory, many compilers produce the set of machine-executable instructions on punched cards, magnetic tape, or other medium suitable for subsequent reentry of the information into the computer. The sequence of phases is as follows (refer to Figure 1-8):

1 *Compilation phase.* The compiler is entered into memory, followed by the statements written in the programming language (these statements are called the *source program*). The compiler generates the machine-executable instructions on some medium from which they can be subsequently reentered into the computer. This set of instructions is generally referred to as the *object deck* (if cards) or *object program*.

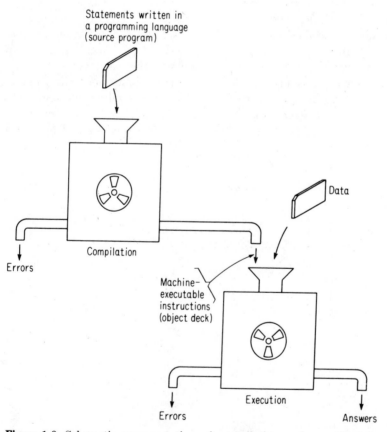

Figure 1-8. Schematic representation of compilation and execution phases for a compiler that generates an object deck.

2 *Load phase.* Before the set of instructions can be executed, they must be entered into memory. The *loader* is a small program that reads the instructions and places them in memory. Since the compiler's task has been completed, these instructions can be placed in the same area of memory that was used for the compiler.

3 *Execution phase.* Upon completion of the load phase, the loader directs the CPU to the first instruction in the user's program.

As for the relative advantages of the two types of compilers, the following observations are pertinent:

1 Although we will not consider errors in detail until a later chapter, load-and-go compilers are generally able to provide the programmer more information concerning errors, especially during the execution phase. Compilers that produce object decks are poorer in this respect.

2 The load-and-go compiler resides in memory during the execution of the program. Compilers that produce an object deck need not reside in memory past the compilation phase, freeing this memory for use by the program. Thus, larger programs can be run.

3 If the same program is to be executed several times, an object deck can be saved and the compilation phase avoided in all except the first run. Since a load-and-go compiler produces no object deck, the compilation phase must be repeated. However, compile time for load-and-go compilers is generally short.

Although a number of other observations could be made, for small- to medium-scale programs a load-and-go compiler has definite advantages, particularly with respect to the error messages generated. Large users and programmers in production-oriented centers prefer compilers that produce an object deck.

1-6. BATCH PROCESSING SYSTEMS

Computing systems can be divided into two broad categories with respect to orientation toward users: batch processing systems versus conversational time-sharing systems. Since batch processing appeared first chronologically, we shall consider it before considering conversational time-sharing.

As the operational complexity of general-purpose computing systems continued to increase, centers began to use professional computer operators to operate the machines instead of permitting individual programmers to operate them. Furthermore, the load at most centralized facilities is such that some jobs are almost always waiting to be run. The programmer brings his program to the center, leaves it to be run by the professional operators, and returns for it at some later time. The term *turnaround* encompasses these steps. How long he has to wait (referred to as the *turnaround time*) depends upon a number of factors: the current load on the center, the priority of his work, the running time and memory requirements of his program, etc. The number of times he can have his program run during a day is determined by the turnaround time. Centers at which the programmer is limited to four turnarounds or less per day are not unusual, although many centers do considerably better.

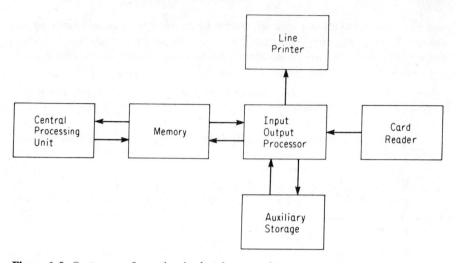

Figure 1-9. System configuration for batch processing.

In explaining the batch processing mode of operation, we shall use the system in Figure 1-9 as the basis of our discussion. This is a relatively minimal configuration, but it will suffice for our purposes.

In the system of Figure 1-9, programs are submitted in the form of punched cards such as the one illustrated in Figure 1-10. This is the so-called Hollerith card, named after Dr. Herman Hollerith who developed the concepts basic to this type of punched card for use in the compilation of the 1890 census. (The 80-column card itself dates back to the 1930s.) The punched card is a cheap and versatile type of input/output medium. It has 80 vertical columns and can hold 80 characters of information—either letters, numbers, or punctuation. The standard card contains ten "number" rows for representing any number from 0 to 9. The ten number rows have above them two zone rows, 11 and 12. The punched card is arranged so that a punch in a single

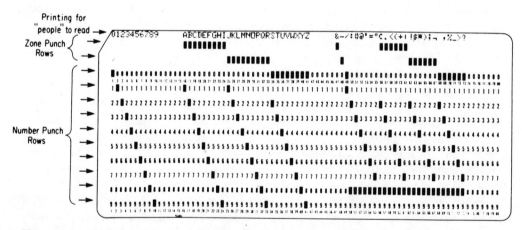

Figure 1-10. A typical punched card shows typical FORTRAN character code. This punched code varies slightly, depending on the specific computer.

number column will represent a digit; by making two or three punches in a single column it is possible to represent any letter of the alphabet or one of the special characters. This is seen vividly in Figure 1-10. The symbolic language of the punched card is automatically translated by the computer into binary information for its internal use.

In a batch processing environment, a supervisory-type program often referred to as the *operating system, executive,* or *monitor* is responsible for directing the computing system through whatever sequence of events is necessary to process the job, as illustrated in Figure 1-11.

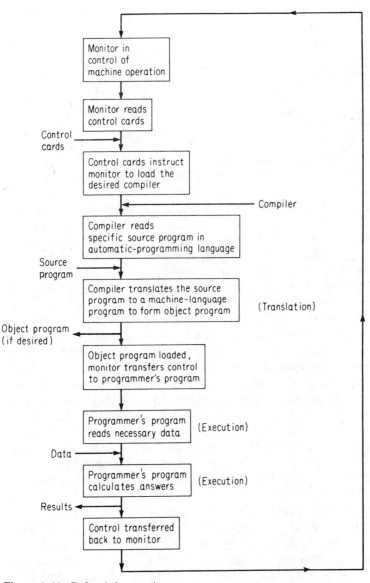

Figure 1-11. Role of the monitor.

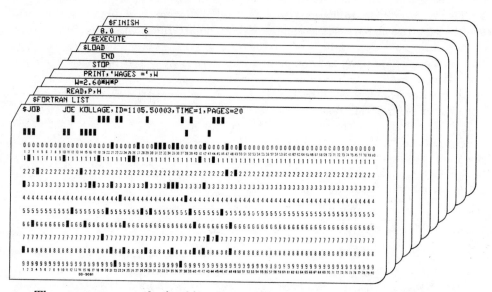

The programmer submits his program along with any necessary *control cards* with which he informs the operating system as to the nature of his program and what actions will be necessary to process it. Figure 1-12 illustrates a typical deck complete with control cards for processing a FORTRAN program. In computer terminology this complete deck is called a "job."

In the deck illustrated in Figure 1-12, each control card begins with the character $. The $JOB control card indicates the beginning of a new job. The programmer's name is given along with his identification number for bookkeeping purposes, an estimated maximum run time (1 minute), and an estimated maximum for pages of output (20 pages). Should this program run more than one minute or print more than 20 pages of output, the job will be "aborted," i.e., terminated, and the next job begun.

The next control card, $FORTRAN, indicates that the programmer is submitting a FORTRAN program. In response to this card, the operating system directs the CPU to copy into memory the FORTRAN compiler from an auxiliary storage device. Once this is completed, the statements comprising the FORTRAN program are processed. The LIST option on the $FORTRAN card instructs the compiler to list the source program as it is being compiled. If the compiler produces an object deck, it will be written into a preassigned area on the auxiliary storage unit.

Encountering the $LOAD card, the operating system copies into memory the loader from the auxiliary storage device. The loader in turn copies into memory the object deck from the auxiliary storage device. If a load-and-go compiler were used, this step would be unnecessary.

Upon processing the $EXECUTE card, the operating system directs the CPU to the first instruction in the program. If the FORTRAN program contains any READ statements, the actual READ operation does not occur until the program is executed. The program in Figure 1-12 is identical to the program in Figure 1-6 except that numerical values for D and H are entered via a READ statement. Therefore, one data card containing the two numerical values is placed immediately after the $EXECUTE card.

Upon completion of the job, the operating system proceeds to the next control card to ascertain what other actions are needed. The $FINISH card informs the system that nothing else is to be done. Were another job waiting to be run, the $FINISH card could be removed and the next job immediately fed into the card reader.

While the batch processing system described in this section is fairly representative of one used on small- to medium-size computers, larger computers provide much more flexibility and capability in manipulating the processing of jobs to achieve maximum efficiency. However the basic process, at least as far as the programmer is concerned, is little different from that presented here.

One user might find this mode of operation very convenient, another might find it very inconvenient. Anyone who is running a large problem, or a problem that runs a long time, is generally content to leave his job for someone else to run when his turn comes. For the small user whose program is very short and runs quickly, the waiting time between job submission and return is, to say the least, inconvenient. Conversational time sharing is a more attractive alternative.

1-7. CONVERSATIONAL TIME SHARING

The basic idea behind conversational time sharing is that several users have programs in progress simultaneously on the same computing system. In the simplest implementations, the only components needed in the computing system are the CPU, memory, some auxiliary storage, and a teletype for each of the users. Figure 1-13 illustrates the configuration of a conversational time-sharing system supporting four users simultaneously. The operating system occupies a region of memory, and the remainder is divided among the four users of the system.

In addition to receiving his proportionate share of the system's memory, each programmer gets his proportionate share of the central processing unit's time, which is divided into small increments called slices. A user receives the processor's undivided attention for one time slice, but then receives no attention over the next three time slices. Therefore, he is receiving 25% of the processor's time minus the small overhead entailed in switching from one program to the next. These time slices are so small that each programmer feels he has the computer's continuous services. Although his program runs slower (as measured by the "clock on the wall") than it would if he were the only user, this is more than offset by the added convenience of being immediately able to get his fraction of the machine's services. He need not wait to have the entire computer at his service.

Although conversational time-sharing systems are commercially available in configurations similar to the one in Figure 1-13, machines with larger configurations can offer a wider spectrum of services. Large conversational time-sharing systems can simultaneously serve 50 or more users. If a large auxiliary storage unit is available, each user can be assigned some space in which he can store programs or data to be available the next time he uses the system. Large systems generally offer other programming languages in addition to FORTRAN.

In many systems the communication between terminal and computer is over telephone lines; this permits the user to be located hundreds of miles from the computer. When the user wants to use the computer, a telephone number is dialed in the same manner as other telephone calls.

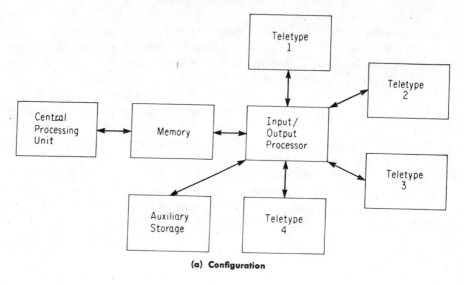

(a) Configuration

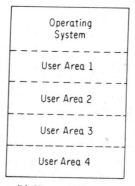

(b) Memory allocation

Figure 1-13. Small conversational time-sharing system for running FORTRAN.

To illustrate the conversational nature of the dialogue between the user and the computer, a typical teletype printout is shown in Figure 1-14. All computer responses are underlined. In the left margin, numbers have been added to facilitate explanation of the printout.

1 After the call has been initiated, the computer responds with a message identifying the system along with other data of general interest such as the time of day and the number of other users.

2 The user must enter his identification number for bookkeeping purposes. To prevent the unauthorized use of this number by other, a password that is not printed on the teletype output must be entered. A proper identification number followed by an improper password will not be accepted as valid.

3 The user informs the computer that he wants to run a FORTRAN program.

17

```
1 { HILBILLY TIME-SHARING SERVICE
    ØN AT 10:27    TTY:   07

2 { ENTER USER NØ:   X547
    ENTER PASSVØRD:

3   SYSTEM?  FØRTRAN

4   ØLD ØR NEW?   NEW

5 { NEW FILE NAME:   JØHN

    INVALID FILE NAME
    FILE NAME IN USE

    NEW FILE NAME:   MARY

    READY

6 { 10 ACCEPT,H,P
    20 W=2.60*H*P
    30 PRINT,"WAGES =",W
    40 STØP
    50 END

7 { SAVE

    READY

8 { RUN

    ?   8.0,6

    WAGES =      124.80

    READY

9 { BYE

    ØFF AT 10:51
```

Figure 1-14

4 By entering NEW, the user indicates that the program is to be created at the terminal.

5 The first file name, JOHN, that is entered is not accepted because the user already has a file by that name in the system. The name MARY is acceptable. Upon completion of the necessary housekeeping chores associated with creating a new file, the computer types READY to inform the user that he can proceed.

6   The FORTRAN program is entered from the terminal. Many systems scan the statements for syntax errors as they are entered, thus indicating errors immediately so that they can be corrected before proceeding.

7   By entering SAVE, the user instructs the computer to store a copy of the program on the auxiliary storage unit. Upon completion, the computer again types READY.

8   The command RUN instructs the computer to execute the program. The FORTRAN program in Figure 1-14 is identical to the one in Figure 1-6 except that the values of D and H are entered via an ACCEPT statement. Upon processing this statement during execution, the computer types the ? character, and then the programmer enters the appropriate numerical values. The answers are then typed by the computer as they are generated. Upon completion of the program execution, the computer again types READY.

9   When the user has completed his work at the terminal, he enters BYE and the computer changes his status from an active to an inactive user.

Most time-sharing systems provide the programmer with more features than are used in the example in Figure 1-14. Programmers can readily add to programs or make changes using editing features available at the terminal.

For the small or occasional computer user, the conversational time-sharing mode of operation is far more desirable than batch processing. For this reason the popularity of conversational time sharing has increased rapidly, and it probably will increase even more in the future. Batch processing is attractive only to the user with a very large program that requires virtually the entire machine in order to run it and to the user whose program runs so long that the wait at the terminal would approach the turnaround wait in the batch processing environment. The number of small users far exceeds the number of users in the later two situations.

1-8. PERIPHERAL DEVICES

A peripheral unit serves one of two functions: as a programmer communication device or as an auxiliary storage unit. In this section we shall give a brief description of several peripheral devices and their use in computing systems.

In time-sharing systems the teletype or typewriter is a very popular unit. Although these units operate at the rather slow speed of 10–30 characters per second, they are so inexpensive that in some cases a single programmer can be provided with a terminal for his or her exclusive use. Although they are most popular with time-sharing systems, many batch processing systems permit programs to be submitted over these units. In these systems, editing features must be available at the terminal to permit the programmer to make corrections readily without having to reenter the entire program.

In many cases the main disadvantages of teletypes or typewriters are their low output speed and the noise levels associated with their operation; both of these can be eliminated by using a cathode-ray tube unit. In simplest terms, this device consists of a keyboard for entry of data and a screen similar to that of a TV except that only characters can be displayed. These units are competitive in price, but they do not directly produce a *hard copy*, i.e., something that can be saved if desired.

Figure 1-15. High-speed printer capable of 800 lines/minute (photo courtesy of J. R. Langley).

In batch processing systems the most popular medium for the preparation of programs has been the punched card, as illustrated in Figure 1-10. Large computers are equipped with on-line card readers that can read cards at rates of 1000 cards per minute or higher and on-line card punches that can punch cards at about half this rate. Programmers punch cards off-line using a device called a keypunch machine. To eliminate the expense and bother of cards, some large centers are currently considering reusable cassette tapes as replacements for cards. To what extent this will prove successful is uncertain at this writing.

The most important method for getting information out of a computer is via *high-speed printers*. A photograph of a high-speed printer is shown in Figure 1-15. These printers are designed to print an entire line of information rather than a single

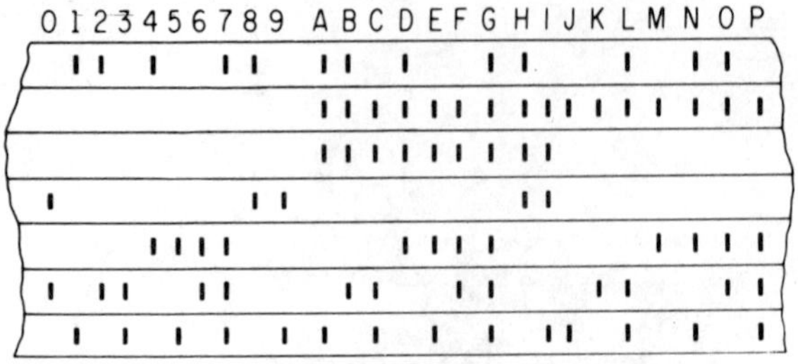

Figure 1-16. Magnetic recording of binary coded decimal information. (*Reprinted by permission from* IBM *Magnetic Tape Units, Publication No. A22-6589-1,* © *by International Business Machines Corporation*).

character at a time as is common in most typewriters. Many of them are capable of printing rates up to 1200 lines a minute. The paper used in the high-speed printer may be of a special format for handling accounting information, statistical reports, warehouse data, etc., or it may be plain unruled paper in which the programmer is allowed to use his own individual format.

A second major means of communicating with a digital computer is via a roll of *magnetic tape* such as is illustrated in Figure 1-16. Magnetic tape has two major advantages which make it highly desirable for use with digital computers. The first is that it can be read into the computer at extremely rapid rates. Some computers are capable of reading 120,000 characters per second from magnetic tape, which is approximately a hundred times faster than is possible from punched cards. The second major advantage is that a very small amount of tape can record huge amounts of information; e.g., a single 10 1/2-inch reel of tape can hold the contents of 250,000 punched cards. This magnetic tape is very similar to the type of tape used in home tape recorders. It is a plastic ribbon with an iron oxide coating that can be magnetized by external heads. A tiny area of the iron oxide coating can be magnetized to represent a "1" in the binary code, and if it is an unmagnetized area, it can be used to represent a "0." A pattern of symbols can be arranged in vertical columns on the tape in a manner very similar to that of the punched card. The magnetic tape symbols that are commonly used are "pure binary" and normally can be read directly by the computer. This allows magnetic tape to be used as a computer's external memory. The following analogy between magnetic tape and books is often used: The magnetic tape provides a sort of computer library, just as an individual's personal books provide a source of external memory for the individual. Magnetic tape is relatively inexpensive and it may be easily erased and reused.

One type of storage device used by the computer which might fall into the category of an input-output device to the central memory of the computer is the *magnetic disc*. These discs look like large phonograph records and have a surface that can be magnetized. Very large amounts of information may be stored on the magnetic surface of these discs, and they provide a type of external memory that is very similar to magnetic tape. The main advantage of the disc is that it transfers information into and out of the computer much more rapidly than is possible from magnetic tape. A *magnetic drum* offers similar advantages.

Another type of input-output device which has gained large usage in business

Figure 1-17. Magnetic-ink characters.

work is *magnetic ink*. The most common example of magnetic ink is the coded personal check which many people have in their bank checking account, and this is illustrated in Figure 1-17. Magnetic ink can be "read" in much the same manner as magnetic tape, but it has the additional advantage that the magnetic ink can be read by people as well as by computers.

The *optical scanner* is another type of input device. The scanner is a device which can read typed or written numbers and words, not just those printed in magnetic ink. The primary advantage of such devices is that they eliminate the manual translation of information into special computer codes. Optical scanners are still in a rudimentary stage of their development: They work by allowing a photoelectric cell to scan material and convert characters into electronic pulses which are compared to patterns that are already stored in the computer's memory. As their development progresses, optical scanners will provide a very important adjunct to the use of the computer, and it will be much more feasible for individuals to communicate directly with the computer.

This section has by no means covered all types of peripheral units. For example, paper tape units were once very popular, but they have virtually disappeared except on very small systems. Incremental plotters enable the computer to prepare line drawings. The list is very long, and it is steadily growing.

THE FORTRAN STATEMENT

The previous chapter introduced the role of automatic-programming languages. It will be the function of this chapter to illustrate the elementary programming concepts associated with FORTRAN. The main thrust of all the material presented in this chapter will be toward the development of skills related to the writing of simple arithmetic-type statements in FORTRAN. It is not the purpose of this chapter to try to develop skills in writing complete programs or even complete sections of programs; rather, the intention is to write statements to carry out simple, specific arithmetic calculations. In order to do this it will be necessary to gain a clear understanding of the use of constants, variables, operations, expressions, functions, and correct statement layout in FORTRAN.

While much of the material presented in this and subsequent chapters is applicable to all versions of FORTRAN, all of this material will be developed in terms of its application in FORTRAN IV. This is implied throughout the book unless stated to the contrary.

In studying the material in this chapter, it is strongly recommended that the student pay special attention to the distinction between integer and real. In fact, this distinction is so important that the final section of this chapter is dedicated to this topic.

2-1. FORTRAN **CONSTANTS**

In the working of everyday problems in data processing, it is always necessary to make use of numerical constants. Upon a little reflection it becomes evident that there are inherently two types of constants involved in what we do: numerical constants related to the *counting* of quantities and numerical constants related to the *measurement* of quantities. In our day-to-day usage of these two types of numbers, we normally switch back and forth between them without really paying much attention to their inherently different nature. The digital computer in its operation, however, will make quite different usage of these types of numbers. They must be handled differently in the computer, and normally they are not interchangeable with one another. It is therefore necessary to have a good understanding of these two different types of numbers.

When we refer to counting numbers, we indicate implicitly that they have no fractional part. For example, we count the number of apples in a barrel, the number of paper clips in a box, the number of people in a room, etc., and we make no provision for fractional parts. It is understood that the decimal point in any such number is fixed. These numbers are always integer numbers, and the decimal point is implied to be immediately to the right of the last digit, although the decimal does not normally appear. In FORTRAN language these numbers which have been indicated as counting numbers are referred to as *integer numbers* which are a particular case of *fixed-point numbers*. Both of these terms are often used interchangeably. FORTRAN also recognizes double precision and complex constants; but these will be described only in Appendix A.

In FORTRAN, in order to distinguish integer numbers from other numbers, they are simply written without a decimal point, and it is not even allowable to have a decimal point associated with an integer number. It should also be noted that embedded commas within a number are not allowed. Arithmetic operations can be carried out using integer numbers, but the arithmetic is inherently integer in its nature; therefore, fractional parts cannot be shown and will be dropped by the computer. For example, in integer arithmetic if we divide 10 by 3 the answer is 3. Both positive and negative integer numbers are allowable, and the largest integer number that is permissible varies widely from one computer to the next. The appropriate limits are shown in Appendix B, but a typical value is that of the IBM System 360 which allows up to 2147483647, or $2^{31} - 1$. (This number is a result of the use of binary arithmetic in the operation of the computer.)

The following list is an example of some valid integer numbers:

        576
      -200
          0
          6
    12345678
     -127982

The following integer numbers are incorrect:

76.2	(decimal present)
21.	(decimal present)
10000000000	(normally too large)
127,924	(embedded comma)

The second type of number encountered in FORTRAN is the type of number normally used for measuring. These numbers have the provision for expressing a fractional part. For example, if we want to measure the dimensions of a desk top it may be 27.2 inches, 26.9 inches, or 27.0 inches. These numbers for measuring quantities not only must express a fractional part, but it is also necessary that this part be preserved in any arithmetic calculations. For this reason these numbers are more useful for actual computational work in the computer. In FORTRAN these numbers are referred to as *real* or *floating-point* numbers. The decimal point does exist, and its location inside the number is not fixed but may have any location assigned to it by the programmer. The use of floating-point numbers is very common in scientific work, where a number is often thought of as a fraction between 0.1 and 1.0 times a power to 10. In most systems the *magnitude* (sign not considered) of a floating-point number may be zero or somewhere between approximately 10^{-76} and 10^{76}. (See Appendix B for various actual limitations.) The terms *floating-point numbers* and *real numbers* are normally used interchangeably.

FORTRAN numbers can only contain a finite number of digits, and thus they must be rational numbers. Irrational numbers may only be approximated, i.e., represented by a finite number of digits.

FORTRAN real numbers may have an integer value or they may have a fractional part. Even if a real number has an integer value in FORTRAN, it must be written with a decimal point to indicate that it is a real number. In the calculations inherent in FORTRAN the computer will take care of all questions of "lining up" decimals before addition, subtraction, etc., and this is not something with which the programmer must be concerned. Embedded commas are not allowed in real numbers, and real numbers are considered to be positive if they are unsigned. It is permissible for them to be positive, zero, or negative.

The following are permissible floating-point numbers:

96.7
−200.
.00001
−999999.

The following are not acceptable real constants:

2,782.	(embedded comma not allowed)
+6	(no decimal present)

There is no restriction on the number of digits that may be written with a real constant; but no more than seven or eight significant figures will normally be retained by the computer: therefore, there is no need to write more than approximately eight significant figures on most systems.

It is also possible to have a real constant written in exponential format in which the real constant is followed by the letter E and a one- or two-digit number (some versions even allow a three-digit number) which may be positive or negative. This indicates an integer power of ten by which the number is multiplied. This facilitates writing very large or very small real numbers.

The following are acceptable real numbers in exponential form:

$$5.0\mathrm{E}+2 \qquad (5. \times 10^2)$$
$$-50.\mathrm{E}-21 \qquad (-50. \times 10^{-21})$$
$$-.7\mathrm{E}2 \qquad (-.7 \times 10^2)$$
$$12.345\mathrm{E}21 \qquad (12.345 \times 10^{21})$$

The following are not permissible real numbers in exponential form:

$\mathrm{E}+2$ (exponent alone not permissible)
$5\mathrm{E}-1$ (no decimal—rejected by most Fortrans)
$5.\mathrm{E}76$ (too large for most versions)
$5.1\mathrm{E}2.1$ (exponent must be integer)

2-2. FORTRAN **VARIABLES**

Variables are used in FORTRAN to denote a quantity that is to be referred to by name rather than by its appearance as a value. An arithmetic variable in FORTRAN refers to the memory address of a number. The number in the memory address is the value of the variable, and thus during the execution of a program this variable may take on many different values as different integer or real constants are stored in the address reserved for the variable. Note that a constant is restricted to a single value, but a variable may take on many different values.

Arithmetic variables in FORTRAN may denote the address of a number which may be either an integer constant or a real constant, and therefore arithmetic variables are said to have *type*, i.e., integer or real, depending on the kind of number which it names. (There are also the possibilities of double-precision, logical, and complex variables in addition to other types, but these are discussed in Appendix A.) There are two ways to denote the type of a variable. One is an implicit method and the other is an explicit method. The explicit method is based upon a *type declaration* (which is taken up in Chapter 5), and this is the only way to handle the specification of complex, logical, or double-precision variables. For integer or real variables the type declaration is normally not given explicitly, but it is implied by the nature of the name of the variable. An integer variable, of course, may take on any of the values permitted for an integer constant, and a real variable may take on the values permitted of real constants.

The name of an integer variable is composed of from one to six letters or digits. (The maximum allowable number of letters or digits may vary in some versions of FORTRAN.) The FORTRAN compiler places no "type" significance on the arrangement of the letters and digits beyond inspecting the first letter of the variable name. The first character of an integer variable must be a letter and must be either I, J, K, L, M, or N. Examples of acceptable integer variables are as follows:

JACK
NUTTY
LIT1
LIT200
JKL
KJL
LJK
I

Some examples of incorrect integer variables are as follows:

ANS	(does not begin with the correct letter)
I*JK	(contains a character other than a letter or digit)
M2.222	(contains a character other than a letter or digit)
NUTHOUSE	(contains more than six characters)
2I	(does not begin with a letter)

Real variables represent real constants inside the computer, i.e., as a fraction times a power of ten. The name of a real variable may be composed of from one to six letters or digits. The first character of the name of a real variable must be a letter, and it may be any letter except I, J, K, L, M, or N.‡ From this it becomes quite obvious that the FORTRAN compiler uses the first letter of the variable name in order to determine the type of variable being named. Therefore, by proper selection of the first letter of the variable name, there is an implicit declaration of variable type. Valid names for real variables are as follows:

ANS
ANSWER
X
X1
X2
ABC
CBA
BCA

Some examples of invalid names for real variables are as follows:

1ANS	(does not begin with a letter)
X − Y	(contains a character other than a letter or digit)
X123456	(contains too many characters)

---

‡ In some FORTRANS the character $ is considered to be alphabetic. It may be used in variable names, and a variable whose first character is $ is considered to be real.

It might be noted that the FORTRAN compiler will place no special meaning or significance on the letters and digits selected to form variable names (other than to make the implicit decision as to type specification). For example, when the computer sees A2 it does not consider this to be A squared, A "times" two, or A with a subscript two, i.e., a_2. It simply assumes this to be the name of a single real variable. This allows the programmer a great deal of freedom in the selection of variable names throughout his program, and it makes available a very large set of variable names. It also allows the programmer to make use of mnemonic names. For example, instead of calculating a variable which will be assumed by the programmer to mean answer, he may calculate a variable whose name is ANSWER.

One of the most common errors made by new programming students is the incorrect selection of the first letter of a variable name.

2-3. OPERATIONS

FORTRAN provides for five basic arithmetic operations. These are addition, subtraction, multiplication, division, and exponentiation, each represented by a separate and distinct symbol

Addition	+
Subtraction	−
Multiplication	*
Division	/
Exponentiation	**

These are the only mathematical operations that are allowed in FORTRAN, and all other mathematical operations must be built from these basic five. (The only apparent exception to this is the use of special mathematical "functions" that will be discussed in a subsequent section.)

Note that since the letter x is allowable as a variable name and since we do not use a lowercase "x," another character (the asterisk) must be used to indicate multiplication. The exponentiation combination ** is considered as two characters but as a single symbol, and it is never correct to write two consecutive mathematical operation symbols in a FORTRAN statement.

These arithmetic operations are useful in combining constants, variables, and functions (discussed later) into meaningful arithmetic *expressions*. The formulation of these expressions is the subject of the next section.

2-4. EXPRESSIONS

Expressions are used in FORTRAN to specify the computation of a numerical value. An expression may consist of a single constant, a single variable, or a single function. In addition, it may specify a combination of two or more constants, two or more variables, a combination of constants and variables, or a combination of constants, variables, and functions (discussed later). Table 2-1 contains some examples of valid FORTRAN expressions.

Table 2-1. Valid FORTRAN **Expressions**

FORTRAN *Expression*	*Its Meaning*
J	The value of the integer variable J.
54.40	The value of the real constant 54.40.
x + 26.5	The sum of the value of x and 26.5.
SAM − BILL	The difference in the values of SAM and BILL.
x * y	The product of the values of x and y.
GO/1.234	The quotient of the values of GO and 1.234.
z ** 2	The value of z raised to the second power.
(x + 1.)/(y + z)	The sum of the values of x and 1. divided by the sum of the values of y and z.
1./(x ** 2)	The reciprocal of x².

By using parentheses with arithmetic operation symbols, it is possible to build up very complex FORTRAN expressions, and there are certain rules which the programmer must follow in order to calculate the exact numerical value intended. The following rules apply:

1   Parentheses may be used to indicate groupings just as in ordinary algebraic manipulations. Parentheses force the inner operation to be carried out first (just as in ordinary algebra), i.e., parentheses are cleared before other operations are performed. There is no penalty for the use of unnecessary parentheses; therefore, the student should not attempt to minimize the number of parentheses in an expression.

2   When the hierarchy of operations in an expression is not controlled by the use of parentheses, the computer follows the following hierarchy:

  a. Exponentiation
  b. Multiplication and Division
  c. Addition and Subtraction

  That is, all exponentiations are performed first, then all multiplications and divisions, and finally all additions and subtractions. For example, the expression A + B * C is interpreted as A + (B * C). Similarly, A ** C * B is (A ** C) * B.

3   In some cases the hierarchy rules stated above are not sufficient to specify the order in which operations are performed. For example, the expression A/B/C could be interpreted as either (A/B)/C = A/(B * C) or A/(B/C) = (A * C)/B, completely consistent with the rules of hierarchy. This dilemma is resolved by adding the following rule: *Operations on the same level of the hierarchy are performed from left to right.* Therefore, A/B/C is interpreted as (A/B)/C = A/(B * C). The expression A/B * C is (A/B) * C = (A * C)/B. Also note the seventh entry in Table 2-2.

4   In early computers, expressions were restricted to containing either all integer variables *or* all real variables. Mixing integers and real variables in an expression resulted in *mixed mode arithmetic* which was not allowed. Most current systems have removed this restriction, but there are some pitfalls for the beginning programmer as discussed in the last section of this chapter.

Table 2-2. Invalid FORTRAN **Expressions**

Conventional Mathematical Notation	*Incorrect Fortran Expression*	*Correct Fortran Expression*
$x \cdot y$	XY	X * Y
$x \cdot (-y)$	X * −Y	X * (−Y) or −X * Y
$-(x + y)$	−X + Y	−(X + Y) or −X − Y
x^{i+1}	X ** I + 1	X ** (I + 1)
$x^{y+1} \cdot z$	X ** Y + 1. * Z	X ** (Y + 1.) * Z
$\dfrac{x \cdot y}{z \cdot s}$	X * Y/Z * S	X * Y/(Z * S) or X/Z * Y/S
$\left[\dfrac{x + y}{z}\right]^{3.14}$	(X + Y)/Z ** 3.14	((X + Y)/Z) ** 3.14
$x[r + y(r + z)]$	X(R + Y(R + Z))	X * (R + Y * (R + Z))
$\dfrac{x}{1 + \dfrac{y}{16.2 + z}}$	X/(1.0 + Y/16.2 + Z)	X/(1.0 + Y/(16.2 + Z))
x^{y^z}	X ** Y ** Z	X ** (Y ** Z) or (X ** Y) ** Z whichever is intended

5 One exception to the above definition of mixed mode arithmetic is that raising a real variable to an integer exponent is not mixed mode arithmetic. Although real variables can be raised to real exponents, only positive real numbers can be raised to real exponents. Recall that an expression such as $1.4^{2.6}$ would be evaluated using logarithms, i.e.,

$$1.4^{2.6} = \exp (2.6 \cdot \ln 1.4)$$

The problem with negative numbers is that their logarithm does not exist. When numbers are raised to integer exponents, results are effectively computed by successive multiplication, thus avoiding logarithms. Therefore A ** J is computable for negative A, but A ** B is not. Even though B may not have a fractional part, it is a real variable, and the operation will be performed with logarithms as indicated above.

As mentioned earlier, operation symbols may never appear next to one another. Parentheses indicate grouping, and they do not specify or imply multiplication. Some mathematical operations must have a number of parentheses in order to achieve the desired numerical result. Table 2-2 gives examples of invalid FORTRAN expressions.

The value of an arithmetic expression will be a number, and the mode of that number will either be integer or real, depending on the mode of the expression itself. When all of the variables and constants in an expression are of the same mode, the mode of the expression will be the mode of the numerical quantity calculated as the value of the expression. For mixed mode expressions, the mode of the result will be real, a point we shall examine in more detail in the last section of this chapter.

It is very important that the programmer develop a good "feel" for the specific rules for the formulation of arithmetic expressions, because there are numerous specific problems that can be created by an inadequate understanding of arithmetic expressions. Some examples of these are appropriate.

The programmer should appreciate the difference between *accuracy* and *precision*. As indicated in earlier sections, most digital computers work with approximately eight digits of precision. This does not imply that every answer will be accurate to eight digits. As an example, 0.12345678 minus 0.12345670 would give an answer of 0.00000008, a result that has eight digits of precision but only one digit of accuracy.

Arithmetic operations, because of the way in which they are carried out, do not obey all of the normal rules of arithmetic. For example, the expression 0.5 + 12345678. − 12345670. would yield 8.0 if evaluated from left to right and 8.5 if evaluated from right to left. The use of parentheses here would have an obvious advantage in forcing the evaluation of the expression from right to left.

Another type of problem that might be encountered in a FORTRAN statement would be the situation in which it would not be possible to get any answer whatsoever from an arithmetic expression. For example, consider the expression x * y/z in which x, y, and z have values of the order of magnitude of 10^{50}. Without any parentheses the operation could be performed by multiplying x times y and the intermediate answer would be of the order of magnitude of 10^{100}. On many machines the multiplication would cause an *overflow*. Overflow occurs when the resultant magnitude (that is, the exponent) of an arithmetic operation exceeds the upper limit of numbers that can be accommodated by the computer. It often occurs when the programmer attempts to divide by a variable which may take on the value of zero. In the particular situation just noted, overflow could be corrected by writing the expression as x * (y/z). It might also be noted that the reverse of overflow is *underflow*, which occurs when a number is too small for the computer. It is up to the programmer to avoid both overflow and underflow by properly structuring his program.

There are some very special problems that arise in the course of performing arithmetic in the integer mode. Division is the most common source of error in this type of expression. In integer division a quotient having a fractional part will be *truncated*, that is, dropped. For example, 10/3 is 3, 8/5 is 1, and −7/3 is −2.

The equivalent of the above situation can also occur in real arithmetic, where, for example, the sum (1.0/3.0 + 1.0/3.0 + 1.0/3.0) yields the result of 0.99999999 instead of 1.00000000. This is caused by each of the individual parts of the expression being evaluated as 0.33333333.

All of the above problems are nothing more than inconveniences, and in every case they can be overcome by proper programming. The most important problem is to appreciate and anticipate such difficulties.

2-5. FUNCTIONS

There are many operations normally encountered in programming that involve rather common mathematical functions. Some examples of these are square roots, logarithms, double precision functions, absolute values, and truncations. Each of these represents a mathematical function that can be evaluated by the programmer through proper use and structure of the five basic mathematical operations. But since these are so commonly encountered, the FORTRAN system has special "subprograms" or equivalent machine language instructions which are useful for evaluating them. The exact list of functions available in any version of FORTRAN will vary; but there are some functions that are common to virtually all computers and compilers using FORTRAN. An extensive list is given in Appendix C.

The use of a FORTRAN function in an expression is very simple. The FORTRAN function's name is written, and it is followed by an expression enclosed in parentheses. The compiler interprets this to mean that the expression contained in parentheses will be computed according to the function. As an example, suppose it is necessary to compute the natural logarithm of a variable X. This could be written as ALØG(x). The logarithm function for the base 10 is ALØG10(x).

ABS(x) is the function for finding the absolute value $|x|$ of a real function x. IABS(j) is the corresponding function for an integer function j where $|j|$ is desired. (Absolute value is value without regard to sign.)

It is possible that the argument of a function may be an expression involving other mathematical operations and/or functions. In most cases it is necessary that the expression which comprises the argument of the function be a real expression, and the functional value computed will appear in real form.

There are restrictions associated with the arguments of most FORTRAN functions, and these restrictions depend on the compiler and the specific computer installation. Typical of these kinds of restrictions is the fact that the argument of the square-root function SQRT(x) may not be negative. When these restrictions on function usage are violated, the results are unpredictable. In some cases erroneous values will be computed and used in the program, and in other cases an error comment may be generated and the program stopped. See Appendix C for comments and restrictions.

It might be noted that some FORTRAN functions are not available in the form of subprograms, but are translated into machine-language instructions. A simple example is the absolute-value function. The distinction between these types of functions is of no importance to the programmer.

2-6. FORTRAN **STATEMENTS**

The general statements that comprise a program in FORTRAN may be classified in the following four categories:

1 Arithmetic assignment statements

2 Input-output statements

3 Flow of control statements

4 Informational statements

The statement that will be discussed in most detail in this section is the arithmetic assignment statement with which a new value of a variable may be computed. In general it is of the form A = B, in which A is a variable name written without a sign, and B is any expression as discussed in Section 2-4. The arithmetic assignment statement is interpreted by the FORTRAN compiler as meaning: evaluate the expression on the right-hand side of the equals sign and store the numerical value computed in the memory cell reserved for the variable indicated on the left-hand side of the equals sign.

From the above statement it is quite obvious that the equals sign in an arithmetic assignment statement is not equivalent to the equals sign normally used in conventional arithmetic and algebra. It is perfectly permissible, for example, to write a statement N = N + 1, which means to take the old value of N, add 1 to it, and store it in the storage location reserved for the variable N. This is quite obviously not true from an algebraic viewpoint, but it is perfectly permissible to use such a statement in FORTRAN.

Since the computer will interpret an arithmetic assignment statement as an operation in which the expression on the right will be evaluated and stored in the variable location indicated on the left of the equals sign, it is therefore illegitimate to try and do any kind of arithmetic operation on the left-hand side of the equals sign. For example, X − Y = A + B would be an incorrect arithmetic assignment statement.

The variables involved in the expression on the right-hand side of an arithmetic assignment statement will be read from memory and will not be destroyed, i.e., they are still available for subsequent calculations. The numerical value of the expression evaluated will be stored in the single-variable address associated with the variable on the left-hand side of the expression, and consequently the old value of the variable on the left-hand side of the arithmetic assignment statement is destroyed and is not available for subsequent computations. It is also very important to note that all of the variables named in the expression on the right-hand side of the statement must

---

Table 2-3. Some Valid Arithmetic Assignment Statements

Meaning	*Statement*
$\nu = 16$	V = 16.
$\alpha = -\dfrac{3}{x^2} + \dfrac{a}{2x}$	ALPHA = −3./X ∗∗ 2 + A/(2. ∗ X)
$a = q_c \dfrac{m_1 m_2}{m_1 + m_2}$	A = QC ∗ XM1 ∗ XM2/(XM1 + XM2)
$g = \dfrac{x(x^2 + y^2)}{x^2 - y^2 + 2}$	G = X ∗ (X ∗∗ 2 + Y ∗∗ 2)/(X ∗∗ 2 − Y ∗∗ 2 + 2.)
$x = (3 \cdot 10^{-12} + 2x^4)^{1/3}$	X = (3.E−12 + 2. ∗ X ∗∗ 4) ∗∗ (1./3.)
$a = \sqrt{x}$	A = SQRT(X)
$i_{\text{new}} = i_{\text{old}} + 1$	I = I + 1
$x_{\text{new}} = x_{\text{old}} + .1e$	X = X + .1 ∗ E
$y = e^x$	Y = EXP(X)
$t = \log_{10} x$	T = ALØG10(X)

Table 2-4. Some Invalid Arithmetic Assignment Statements

X = 3.Y + 2.	* missing.
2.14 = PI = 1.	Left side must be a variable; only one equals sign permitted.
Z = ((X + Y) ** 2	Unequal number of right and left parentheses.
−J = I ** (−2)	Integer quantities raised to negative powers always give a zero result; variable on left must not be written with a sign.
X = 1./−2. * Y	Two operation symbols side-by-side are not permitted, even though the minus sign here is not intended to indicate subtraction.
A = N * X ** (N − 1)	Mixed modes in multiplication; not accepted by some compilers.
A * X = Y	Left side must be a single variable.
sqrt(X) = X ** 0.5	The left side must be a variable name.

be available at the time the arithmetic assignment statement is executed, i.e., all of the variables must have numerical values available in their storage addresses. If not, an "undefined variable" error will occur and be detected by some computers but not detected by others.

As pointed out earlier, some computers do not permit mixing of the modes of arithmetic that occur in an expression. It is always permissible, however, to "mix modes" of arithmetic across an equals sign in an arithmetic assignment statement. For example, an integer expression on the right-hand side may be set equal to a real variable on the left-hand side of an arithmetic assignment statement. The reverse is also allowable. When such a statement is encountered, the computer will evaluate the expression on the right-hand side in the appropriate mode of arithmetic and then convert it to the other mode of arithmetic before it is stored. One comment might be made about the conversion of the results of real expressions to integer values. If an arithmetic assignment statement is written to compute a real number which is to be converted to integer form before storage, the real number always will be truncated past the decimal point. In order to obtain rounding, a statement such as I = A + 0.5 is sufficient to round the real number A to the integer number I if A is positive.

Table 2-3 shows examples of arithmetic assignment statements, and Table 2-4 shows some errors which are commonly made in arithmetic assignment statements. A very careful review of these two tables is important to the reader.

The other types of FORTRAN statements discussed at the beginning of this section will be discussed in much greater detail during subsequent chapters of this book.

2-7. STATEMENT FORMAT

A FORTRAN program is a series of individual instructions or statements arranged in the order in which they are to be encountered and executed by the computer. For batch processing systems the arrangement of the statement on the card has become highly standardized. Therefore, we shall consider these systems first, followed by time-sharing systems.

Batch Processing Systems. Normally there is one statement prepared for each individual input card, i.e., there is a punched card (or its equivalent) for each statement that is to be fed to the FORTRAN compiler. It is necessary for the programmer to write on a FORTRAN *coding form* the instructions that are to be punched on the cards by a *keypunch operator*. There are some general guidelines that must be observed in preparing these FORTRAN coding forms for interpretation by the keypunch operator. A typical FORTRAN coding form is shown in Figure 2-1. Each line or row on the programming form corresponds to one card that will be punched by the keypunch operator. The two arithmetic assignment statements shown in Figure 2-1 are assumed to be part of a much greater program that will be run by the computer. The first statement calculates an individual's pay as being equal to his rate of pay times the time that he has worked, and then the net pay that the individual will receive will be equal to his gross pay minus whatever taxes he must pay and whatever other deductions he might have in his payroll computation.

These two arithmetic assignment statements will each appear later as an individual punched card. Their layout on the FORTRAN coding form is sufficient to illustrate the usage of the various columns on the coding form, but a few general statements about the program coding form are appropriate. Note that each row is marked off into a series of individual spaces. On the coding form shown there are 72 such spaces in each row. Only one symbol may be written in each space, and each symbol

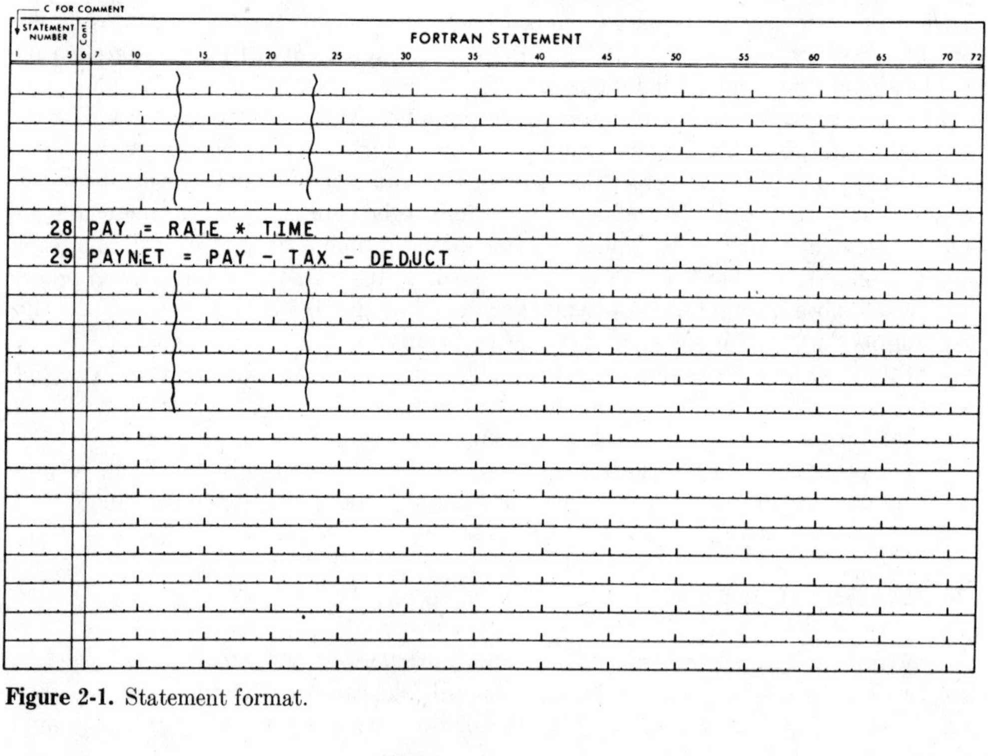

Figure 2-1. Statement format.

must be written separately in its own individual space. It does not make any difference if the symbol is a letter, a digit, a comma, a period, a parenthesis, or an arithmetic operation sign, etc. Each individual symbol must have its own individual space. The reason for this is obvious when it is recalled that each line on the coding form will correspond to a punched card at a later time in the development of the program, and consequently each individual space will correspond to a punch on a card. It might also be noted in the statements shown in Figure 2-1 that a number of blank spaces are present in the arithmetic assignment statements. These blanks are ignored by FORTRAN (except in the Hollerith format specification discussed later).

Columns 1–5 of the typical FORTRAN statement are reserved for a statement number which identifies an individual statement. It is not necessary that all statements have a statement number nor is it necessary that these statement numbers follow any distinct order or sequence. There are additional uses for column 1; but these will be discussed subsequently. The actual FORTRAN statement itself begins in column 7 and continues to the right, but may not go past column 72. If it requires more characters to form the FORTRAN statement than can be placed in columns 7–72, then it is possible to continue a FORTRAN statement on the next line, i.e., the next card. Column 6 of the FORTRAN coding form is provided for this purpose. If there is any character punched in column 6 (except a 0 or blank), it will serve as a "flag" to the FORTRAN compiler that this card is a *continuation card* for the statement above.

It might be recalled from Chapter 1 that punched cards normally have 80 columns on them. In FORTRAN programming, columns 73–80 of punched cards are not used. They *may* be used to punch identifying characters and/or sequence numbers into the cards for a direct indication of the numbered sequence of the cards. The FORTRAN compiler will ignore any information punched in columns 73–80, and for this reason many coding forms do not even show these columns on the coding form itself.

In general, FORTRAN programs will consist of a series of statements in the following typical structure. First, an input section; second, a series of calculations performed on the data read into the computer via the input section (these calculations may involve flow of control statements and arithmetic assignment statements); and third, an output section in which the results of the calculations will be obtained from the computer. All of these sections may contain informational statements. Most of the statements involved in the sections of the FORTRAN program will use the general format shown in Figure 2-1 (with a few possible exceptions which will be discussed as they are encountered).

It is very important for the beginning programmer to get a firm understanding of the typical card format for FORTRAN programming. It is equally important in the preparation of his FORTRAN coding form that he be very particular and neat in the preparation and writing of the symbols in the individual spaces on the form. For example, it is very common to confuse a 1 with an *i*, a 1 with a /, a 5 with an S, a 2 with a Z, or a "zero" with an "oh." Many computer installations require that the "oh's" be written with a slash through them to avoid confusion; but the reader is cautioned that the opposite convention is used at some sites, i.e., the zero is often written with a slash. In computer listings in this text the letter O appears with a slash. These individual details require the undivided attention of the beginning programmer because any one of the above mentioned errors or violations of the programming rules will be sufficient to reject the execution of an entire program.

```
END
STOP
57  FORMAT(' HAROLD =',F10.4,5X,'ALPHA =',F14.4)
14  WRITE(6,57) HAROLD,ALPHA
  1 5.12778)*HAROLD+1.457766)*HAROLD+0.451134
643 ALPHA=((((2.44532*HAROLD+12.44512)*HAROLD-1.24511)*HAROLD-
C   COME HERE IF HAROLD IS NEGATIVE
    GOTO14
  1 2.44511)*HAROLD+0.274333)*HAROLD+0.742355
    ALPHA=((((1.52347*HAROLD+22.1687)*HAROLD-0.012954)*HAROLD+
C   COME HERE IF HAROLD IS POSITIVE
    IF(HAROLD.LT.0.) GOTO643
28  FORMAT(F10.0)
    READ(5,28) HAROLD
C   CONTINUATION CARDS.
C   THIS PROGRAM ILLUSTRATES STATEMENT NUMBERS, COMMENT CARDS, AND
```

Figure 2-2. Card deck for FORTRAN program.

Figure 2-2 illustrates a complete card deck for a simple FORTRAN program. Note the appearance of statement numbers, comment cards, and continuation cards.

Time-Sharing Systems. In batch processing systems, the program is in the form of a card deck. In order to add, delete, or change statements in the program, the programmer simply locates the proper cards and makes the desired changes. In time-sharing systems, no card deck as such exists, but the programmer must still be able to make program modifications in a convenient manner, a process often referred to as program editing.

To facilitate this process, each statement in the FORTRAN program for time-sharing systems is given a *line number* (not to be confused with or equated to a *statement number*). The line number is generally restricted to a five-digit number and always appears prior to the FORTRAN statement. In essence the line number is not part of the FORTRAN statement, and it is present only to facilitate program editing.

Although some time-sharing systems adhere strictly to the statement format presented earlier in this section for batch processing systems, many systems use a freer statement format. As illustrated in Figure 2-3, the rules are as follows:

A comment line is designated by a C immediately following the line number.

A continuation line is designated by an ampersand (&) immediately following the line number.

```
10C THIS PROGRAM ILLUSTRATES STATEMENT NUMBERS, COMMENT LINES,
20C AND CONTINUATION LINES.
30 ACCEPT,HAROLD
40 IF(HAROLD.LT.0.) GOTO643
50C COME HERE IF HAROLD IS POSITIVE
60 ALPHA=((((1.52347*HAROLD+22.1687)*HAROLD-0.012954)*HAROLD+
70& 2.44511)*HAROLD+0.274333)*HAROLD+0.742355
80 GOTO14
90C COME HERE IF HAROLD IS NEGATIVE
100 643 ALPHA=((((2.44532*HAROLD+12.44512)*HAROLD-1.24511)*HAROLD-
110& 5.12778)*HAROLD+1.457766)*HAROLD+0.451134
120 14 PRINT57,HAROLD,ALPHA
130 57 FORMAT("HAROLD =",F10.4,5X,"ALPHA =",F14.4)
140 STOP
150 END
```

Figure 2-3. FORTRAN program for time-sharing system.

A blank column normally separates the statement from the line number.

A blank column separates the statement number and the line number, and another blank column separates the statement number from the remainder of the statement.

Unfortunately, these rules are by no means universal, so the reader should not be surprised if a specific system does not follow them. Since these rules are not standardized, in this manual we shall always use the previously presented rules for punched cards.

In effect, the system maintains a program file that may be modified from the terminal by the programmer. To facilitate editing a program, the line numbers are generally entered in increments of 10, as shown in Figure 2-3. Editing is accomplished as follows:

To add a statement, simply give it a line number appropriate to its intended position in the program and type it in. The system will always maintain the program file with the statements in ascending order according to the line numbers.

To delete a statement, simply type its line number and depress RETURN.

To change a statement, simply reenter it. In essence, only the last statement entered with a given line number is retained.

Most systems provide special editing commands that permit listing the entire program or parts thereof, resequencing the line numbers, linking one program file with another, etc. For these, a manual for the specific system being used is required.

2-8. INTEGER VERSUS REAL

Before discussing the pitfalls for beginning (and experienced) programmers that stem from the existence of integer and real variables in FORTRAN, some explanation as to their origin may be enlightening. The tendency of FORTRAN to conform to the computing hardware is the primary reason for the two modes of variables. For scientific computations, numerical values can be represented in one of two ways (integer versus real) in storage. In integer form the number is stored directly; but fractional parts are not permitted. In real form the number is expressed as a fraction and an exponent, and the storage location is partitioned so that both the fraction and the exponent are stored in the same storage location.

Virtually all modern scientific computers use the binary number system as the basis for performing numerical operations. We shall, however, discuss only the three characteristics of the binary number system that are pertinent to our present subject.

A decimal number without fraction can be precisely represented in integer format in the binary number system. Arithmetic operations involving integer numbers can be performed precisely if we recognize the fact that any fractional parts resulting from divisions are lost. The equation

$$2 + 2 = 4$$

is true for integer variables; but, as we shall see in the next paragraph, it is not quite true for real variables.

To store a numerical value in real format, the decimal number is converted to binary, the decimal point (or binary point, to be precise) is "floated" to obtain a fraction and an exponent, and the result is stored. Unfortunately, very few decimal numbers with fractional parts can be accurately represented in the binary number system. For example, if the decimal number 0.1 is converted to binary, the result stored in real format, and the value in storage converted back to decimal, we would obtain the number $0.0999999930295\cdots$ from one specific commercial computer. While the result is close to 0.1, it is not *exactly* 0.1. If we add 0.1 (as stored) to itself ten times and then have the computer check to see if the result is 1.0, the answer is *no*. Similarly, using real arithmetic, the equation

$$0.2 + 0.2 = 0.4$$

is not quite true. The error is typically in the seventh or eighth decimal place, which is negligible in most calculations *except* for counting purposes. In counting, if we add 1 to itself ten times, the result had better be *exactly* 10, not *almost* 10. Since counting numbers never have a fractional part, and since integer arithmetic is exact, integer variables and constants should always be used for counting. Integers should be used whenever fractional parts will not be encountered.

For many constants in FORTRAN, the integer and real expressions have nearly the same appearance, but results can often be significantly different. Consider the following two examples:

A ** 2   A ** 2.

Although these two expressions are quite similar, the difference between them is very significant. The exponent in the expression on the left is written without a decimal point, which defines it to be integer. The exponent in the expression on the right is written with a decimal point, which defines it to be real. We ask the question "What if A is negative?" to see that this difference is significant. The expression on the left is a real number raised to an integer exponent, i.e., A ** J, which is computable for all values of A, positive or negative. However, the expression on the right is a real number raised to a real exponent, i.e., A ** B, which is computable only for positive A. The fact that the real exponent does not have a decimal fraction is immaterial since the computer performs all arithmetic operations in the binary number system without making such a test. If the exponent is real, the evaluation is made according to the procedure for computing A ** B even though B may, in fact, not have a fractional part. Therefore, in exponentiations, integer exponents should be used in *all* cases where the exponent does not have a fractional part. A ** 2 is preferred over A ** 2. in all cases.

The prohibition on mixed mode arithmetic stems from the computing hardware. Arithmetic units in computers do not generally perform operations on mixed variables. Hardware logic is available to add an integer number to an integer number, to add a real number to a real number, but *not* to add a real number to an integer number or vice versa. A similar situation exists with respect to subtraction, multiplication, and division. Exponentiation is usually performed by routines similar to library functions; therefore, a real variable can be raised to either an integer or real exponent.

In view of this situation, most early FORTRAN compilers simply did not allow mixed mode arithmetic. If the product of variables A and N had to be computed and the result stored in B, two statements such as the following were typically used:

```
X = N
B = A * X
```

The numerical value stored in variable N is converted to real and stored in variable X by the first statement (the content of variable N is not changed). The second statement computes the desired product.

Mixed mode arithmetic applies only to an expression. It is always permissible to set an integer variable equal to a real expression or a real variable equal to an integer expression.

While most programmers follow the practice illustrated above, using two statements to avoid mixed mode arithmetic, an alternate approach is to use the two library functions INT and FLØAT, described below:

INT(x)   Computes the integer equivalent of the real variable or expression used as the argument.

FLØAT(J)   Computes the real equivalent of the integer variable or expression used as the argument.

In effect, the statement

```
X = N
```

in the above example is in essence

```
X = FLØAT(N)
```

with the function FLØAT inserted by the compiler.

Mixed mode arithmetic can be avoided in this example by using the following statement:

B = A * FLØAT(N)

If the result must be integer, a statement such as the following can be used:

J = INT(A) * N

The INT and FLØAT functions are available in all versions of FORTRAN, and can be used whenever the need arises.

As FORTRAN compilers continued to be developed, they steadily became "smarter." It was easy to insert a FLØAT or INT function and continue, instead of printing an error message on encountering mixed mode arithmetic. However, instead of attempting to decide which function would be more appropriate, most compilers simply insert the FLØAT function, changing *all* mixed mode arithmetic to real arithmetic. The statement

B = A * N

became perfectly acceptable, being computed as follows:

B = A * FLØAT(N)

which is quite appropriate.

Unfortunately, the unilateral insertion of the FLØAT function does not always lead to the most appropriate result. For example, the statement

J = A * N

is computed as

J = INT(A * FLØAT(N))

That is, variable N is floated, the result multiplied by A using real arithmetic, and the result (in real) converted to integer. An alternative approach would be to compute the statement

J = A * N

as follows:

J = INT(A) * N

In this case the value stored in variable A is converted to integer, the result multiplied by N, and the result stored in J. How do the two statements

J = INT(A * FLØAT(N))
J = INT(A) * N

compare? The latter statement does not require a conversion from integer to real, and is therefore computationally more efficient. However, the important difference is that these two statements do *not* always produce the same answer. Suppose A equals 2.5 and N equals 3. The statement

J = INT(A * FLØAT(N))

computes a value of $2.5 \times 3 = 7.5 = 7$ (integer) for J, whereas the statement

J = INT(A) * N

computes a value of $2 \times 3 = 6$ for J. Which is correct? That depends upon the problem, and it is therefore the responsibility of the programmer. If the value 7 is correct, the mixed mode statement

J = A * N

is appropriate; but the second statement must be used when the value 6 is correct.

Another problem with the use of mixed mode arithmetic is that the insertion of the FLØAT function is not consistent from compiler to compiler. In compilers that use real arithmetic for all computations in a mixed mode expression, the statement

A = J/N * 100.

would be computed as follows:

A = FLØAT(J)/FLØAT(N) * 100.

Other compilers perform the computations as dictated by the hierarchy and left-to-right rule discussed in Section 2-4, and they insert the FLØAT function only when a mixed mode operation is encountered. For the statement

A = J/N * 100.

the sequence of operations would be to divide J by N and multiply the result by 100. Since J and N are both integer, their division does not involve mixed mode arithmetic. Therefore the FLØAT function is needed only when their result is multiplied by 100. Therefore, some compilers would treat the statement

A = J/N * 100.

as

A = FLØAT(J/N) * 100.

Is the statement above equivalent to the statement below?

A = FLØAT(J)/FLØAT(N) * 100.

Suppose J equals 2 and N equals 5. The first statement computes a result of 0.0 for A (dividing 2 by 5 in integer gives a result of 0). The second statement computes a result of 40.0 for A. Which is correct? That depends upon the problem and is, therefore, the responsibility of the programmer.

To summarize this discussion, mixed mode arithmetic is a convenient feature, but it is not without its pitfalls. Many experienced programmers avoid its use, partly out of habit, since it was forbidden on earlier systems, and partly because of the pitfalls discussed above. The beginning programmer must be cautious.

One final note: The fact that the fractional part is always truncated when a real number is converted to integer in FORTRAN seems unnatural to many students, primarily because rounding is emphasized in many mathematics courses. In reality, there is a large number of problems in which truncation, as opposed to rounding, is required. Consider the following problem:

> A boy takes $1.00 into a department store to purchase as many baseballs as his money will buy. He discovers that baseballs cost 35¢ each. How many can he buy?

To solve this simple problem, we divide 100 by 35, obtaining 2 30/35 or 2 5/6. Do we round (obtaining 3) or truncate (obtaining 2) for the answer? Truncation is appropriate for this problem.

2-9. IN SUMMARY

This chapter has introduced FORTRAN statements in general and has presented a general discussion of the arithmetic assignment type of FORTRAN statement. FORTRAN constants, variables, operations, expressions, and functions have all been discussed along with many of the individual rules that must be followed in using these FORTRAN elements. Some of the numerous idiosyncrasies that may be present in many compilers have been mentioned. Various compilers have been written by different people at different times for different machines and with some variation in objectives. Specific limitations, rules, and regulations for individual compilers are always available in the form of individual programming manuals for compilers on specific machines. It is not necessary (or desirable) to get involved in individual idiosyncrasies at this point.

After this chapter has been carefully read, the student should be thoroughly familiar with the techniques and the rules governing the writing of arithmetic assignment statements. The next chapter will make these arithmetic assignment statements the basis of FORTRAN calculations and couple them with the necessary input-output statements to write simple programs for a FORTRAN compiler.

Exercises ‡

2-1 Write the following as FORTRAN integer constants:

$$-2,486 \qquad 4 \times 10^2 \qquad -16.\dagger \qquad 86,487.0\dagger$$

2-2 Write the following as FORTRAN integer constants:

$$27.0 \qquad -2,726 \qquad 5.86 \times 10^2 \qquad -16,262.0$$

---

‡ Solutions to Exercises marked with a dagger † are given in Appendix G.

2-3 Write the following as FORTRAN real constants (using either decimal or exponential format):

10^{21} 0.0000082† -10^2 26,286.3

2-4 Write the following as FORTRAN real constants (using either decimal or exponential format):

$-27,281$† 10^{-17} 0.298612 27.83×10^4

2-5 Why are the following unacceptable as FORTRAN integer constants?

-121.8 5,241   27E21†   29342641893

2-6 Why are the following unacceptable as FORTRAN integer constants?

27E–03   16.8   27,243† 10^{14}

2-7 Why are the following unacceptable as FORTRAN real constants?

$-2871.$ 27.8E $+$ 92† $+21$ 6E02

2-8 Why are the following unacceptable as FORTRAN real constants?

9.12 $-$ E01   281E3.2 $-18,342$†   16,221.3

2-9 From the following list of variable names you are to select those that are integer variable names, those that are real variable names, and those that are unacceptable as variable names.

(a)	2EASY	†(b)	TWØ
(c)	IKE	(d)	ANSWER
†(e)	ANSWER 1	(f)	TØ.JØ
(g)	IDIØT	(h)	UNCLE
†(i)	RØØT	(j)	A — B
(k)	(LAST)	(l)	I

2-10 From the following list of variable names you are to select those that are integer variable names, those that are real variable names, and those that are unacceptable as variable names.

(a)	ADDITIØN	†(b)	23SKEEDØ
(c)	T	(d)	TEE
†(e)	A * B	(f)	(X)
(g)	MUST	(h)	GAMMA
(i)	CØBØL	†(j)	JERK
(k)	DIRTY	(l)	GØ-GØ

2-11 Write FORTRAN expressions to accomplish the following:

(a) $\dfrac{a + b}{c + d}$ (b) x^3

(c) $a + \dfrac{b}{c + d}$ †(d) $\dfrac{a \cdot b}{c + 10}$

(e) $\dfrac{x + 2}{y + 4}$ (f) $\dfrac{i + j}{k + 3}$

2-12 Write FORTRAN expressions to accomplish the following:

(a) $\dfrac{i+j}{k+n} + m$ †(b) $\dfrac{a+b}{c+(d/e)}$

(c) $1 + x + \dfrac{x^2}{2} + \dfrac{x^3}{6}$ (d) $\dfrac{3+y+y^2+4y^3}{x+4}$

†(e) $\dfrac{a}{b} + \dfrac{c \cdot d}{e \cdot f \cdot g}$ (f) $\dfrac{1}{x^2}\left(\dfrac{y}{10}\right)^z$

2-13 Write FORTRAN expressions to accomplish the following:

(a) $2\pi r^2$ (b) $a + x[b + x(c + dx)]$

(c) $\left(\dfrac{a}{b}\right)^{.86c+1}$ †(d) $\left[p\left(\dfrac{r}{s}\right)\right]^{t-1}$

(e) $k^3 + \left(\dfrac{m \cdot n}{2i}\right)^{2k}$ (f) $\left(-\dfrac{-x+y+27}{z^2}\right)^4$

2-14 State the numerical value of J that will be transferred to memory by the following arithmetic assignment statements:

†(a) J = 5 * 5/7
(b) J = 5 * (5/7)
(c) J = 2/3 + 2/3
(d) J = 2./3. + 2./3.
†(e) J = 2000 * (1999/2000)
(f) J = (2000 * 1999)/2000

2-15 State the numerical value of x that will be transferred to memory by the following arithmetic assignment statements:

(a) x = 5 * 5/7
†(b) x = 5/7 * 5
(c) x = 5. * 5./7.
(d) x = 4 ** (3 ** 2)
(e) x = (4 ** 3) ** 2
†(f) x = 5./3. + 3./3. + 5./3.

2-16 Identify the error(s), if any, in each of the following arithmetic assignment statements:

(a) X = I ** Y
(b) X − 3 = Y * Z + 6
†(c) X = Y * −Z + 6.
(d) X = I + 3 = J + 4
(e) X = 27z
†(f) X = (Y + 3) ** 2

2-17 Identify the error(s), if any, in each of the following arithmetic assignment statements:

(a) 4 = X − Y
(b) −X = (Y + Z) * 12.
†(c) X * Y = I ** 2

(d) x = 2,763 * a
(e) 3x + ı ** 3
†(f) x = (y + 4) ** 2
(g) x = (−3.5 * ABS(D + G)) ** B
(h) A = B ** (1/4)

2-18 The consumption function in economic theory relates the consumer expenditures to income. Suppose for a certain situation the relationship is as follows:

consumer expenditure = 92.4 + 0.85 × income

Develop an arithmic assignment statement devising appropriate variable names so that both consumer expenditure and income are real.

2-19 The total price of an automobile is computed as the sales price plus a sales tax of 4%. The relationships are

sales tax = 0.04 × sales price
total price = sales price + sales tax

Write the appropriate arithmetic assignment statements using real variables.

2-20 Joe is a diligent employee whose number of regular hours worked for the past week is stored in variable REG, overtime hours in OV and regular hourly pay rate in RATE. For overtime hours, he receives $1\frac{1}{2}$ times his regular hourly pay rate. The witholding for taxes is 13% and for medical insurance is $19.27. Write the arithmetic assignment statements to compute Joe's take-home pay.

†**2-21** If you divide 43 by 9, you obtain a quotient of 4 and a remainder of 7. Write the necessary arithmetic assignment statements to store the quotient in variable JQ and the remainder in variable JR. Note that if you divide 43 by 9 using integer arithmetic, you obtain the quotient 4. Multiplying the quotient by 9 and subtracting from 43 gives the remainder.

2-22 Revise the above program assuming 43 is initially stored in variable JA and 9 in variable JB.

2-23 Suppose you have a three-digit positive integer stored in variable IV. We would like to store the first digit in L1, the second in L2, and the third in L3. For example, if the value of IV is 825, then the values of L1, L2, and L3 should be 8, 2, and 5, respectively. Proceed as follows (illustrated for 825)

825/10   = 82
825 − 10 * 82 = 5 = L3
82/10   = 8 = L1
82 − 8 * 10   = 2 = L2

Write the necessary arithmetic assignment statements to do the same for any three-digit positive integer.

2-24 Revise the above procedure for a four-digit positive integer number.

2-25 Suppose the date July 12, 1974 is stored in variable IDATE as 071274. Write the necessary arithmetic assignment statements to store the month in variable MØNTH, the day of the month in IDAY, and the year in variable IYEAR. For the above example, the values of MØNTH, IDAY, and IYEAR should be 7, 12, and 1974, respectively.

SIMPLE FORTRAN PROGRAMS

The previous two chapters have introduced the concept of automatic programming languages and developed the basic tools that are necessary to formulate some of the simpler individual statements of FORTRAN. The last chapter gave attention to the development of the arithmetic assignment statement, and it is the purpose of this chapter to carry this development forward and to explain some of the other types of FORTRAN statements. Based on this, some simple FORTRAN programs will be written. In this chapter statements will be introduced that are sufficient to write only a very elementary type of FORTRAN program.

It might be reemphasized that the procedures, formats, and rules given are those that are peculiar to FORTRAN IV.

3-1. FORMAT-FREE INPUT STATEMENTS

If a problem is to be done only one time, all of the necessary data associated with the problem can be entered into the FORTRAN program directly in the form of constants in the individual statements. This is not normally done, however, since a digital computer is best suited for doing repetitive-type calculations, and most problems en-

46

countered in the application of digital computers are those in which the program is to be executed a number of separate times on different data. This is usually handled by having the program read the data associated with an individual problem from cards (or their equivalent) at the time the program is to be executed. Constants are used in the program only for those quantities that are in fact constant, i.e., they are not dependent upon the input data. If the program is set up in this general format, the same program can be used for many different sets of input data. This means that the FORTRAN program must handle the input of data into the computer. This becomes a significant portion of the programmer's task and it will now receive our attention.

The primary thing to appreciate in considering input statements is the fact that the input data for the program may be entered into the machine from any number of different input units, e.g., from card reader units, from magnetic tape units, from paper-tape units, or perhaps even from a console typewriter. Furthermore, the individual numbers which comprise the input data for the program may appear in different layouts, i.e., formats.

In general there are two approaches to handling input and output statements: the format-free approach and the format approach. Both will be presented briefly. It is important to note that either one may be used in any given problem‡; the choice is up to the programmer. The format-free approach is simpler and easier to use, and the format approach is more general and more powerful.

First, the format-free approach. An input statement can take the form

READ, NHØURS, BRATE, DEDUC

where NHØURS, BRATE, and DEDUC comprise a *list* of variables whose value is to be read into the computer. By implication, NHØURS is an integer variable and BRATE and DEDUC are real variables. The execution of this statement will cause the standard input unit for the computer, usually a card reader, to read in a card and to scan this card for the numerical values to assign to these variables. If the computer finds all three numerical values, then it will execute the next statement in the program. If it does not find all three, it will read in additional data cards until it has found three numerical values. These numerical values will be assigned in order to NHØURS, BRATE, and DEDUC. The first numerical value should be, therefore, integer, and the second and third numerical values should be real. The numerical values on the input card(s) may be punched anywhere, but successive values should be separated from each other by blanks or commas.

Several comments apply to this format-free approach:

There is no need for the first numerical value to start in column 1.

A numerical value may not be continued across two cards.

Successive cards will be read until enough items have been found to satisfy the requirements of the list part of the READ statement.

Any numerical values remaining on the last data card read for a particular READ statement will be ignored.

---

‡ This assumes that the FORTRAN IV compiler in use by your computer center has available on it both of these capabilities.

The type (real or integer) of a data item should match the type of variable to which it is being assigned.

For integer values either signed or unsigned integer constants are acceptable.

For real values either exponential or floating-point constants are acceptable.

Format and format-free input-output statements may be mixed within the same computer program.

The general form of the format-free input statement is

READ, *variable list*

As indicated earlier, the value of the format-free statement is based on its simplicity and the ease with which it may be used.

For input via the teletype, many time-sharing systems use the ACCEPT statement. For example, to enter values for variables x, J, and c, the appropriate statement is

ACCEPT, X,J,C

Upon processing this statement the computer waits for the programmer to enter numerical values for x, J, and c. Most terminals have a light or other mechanism by which the user is aware that the system is ready to accept input. Many programmers precede the ACCEPT statement with a PRINT statement to tell them which variables appear in the ACCEPT statement.

The rules regarding entry of values for the ACCEPT statement are essentially the same as for the format-free READ statement. That is, the numerical values are separated by a comma or one or more blank spaces. Only integer constants may be entered for integer variables, but either exponential or floating-point constants may be entered for real variables. After all values have been entered and the RETURN key depressed, the computer continues processing the statements in the program.

3-2. FORMATTED INPUT STATEMENTS

Perhaps the easiest way to illustrate the nature of the standard formatted input statement is by way of example:

```
     READ (5,297) NHØURS, BRATE, DEDUC
297  FØRMAT (I10,F10.2,E20.7)
```

These two statements are interpreted in the following manner. The READ indicates to the computer that data is to be entered into the computer memory from one of the many possible input units and in one of the many possible data formats that might exist on the typical input card (or its equivalent). The number 5 is a number whose value specifies the particular input unit to be used. This is an assignment that is made in a more or less arbitrary fashion with regard to specific machine configurations.

The 297 refers to the statement number of an associated FØRMAT statement for the input READ statement. This FØRMAT statement is not a statement that is executed by the computer; it is a statement which provides information to the computer telling it the arrangement of the various items of data on the input card (or its equivalent). The three variables in the list following the parentheses in the READ statement have the names NHØURS, BRATE and DEDUC. These variables are assigned values from the data card when the READ statement is executed.

In statement 297 (the FØRMAT statement) there are *field specifications* for the variables in the READ statement.

The FØRMAT statement dictates the layout of data on the input card (or its equivalent), and there must be a format field specification for *each* of the variables in the input READ list. In the list shown, the variable NHØURS is an integer variable, and the field specification associated with the variable NHØURS is given as I10. The I10 indicates that the first variable in the list is an integer variable, and it will be found in the first 10 columns of the input data card.

The variable BRATE is a floating-point variable, and the F10.2 is the field specification associated with the data layout for the value of BRATE to be read into the computer. The F indicates that BRATE is floating-point, and therefore the field specification is for a real number. The 10 indicates that the value of BRATE will be found in the next 10 columns on the data card, i.e., columns 11–20, and the 0.2 indicates that when the number is processed, the decimal point will be assumed between the numbers in columns 18 and 19, i.e., two places will be found to the right of the decimal. It is better programming practice to actually write the decimal in the number on the data card rather than to rely on its assumed location. If the decimal is explicitly written, it would normally appear in column 18; but if it is placed in any other column, its actual column location will *override* the format specification given in statement 297. This freedom is, of course, limited by the fact that the entire numerical value of BRATE, including the decimal point, must be completely contained within columns 11–20.

The variable DEDUC is also a real variable, and it could have been given in the floating-point or F-type of field specification. For sake of illustration, the variable DEDUC is shown here in an alternate type of real-number field specification—the exponential or E-type of field specification. The E-type of field specification calls for a numerical value plus an exponent raised to a power of 10. The 20 specifies a total of 20 columns for the field, and the 0.7 indicates that seven places will be assumed to the right of the decimal in the input number. The number must also contain an exponent giving the power of 10 by which the fractional part of the number is to be multiplied. As before, it is better programming practice to actually write the decimal in the numerical value of DEDUC on the data card. The input information for this particular number might appear as 0.526E01 which would indicate the real number 5.26. Note in this instance that the number of decimal places indicated in the input number is less than that indicated in the field specification. This is perfectly permissible and the actual location will override the field specification given in statement 297. Also note that the input number proposed did not occupy the full 20 columns allowed, i.e., columns 21–40. This is permissible and perhaps even desirable because it allows the programmer to leave blank spaces (within limits) between his input data on the cards, and thus make the data easier for people to read. Since blanks on the input data card will be read by the computer as zeros, all numbers on the input card should be placed in the columns at the right of the field provided and all blank columns should be at the left of the field provided, i.e., the input should be *right justified*.

Table 3-1.   Formatted Input Statements

Input Unit	Standard Form	Alternate Form
Card reader, on-line		READ n, *list*
Magnetic tape (cards off-line)		READ INPUT TAPE j, n, *list*
	READ (j,n) *list*	
Paper tape		ACCEPT TAPE n, *list*
Console typewriter		ACCEPT n, *list*

Note: j stands for an integer whose value specifies the input unit, n stands for the statement number of the FØRMAT statement, and *list* stands for the input variables.

Summarizing, the individual input statements shown in the previous example would direct the computer to go to input unit number five and read in a single card which will contain the integer variable NHØURS and the real variables BRATE and DEDUC. They will be contained on a single card (or its equivalent) whose format is laid out in the arrangement shown in statement 297 of the program. The integer variable NHØURS will be contained in columns 1–10, the real variable BRATE will be shown in normal decimal notation in columns 11–20, and the real variable DEDUC will be shown in exponential notation in columns 21–40.

There are many modifications to the nature of input READ statements depending on the individual compiler. More recent FORTRAN compilers have arrived at a single standard statement for use as a formated input statement, and that is the preferred form. Older FORTRAN compilers use different statements to identify different input units, and in general, different computer laboratories have preferred input units for standard jobs. A listing of possibilities is shown in Table 3-1. If the standard form of the READ statement shown in Table 3-1 is available, then its use is preferred.

3-3. FORMAT-FREE OUTPUT STATEMENTS

The general procedures associated with output statements are much the same as those presented in the previous sections on input statements. Again, there is a format-free and a format approach.

Suppose that the three variables NHØURS, BRATE, and DEDUC are read into the computer as indicated in the previous section, and an answer to a simple problem is calculated. It is then desired to obtain from the computer both the value of this answer and the values of NHØURS, BRATE, and DEDUC which were used to produce this answer. The format-free output statement would be

PRINT, NHØURS, BRATE, DEDUC, ANS

The numerical values of these four variables in the output list will then be printed across a page on the printer. Each value will be printed to full precision with blank spaces inserted between values for clarity. Eight values are typically printed across an output page; but this varies from one installation to another. Real numbers are normally printed in exponential format with seven significant figures. Typical output for the above statement might be

12   0.1623000E01   0.1000000E−01   0.4210000E02

When the PRINT statement has more output variables than may be printed on a single line, output is continued on the following line.

The general form of the PRINT statement is

PRINT, *variable list*

There is also an output PUNCH statement which produces output on cards and has the general form

PUNCH, *variable list*

It is also possible to produce explanatory messages in format-free output by inserting the material within single quotation marks in the output variable list. For example:

PRINT, 'THE ANSWER IS', ANS

would produce

THE ANSWER IS 0.4210000E02

This will be illustrated further.

3-4. FORMATTED OUTPUT STATEMENTS

By using the earlier example, the formatted output approach would use the following two statements:

```
    WRITE (6,28) NHØURS, BRATE, DEDUC, ANS
28  FØRMAT (1X,I10,F10.2,E20.7,E20.5)
```

The WRITE statement is very similar to the READ statement. The WRITE statement directs the computer to write the variables using unit number 6. The layout of the variables will be given by FØRMAT statement number 28, and the individual variables to be written are NHØURS, BRATE, DEDUC, and ANS.

For line printer output, the output FØRMAT statement has one slight difference from the input FØRMAT statement. The first column of an output list is used as a *carriage control indicator*, and the carriage of the output printer (which will ultimately produce a printed list of these variables) will be controlled by the character found in column 1. Here an x-type format specification indicates that the first column is blank. The x-type field specification is a convenient way to indicate blank spaces in the output list. The width of the field specification for an x-type format is given in front of the x specification, and a 1X field specification makes the first column in the output list a blank. Having column 1 blank will produce an output list that is single spaced. It might also be noted that the X-type format is not associated with any of the variables in the output variable list shown in the WRITE statement.

The carriage control indicator does not apply to teletypes such as those used in time-sharing systems, nor does it apply to card punches, magnetic tapes, etc.

The next field specification in the FØRMAT list is the I10 specification associated with the integer variable NHØURS, and the F10.2 field specification is for the real variable BRATE. The E20.7 is the exponential format specification associated with the real variable DEDUC, and the E20.5 field specification is for the output variable ANS. Since it is possible that the size of the numerical value of the variable ANS is unknown, it is desirable to have it come out in an exponential format to take care of extremely small or extremely large numbers. The field specification E20.5 takes care of this and allows 20 columns with five significant figures.

Summarizing these output statements, they indicate to the machine that it should use output unit number 6 to list the four variables NHØURS, BRATE, DEDUC, and ANS according to the output format given by statement 28. Statement 28 indicates that in the output record the first column should be blank, columns 2–11 should contain the integer variable NHØURS, columns 12–21 should contain the floating-point variable BRATE with two places to the right of the decimal, columns 22–41 should contain the real variable DEDUC in exponential notation with seven places to the right of the decimal and with the fraction to vary between 0.1 and 1.0, and columns 42–61 should contain the variable ANS in exponential format with five places to the right of the decimal and with the fraction to vary between 0.1 and 1.0.

There are many alternate possibilities for output statements just as there are many alternate forms for input statements, and alternate forms are shown in Table 3-2.

One additional comment about input and output listings might be appropriate. As indicated earlier, there are more columns specified in many of the field specifications than are necessary to contain the variable. For example, in the sample output listing it is possible that the output variable BRATE will require only four columns to contain the value of the variable. If the variable BRATE took on the value 8.10, then it could be held in four columns and there would be six columns left over in the output field

Table 3-2. Formatted Output Statements

Output Unit	Standard Form	Alternate Form
Card punch, on-line		PUNCH *n*, *list*
Printer, on-line		PRINT *n*, *list*
Magnetic tape (for off-line printing and punching)	WRITE (*j,n*) *list*	WRITE ØUTPUT TAPE *j, n, list*
Paper tape		PUNCH TAPE *n*, *list*
Console typewriter		TYPE *n*, *list*

Note: j stands for an integer whose value specifies the output unit, *n* stands for the statement number of the FØRMAT statement, and *list* stands for the output variables.

specification. In all cases such as this the computer will *right justify* the output. This means that the computer will take the output number and push it as far to the right as it can in the output field specification, i.e., all of the output blanks will be on the left-hand side of the field. For the value of BRATE above, columns 2–7 would be blank.

On input statements the computer does not control whether the data are right justified or left justified; this is up to the programmer. He may use any spacing within his given field width that he desires for his real variables. In the input READ statement the BRATE could be placed either extremely to the left, i.e., *left justified*, or it could be right justified within the columns allotted. If the number of places to the right of the decimal in the actual value of BRATE given is different from that called for in the field specification, then the format of the input variable itself will override the number of decimal places called for in the FØRMAT statement field specification.

In the case of integer variables and real variables using exponential format the problem is more complicated, however, because the computer will recognize blank spaces as zeros. For this reason it is necessary that all integer variables and all real variables using exponential form must always be right-justified for input, or otherwise the computer will inadvertently enter an input constant that is orders-of-magnitude larger than intended. The basic format specifications discussed in this and the previous section are summarized in Table 3-3.

Table 3-3. Format Field Specifications

General form of the FØRMAT statement for numerical data is

$$n \text{ FØRMAT } (S_1, S_2 \ldots S_k)$$

where n stands for a statement number, and each S_i is a format specification.

The following format specifications are available for single line input and output of real and integer data and to skip a field on the input and output record.

Format Code	External Representation	Internal Representation	Suggested Minimum Output Field Width
Iw	Integer, $\pm$xxxx	Fixed-point number	Number of significant digits $+ 1$
Fw.d	Real number without exponent, $\pm$x.xxxx	Floating-point number	Depends on number size, at least $d + 3$
Ew.d	Real number with exponent, $\pm$x.xxxE $\pm$ xx	Floating-point number	$d + 7$ for most computers
wX	Skip field	None	Any

In the above, w stands for an unsigned integer constant which specifies the field width, d stands for an unsigned integer constant which specifies the number of digits in the fractional part of the number, and x stands for any decimal digit or a blank character which is interpreted as a zero.

3-5. PAUSE, STØP **AND** END **STATEMENTS**

There are several statements available for program termination and/or interruption. This termination and/or interruption may come during the compilation or during the execution of a program, and there are different statements available for these different purposes. As described in Chapter 1, the first phase of running a FORTRAN program will be the compilation of the program to produce an object program. There must be some way for the FORTRAN compiler to recognize the end of the program that it is compiling. This is true since a number of different programs may be stacked together and put into an input unit for compilation. Unless there is some way for the compiler to recognize the end of one program, it might try to compile all of these individual programs together as one large program. The compiler recognizes the end of a program by an END statement. This statement is not executable and does not itself produce any machine-language instructions. The END statement is the last statement in the list of the FORTRAN source program. This does not imply that it is the last statement to be executed; but it does indicate that there are no further statements in this particular program list. Saying this another way, there must be only one END statement in a program, and it must be the very last statement in the program listing (disregarding the fact that there may be data cards following the program itself).

Once the FORTRAN program has been compiled and the object program is ready for execution, there also must be a means to terminate and/or interrupt the execution of the program. The PAUSE and STØP statements are provided for these purposes. One of the most logical applications of a STØP statement is at the termination of the executable statements in the program. This says that the execution of a particular program is complete, and all of the instructions for this individual program have been executed, i.e., the machine has completed running the program. A STØP statement is sufficient for this purpose. Normally the computer cannot be made to continue within the given program after a STØP statement has been executed. In computers using a monitor the STØP statement normally shifts control back to the monitor to start a new program job. Note that the STØP statement is such that it stops the execution of the object program and can only take effect while the object program is being executed. The STØP statement does not cause termination of compilation.

It might be noted that in some FORTRAN compilers the END statement automatically causes the FORTRAN compiler to generate a STØP statement at the end of the object deck.

There are many additional useful applications of the STØP statement. For example, in many cases a program will direct the computer to read a set of input data and check all of these data for consistency. If some of the data are inconsistent, then the programmer might direct the computer to go to a STØP statement and not try to process the data. In such an application a STØP statement would be contained within the body of the program, and if it were ever executed, it would actually stop the running of the program before it had completed the entire sequence of calculations called for by the program. Note that this implies that the STØP statement will be compiled and will generate machine-language instructions that will appear in the object deck.

One of the difficulties with the STØP statement, as indicated earlier, is that the computer cannot conveniently be made to continue within the same program after the STØP statement has been executed. The PAUSE statement allows the operator to overcome this inconvenience and to restart the program. The PAUSE statement does, in fact, stop the computer; but it does allow restarting possibilities. This is usually done by pressing a button on the computer console, and, when this is done, the computer will resume the execution of the object program beginning with the statement just after the PAUSE statement. The PAUSE statement might be used to interrupt a program temporarily in order to check intermediate results, to mount a new magnetic tape, or to take other action.

There are many differences in computer centers as to their choice between the use of STØP and PAUSE statements. Many large computer centers will try to avoid the wasted (expensive) computer time that is consumed by encountering a STØP or PAUSE statement, and they may actually modify the basic FORTRAN compilers so that these statements are not acceptable. Large computer centers often have computers which are run under the control of a monitor program as discussed in Chapter 1. The monitor program normally does not provide for a STØP when a program reaches the normal completion of its execution: It is more desirable for the computer to return control to the monitor program. This is better than stopping execution completely. A convenient way to provide for return of control from the individual program to the monitor's control is through the use of the CALL EXIT statement. The CALL EXIT statement has the effect of simply returning the control of the computer to the monitor. Many compilers are set up so that a STØP statement has the same effect as a CALL EXIT statement, and the machine does not stop its operation. This point should be checked with any local computer center before use is made of the STØP statement.

Summarizing, the END statement must be the last statement in the source program. There may only be one END statement, and it is a signal to the compiler that it is the end of the program being compiled into an object program. It is not a statement that is executed during the running of the object program, and it does not generate any machine-language instructions in the object program. The PAUSE and STØP statements are statements that appear within the body of the program. There may be more than one of them within any individual program: They do generate machine-language instructions for the object program, and they may be executed during the course of running the object program.

3-6. AN EXAMPLE PROGRAM

With the example statements discussed so far, it is now possible to write a sample FORTRAN program. We might, for sake of a simple example, assume that it is desirable to write a simple "payroll" program to calculate weekly paychecks for employees of a company. For each employee the program should read in the number of hours (NHØURS) which the individual had worked, the basic hourly rate (BRATE) at which the employee is paid, and the dollar value of any deductions (DEDUC) which should be subtracted from the employee's "take home" pay. The program should be written to pay the employee at the basic rate for the first forty hours per week worked, and then pay should be "time-and-a-half" for all overtime. The employee's income tax should be calculated at a flat rate of 16%, and then "net pay" should be calculated as "gross pay" minus deductions and minus income tax. Finally, the program should write out NHØURS, BRATE, DEDUC, income tax (TAXIC), and the net pay (PAYNET).

If only one pay check were ever to be calculated, it would be possible to write the program with the values of NHØURS, BRATE, and DEDUC appearing as constants within the program, but knowing it will be desirable to make this calculation quite often, it is feasible to write the program to read in values of NHØURS, BRATE, and DEDUC. For sake of illustration in this particular section, assume that we will only read in one set of values of NHØURS, BRATE, and DEDUC, and, based on these, calculate one set of numerical answers. To take care of many additional sets of input data, one or two additional statements will have to be added to our program at a later time.

In order to write the program one additional statement might be discussed. This is the so-called comment card or comment line. This comes under the heading of an informational type of statement in a FORTRAN program as discussed in an earlier chapter. The comment card or comment line has a C in column 1 of the statement. When the FORTRAN compiler encounters a card which has a C in column 1, it does not process the information contained on the card. In other words, it is not treated as an executable statement or a statement to be compiled; but if the computer does provide a "listing" of the program (a printed version of the program which will be produced during the compilation phase), then the comment cards will be provided in the listing. The use of the comment card is to make the program more easily understandable by the programmer. It does not provide explicit information for use by the computer. Very liberal use of these comment cards will make the program more easily understandable by the original programmer if he should return to the program some period of time after its original conception, and it also will make it easier for someone other than the original programmer to interpret the program, i.e., it will improve the documentation. Comment cards are not too necessary in very short programs, but they become almost mandatory in very large and complex programs. In order to help the reader get into the habit of using them, this entire book will make very liberal use of comment cards. *Comment cards must not appear in input data.*

Based on the few previous comments it might be desirable to look at an example program to carry out the objective indicated earlier. This example program is shown in Figure 3-1. Both format and format-free I/Ø statements are shown. Note that comment cards have been used to indicate the name of the program and to indicate the input statements, the calculation statements, the output statements, and the terminal statements in the program. The input statements for the program are as discussed in Sections 3-1 and 3-2, the output statements are similar to those discussed in Sections 3-3 and 3-4, and the terminal statements are as discussed in Section 3-5. The calculation statements for the program are indicated and the calculation itself is broken up into three statements. The first statement calculates gross pay, i.e., GRSPAY is done in mixed mode arithmetic. ‡ The GRSPAY statement pays the employee at the basic rate for 40 hours, and all over 40 hours is paid at time-and-a-half, i.e., 50% extra.

---

‡ In many present-day compilers this mixed mode is acceptable; but often it is wasteful of machine time. In most current compilers the presence of the real constant in the expression will signal the compiler to evaluate the entire expression in real arithmetic, i.e., convert all constants and variables to real quantities and then perform the arithmetic operations. This mixed mode is inserted and illustrated here to point out a potential programming problem for some compilers.

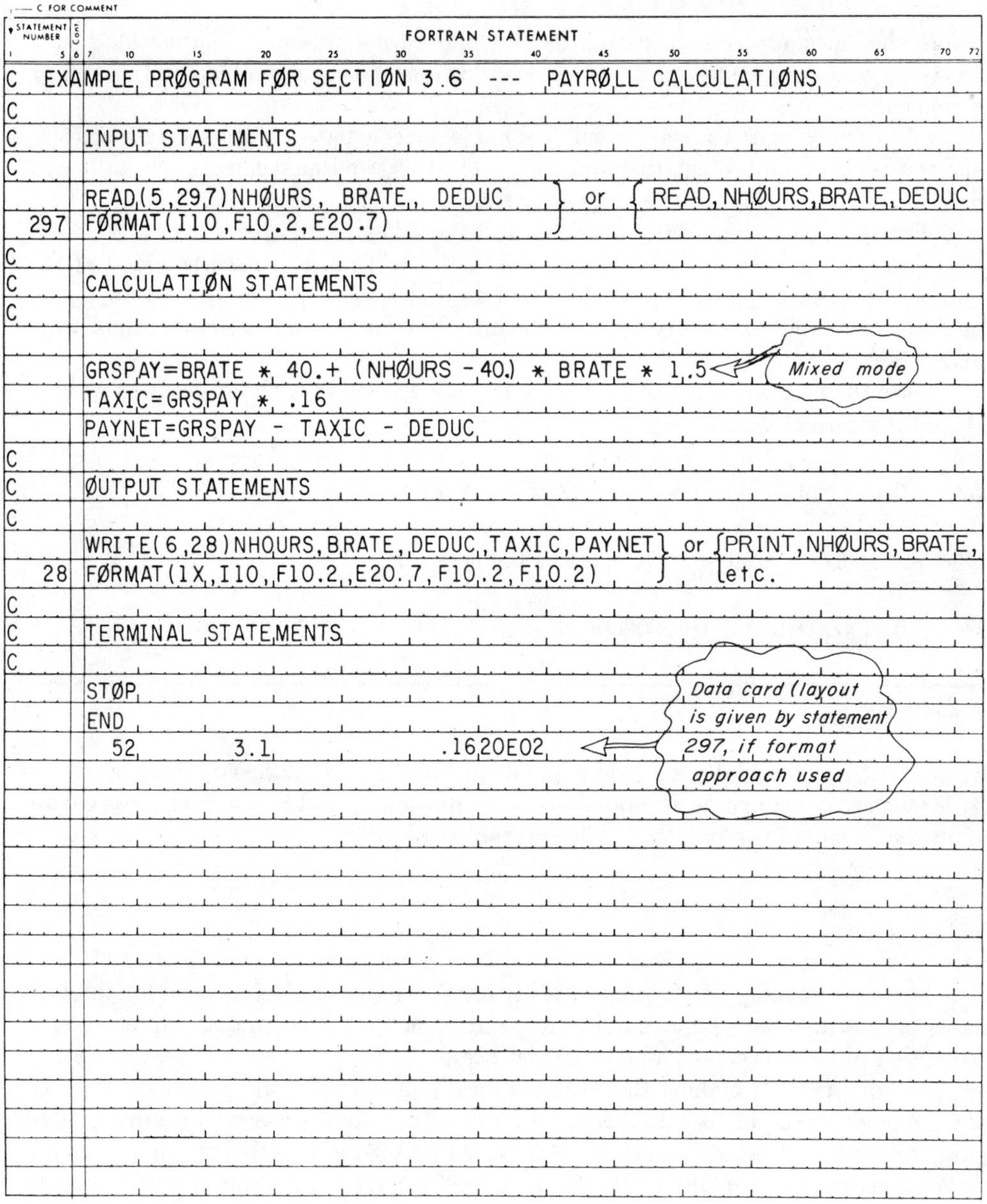

```
C   EXAMPLE PRØGRAM FØR SECTIØN 3.6 --- PAYRØLL CALCULATIØNS
C
C       INPUT STATEMENTS
C
        READ(5,297)NHØURS, BRATE, DEDUC     } or {  READ,NHØURS,BRATE,DEDUC
  297   FØRMAT(I10,F10.2,E20.7)             }      {
C
C       CALCULATIØN STATEMENTS
C
        GRSPAY=BRATE * 40.+ (NHØURS -40.) * BRATE * 1.5   (Mixed mode)
        TAXIC=GRSPAY * .16
        PAYNET=GRSPAY - TAXIC - DEDUC
C
C       ØUTPUT STATEMENTS
C
        WRITE(6,28)NHØURS,BRATE,DEDUC,TAXIC,PAYNET} or {PRINT,NHØURS,BRATE,
   28   FØRMAT(1X,I10,F10.2,E20.7,F10.2,F10.2)    }     {etc.
C
C       TERMINAL STATEMENTS
C
        STØP
        END
     52      3.1          .16 20E02  <-- Data card (layout
                                         is given by statement
                                         297, if format
                                         approach used
```

Figure 3-1. Coding form for example program in Section 3-6.

The GRSPAY statement is shown with an intentional mixed mode statement (since it contains NHØURS) which a few compilers will treat as an error. This is done in order to illustrate some of the problems that may be encountered. The expression on the right-hand side of the equal sign will, of course, be done in real arithmetic. In order to avoid this mixed-mode problem, we could insert a statement

TØTHRS = NHØURS

before the calculation of GRSPAY. TØTHRS could then be used in the calculation of GRSPAY in place of NHØURS, and there would be no mixed-mode problem in the GRSPAY statement.

As the original problem was stated, income tax is calculated at a fixed rate of 16%, and this is the second calculation statement. The third and final calculation statement determines the net pay for the employee.

The FORTRAN coding form is written to have a keypunch operator produce all of the cards for the entire computer program, and a typical data card is added at the end of the form. Once this complete set of cards has been prepared by a keypunch operator, the program is ready for insertion into the computer for its actual compilation and execution.

Once the program has been run, the data shown will give the results shown here (layout for formatted output case):

52   3.10   0.1620000E+02   28.77   134.83

The format-free output would appear as follows:

52   0.3100000E01   0.1620000E02   0.2877000E02   0.1348300E03

EXAMPLE 3-1

It is desired to calculate the yearly payment that will be necessary to amortize a $10,000 loan over 20 years at annual interest rates of 6% and 8%. Under these conditions the formula for repaying $1 over n years at i% interest is:

$$\frac{i}{1 - (1 + i)^{-n}}$$

The purpose of example is to prepare a program to make this calculation for the two cases proposed. Read in the number of years N in I5 format and the interest rate RATEIN in F10.5 (not expressed as a percentage).

The program for making these calculations is shown in Figure 3-2. It is set up so that program reads in the number of years and the rate of interest in order that it can be used for situations other than 20 years and 6% or 8%. This flexibility could be extended to the amount of the loan ($10,000), but is not done in this example.

Note that, in effect, the basic program is executed twice—once for 6% and once for 8%. (Chapter 4 will introduce transfer of control statements that will eliminate the need for so many statement repeats.)

In the statements for case 1 the PAY calculation is broken down into two arithmetic assignment statements simply as a matter of illustration. In the equivalent calculation in case 2, the calculation is all done in one arithmetic assignment statement. Also note in case 2 that the input READ and the output WRITE statements refer to earlier FØRMAT statements, i.e., there is no need to repeat these FØRMAT statements.

When executed each of these read statements brings in a data card, and therefore, two input data cards are necessary. These data cards could be altered to run

```
C FOR COMMENT
STATEMENT NUMBER | CONT | FORTRAN STATEMENT
C EXAMPLE PRØGRAM TØ CALCULATE PAYMENT NECESSARY TØ AMØRTIZE A LØAN
C
C READ IN DATA FØR CASE 1
      READ(5,10,)N,RATEIN       }  or  { READ,N,RATEIN
   10 FORMAT(I5,F10.5)          }      {
C
C CALCULATIØNS FØR CASE 1
C
      TERM = (1. + RATEIN)**N
      PAY = 10000.* RATEIN/(1. - 1./TERM)
C
C ØUTPUT ØF RESULTS FØR CASE 1
C
      WRITE(6,100)N,RATEIN PAY  }  or  { PRINT,N,RATEIN,PAY
  100 FØRMAT(1X,I5,F10.5,F10.0) }      {
C
C READ IN DATA FØR CASE 2
C
      READ(5,10)N,RATEIN           or    READ,N,RATEIN
C
C CALCULATIØNS FØR CASE 2
C
      PAY = 10000.*RATEIN/(1.-(1.+RATEIN)**-N)
C
C ØUTPUT ØF RESULTS FØR CASE 2
C
      WRITE(6,100)N,RATEIN,PAY      or    PRINT,N,RATEIN,PAY
C
C TERMINAL STATEMENTS
C
      STØP
      END
   20     .060
   20      .080
```

Figure 3-2. Coding form for Example 3-1.

any two equivalent cases, e.g., 10 years at 3% and 30 years at 9%. The important concept is that each time a READ statement is executed, it will bring in a new data card.

In the output FØRMAT statement number 100 the first column is left blank to prevent any undesired spacing of the carriage on the output printer for the computing system. In general, as indicated earlier, the contents of column 1 in an output line will control the line printer's operation. The printer uses column 1 for carriage control, and thus the contents of this column do not appear on the printed sheet. Generally speaking the following printer actions are appropriate:

Contents of Column 1	Action of Printer
Blank	Single spacing before printing.
Zero	Double space before printing.
1	Skip to the top of a new page before printing.
+	Print without advancing carriage

The usage of these symbols to control carriage spacing on the output line printer will be illustrated further in many examples throughout this book.

For the example program the results are given below (using format approach):

```
20     0.06000     872.
20     0.08000     1019.
```

The format-free output would appear as follows:

```
20     0.6000000E−01     0.8720000E03
20     0.8000000E−01     0.1019000E04
```

EXAMPLE 3-2

A store has a number of charge accounts which contain unpaid bills and some of these bills have as much as six months of unpaid charges. The store has a policy of charging interest on these unpaid bills at the rate of 1.5% per month on the unpaid balance. In an effort to collect these bills the store decides to let the customers pay one-fourth of the total bill (including interest charges) now and one-fourth (plus additional accumulated interest) during each of the next three months. It is desired to write a computer program to read in the monthly charges (if any) for each of the last six months and calculate the total bill due now (including interest). It is also desired to have the computer program calculate the portion of the bill to be paid now and in each of the next three month periods.

The computer program necessary to carry out the indicated calculations is shown in Figure 3-3 which includes numerous comment cards (some of which are even blank) to indicate the different portions of the program and make it easier to follow the contents of the FORTRAN statements themselves. Note the use of continuation cards in the arithmetic assignment statements associated with calculations of TØTNØW. This arithmetic assignment statement would have run past column 72 on the FORTRAN coding form, and a continuation statement was necessary. It is good programming practice to use a number in column 6 to indicate the number of the continuation line rather than some other arbitrary symbol. This is, however, a matter of convenience and personal preference, since any symbol could have been used in column 6 to indicate that the card is a continuation card.

```
C EXAMPLE PRØGRAM TØ CALCULATE CHARGE ACCØUNT BILLS
C
C INPUT ØF PREVIØUS SIX MØNTHS BILLS

      READ(5, 1000)B6MØLD,B5MØLD,B4MØLD,B3MØLD,B2MØLD,B1MØLD
1000  FØRMAT(6F10.2)
C
C CALCULATIØN ØF TØTAL AMØUNT DUE NØW
C
      TØTNØW = B6MØLD*1.015**6 + B5MØLD*1.015**5 + B4MØLD*1.015**4 +
1B3MØLD*1.015**3 + B2MØLD*1.015**2 + B1MØLD*1.015
C
C CALCULATIØN ØF AMØUNTS TØ BE PAID IN THE FØUR INSTALLMENTS
C
      DUENØW = TØTNØW/4.
      DUE1MØ = TØTNØW/4. + 3./4.*TØTNØW*0.015
      DUE2MØ = TØTNØW/4. + TØTNØW/2.*.015*1.015
      DUE3MØ = TØTNØW/4. + TØTNØW/4.*.015*1.015**2
C
C ØUTPUT ØF RESULTS
C
      WRITE(6,2000)TØTNØW,DUENØW,DUE1MØ,DUE2MØ,DUE3MØ
2000  FØRMAT(1X,5F10.2)
      STØP
      END
72.45     16.24     8.09     104.21     0.00     21.08


      The  format-free  I/Ø  statements  would  be:

      READ, B6MØLD, B5MØLD, B4MØLD, B3MØLD, B2MØLD, B1MØLD
                and
      PRINT, TØTNØW, DUENØW, DUE1MØ, DUE2MØ, DUE3MØ
```

Figure 3-3. Coding form for Example 3-2.

In both the input and output portions of the program a *repetition number* in the format statements is employed. In statement 1000 the F10.2 is used six times and rather than repeat it each time the 6F10.2 is used. The repetition number 6 saves this unnecessary writing. In statement 2000 the 5 is a repetition number.

The results of running this program for the sample data card of Figure 3-3 are shown below:

235.67   58.92   61.57   60.71   59.83

The format-free output would appear as follows:

0.2356700E03   0.5892000E02   0.6157000E02   0.6071000E02   0.5983000E02

3-7. HANDLING PROGRAM DECKS

The physical arrangement of programs and data is dependent on the computer and monitor employed in a given center. The equipment associated with the computer and individual preference of the local computer center are also important. Because of this it is very difficult to generalize about the actual physical arrangement of programs and data; but several example situations will be discussed. As an example of how the operation might be handled, consider a case in which a digital computer is used with an off-line printer, i.e., a printer that is not physically connected to the computer. Also assume that the installation is one in which all input to the computer is done primarily via punched cards and output also is obtained primarily via punched cards. In such an installation the compilation and execution of programs such as those illustrated

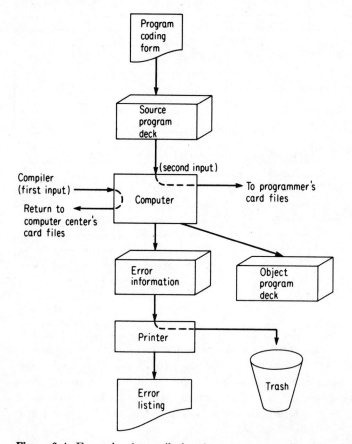

Figure 3-4. Example of compilation (a one-pass compiler illustrated).

in Examples 3-1 and 3-2 will be as follows. The coding form would be used to prepare a source program deck, and the source program deck would be fed through the computer along with the compiler program (and assembler program, if necessary) in order to produce an object program deck and, if appropriate, information on errors made in the language of the source program. This is illustrated in Figure 3-4. If source program language errors are encountered in the compilation of the program, the object program deck will not be one that is suitable for execution. The error information is taken to a printer to produce a listing or a hard copy of the information. As the object deck itself is in binary, it is not listed. (If too many errors are present, an object deck may not be produced.) The common thing to do at this stage if errors are present is to go back and make changes to individual cards in the source program deck and recompile the source program deck. It is possible to go into the object program deck and make corrections in it; but it requires a deep understanding of absolute machine language on the part of the programmer. Consequently, except in the rarest cases, the source deck is modified and recompiled to eliminate any source program language errors, or *bugs*, that might have been encountered in the original compilation. Once this phase of *debugging* is complete, the program is ready for execution.

In order to be executed, a program similar to those discussed in the previous

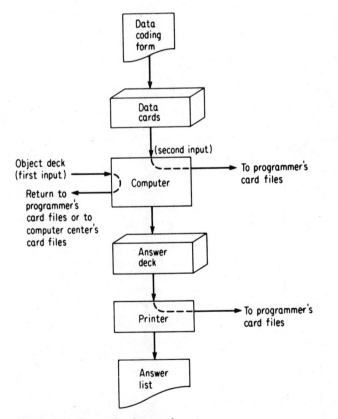

Figure 3-5. Example of execution.

sections will require data cards in addition to the program itself. The data are prepared on coding forms much like the FORTRAN program itself, but with no restrictions on the use of the various columns. These forms are converted into data cards by the keypunch operator. The object program and the data cards are then fed into the computer. The object deck will be introduced, followed by the data cards. The results of the object program's execution on the specific data provided will produce answers in the form of an answer deck which may be taken to an off-line printer to produce a printed list or hard copy of the results obtained. This is shown schematically in Figure 3-5. In the execution of the program it is possible that execution errors will be encountered, and further source program debugging will be necessary. (This is discussed further in Section 3-8.)

In Chapter 1 it was indicated that it may be desirable to have a load-and-go compiler in which no output object deck is produced. An example of a load-and-go compiler's operation on a card-input and card-output computer system is shown in Figure 3-6. Note in Figure 3-6 that the compiler is entered first, followed by the source program and then by the data cards. There is no object deck produced; there are no intermediate results produced; the answer cards are produced directly (assuming no

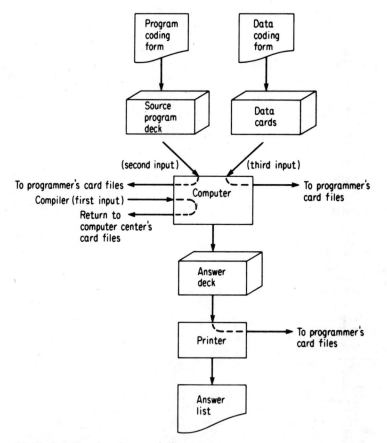

Figure 3-6. Load-and-go compiler.

program errors). These answers are taken to an off-line printer for preparation of an answer list or hard copy. The load-and-go compiler has the advantage of not requiring the time necessary to punch out an object deck, although the object program is internally prepared and stored in memory. The load-and-go compiler is simpler in operation and requires fewer steps in handling information external to the computer's memory. It has the obvious disadvantage that the program must be recompiled every time it is to be executed, and the compilation phase requires machine running time. If a program is to be used over and over again, then the load-and-go compiler is not very efficient. Load-and-go compilers are very useful in student programming laboratories where programs are normally run only once and where there are very large numbers of relatively simple programs to be handled. Also, a student may have several runs on the same program before it is bug-free.

Large computers operating under the control of a monitor system are more complex than the previous examples. Typically these larger machines have magnetic tape input and output because of the slow speed of the card-handling equipment. Programs and data must have *control cards* associated with them to make certain that the monitor understands when the program is to be compiled, when it is to be executed, and which input unit contains data for a program. It is not desirable to discuss control cards further because their use varies so widely from one computer to another. These control cards typically carry the name of the programmer or the number of the job, the maximum amount of time the program is expected to run, and other types of similar information. They also contain an indication as to the specific compiler that is necessary for the program, which input units and output units are assigned for the program, etc. In some installations some portion of this information is assigned by the monitor, and in other cases they are dictated by the control cards directly.

3-8. DEBUGGING THE SOURCE PROGRAM

It can happen to the best of us! The original program as prepared, punched, and compiled on the computer is not properly written and errors exist in the program. These errors must be removed or the computer will not provide an object deck that is acceptable for actual execution. The purpose of this section is to give some insight into these errors.‡

There are three different types of errors that might be present in a computer program. There are source program language errors that prevent the compilation of the program, and these must be removed before compilation can be successfully completed. There are execution errors which will not be encountered until the actual execution of the program. For example, some of the most common execution errors are due to the programmer's use of inadequate field specifications in FØRMAT statements. All of these execution errors must be removed before the computer will produce any complete answers. Finally, there are errors in the logic and formulation of the program or of individual statements by the programmer. These latter errors are the

---

‡ Debugging can be greatly assisted if a FORTRAN compiler such as the WATFØR or WATFIV compiler is used. (See Appendix E.)

insidious ones that appear when a programmer writes a program that is perfectly acceptable to the computer and is a good program—except that it causes a computation to be made which is different from the one intended by the programmer. ‡ The only way that these errors of intent can be corrected is for the programmer to make a thorough check for consistency and reasonableness in the answers that are produced by the computer. There may be some kinds of internal checks in the program which the programmer may provide; but in general, there must be a final and thorough review of some typical answers of the program to see if the program is actually doing what the programmer intended.

Most compilers provide "error scans" in order to detect compilation and execution errors, and they give an indication to the programmer as to the nature of the error and its location in the program. In Section 3-6 the program given in Figure 3-1 contains a mixed mode. In the actual running of this program by some compilers an error will be detected and the actual execution of the program deleted. The compiler would indicate an error of "mixed mode" in statement 297 + 1 (which refers to the first line past statement number 297, not including comment cards). In many cases the compiler also will assign a *line number* to every statement in the FORTRAN program and provide an output listing of the source program with the associated line numbers and error messages (referenced to the appropriate line). The completeness of an error scan on any given computer depends on both the desires and operating procedures of the computer center, the nature of the compiler, and the nature of the computer. It might be recognized that the larger the error scan, the more memory its programming will require in the computer. Also, the larger the error scan, the more time it will take to check for errors. Generally speaking, error scans are very complete in load-and-go type compilers such as WATFØR or WATFIV which are usually used in student installations.

Sometimes an error made during compilation in one statement will produce a whole series of apparent errors in subsequent statements. For example, the potential error indicated in the example program of Section 3-6 was a mixed mode that could prevent some compilers from calculating the variable GRSPAY. Subsequently to this, GRSPAY appears on the right-hand side of the statement which calculates TAXIC and the statement which calculates PAYNET. Since the compiler has no record of GRSPAY being defined (calculated), the compiler finds errors in the arithmetic assignment statements for the calculation of TAXIC and PAYNET because GRSPAY is not defined. Therefore, it is an *undefined variable*. This means that the compiler has no record of GRSPAY, TAXIC, and PAYNET being defined (calculated), and therefore, in the WRITE statement at the end of the program, they are not available for output. Thus, undefined variables are encountered in the output list. The simple correction of the mixed mode in the calculation of GRSPAY will remove all of these error indications.

For the exact error code for an individual computer, it will be necessary to contact the computer center itself. (In some cases, manufacturer's programming manuals contain error codes.) These codes are normally prepared in the form of handouts for all users.

A number of general conclusions are possible concerning the debugging of com-

---

‡ The statement has been made that the ultimate computer is one that does what we want it to do, not necessarily what we tell it to do.

puter programs and the accompanying usage of error messages. These rules are as follows:

1 Never assume that a program is completely correct even though it may be accepted by the computer, completely compiled, and numerical results are achieved. It is possible that logical errors are present.

2 The checking or debugging of a computer program is made much simpler if values of intermediate variables are available. This means that quite often in the writing of a computer program there are extra WRITE statements to make these values available for debugging. Once the program is satisfactorily running, these extra WRITE statements can be removed and the program recompiled for routine use.

3 The tendency is to write a program on a "once-through" basis and present it immediately for keypunching and running on the computer. The programmer should resist this temptation and spend some time in making a careful check of his programs before they are punched and run.

4 When attempting to debug a computer program, there is a big temptation to assume that all aspects of a program are correct because it gives correct answers for an individual set of data. Make certain when choosing data for trial runs of your program that you select data which will execute every portion of your program.

5 When you are in the process of debugging a program, correct every error encountered before you attempt to return it to the machine to have the program recompiled. There is a temptation to make a single (or at least minimum) correction before recompiling. Avoid this temptation and try to approach the computer with as perfect a program as possible.

6 In writing your program make liberal use of comment cards, and for more complex programs be certain that you have the flowchart complete before you attempt to write any portion of the program. (Flowcharts will be discussed in more detail in Section 4-1.) In other words, make every possible effort to make your program as easy to interpret as possible, both for yourself and for others who may attempt to work with the program. This time is well spent and will make it much simpler for the individual to debug the program: It will result in a saving of both programmer and machine time.

3-9. IN SUMMARY

This chapter has proposed to introduce simple input and output statements and the termination and/or interruption statements that are necessary in the compilation and execution of a program. All of these have been combined into some simple sample programs. Finally, the arrangement of individual programs for execution has been discussed briefly along with some error messages that may be encountered. Unfortunately, many of the items discussed in this chapter are dependent on the individual computer center and will vary from one installation to the next.

It is hoped that the reader has gained an insight into the structure of FORTRAN programming. Rather than go on to more complex programs or get involved in the complexities of large programs, it is to the advantage of the student programmer to write many small programs rather than a few very large ones. The exercises associated with this chapter are structured with this in mind.

Exercises ‡

Where you use formatted I/Ø in these exercises you are to assume that all input real variables are in F10.2 FØRMAT, all input and output integer variables are in I10 format, and all output real variables are to be E20.7 format.

3-1 Write the FORTRAN format-free and formatted input statements necessary to read in the following:

(a) A, B, CAT, DØ

(b) I, J, KID

†(c) X, J, YES

(d) A, SIMPLE, GØ, I

3-2 Write the FORTRAN format-free and formatted input statements necessary to read in the following:

(a) IN, ØUT, UP, DØWN

(b) R, S, TEE, J

(c) X, Y, ZEE, ALPHA

†(d) CØNST, ØUKID, A, J

3-3 Prepare the FORTRAN format-free and formatted output statements necessary to write out the variable lists of Exercise 3-1 plus a new variable ANS in each set. Assume the variables given are input and ANS is the result of calculations performed on the input variables.

3-4 Prepare the FORTRAN format-free and formatted output statements necessary to write out the variable lists of Exercise 3-2 plus a new variable ANS in each set. Assume the variables given are input and ANS is the result of calculations performed on the input variables.

†**3-5** Repeat Exercise 3-3, except provide an additional three blank spaces between each output variable written. Do for formatted output only.

3-6 Repeat Exercise 3-4, except provide an additional three blank spaces between each output variable written. Do for formatted output only.

Note: For the following exercises you are to read in the given variables, perform the desired calculations, and write out the results as directed. Write complete FORTRAN programs including a trial data card. Watch for inadvertent cases of mixed modes, and where necessary change variable names inside the program to avoid mixed mode errors. Your instructor will indicate whether to take a format-free or a formatted approach in each case.

3-7 Read: x, y, z

Calculate: RESULT $= \dfrac{2x^2 + 16y}{z}$

Write: x, y, z, RESULT

---

‡ Solutions to Exercises marked with a dagger † are given in Appendix G.

†**3-8** Read: a, b, c, s

Calculate: $t = a \cdot \sqrt{s} + b \cdot s + c \cdot s^2$

Write: a, b, c, s, t

3-9 Read: x, y, z

Calculate: $\text{SØLN} = x^{17} + y^2 + 1/z$
$\text{BEST} = (\text{SØLN})^{0.5}$

Write: $x, y, z, \text{SØLN}, \text{BEST}$

3-10 Read: TØP, XMID, BØT

Calculate: $\text{TM} = (\text{TØP})^2 + \dfrac{1000.}{\text{XMID}} + \text{BØT}$

$\text{LM} = \text{TØP} + \dfrac{1000.}{\text{XMID}} + (\text{BØT})^2$

Write: TØP, XMID, BØT, TM, LM

3-11 Read: x, y, z

Calculate: $a = \sqrt{x^2 - 6}$
$b = |\, y^2 + 112.8\,| + z^2$

Write: x, y, z, a, b

†**3-12** Read: a, b, c

Calculate: $\text{A}1 = \left(1 - \dfrac{1 + abc}{1 + (a^2/bc)^{1/3}} \right)^{-1}$

$\text{A}2 = \dfrac{\text{A}1 + 3}{\text{A}1 - 5}$

Write: $a, b, c, \text{A}1, \text{A}2$

3-13 Read: x, y, i

Calculate: $\text{GØ} = x^2 + y + (i)^{1/2}$
$\text{STØP} = i^2 + y + (x)^{1/2}$

Write: $x, y, i, \text{GØ}, \text{STØP}$

3-14 Read: h, i

Calculate: $g = (h)^{.16} + (i)^2 + hi$
$j = i \cdot \sqrt{h} + hi + \sqrt{hi}$

Write: h, i, g, j

†**3-15** Read: x, y, z

Calculate: $\text{A}1 = x^3 + x^2 + x + 1$
$\text{A}2 = y^3 + y^2 + y + 1 + \text{A}1$
$\text{A}3 = z^3 + z^2 + z + 1 + \text{A}2$

Write: (Line 1) x, y, z
(Line 2) A1, A2, A3

3-16 Read: r, s, t, u, ν

Calculate: $\text{HE} = r + \dfrac{st}{u - \nu}$

$$\text{SHE} = |r| + \dfrac{(tu)^4}{1 - \nu}$$

$$\text{DEL} = \text{HE} - \text{SHE}$$

Write: (Line 1) r, s, t, u, ν
(Line 2) HE, SHE
(Line 3) DEL

3-17 Read: (Card 1) x, y
(Card 2) a, b
(Card 3) i

Calculate: $\text{SØLN} = ax + by + i$

Write: (Line 1) x, y, a, b
(Line 2) i, SØLN

†3-18 Read: (Card 1) r, s
(Card 2) t, u
(Card 3) x, y

Calculate: $\text{UP} = (r - s) + (t - u) + (x - y)$
$\text{DØWN} = (r + s) + (t + u) + (x + y)$
$\text{FIRST} = r + t + x$
$\text{SEC} = s + u + y$

$$\text{FINAL} = \text{UP}^2 + \sqrt{\text{DØWN}} + \dfrac{1}{\text{FIRST}}$$

Write: (Line 1) r, s, t, u, x, y
(Line 2) UP, DØWN, FIRST
(Line 3) SEC, skip thirty blank spaces, FINAL

3-19 Read: (Card 1) a, skip ten blank spaces, b
(Card 2) x, skip ten blank spaces, z

Calculate: $\text{ANS} = ax + bz$
$\text{DIF} = a - b$
$\text{SUM} = x + a$

Write: (Line 1) a, b, skip twenty-five blank spaces, x, z
(Line 2) SUM, skip twenty-five blank spaces, DIF
(Line 3) skip twenty-two blank spaces, ANS

3-20 Read: (Card 1) a (Card 4) d
(Card 2) b (Card 5) e
(Card 3) c (Card 6) f

Calculate: $\text{SUM} = abcdef + abcde + abcd$
$\text{SUMRT} = \sqrt{a} + \sqrt{b} + \sqrt{c}$
$\text{SUMSQR} = d^2 + e^2 + f^2$
$\text{MINØR} = abc + ab + a$

Write: (Line 1) SUM
(Line 2) skip twenty blank spaces, SUMRT
(Line 3) skip forty blank spaces, SUMSQR
(Line 4) skip sixty blank spaces, MINØR

3-21 Write a complete FORTRAN program to read in a student's identification number and his marks on "test one," "test two," and "test three." Also read in "homework average," "mid-term exam," and "final exam." Calculate "test average" for the three tests. Also calculate "composite average" based on 40% credit to test average, 10% credit to homework, 20% credit to the mid-term exam mark, and 30% credit for the final exam mark. Write out the student's identification number, his test average, and his composite average. If format is used for input and output, use I5 format for the identification number and F10.1 for all other variables.

†3-22 A student's grade point average is calculated by assigning A = 4.0, B = 3.0, C = 2.0, D = 1.0, and F = 0.0 and weighting the results based on the number of hours credit (semester or quarter basis) for the course to which the grade is applied. Write a computer program to read in a student's identification number, his old grade point average, and the number of hours to which this old grade point average applied. The purpose of the program is to up-date this grade point average based on the results of five courses just completed. The program must read in the hours credit and the numerical value of the grade awarded for each of these five courses. The purpose of the program is to calculate a new grade point average for the student. Write out the student's identification number, the new total number of hours to which the new grade point average applies, and the new grade point average itself.

3-23 Write a complete FORTRAN program entitled "Party Game." The calculations to be made are as follows:

1 Read into the machine two numbers. The first number will represent the date and month of your birth, e.g., if you were born on July 10th this would be 107. The second number is to be your age at your last birthday.

2 Multiply the first number by 2.

3 Add 5 to the results.

4 Multiply the results by 50.

5 Add your age to the results.

6 Add 365 to the results.

7 Subtract 615 from the results.

8 Write out the two numbers you read in and the results of step 7.

The "answer" calculated by these steps will give one number as the day and month of your birth and your current age.

3-24 A man needs a program to calculate the total taxes which he has paid during the course of a year. The final answer will indicate his relative "tax burden," i.e., the ratio, expressed as a percentage, of the total taxes which he pays divided by his total income. Read in his gross pay. Assume his income and social security taxes are 16% of his gross pay. Assume he drives an auto 10,000 miles per year, gets 15 miles per gallon, and pays 12¢ tax per gallon. Assume he pays 4% retail sales tax on purchases which amount to about 56% of his gross pay. His property tax is $175. Assume he pays miscellaneous taxes of about 3% of his gross pay per year. Calculate and write out his total taxes, and the tax burden ratio as defined earlier.

3-25 Prepare a program to read a measurement in feet and print this measurement in centimeters, meters, inches, feet, and yards. The conversion factors are

1 foot   = 12 inches
1 yard   = 3 feet
1 inch   = 2.54 centimeters
1 meter = 100 centimeters

The output should be similar to the following (for 3 feet):

0.9144 METERS
 91.4 CENTIMETERS
  36 INCHES
   3 FEET
   1 YARDS

Run the program for 1.7 feet.

†3-26 Prepare a program to read a volumetric measurement in cubic feet and convert to gallons (1 cu ft = 7.48 gal), liters (1 cu ft = 28.316 liters), cubic yards (27 cu ft = 1 cu yd), bushels (1 cu ft = 0.8036 bushels), and U.S. liquid barrels (1 bl = 31.5 gal). The output should be analogous to that in the previous exercise. Run the program for 10 cu ft.

3-27 A man borrows P dollars for n years at an interest rate of i. At the end of n years, he owes $P(1 + i)^n$. Prepare a program that reads P, i (in percent), and n, and calculates the final amount owed. Run for $P = \$100$, $i = 8$ percent, and $n = 5$.

3-28 A man borrows a sum of money P. He proposes to repay this amount in n annual installments at an annual interest rate of i. The annual payment is given by

$$M = \frac{Pi(1 + i)^n}{(1 + i)^n - 1}.$$

The total amount of interest he pays is

$nM - P$.

Prepare a program to compute the annual payment and total interest paid if $5000 is borrowed at 7% interest for 5 years.

†3-29 Write a program that reads a three-digit integer number, reverses the digits, and prints the results. For example, reversing the digits in 829 gives 928.

3-30 Write a program that computes the sum of the digits in a four-digit integer number. For example, the sum of the digits in 1824 is $1 + 8 + 2 + 4 = 15$.

3-31 Prepare a program to evaluate the polynomial

$$f(x) = ax^3 + bx^2 + cx + d$$

for given values of a, b, c, d, and x. The number of calculations can be minimized by programming this equation as follows:

$$f(x) = ((ax + b)x + c)x + d.$$

Run this program for $a = 1$, $b = 2$, $c = 7$, $d = 4$, and $x = 3$.

3-32 A cubic equation of the form $x^3 + bx^2 + cx + d = 0$ can be reduced to the form $y^3 + py + q = 0$ by the substitution $x = y - b/3$. The equations for p and q are

$$p = (3c - b^2)/3$$
$$q = (27d - 9bc + 2b^3)/27$$

Prepare a program to compute p and q for $b = 5$, $c = 7$, and $d = 2$. For output print the answer in equation form similar to the following:

$$\text{Y} ** 3 + (-1.333)\text{Y} + (-0.407)$$

†3-33 An arithmetic progression is a sequence of the type $a, a + d, a + 2d, \ldots, a + (n - 1)d$ in which each term differs from the preceding term by d, called the *common difference*. The sum of n terms is given by

$$s = \frac{n}{2}[2a + (n - 1)d]$$

Prepare a program to compute s for $n = 20$, $a = 1.5$, and $d = 2$.

3-34 A geometric progression is a succession of terms of the type $a, ar, ar^2, \ldots, ar^{n-1}$, where $a =$ first term, $r =$ ratio of successive terms (called the *common ratio*), $l =$ last term, $n =$ number of terms, and $s =$ sum of the terms. Prepare the flowchart for a program to compute l and s according to the following equations:

$$l = ar^{n-1}$$
$$s = \frac{a(r^n - 1)}{r - 1}$$

Use $a = 1.5$, $r = 0.8$, and $n = 20$.

3-35 A combined arithmetic and geometric progression is of the form $a, (a + d)r, (a + 2d)r^2, \ldots, [a + (n - 1)d]r^{n-1}$. The sum of n terms is given by

$$s = \frac{a - [a + (n - 1)d]r^n}{1 - r} + \frac{rd(1 - r^{n-1})}{(1 - r)^2}.$$

Prepare a program to compute s for $a = 1.5$, $d = 2$, $r = 0.8$, and $n = 20$.

3-36 For given values of F and T, the value of k_s can be computed by the following equation:

$$k_s = 0.57827(1.8081 - 0.03698F + 0.00198T + 0.0003056F^2$$
$$- 0.000005184T^2 - 0.00001872FT).$$

Write a program to compute k_s for values of 45 and 25 for T and F, respectively. Print T, F, and k_s.

3-37 For a value of t between 50 and 347.11, the value of p can be computed by the following relationship:

$$\log_{10} \frac{p}{p_c} = -\frac{x}{T}\left[\frac{a + bx + cx^3 + ex^4}{1 + dx}\right]$$

where $p_c = 218.167$
$T = t + 273.16$
$x = T_c - T$
$T_c = 647.27$
$a = 3.3463130$
$b = 4.14113 \times 10^{-2}$
$c = 7.515484 \times 10^{-9}$
$d = 1.3794481 \times 10^{-2}$
$e = 6.56444 \times 10^{-11}$

Compute p for $t = 75$. *Hint:* If $\log_{10} y = z$, then $y = 10^z$.

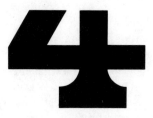

TRANSFER OF CONTROL

In the preceding chapter some very simple FORTRAN programs were illustrated and developed, and each of these had one aspect of their development in common. Each operated on a more or less "once-through" basis, and there were no loops or branches in the structure of the program's logic. Programs such as these are quite often encountered; but the more common situation is the one that takes advantage of the very powerful possibilities of logical decision-making in the digital computer itself. There are times when the programmer would like to skip certain statements in the program under one set of conditions, or execute those statements under another set of conditions. In other situations the programmer might prefer to go back to the very beginning of the program and read in new sets of data; transfer to the end of the program and terminate its operation; or go to some other intermediate point in the program to begin a new series of calculations. These situations described above give rise to the need for *transfer of control* statements, and the purpose of this chapter is to introduce this type of statement and show its usage in FORTRAN programming. Before tackling this problem directly, however, it is desirable to introduce the subject of flow charts.

4-1. FLOWCHARTS

With the possibilities for branches and loops within the structure of a computer program, it becomes increasingly difficult for the programmer to mentally account for all the possible loops and branches. The programs that have been illustrated previously in this book have been relatively simple; but with the introduction of transfer of control statements, they can be made so complex that it is virtually impossible for the programmer to visualize all of the logical decision loops via a purely mental memory process. Flowcharts provide an answer to this problem.

The flowchart is a very simple type of schematic diagram or "road map" which allows the programmer to chart out on paper the logical structure of his computer program. He may indicate all the branches and loops and their interrelationships with one another. The flowchart or block diagram provides a visual representation that not only is helpful to the individual programmer; but it is a valuable part of the documentation of his program and will allow someone else to interpret and use the program with a minimum of difficulty.

Flowcharts indicate the "flow of control" between the various executable statements that comprise the program. The flowchart is normally made up of a set of boxes or shapes which are coded to indicate the nature of the operations involved.

Appendix D at the end of the book gives a complete list of the American Standard flow-chart symbols, but for the purposes of this chapter, the following simple list is sufficient.

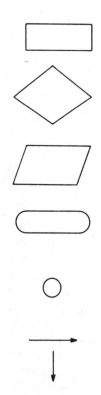

A rectangle is used to indicate a processing symbol (typically arithmetic operations).

A diamond is used to indicate a decision and the lines leaving the corners of the diamond are labeled with the decision results that are associated with each path.

The parallelogram is used to indicate any basic input or output symbol. There are, in addition, many special symbols for input-output operations.

An oval is used to indicate either the beginning or the end of a program, i.e., a terminal STØP or START.

A small circle is used to indicate a connection between two points in a flowchart in situations in which a connecting line between them would clutter the basic flowchart.

Arrows are used to indicate the direction of flow through the flowchart. Every line should have an arrow on it, but the length of the arrow is not important.

Any text or notes may be placed beside or in these symbols. It is especially helpful to indicate numbers beside appropriate processing symbols to indicate the statement number that will be associated with that particular operation in the FORTRAN program.

Throughout the remainder of this book are examples of flowcharts which should be sufficient to illustrate completely their usage.

It cannot be overemphasized to the beginning programmer that the flowchart represents the *first* step in the formulation of the program. Many beginning students participate in the very foolish habit of first trying to write their program and *subsequently* constructing a flowchart to illustrate the logic of the program. This is exactly the opposite of the recommended route. It should be noted that beginning programmers cannot always anticipate everything. Hence, often it is not until they have drawn a flowchart and tried to write the FORTRAN statements that they begin to find flaws in the flowchart.

4-2. UNCONDITIONAL GØ TØ

The primary purpose of the unconditional GØ TØ statement (and every other transfer of control statement) is to allow the programmer to shift the execution of the program to some statement other than the one that would normally be executed next in a straight-through sequence. As has been pointed out in earlier chapters, a digital computer will execute each statement in sequence according to the list encountered. The general form of the unconditional GØ TØ statement is:

GØ TØ *n*

where *n* is the number of an executable statement somewhere else in the program— either before or after the GØ TØ statement. When the GØ TØ statement is encountered it transfers the program to statement number *n*, and statement number *n* will be the next statement executed in the program. After statement *n* has been executed, the statement immediately following statement *n* will be executed unless statement *n* is a transfer-of-control statement.

Every statement in FORTRAN programming may be classified as either executable or nonexecutable, and statement *n* must be an executable statement. No transfer-of-control statement may direct transfer to a nonexecutable statement. Nonexecutable statements include some definition statements, certain specification statements, and the FØRMAT statement.

The statement number *n* illustrates quite vividly the only purpose which statement numbers serve in a FORTRAN program. Statement numbers, as pointed out earlier, are positive integer numbers of five digits or less, written in columns 1–5 of the FORTRAN coding form, and punched in columns 1–5 of the input card or its equivalent. The maximum value of the statement number varies with some versions of FORTRAN allowing up to 99999. The statement numbers in FORTRAN programs simply provide a *cross-reference* to allow statements to refer to one another within the program. As indicated in earlier examples, there is no necessary numerical sequence in FORTRAN statement numbers, and it is not necessary that every statement be numbered. It is not permissible, however, for any two statements to have the same number.

The main use of the unconditional GØ TØ statement is to allow the programmer to return execution from logical "branches" in which he has been operating to the "main body" of the program. There might be several such side branches in the program, and each of these normally will be terminated either by a STØP statement or by an unconditional GØ TØ statement.

EXAMPLE 4-1

To illustrate the use of the unconditional GØ TØ statement, consider the problem of calculating the numerical grade of a student in a class. Assume that the final grade for the student is based on the following considerations:

Test No. 1 counts	10%
Test No. 2 counts	10%
Test No. 3 counts	10%
Homework Average Grade counts	20%
Student Special Project counts	15%
Final Examination counts	35%
	100%

Write a computer program to read in these six items of information along with the individual student's identification number and, for that student, calculate his final numerical grade for the course. The output should be the student identification number and this final numerical grade. Consider for the moment that there will be an unlimited number of these sets of input data.

The flowchart for such a calculation might appear as shown in Figure 4-1 and the program as given in Figure 4-2. The program is relatively straightforward except that in output FØRMAT statement 20 there is the provision to leave column 1 blank, to write the identification number in i5 format, and then to provide for 10 blank

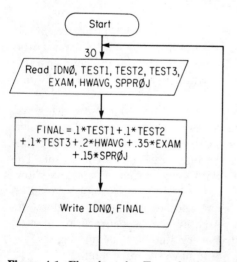

Figure 4-1. Flowchart for Example 4-1. (Calculation of final grade.)

```
┌─ C FOR COMMENT
│STATEMENT│C│                    FORTRAN STATEMENT
│ NUMBER  │O│
│1      5 6 7  10   15   20   25   30   35   40   45   50   55   60   65   70  72

C EXAMPLE PRØGRAM TØ CALCULATE THE NUMERICAL FINAL GRADE FØR A
C        STUDENT IN A CØURSE
C
C INPUT ØF STUDENT I.D NUMBER, TEST SCØRES, HØMEWØRK AVERAGE AND
C        GRADE ØN THE STUDENTS SPECIAL PRØJECT
C
   30 READ(5,10)IDNØ,TEST1,TEST2,TEST3,EXAM,HWAVG,SPPRØJ
   10 FØRMAT (I5,6F10.1)
C
C CALCULATIØN ØF FINAL GRADE
C
   40 FINAL = .1*TEST1 + .1*TEST2 + .1*TEST3 + .2*HWAVG + .35*EXAM +
      1.15*SPPRØJ
C
C ØUTPUT ØF ID NUMBER AND FINAL GRADE
C
   50 WRITE(6,20)IDNØ,FINAL
   20 FØRMAT(1X,I5,10X,F10.2)
C
C TRANSFER ØF CØNTRØL BACK TØ READ IN A NEW DATA CARD
C
   60 GØ TØ 30
      END
7321       63.2       78.3       27.8       45.       83.49       85.
7322       94.1       91.        91.3       27.       27.86       70.
7323       100.       62.3       82.1       72.       72.47       65.

         The  format-free  I/Ø statements would be :

      READ, IDNØ,TEST1,TEST2,TEST3,EXAM,HWAVG,SPPRØT

              and

      PRINT, IDNØ, FINAL
```

Figure 4-2. Coding form of Example 4-1.

spaces in the output line before writing the final grade in F10.2 format. After the final output statement the program has an unconditional transfer-of-control statement, GØ TØ 30, in which the execution of the program is referred back to statement number 30 and a new card is read into the machine, i.e., a new set of data introduced. This program will continue to operate indefinitely as long as data cards are available.

When the last of the data cards has been read, the FORTRAN compiler will give an execution error indicating that there is a "last-card error" (or something equivalent). This execution error indicates that the computer has transferred control back to the READ statement, the READ statement has tried to bring in a new set of data, and the input data card is not available. From the viewpoint of the programmer this error is rather trivial though it is not especially pleasing from an esthetic viewpoint. There are, of course, many ways to circumvent this type of error, and these will be discussed in detail in subsequent sections.

In order to illustrate the use of this program, some sample data are given and the program is run to calculate some final grades. In an actual problem, of course, there would be much more data than these, but these values will be sufficient to illustrate the results of using this program. Results for the running of these data are

7321   62.13
7322   53.16
7323   73.88
ERROR (STATEMENT $30 + 0$ LINES)

The error in this case simply indicates that the computer tried to read another data card and none was available.

The very important thing to note about this program is the permanent loop which has been formed into the program in which the computer continues to iterate through identical calculations because of the transfer-of-control statement which appears as the last executable statement in the source program. This program will continue to run indefinitely as long as data cards are available for processing. Note that if the GØ TØ statement had inadvertently been GØ TØ 40, a permanent loop would have been formed from which there is no exit. There would have been an unending execution of statements 40, 50, and 60, and on each pass through this loop there would have been resultant output (unchanging) associated with statement 50.

4-3. COMPUTED GØ TØ

The unconditional GØ TØ statement causes a transfer of control to some other statement in order to break the normal sequential execution of the program. The logical extension of the unconditional GØ TØ is to allow transfer of control to multiple branches within the program depending upon the value of an integer variable. The computed GØ TØ statement extends the capability of FORTRAN by providing the possibilities of entering multiple branches. The general form of the computed GØ TØ statement is

GØ TØ $(n_1, n_2, \ldots, n_k)$, i

where $n_1, n_2, \ldots, n_k$ (integer numbers, not variables) will stand for statement numbers of executable statements elsewhere in the program. The i stands for a simple integer variable which is written without a sign and must be in the range of values of 1 to k where k indicates the number of statement numbers that are enclosed within parentheses.

The operation of the computed GØ TØ statement is as follows. When the computed GØ TØ statement is executed the value of the variable i may have any integer value within the range indicated earlier. If the value of the variable i is j, then the next statement to be executed in the FORTRAN program will be statement number n_j, and subsequently, the statement next in line for execution will be the statement following n_j in the FORTRAN statement list, unless n_j is a transfer-of-control statement.

As an elementary example of the use of the computed GØ TØ statement, consider the statement:

GØ TØ (7, 127, 68, 41), LEAP

If the value of the integer variable LEAP is 2 when the computed GØ TØ statement is executed, the next statement to be executed will be 127; if the value of the integer variable is 4, the next statement to be executed will be statement number 41; etc. If the value of the integer variable LEAP has been greater than 4, i.e., if it had been above the number of statement numbers contained within the parentheses in the computed GØ TØ statement, the results are unpredictable. (Some compilers execute the statement immediately following the computed GØ TØ statement, and some cause termination of execution.)

EXAMPLE 4-2

As an example of the use of the computed GØ TØ, consider the problem in which a number of college students are given identical tests and *raw scores* from these tests are recorded in order to calculate *percentile scores* to compare one student against another. It is necessary to weight the raw scores depending on whether the individual student tested was a freshman, sophomore, junior, or senior. Assume that all of the information on a particular student including his college level and his test scores are input data.

The flowchart for the computer program might appear as shown in Figure 4-3. The FORTRAN program itself for this calculation is outlined in Figure 4-4. The variable LEVEL is fed into the program along with all additional necessary information. LEVEL is used as the integer variable to determine which one of four possible branches might be used in the overall structure of the program. If the value of LEVEL is 1 (indicating a freshman) the program transfers control to statement number 100 where all the

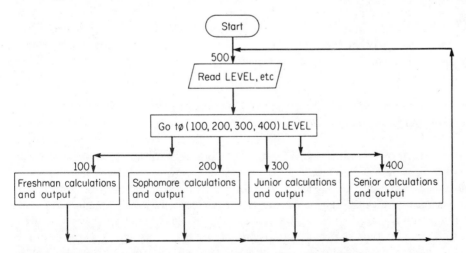

Figure 4-3. Flowchart for Example 4-2. (College Test Score Evaluation.)

```
┌─ C FOR COMMENT
│ STATEMENT │C│                          FORTRAN STATEMENT
│  NUMBER   │O│
│1        5│6│7    10    15    20    25    30    35    40    45    50    55    60    65    70  72
C  EXAMPLE PRØGRAM TØ SHØW USE ØF CØMPUTED GØ TØ IN SELECTING PRØGRAM
C          BRANCHES FØR CØLLEGE TEST SCØRE EVALUATIØN
C
C  INPUT ØF "LEVEL" PLUS ØTHER DATA INCLUDING SCØRES
C
  500 READ(5,1)LEVEL, plus other variables       }      { READ,LEVEL, ···
    1 FØRMAT(I5, plus other field specifications}  or   {
C
C  CØMPUTED GØ TØ FØR BRANCH SELECTIØN
C
      GØ TØ (100,200,300,400) LEVEL
C
C  BRANCHES
C
  100 Calculations for freshmen and output of results
      GØ TØ 500
  200 Calculations for sophomores and output of results
      GØ TØ 500
  300 Calculations for juniors and output of results
      GØ TØ 500
  400 Calculations for seniors and output of results
      GØ TØ 500
      END
```

Figure 4-4. Coding form for Example 4-2.

necessary calculations are made on the raw scores of the freshman student. Once these calculations have been completed and the appropriate results have been printed out by the computer, control is transferred back to the initial READ statement for a new set of data. The overall function of the program is the same for sophomores, juniors, and seniors, and the particular branch involved only depends on the value of LEVEL. There is a terminal END statement at the end of the FORTRAN program list. It might also be noted that this program will suffer the same "error" noted in Example 4-1 in which the compiler indicates an execution error when no more data cards are available for processing.

4-4. ARITHMETIC IF

Upon a little reflection it will be seen that the unconditional GØ TØ statement discussed in Section 4-2 provided a means for returning from a branch of the logical structure of a FORTRAN program while the computed GØ TØ statement of Section 4-3 provided a means of entering one of many possible branches in the logic structure. This section will discuss the arithmetic IF statement which is similar to the computed GØ TØ statement in that it provides a means of branching to one of three possible branches. The IF statement and the computed GØ TØ statement appear quite different; but their operation and usage are often closely related.

The IF statement provides a means of branching to one of three statement numbers by means of examining an arithmetic expression. It causes transfer to one of the possible branches depending on whether the expression evaluated is less than zero, equal to zero, or greater than zero.

The arithmetic IF statement is of the following general form

IF (e) n_1, n_2, n_3

where e stands for any expression and the n_1, n_2, and n_3 are numbers (not variables) of executable statements in the FORTRAN listing that may appear either before or after the IF statement. If the value of the expression within the parentheses is negative, the next statement to be executed will be n_1; if the value of the expression within the parentheses is zero, the next statement to be executed is n_2; and if the value of the expression in the parentheses is positive, the next statement to be executed is n_3.

It is possible for any two of the statement numbers in the arithmetic IF statement to be the same. (It is also possible for all three to be identical; but in such a case the result would comprise a trivial statement in the program content.) It is necessary that every statement number in the IF statement be the number of an executable statement in the FORTRAN listing. It is possible in some situations that one branch of the IF statement will never actually occur in execution with consistent data, but in any event it is still necessary to provide a statement number for this possibility, even though it does not exist from a practical viewpoint. Mixed modes of arithmetic are not normally allowed in the expressions found as the argument to an arithmetic IF statement. Either real or integer expressions are allowed, however. Complex expressions (to be discussed later) may not be used in arithmetic IF statements, and if a complex expression is inadvertently placed in an IF statement, the real part is tested.

One problem that may arise in the use of the arithmetic IF statement results from the computer requirement that the arithmetic expression which comprises the argument of the IF statement be *identically* 0 before the second statement in the list of statements is executed. There may be some problems created in this situation because of the inherent manner in which the transition from binary to decimal arithmetic is accomplished. Problems also may be created by truncation and round-off errors in the representation of numbers (such as 1./3.). These do not present any difficulties when the IF statement is applied to integer expressions, since fixed-point representation of integers is inherently exact. When the argument of the IF statement is a real expression, however, problems may be present due to the fact that the computer may not have the argument *exactly* 0, and it may be to the advantage of the programmer to place some checks to avoid inadvertent errors caused by the inherent operation of the arithmetic calculations in the computer.

EXAMPLE 4-3

To illustrate the arithmetic IF statement, consider the typical "withholding" calculation for state income tax payment. Assume the withholding formula is:

If taxable income is less than $2000, the withholding is zero.

If taxable income is greater than $2000 but less than $5000, the withholding is 2% of the taxable income above $2000.

If taxable income is greater than $5000, the withholding is $60 plus 3% of the taxable income above $5000.

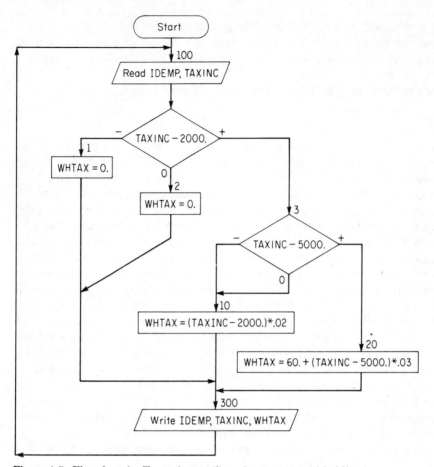

Figure 4-5. Flowchart for Example 4-3. (State income tax withholding.)

It is desired to prepare a computer program to calculate the amount of potential tax, i.e., the amount of state income tax to be withheld, for all of the employees of a company. The flowchart of a program to do this is shown in Figure 4-5 and the program is given in Figure 4-6.

In the computer program a check is first made to see if the employee made less or more than $2000. An arithmetic IF statement is used for this purpose, and if the employee earned less than $2000 of taxable income the logical flow is to statement 1 where his withholding tax is defined as zero and transfer of control is directed to the output statements. If the employee earned exactly $2000 his withholding tax is also zero. In this particular situation, the next instruction could be either 1 or 3— the student should verify this—but for illustrative purposes a separate branch is shown in this example, i.e., control is transferred to statement 2 and then to the output statements.

If the employee earned in excess of $2000, a check must be made to see how his computation should be made, i.e., did he earn over $5000 of taxable income? This check is made in statement 3 which is another arithmetic IF statement. If he earned between $2000 and $5000, control is transferred to statement 10; if he earned more

C FOR COMMENT

STATEMENT NUMBER	FORTRAN STATEMENT

```
C  EXAMPLE PRØGRAM TØ CALCULATE STATE INCØME TAX  —   ILLUSTRATIØN ØF THE
C     ARITHMETIC  IF STATEMENT
C
C  INPUT ØF TAXABLE INCØME DATA AND IDENTIFICATIØN NUMBER
C
  100 READ(5,200)IDEMP,TAXINC  } or {   READ,IDEMP,TAXING
  200 FØRMAT(I5,F15.2)
C
C CHECK TØ SEE IF TAXABLE INCØME EXCEEDS $2000.
C
      IF(TAXINC - 2000.)1,2,3
C
C TAXABLE INCOME IS LESS THAN $2000 AND TAX IS ZERØ
C
    1 WHTAX = 0.
      GØ TØ 300
C
C TAXABLE INCØME IS $2000 AND TAX IS ZERØ
C
    2 WHTAX = 0.
      GØ TØ 300
C
C TAXABLE INCØME IS ABOVE $2000 — CHECK TO SEE IF ABOVE $5000
C
    3 IF(TAXINC - 5000.)10,10,20
C
C TAXABLE INCØME IS BETWEEN $2000 AND $5000 OR EQUAL $5000
C
   10 WHTAX = (TAXINC - 2000.)*.02
      GØ TØ 300
C
C TAXABLE INCØME GREATER THAN $5000
C
   20 WHTAX = 60. + (TAXINC - 5000.)*.03
C
C ØUTPUT ØF TAXABLE INCØME AND WITHHØLDING TAX
C
  300 WRITE(6,400)IDEMP,TAXINC,WHTAX  } or {   PRINT, IDEMP, TAXING,WHTAX
  400 FØRMAT(1X,I5,2F15.2)
      GØ TØ 100
      END
  221       1234 .27
  222       6248.94
  223       3219.21
```

Figure 4-6. Coding form for Example 4-3.

than $5000, control is transferred to statement 20; and if he earned exactly $5000, control may be transferred to either statement 10 or 20 (statement 10 is illustrated).

Note that control always ends up in the output section of the program, and after writing out the information on taxable income and withholding tax calculated for the individual employee, control is then transferred back to the input section to get new data on another employee (along with his employee identification number).

This program also suffers from the last card execution error shown in Examples 4-1 and 4-2.

In order to illustrate this program, some typical data are shown and for these three sets of data, the output results are as shown herewith.

$$
\begin{array}{lll}
221 & 1234.27 & 0.00 \\
222 & 6248.94 & 97.47 \\
223 & 3219.21 & 24.38
\end{array}
$$

ERROR (STATEMENT 100 + 0 LINES)

4-5. LOGICAL IF

The logical IF statement is the last statement for transfer of control that is considered in this chapter. The logical IF statement has the general form

IF (e)S

where e is a Boolean (logical) expression with the value of true or false, and the S is any statement except another logical IF statement, an arithmetic IF statement (allowable in some versions), or a DØ statement. (The DØ statement is considered in the next chapter). If the expression which comprises the argument of the logical IF statement is true, statement S is executed next, and then the next statement following the logical IF statement is executed unless the S statement itself is an arithmetic IF (if allowed) or a GØ TØ statement which would modify the normal sequence of execution. If e is false, the statement immediately following the logical IF statement is executed next. The Boolean expression e is a *logical expression* and these logical expressions are normally formed by the use of *relational operators* in order to write *relational expressions*. Typical questions are, for example, "is x greater than or equal to 3.14?" or "is i equal to j?" In order to form such logical expressions the following relational operators are available:

Relational Operator	Meaning
.LT.	Less than
.LE.	Less than or equal to
.EQ.	Equal to
.NE.	Not equal to
.GT.	Greater than
.GE.	Greater than or equal to

These relational operators may be used for both real and integer variables; but a change of mode is not normally permitted across a relational operator.

The "periods" in these relational operators are essential and are inserted to differentiate relational operators from variable names which may inadvertently have been chosen by the programmer.

The logical IF statement's usefulness is extended measurably by the combination of *logical operators* such as .AND., .ØR., and .NØT. with relational operators. The use of these logical operators might be as follows: Suppose that we desire to go to statement number 267 if x is greater than y and if x is also greater than or equal to z. If both of these conditions are not met, then the next statement to be executed should be the statement following the logical IF statement. This situation can be programmed into a single logical IF statement:

IF(X.GT.Y.AND.X.GE.Z) GØ TØ 267

If *both* conditions are met, statement 267 will be executed; and if *either* of the conditions are not met, the next statement to be executed will be the one immediately following the logical IF statement.

Although it is not normally possible to mix arithmetic modes in logical expressions, it is normally allowable to have logical expressions of different arithmetic modes to be connected by a logical operator, e.g., the following example is correct:

IF(X.GT.Y.AND.I.GE.J) GØ TØ 267

In a similar fashion the .ØR. operator is satisfied if *either or both* of the logical expressions it connects are true, and the .NØT. operator reverses the truth value of the expression it modifies. As an example of the use of the .NØT. operator, consider the expression:

IF(.NØT.(X.LT.Y)) X = Z

has exactly the same value as the logical IF statement:

IF(X.GE.Y) X = Z

since "not less than" means the same as "greater than or equal to."

Logical IF statements are very potent tools which are available to the user of FORTRAN IV (they are not available in earlier versions of FORTRAN) and the student should become very familiar with them. Questions relative to the hierarchy of relational expressions and logical operators will be covered later.

EXAMPLE 4-4

As an example of the logical IF statement, consider the problem in which we intend to take three readings of a person's body temperature during a six-hour period and then use the computer to select the largest (highest) of these three temperatures. The computer will be asked to do nothing more than select the largest of the temperatures and write it out as an "answer." The three input temperatures are in F10.2 format and the output answer is to be in F20.2 format. The flowchart is shown in Figure 4-7, and the computer program necessary is shown in Figure 4-8.

The general structure of the computer program shown is based on the idea of using a logical IF statement to compare two of the temperatures and select the largest of these two. The largest of these two temperatures is then compared to the third temperature in order to select the highest temperature for the six-hour period. To select the largest of two temperatures a logical IF statement is used with the .LE. operator. Based on the use of this operator an intermediate variable BIG2 is calculated. A second logical IF statement is used to compare BIG2 with T3 in order to select BIG3, the highest of the 3 temperatures. In the second logical IF statement the .LT. operator is used although the .LE. operator also could have been used. Note from the alternative in Figure 4-8 that the manner in which the programming is done has a significant effect on the number of statements required.

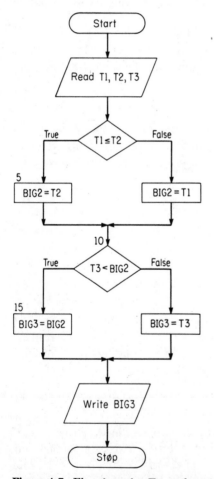

Figure 4-7. Flowchart for Example 4-4 (selecting the largest of three temperatures).

```
C FOR COMMENT
STATEMENT    FORTRAN STATEMENT
NUMBER
  5 6 7   10    15    20    25    30    35    40    45    50    55    60    65    70  72
C    EXAMPLE PRØBLEM TØ SELECT THE LARGEST ØF THREE TEMPERATURES
C
C    READ IN THE THREE TEMPERATURES
C
     READ(5,1)T1,T2,T3         { or {  READ, T1,T2,T3
  1  FØRMAT(3F10.2)
C
C    SELECT THE LARGER OF TWØ
C
     IF(T1.LE.T2)GØ TØ 5
     BIG2 = T1
     GØ TØ 10                              {BIG3=T1
  5  BIG2 = T2                         OR {IF(T2.GT.BIG3)BIG3=T2
C                                          IF(T3.GT.BIG3)BIG3=T3
C    CØMPARE THE LARGER ØF TWØ WITH THE THIRD
C
 10  IF(T3.LT.BIG2) GØ TØ 15
     BIG3 = T3
     GØ TØ 20
 15  BIG3 = BIG2
C
C    ØUTPUT ØF RESULTS
C
 20  WRITE(6,2) BIG3         { or {  PRINT, BIG3
  2  FØRMAT( F20.2 )
     STØP
     END
 98.86     101.20     99.47
```

Figure 4-8. Coding form for Example 4-4.

In the output format statement the single temperature that was selected as being the highest is written out as BIG3 in F20.2 format. Since this variable, of necessity, is one of the original three temperatures read into the computer, it cannot possibly occupy 20 spaces since there were only 10 spaces in the input field. The output answer will be right justified in the space available, and consequently, there will be at least 10 blank spaces to the left of the output field. Since this is "guaranteed" there is no need to provide a blank space in column 1 of the FØRMAT statement of the output record. Unpredictable carriage control is prevented since this column will always be blank. The output results for the example set of data on this problem is, of course, 101.20.

This example illustrates the nature of the logical IF statement and its usage in a simple program. It must be pointed out that the problem proposed is a rather trivial one in terms of justification for the usage of the computer; but it does illustrate the programming concepts.

4-6. HEADINGS

In many problems the most appropriate format for the output of a program is in the form of a table. Above, each column of output should appear a heading. For some problems, the last line of output should provide a total of one or more of the columns of the table.

To illustrate, we shall consider the following example. Suppose a company has prepared punched cards for each of its employees containing the following information:

a. Employee ID number

b. Regular hours worked for the past week

c. Overtime hours worked for the past week

d. Hourly pay rate

From these data, the gross pay is computed, allowing time-and-a-half for overtime.

Figure 4-9 provides the flowchart and program for solving this example. In essence, a card is read, the gross pay computed, the gross pay printed, and then another card is read. As illustrated by the flowchart, the program logic consists of a loop from which no exit is provided. Of course, the program eventually runs out of data cards, which results in the "error message" indicating the encounter of a control card by the card reader. This message is not an "error message" in the usual sense because the programmer anticipated that the program would terminate in this manner.

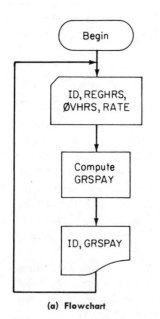

(a) Flowchart

Figure 4-9. Program for computing gross pay.

format-free

```
1      READ,ID,REGHRS,OVHRS,RATE
2      GRSPAY=RATE*(REGHRS+1.5*OVHRS)
3      PRINT,ID,GRSPAY
4      GOTO20
5      END
```

format

```
1  20  READ(5,21)ID,REGHRS,OVHRS,RATE
2  21  FORMAT(I5,3F5.0)
3      GRSPAY=RATE*(REGHRS+1.5*OVHRS)
4      WRITE(6,25)ID,GRSPAY
5  25  FORMAT(1X,I10,F10.2)
6      GOTO20
7      END
```

(b) Program

format-free

```
1154,40.,0.,4.75
1276,40.,9.,6.20
1189,35.,0.,5.20
2122,40.,0.,3.85
1750,40.,5.,7.15
```

format

```
1154 40.  0.  4.75
1276 40.  9.  6.20
1189 35.  0.  5.20
2122 40.  0.  3.85
1750 40.  5.  7.15
```

(c) Input data

format-free

```
1154    0.1900000E 03
1276    0.3317000E 03
1189    0.1820000E 03
2122    0.1540000E 03
1750    0.3396248E 03
***ERROR***  CONTROL CARD ENCOUNTERED ON UNIT    5 AT EXECUTION.
```

format

```
1154    190.00
1276    331.70
1189    182.00
2122    154.00
1750    339.62
***ERROR***  CONTROL CARD ENCOUNTERED ON UNIT    5 AT EXECUTION.
```

(d) Output data

Figure 4-9. *Continued.*

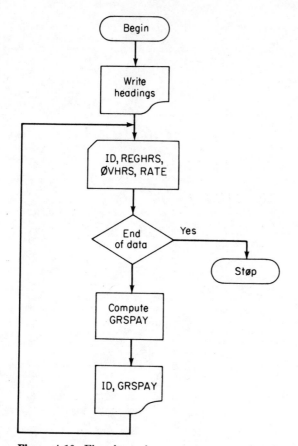

Figure 4-10. Flowchart for program to print headings.

Some programmers prefer their programs not to end on an error message. One approach to avoid the error message is to provide a special card commonly called a "trailer card" at the end of the data deck that can be detected within the program. For our example, a convenient approach would be to add a card containing a zero for the employee ID number. Immediately following the READ statement in the program in Figure 4-9, we should add the following statement:

IF (ID.EQ.0) STØP

The program now terminates after processing the trailer card and no error message would be generated.

We shall now consider how to provide headings for the output from the program in Figure 4-9. To illustrate, suppose we wish to provide the heading ID-NUMBER above the first column and GRØSS PAY above the second. The resulting flowchart is shown in Figure 4-10; but we need to consider the problem of how to determine the proper spac-

COMM.	STATEMENT NUMBER	CONT.																										
			I D − N U M B E R						G R Ø S S		P A Y																	
			X X X X						0 . X X X X X X X E		X X																	

(a) Spacing for headings

```
1            PRINT,'       ID-NUMBER      GROSS PAY'
2      20    READ, ID,REGHRS,OVHRS,RATE
3            IF(ID.EQ.0)STOP
4            GRSPAY=RATE*(REGHRS+1.5*OVHRS)
5            PRINT,ID,GRSPAY
6            GOTO20
7            END
```

(b) Program

```
ID-NUMBER       GROSS PAY
      1154       0.1900000E 03
      1276       0.3317000E 03
      1189       0.1820000E 03
      2122       0.1540000E 03
      1750       0.3396248E 03
```

(c) Input data

```
1154,40.,0.,4.75
1276,40.,9.,6.20
1189,35.,0.,5.20
2122,40.,0.,3.85
1750,40.,5.,7.15
0,0.,0.,0.
```

(d) Output data

Figure 4-11. Headings with format-free statements.

ing for the headings. We shall first consider the case when format-free i/ø is used, and then consider the use of the FØRMAT statement.

For format-free i/ø, integer values are always printed right-justified (i.e., positioned as far to the right as possible) in a field that is 12 columns wide. Real values are always printed right-justified in a field that is 17 columns wide. We would like

COMM.	STATEMENT NUMBER	CONT.		
1	2 3 4 5	6	7 8 9 10 11 12 13 14 15 16 17 18 19 20 21 22 23 24 25 26 27 28 29 30 31 32 33 34 35 36 37 38 39 40 41	
I D	- N U M	B E R	G R Ø S S P A Y	
	X X X X		X X X X . X X	
			F Ø R M A T (' 1 I D - N U M B E R G R Ø S S P A Y ')	
			F Ø R M A T (4 X , I 4 , 8 X , F 7 . 2)	
			o r	
			F Ø R M A T (1 X , I 7 , F 1 5 . 2)	

(a) Spacing for headings

```
 1           WRITE(6,15)
 2    15     FORMAT('1ID-NUMBER      GROSS PAY')
 3    20     READ(5,21)ID,REGHRS,OVHRS,RATE
 4    21     FORMAT(I5,3F5.0)
 5           IF(ID.EQ.0)STOP
 6           GRSPAY=RATE*(REGHRS+1.5*OVHRS)
 7           WRITE(6,25)ID,GRSPAY
 8    25     FORMAT(1X,I7,F15.2)
 9           GOTO20
10           END
```

(b) Program

```
1154 40. 0.    4.75
1276 40. 9.    6.20
1189 35. 0.    5.20
2122 40. 0.    3.85
1750 40. 5.    7.15
   0  0. 0.    0.
```

(c) Input data

```
ID-NUMBER        GROSS PAY
  1154            190.00
  1276            331.70
  1189            182.00
  2122            154.00
  1750            339.62
```

(d) Output data

Figure 4-12. Headings with FØRMAT statements.

to position the headings so that they are centered above this output. To obtain the proper spacing, one approach is to first determine the position of the numeric output. For this purpose, we need a form showing columns, and the coding form is quite adequate. The first step is to then indicate on the form how the numeric output will appear, which results in the second line on the form in Figure 4-11a. The next step is to enter the desired headings, which gives the top line. From this we can prepare an appropriate PRINT statement, which results in the program in Figure 4-11b.

When using formatted I/Ø, one may either first select the spacing for the headings and then position the numeric output appropriately, or first select the spacing for the numeric output and then position the headings appropriately. We shall take the former approach. For convenience, we need to lay out the headings on paper such as the coding form that indicates the position of columns. We arbitrarily begin with the heading spacing illustrated by the first line of Figure 4-12a. We then appropriately position the numeric output beneath the headings, as illustrated by the second line. We can then proceed to write the FØRMAT statements, which are also illustrated in Figure 4-12a. Note the inclusion of carriage control in each FØRMAT statement, with the heading line appearing at the top of a page. For the last FØRMAT statement, it is tempting to use

FØRMAT (4x,I4,8x,F7.2)

but all of the X-fields except the one for carriage control should be combined with the numeric fields to give

FØRMAT (1x,I7,F15.2)

The program is given in Figure 4-12b.

As a final point, suppose it is desired to print the total gross pay for all employees. Suppose we choose to use TGP as the variable for this purpose. We must assign TGP a value of zero prior to entering the loop to process the individual cards, and then after computing the value of the gross pay for an employee, we must add the value to TGP. The flowchart and resulting programs are illustrated in Figure 4-13. The spacing for the final line can be readily obtained by extending the approach in Figure 4-11 or 4-12.

Essentially all computing systems require that the data cards be followed by a control card. In fact, the error message in Figure 4-9 is generated upon encounter of this card. Most systems provide some mechanism for detecting this control card and transferring to a statement within the program rather then producing the error message and terminating the run. Unfortunately, the implementation of this feature varies somewhat depending upon the specific computer being used. On IBM systems and in WATFIV, the implementation is via the END = option in the READ statement. For example, to transfer to statement 28, the READ statement in Figure 4-13 should be changed to

READ (5,21,END = 28) ID, REGHRS, ØVHRS, RATE

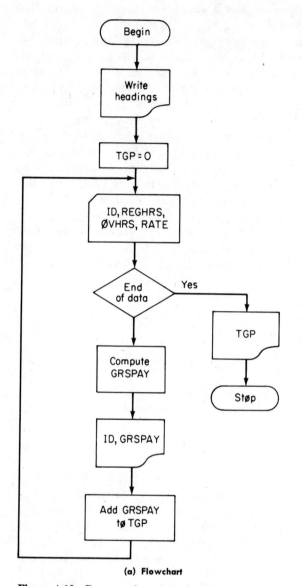

(a) Flowchart

Figure 4-13. Computation of total gross pay.

When using format-free I/Ø in WATFIV, the statement number of the FØRMAT statement should be replaced by an asterisk, giving

READ (5,*,END = 28) ID, REGHRS, ØVHRS, RATE

The resulting programs are shown in Figure 4-14. In this case, the "trailer card" with a zero for the employee ID number is not needed and must be omitted.

```
1        PRINT,'      ID-NUMBER      GROSS PAY'
2        TGP=0.
3  20    READ,ID,REGHRS,OVHRS,RATE
4        IF(ID.EQ.0)GOTO28
5        GRSPAY=RATE*(REGHRS+1.5*OVHRS)
6        PRINT,ID,GRSPAY
7        TGP=TGP+GRSPAY
8        GOTO20
9  28    PRINT,'     TOTAL',TGP
10       STOP
11       END
```

format-free

```
1        WRITE(6,15)
2  15    FORMAT('1ID-NUMBER        GROSS PAY')
3        TGP=0.
4  20    READ(5,21)ID,REGHRS,OVHRS,RATE
5  21    FORMAT(I5,3F5.0)
6        IF(ID.EQ.0)GOTO28
7        GRSPAY=RATE*(REGHRS+1.5*OVHRS)
8        WRITE(6,25)ID,GRSPAY
9  25    FORMAT(1X,I7,F15.2)
10       TGP=TGP+GRSPAY
11       GOTO20
12 28    WRITE(6,30)TGP
13 30    FORMAT(3X,'TOTAL',F15.2)
14       STOP
15       END
```

format

(b) Program

```
1154,40.,0.,4.75
1276,40.,9.,6.20
1189,35.,0.,5.20
2122,40.,0.,3.85
1750,40.,5.,7.15
0,0.,0.,0.
```

format-free

```
1154 40.  0.  4.75
1276 40.  9.  6.20
1189 35.  0.  5.20
2122 40.  0.  3.85
1750 40.  5.  7.15
   0  0.  0.  0.
```

format

(c) Input data

```
ID-NUMBER       GROSS PAY
1154          0.1900000E 03
1276          0.3317000E 03
1189          0.1820000E 03
2122          0.1540000E 03
1750          0.3396248E 03
TOTAL         0.1197324E 04
```

format-free

```
ID-NUMBER       GROSS PAY
1154             190.00
1276             331.70
1189             182.00
2122             154.00
1750             339.62
TOTAL           1197.32
```

format

(d) Output data

Figure 4-13. *Continued.*

(a) Program

```
1        WRITE(6,15)
2   15   FORMAT('1ID-NUMBER      GROSS PAY')
3        TGP=0.
4   20   READ(5,21,END=28)ID,REGHRS,OVHRS,RATE
5   21   FORMAT(I5,3F5.0)
6        GRSPAY=RATE*(REGHRS+1.5*OVHRS)
7        WRITE(6,25)ID,GRSPAY
8   25   FORMAT(1X,I7,F15.2)
9        TGP=TGP+GRSPAY
10       GOTO20
11  28   WRITE(6,30)TGP
12  30   FORMAT(3X,'TOTAL',F15.2)
13       STOP
14       END
              format
```

```
1        PRINT,'      ID-NUMBER      GROSS PAY'
2        TGP=0.
3   20   READ(5,*,END=28)ID,REGHRS,OVHRS,RATE
4        GRSPAY=RATE*(REGHRS+1.5*OVHRS)
5        PRINT,ID,GRSPAY
6        TGP=TGP+GRSPAY
7        GOTO20
8   28   PRINT,'      TOTAL',TGP
9        STOP
10       END
              format-free
```

(b) Input data

```
1154  40.  0.  4.75
1276  40.  9.  6.20
1189  35.  0.  5.20
2122  40.  0.  3.85
1750  40.  5.  7.15
       format
```

```
1154,40.,0.,4.75
1276,40.,9.,6.20
1189,35.,0.,5.20
2122,40.,0.,3.85
1750,40.,5.,7.15
       format-free
```

(c) Output data

```
ID-NUMBER    GROSS PAY
1154          190.00
1276          331.70
1189          182.00
2122          154.00
1750          339.62
TOTAL        1197.32
       format
```

```
ID-NUMBER    GROSS PAY
1154        0.1900000E 03
1276        0.3317000E 03
1189        0.1820000E 03
2122        0.1540000E 03
1750        0.3396248E 03
TOTAL       0.1197324E 04
       format-free
```

Figure 4-14. Use of END- feature.

4-7. SIMPLE COUNTERS

One of the principal applications of integers in FORTRAN programming is in the counting of the repeated execution of a set of instructions, i.e., the counting of *iterations* of a program. In Example 4-1 the use of a loop in the program caused the computer to repeat the calculations over and over. When the last data card was read the computer gave an execution error indicating a "last-card" error which was unavoidable with the programming knowledge available at that time. This problem can be avoided by the use of simple counters.

Suppose it is planned in advance to read in 100 sets of input data to the program of Example 4-1. In such a case a counter could be incorporated into the program for this problem and the program could check itself at the end of each set of calculations to see if it had, in fact, run 100 data sets. Before reading in the first data set a counter variable, defined as I, could be set equal to 0, and on each execution of the READ statement the value of this integer counter I could be incremented by 1. At the end of the program's calculation statements an arithmetic IF statement could be inserted to check on the arithmetic expression (I − 100). If this quantity were negative, control could be transferred back to the beginning of the program; if it were 0 or positive, control could be transferred to a STØP statement at the end of the program. This action would prevent a last-card execution error, and illustrates how counters may be used in digital programming.

Another typical example of a counter is in its use to keep track of the number of times that a computer program is required to iterate through some trial-and-error calculation before an answer is achieved. The value of the counter can be printed out at the end of the calculations to give the programmer an indication of the quality of convergence which has been achieved in the program. Another typical use of the counter is to set an upper limit on the number of trials which may be run in a trial-and-error computation. Since it is entirely possible that these techniques converge very slowly, the programmer may desire to set an upper limit on the number of trials, e.g., 200. It may be desirable to punch out the results at this stage of the trial-and-error calculations regardless of whether exact convergence has been achieved or not. These types of applications of the counter are typical and in no way limit their overall usage. Counters are extremely powerful tools for the digital programmer.

EXAMPLE 4-5

A single example will be sufficient to illustrate two relatively different uses of the counter. Assume there are three separate data cards, each containing the total miles driven by a single company-owned automobile during a given week. These autos are used as a "shuttle service" between two different company offices, and it is desired to roughly estimate the number of round trips each auto made between the two offices. The estimated round trip mileage is 43.8 miles. The purpose of the computer program we are to write is to read in each of these three mileages, one at a time, and subtract 43.8 miles from each one a sufficient number of times to reduce it to a mileage less than 43.8 miles. (This problem could be solved more easily, of course, by simple divi-

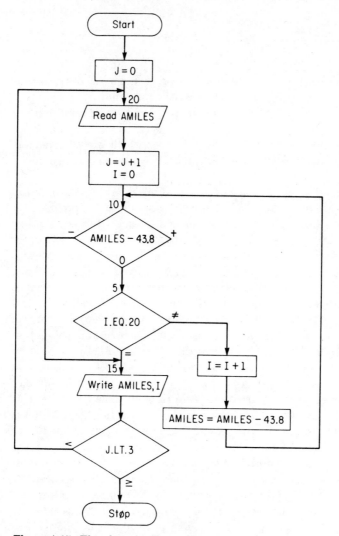

Figure 4-15. Flowchart for Example 4-5 (mileage reduction).

sion, but we will structure it as outlined in order to illustrate the use of counters.) At the end of the "mileage reduction" for each auto, the number of trips and the mileage "left over" will be printed out. A counter also will be used to instruct the computer to READ the three data cards (one at a time) before it completely stops its calculations.

It was previously stated that it also was possible to use a counter as a means of setting an upper limit on the number of trial iterations that might be carried out in a particular loop of a program. The usage of counters also can be illustrated in this particular example by subtracting 43.8 miles from the total mileage no more than 20 times. After having made this reduction in the mileage on 20 separate occasions, if the resulting mileage is still greater than 43.8, the reduced value of the mileage is to be written on the output record.

The problem requires two counters as defined—one to handle the count of the number of data cards that have been read into the machine, and a second to keep

```
C EXAMPLE PRØBLEM TØ REDUCE MILEAGE
C
C INITIALIZE CØUNTER FØR RECØRDING NUMBER ØF DATA CARDS READ
C
      J = 0
C
C INPUT ØF ØNE CARD
C
   20 READ(5,100)AMILES     } or {   READ, AMILES
  100 FØRMAT(F20.5)         }    {
C
C INCREMENT CARD CØUNTER AND SET ITERATIØN CØUNTER FØR THIS CARD
C
      J = J + 1
      I = 0
C
C REDUCE THE MILEAGE AS NECESSARY
C
   10 IF(AMILES - 43.8)15,5,5
    5 IF(I.EQ.20) GØ TØ 15
      I = I + 1
      AMILES = AMILES - 43.8
      GØ TØ 10
C
C ØUTPUT ØF MILEAGE AND NUMBER ØF TRIPS
C
   15 WRITE(6,200)AMILES,I       } or {PRINT, AMILES, I
  200 FØRMAT(1X,F20.5,I5)        }    {
C
C CHECK TØ SEE IF THERE ARE MØRE DATA CARDS
C
      IF(J.LT.3) GØ TØ 20
      STØP
      END
            1273.4
            398.2
            100.00
```

Figure 4-16. Coding form for Example 4-5.

track of the number of iterations made on any single data card. The flowchart for the program is given in Fig. 4-15, and the computer program necessary to make these calculations is shown in Fig. 4-16. It is seen that it is first necessary to initialize the counter for reading data cards. Once this has been done, it is possible to READ a card and set the values of both counters for that particular data card. The reductions of AMILES are then made, and on each reduction of AMILES the counter I (used to keep track of the number of iterations) is incremented by 1. In each iteration through the computation, a check is made on the value of AMILES to see if it is less than 43.8, and a separate check is made on the value of the iteration counter I. Once AMILES falls within its prescribed limits or the necessary number of iterations have been made, control is transferred to the output section of the program where the current values of AMILES and I are written on an output record. After they have been written, a check is made to see if there are more data cards to be processed by using an IF statement on the data card counter J. If more data cards are to be processed, the flow of control is transferred back to the READ statement—if not, transfer is made to the STØP statement.

For the typical values of input data shown, the results are illustrated herewith.

397.40000	20
4.00000	9
12.40000	2

4-8. IN SUMMARY

This chapter has been devoted to some of the most powerful statements that are available in FORTRAN programming, and the usage of these transfer-of-control statements unlocks the really powerful tools of the digital computer. The GØ TØ statements and the IF statements have been discussed in some detail, and it is now assumed that the student has them at his command. As the student becomes more familiar with these powerful transfer-of-control statements, the logical structure of his program becomes much more complex and the usage of flowcharts to illustrate the structure of his program becomes increasingly important.

It is recommended that the student carefully study the example problems worked out in this chapter. As stated at the end of an earlier chapter, it is important that the student make a number of separate, although perhaps simple, uses of the types of statements introduced in order to gain complete confidence in his ability to use them.

With the material now presented, it is logical to extend our coverage of FORTRAN programming to the subject of subscripted variables and DØ statements wherein lies much of the ability of the computer to handle very large arrays of data with minimum problems for the programmer.

Exercises‡

4-1 Most of the exercises at the end of Chapter 3 were presented as cases in which only one set of input data was available. Assume that there are many sets of input data available for these exercises. You are to indicate how the computer programs would have to be written in order to process these multiple data sets using an unconditional GØ TØ statement for

(a)	3-9	(b)	3-13
†(c)	3-15	(d)	3-17
(e)	3-20		

---

‡ Solutions to Exercises marked with a dagger † are given in Appendix G.

4-2 A computer program is set up to calculate insurance premiums for various employees in a plant. The necessary calculations are dependent on the number of children which an employee has, i.e., 0, 1, 2, 3, or "more than 3." Set up the general outline of this program much as is done in Figures 4-3 and 4-4, using a computed Gø Tø statement.

†4-3 The age of a person is one of the principal factors in determining caloric intake requirements. Assume that a person's age is one part of input data to a program to make this type of calculation. Depending on whether the person is 0–10, 10–20,..., or 91–100, there will be an appropriate set of calculations. Use a computed Gø Tø to select the appropriate branch, and outline the program as in Figures 4-3 and 4-4.

Note: For all the following exercises you are to read in the given variables, perform the desired calculations, and write out the results as directed. Write complete FORTRAN programs including a trial data card(s).

4-4 Read in x and y. If $x > y$, set $z = 1$; if $x < y$, set $z = 2$; and if $x = y$, set $z = 3$. Write out x, y, and z. Assume there are many data cards, each containing a value of x and y. Use an arithmetic IF statement(s) to make the necessary decision(s). Be certain to draw a flowchart.

4-5 Repeat Exercise 4-4 using a logical IF statement(s).

†4-6 A number of data cards are available, each containing three numbers which we shall designate as y_1, y_2, and y_3. Use an arithmetic IF statement(s) to check each set to see if $y_2 > y_1$ and $y_2 > y_3$. If so, write out the three numbers. If not, do not write out anything and go to a new data set. Be certain to draw a flowchart.

4-7 Repeat Exercise 4-6 using a logical IF statement(s).

4-8 A number of data cards are available, each containing a value of the variable x. Use a logical IF containing two relational operators with the logical operator .AND. to see if $1 \leq x \leq 99$. If x is within this range, add the value of x to a running sum of all of the values of x contained on the input data cards, write out the current value of the sum, and read in a new data card. If x is outside the specified range, subtract 99 from x, add the reduced value of x to the running sum, write out the value of the sum, and read in a new data card. Be certain to draw a flowchart.

4-9 Repeat Exercise 4-8 using the logical IF.

4-10 Extend Exercise 3-29 by adding tests to verify that the entered number has three digits. That is, the number should be greater than 99 and less than 1000. If either of these is not true for the number entered, write an appropriate message. Use logical IF statements.

4-11 Repeat Exercise 4-10, using arithmetic IF statements.

†4-12 Read in a data card containing an initial value of x, a final value of x, and an increment on x. Write out these three values of x and then calculate y as a function of x:

$$y = 1 + x + \frac{x^2}{2} + \frac{x^3}{6} + \sqrt{x}$$

where x's first value is x initial. Keep calculating y for values of x (in each case adding the increment on x to the old value of x) until x exceeds the final value of x. In each calculation write out y and the value of x used to calculate y. When x exceeds the final value of x, read in a new data card and start over. Be certain to draw a flowchart.

4-13 Repeat Exercise 4-12, except that you are directed to stop calculating y whenever y exceeds 100 *or* when x final has been exceeded, whichever occurs first.

4-14 Set up a counter on Exercise 4-4 to handle four input data cards.

†**4-15** Set up a counter on Exercise 4-6 to handle seven input data cards.

4-16 Set up a counter on Exercise 4-8 to handle five input data cards.

4-17 Set up a counter on Exercise 4-10 to handle six input data cards.

4-18 Set up a counter on Exercise 4-12 to handle three input data cards. Also add an iteration counter to stop calculations on a given set of input data if y is calculated as a function of x more than fifty times.

†**4-19** An alternate way to determine when a particular input data card is the last card is to define a new input variable, e.g., N. Use a value of N as zero as a basis for reading in a new data card and a value of N as 1 as a basis for stopping the program. N will have to be included on each input card when format-free I/∅ is used; but since a zero value indicates further processing, N will only have to be punched on the last input data card when formatted I/∅ is used. Do this for Exercise 4-6.

4-20 Repeat Exercise 4-19 for Exercise 4-8.

4-21 A company bills its customers on the last day of each month. If the customer pays his bill within the first 10 days of the next month he gets a $10.00 or a 2% discount, whichever is more; if he pays in the next ten days of the month, he pays the exact amount of the bill; and if he pays after this second ten day period, he pays the bill plus a penalty of $10.00 or 1% per month on the unpaid balance, whichever is less. As an example, if he paid his bill 25 days after the billing he would pay a $10.00 or 1% penalty. Set up a program to read in the basic amount of a bill and the customer's identification number. Write out his identification number, the amount of the bill if paid in the first ten days, the second ten days, and the third ten days of the next month so that all of this information is available for the statement to be mailed to the customer.

4-22 Repeat Exercise 4-21 using a counter to handle 6 input data cards.

4-23 Repeat Exercise 4-19 for Exercise 4-21.

4-24 Consider a program to compute the coins to be given in change for the following situation:

    a. All purchases are under $1.

    b. Purchaser will always present a dollar bill.

    c. Change should consist of the minimum number of coins.

    d. Only pennies, nickles, dimes, and quarters will be given in change.

The program should be written to run more than one case. Output should be in columns with amount of purchase, number of pennies, number of nickels, etc., with appropriate headings. Run the program for purchases of 97, 78, 54, 21, and 1 cent.

4-25 As published in the 1974–75 General Catalog, the regular semester fee schedule for undergraduate students at Grand State University were as follows:

Hours	University Fee
1–3	$60
4–6	85
7–9	110
10–11	135
12 or more	160

Write a program to read the number of hours taken by an undergraduate student and print the appropriate university fee.

†4-26 Suppose a university teaches ten sections of a course on basket weaving. For each student in this course, a card is punched containing the following information:

a. Section

b. Sex (male—0; female—1)

c. Standing (freshman—1; sophomore—2; junior—3; senior—4, graduate—5)

A card containing a zero for the section indicates last card. Determine the number of students in Section 8.

4-27 Revise the above exercise to determine the number of females in Section 2.

4-28 Revise Exercise 4-26 to determine the number of juniors in Section 9.

4-29 Revise Exercise 4-26, to determine the number of female sophomores taking basket weaving.

4-30 Revise Exercise 4-26 to determine the number of male seniors in Section 5.

4-31 Extend Exercise 3-22 to encompass credit hours earned. In addition to the entries in Exercise 3-22, the old number of credit hours earned should be read. In updating the credit hours earned, no credit is allowed for grades of F. Write the new number of credit hours earned along with the output requested in Exercise 3-22.

4-32 Podunk U. determines an undergraduate student's classification according to the following guidelines:

1 Freshman   less than 30 semester hours

2 Sophomore   30–59 semester hours

3 Junior   60–89 semester hours

4 Senior   90 or more semester hours

Develop a program that reads the number of semester hours earned by a student and prints a 1 if a freshman, 2 if a sophomore, 3 if a junior, or 4 if a senior.

†**4-33** Develop a program that reads the time (expressed in military fashion) into a single variable and then prints the time in civilian fashion. For example, 0845 should be printed as 8:45 AM (use the minus sign if a colon is not available), and 1829 should be printed as 6:29 PM. However, note that 0042 is 12:42 AM and 1219 is 12:19 PM. If the entered hour digits are greater than 24 or if the minutes digits are 60 or greater, print the message "Erroneous time entered" followed by the value entered.

4-34 This exercise entails the preparation of a program to compute the time duration in minutes of an airline flight. The time will be entered in military fashion as in the previous exercise. The first time entered will be the departure time; the second will be the arrival time at the destination. Each time should be checked for erroneous values as in the previous exercise. Furthermore, the program should function properly for flights over midnight. For example, a flight with a departure time of 2240 and an arrival time of 0120 lasts 160 minutes (no flight lasts longer than 24 hours). The program's output should be as follows:

Flight	Hours	Minutes
809	2	15
911	4	20

Use the following as input data:

Flight No.	Departure Time	Arrival Time
17	0915	1245
122	0945	1215
405	2140	0020
101	1710	1850

4-35 Write a program to accept the date in the customary numerical designation and print the date with the month spelled out. That is, 2/14/75 should be written February 14, 1975. In entering the numerically designated date, the three numerical components are entered separately with the month first, the day next, and the year last. The program should also check for unreasonable entries. Specifically, the following checks should be made:

1 The numerical designation for the month should not exceed 12.

2 The entry for the day should be checked against the maximum number of days in the month. For February, the program should consider that leap years occur whenever the year is divisible by 4.

3 The year should not exceed 99.

4-36 Suppose a book company estimates the price of a book by the following guidelines: The basic cost of a book is 50 cents plus 2 cents per page, which assumes that the book will be a paperback. If, however, the number of pages exceeds 300 pages, cloth binding is used, which increases the price by $1.00. Furthermore, if the number of pages exceeds 550, special binding procedures become necessary, which increases the cost another 75 cents. Prepare a program to compute the cost of a book given the number of pages.

4-37 As a follow-on to the previous exercise, suppose 800 pages is the absolute maximum number of pages that can be bound. Therefore, books containing more than 800 pages will be published in volumes of equal length but whose individual length does not exceed 550 pages. Extend the program prepared for the previous exercise to encompass this situation.

†4-38 In selling merchandise, a vendor uses the following procedure in computing prices:

1 The base price is applied to the first twelve units.

2 A 10 percent discount is applied to all units between 13 and 100.

3 A 30 percent discount is applied to all units above 100.

For example, suppose a purchaser orders 200 units of an item selling for $10. The total price would be

$$\$10 \times 12 + \$9 \times 88 + \$7 \times 100 = \$1,612$$

The average price is $1612/200 = $8.06. Prepare a program to read the number of units ordered and the price and compute the total price for all units and the average price.

4-39 Exercise 4-38 presented a formula for applying discounts to identical items in an order. Let's extend it to the situation where several items may appear in a single order, and the formula is to be applied to each. For example, consider the following order:

Item no.	Units	Unit Price
407	42	$4.45
219	7	27.15
375	125	6.25
129	19	13.42

For each item, the program should read the item number, the units ordered, and the unit price. The output should consist of the input followed by the total cost for all units of a given item and the average price. Finally, the program should print the total cost of all items in the order. Signify end-of-data by entry of a zero item number.

4-40 Jalopy Rent-A-Car has decided to computerize its billing procedure. In essence, the operator enters the following information:

1 Total number of hours the customer has kept the car.

2 The daily rate for the particular car.

3 The miles driven.

4 The mileage charge in cents per mile.

5 The discount allowed for this customer.

6 An indication as to whether or not the customer took the complete collision coverage, which costs $2.00 per day. A one indicates he took the coverage; a zero indicates he refused it.

In computing the bill, the following factors must be considered:

1 The minimum rental charge is one day's rental rate.

2 The hourly rate is 20% of the daily rate. Therefore, if a customer kept a car for 27 hours, he should be charged for one day plus 3 hours. However, hourly charges should not exceed the one-day rental rate.

3 If the car is kept for seven days or more, a 10% discount is applied to the daily rental rate (but not the mileage rate).

4 The maximum insurance rate is $10 per week.

5 The customer discount is applied to all but the insurance rate.

6 6% sales tax should be added to the bill.

Prepare the program to compute the bill.

†4-41 Via a method presented in *Puzzles and Paradoxes* by T. H. O'Beirne (Oxford University Press, London, © 1965), the date for Easter can be computed for any year x by the following ten steps:

Step	Dividend	Divisor	Quotient	Remainder
1	x	19	—	a
2	x	100	b	c
3	b	4	d	e
4	$8b + 13$	25	g	—
5	$19a + b - d - g + 15$	30	—	h
6	$a + 11h$	319	μ	—
7	c	4	i	k
8	$2e + 2i - k - h + \mu + 32$	7	—	λ
9	$h - \mu + \lambda + 90$	25	n	—
10	$h - \mu + \lambda + n + 19$	32	—	p

The month in which Easter occurs is given by n and the day of the month by p. For example, using 1972 for x gives a value of 4 and 2 for n and p, respectively, which corresponds to a date of April 2 for Easter. Prepare a program to perform these computations. See Exercise 2-21 for calculating quotients and remainders.

4-42 As an alternate to the procedure given in the previous exercise, O'Beirne proposes the following:

Step	Dividend	Divisor	Quotient	Remainder
1	x	100	b	c
2	$5b + c$	19	—	a
3	$3(b + 25)$	4	δ	ϵ
4	$8(b + 11)$	25	γ	—
5	$19a + \delta - \gamma$	30	—	h
6	$a + 11h$	319	u	—
7	$60(5 - \epsilon) + c$	4	j	k
8	$2j - k - h + \mu$	7	—	λ
9	$h - \mu + \lambda + 110$	30	n	q
10	$q + 5 - n$	(32)	(0)	p

Prepare a program to perform these computations.

4-43 Financial analysts take into account the time value of money via the present value. To illustrate this concept, suppose an investment is expected to yield the returns given in the second column of the following table:

Year	Return	Present Value		
1	\$ 7,000	$7,000/1.08$	$=$	6,481
2	9,000	$9,000/(1.08)^2$	$=$	7,716
3	13,000	$13,000/(1.08)^3$	$=$	10,320
4	20,000	$20,000/(1.08)^4$	$=$	14,701
5	40,000	$40,000/(1.08)^5$	$=$	27,233
		Present value	$=$	66,441

The present value of the return is the amount that would have to be invested now to yield this return, as illustrated in the above table for an interest rate of 8 percent.

Prepare a program to calculate the present value of the above investment for interest rates of 8, 12, and 15 percent.

4-44 Write a program to condense some statistics on the students in a class. One set of data is provided for each student, and contains (1) his or her age; (2) the student's sex, the code being 1–male, 2–female; and (3) the student's standing, the code being 1–freshman, 2–sophomores, 3–junior, 4–senior. The output should be the average age of the students, the percent males, and the percent freshmen, sophomore, juniors, and seniors. The number of entries are not counted, so use a zero set of entries to indicate the end of the data. Use the following data:

19	1	1
24	1	4
20	2	2
21	1	2
18	2	1
27	1	4
20	1	2
21	2	3
21	2	2
20	1	2

4-45 Suppose three temperatures, T1, T2, and T3, are entered into a program via a data card. These temperatures may be in any order, but the program is to print them in ascending order, i.e., smallest first, largest last. Prepare a program to accomplish this objective. Use as data 190, 271, and 147 for T1, T2, and T3 respectively.

†4-46 A man borrows $200 at an interest rate of $1\frac{1}{2}\%$ per month. He proposes to repay this at the rate of $10 per month. How many full payments must he make, and what must be paid in the final month to leave a balance of exactly zero? Program this problem. The calculations for each month should be as follows:

a. Calculate the interest for that month, which is $1\frac{1}{2}\%$ of the current balance.

b. Add the interest to the current balance to obtain the total amount owed at the end of the month (before receipt of payment).

c. Subtract the payment to obtain the new balance. For the first month, the interest is $(1\frac{1}{2}\%) \cdot (\$200) = \$3$. The new balance is $\$200 + \$3 - \$11 = \$193$.

4-47 A man plans to invest $500 per year at 6% interest. How many years will be required to accumulate $10,000? Write a program to compute this. Print the number of years along with the total value of his investments when they first exceed $10,000. The calculations proceed as follows. After the first year, the value of the investment is $\$500 \cdot (1 + 0.06) = \$530$. After the second year, the value is $(\$500 + \$530) \cdot (1 + 0.06) = \$1,091.30$.

†4-48 Consider writing a program that would compute the arithmetic average of the absolute values of a set of data. However, suppose that it is undesirable to count the number of values in this set of data. If it is known beforehand that none of the values will be exactly zero, the computer can be programmed to read successive values until a value of zero is detected as discussed in Section 3-3. Write a program that computes the arithmetic average of the values 0.7, 1.9, −2.2, 7.1, 17.0, −4.2, 7.9, and −5.1. The program should print and appropriately label the total number of values and the arithmetic average.

4-49 Write a program similar to the one in the previous exercise except that the geometric mean of the absolute values is computed. The geometric mean of n values is the nth root of their product.

4-50 Prepare a program to read an integer number and determine if it is even. This can be done by dividing by 2 and checking to see if the result is an integer. If the number is even, print the number followed by IS EVEN. Do likewise if the number is odd. Run the program for -5, -24, 17, and 8. What would this program tell us about zero?

†4-51 To seven decimal places, the fraction 1/7 is given as 0.1428571. Suppose you wanted it expressed to 20 decimal places. Can you devise a procedure to calculate the digits one by one and prepare a program utilizing it?

4-52 One of the following inequalities is incorrect:

$$|a + b| \leq |a| + |b|$$
$$|a + b| \geq |a| - |b|$$
$$|a + b| \leq |a| - |b|$$

Write a program that reads a value for a, a value for b, and checks these inequalities. The program should print the incorrect inequality as it would be programmed in FORTRAN. Running the program for the following values of a and b should check all possibilities:

a	b
1	1
1	-1
-1	-1
-1	1

4-53 Suppose you have a deck of cards each of which contains a single integer value. It is not known how many cards are in the deck, but it is known that the last card has the value 0 and no other card has this value. Write a program to compute and print the sum of the positive values on these cards and the sum of the negative values.

4-54 Modify the above exercise to count the number of cards containing positive even integers.

4-55 One method of finding the square root is to use the iterative formula

$$S_{i+1} = \frac{1}{2}\left(\frac{X}{S_i} + S_i\right)$$

where S_i is the estimate of X on the ith iteration. For $X = 300$ and starting with $S = 15$, continue to iterate until the value of S does not change in the fourth decimal place between successive iterations. As output print the results of this procedure along with the results using the SQRT function. What changes would you make in the program to compute the square root of 10,000,000? Of 0.001? (*Hint:* One way to make the test for changes in the fourth decimal is to express the equation in the form

$$S_{i+1} = S_i + \frac{1}{2}\left(\frac{x}{S_i} - S_i\right)$$

Now when $\frac{1}{2}\,|\,(x/S_i) - S_i\,|$ is less than 0.0001, the solution is found according to our criterion.)

4-56 Another way to formulate the method in the above exercise is as follows. To calculate the square root of a number, say b, select any number, say g_1, and compute another number, say h_1, as follows:

$$h_1 = \frac{b}{g_1}$$

The next step is to average g_1 and h_1 to obtain g_2:

$$g_2 = \frac{g_1 + h_1}{2}$$

Then h_2 is computed as before:

$$h_2 = \frac{b}{g_2}$$

This procedure can be generalized as follows:

$$h_i = \frac{b}{g_i}$$

$$g_{i+1} = \frac{g_i + h_i}{2}$$

The sequences $g_1, g_2, \ldots, g_i$ and $h_1, h_2, \ldots, h_i$ both approach the square root of b. The stopping criterion is whenever

$$|\,g_i - h_i\,| < \epsilon$$

where ϵ is a small but positive number. Use this program to take the square roots of 4 and 2, starting with $g_1 = 1$ in both cases and using $\epsilon = 0.00001$.

4-57 The cube root S of a number X can be calculated using the iteration formula

$$S_{i+1} = \frac{2}{3}S_i + \frac{X}{3S_i^2}$$

The iterative procedure may be initialized by setting $S_1 = 1$. Write a computer program to take cube roots of numbers in this manner. For informative purposes, print the value of S after each iteration. Terminate the procedure when the change in S from one iteration to the next is less than 0.01% of the current value of S. The above formula will work for positive or negative values of X, so your program should work likewise. Run the program for $X = 235$ and $X = -91.6$.

†**4-58** The solution of the simultaneous equations

$$a_1x + b_1y = c_1$$
$$a_2x + b_2y = c_2$$

is known to be

$$x = \frac{c_1b_2 - c_2b_1}{b_2a_1 - b_1a_2}$$

$$y = \frac{a_1c_2 - a_2c_1}{b_2a_1 - b_1a_2}$$

if $b_2a_1 - b_1a_2 \neq 0$. Prepare a program that computes x and y and prints the solution as shown in the figure. If there is no solution, the program should write "No solution."

INTRODUCTION TO DØ LOOPS AND SUBSCRIPTED VARIABLES

The first four chapters of this book have served to introduce the subject of FORTRAN programming and to give the individual student an introduction to many of the possibilities present in simple FORTRAN programming. It now becomes the function of the remainder of this book to build upon this simple programming ability and introduce many of the more powerful features of FORTRAN. One of the most noted of these is the capability of using subscripted variables. Use of subscripted variables in conjunction with the DØ statement will give the programmer a very easy and flexible means to handle complex tasks involving very large amounts of data with a minimum of programming effort. The ability to feel at ease in the use of subscripted variables and DØ statements is essential for a FORTRAN programmer. This chapter introduces the fundamental concepts behind the DØ statement followed by an introduction to subscripted variables. The next chapter treats more advanced material on these two subjects.

5-1. DESCRIPTION OF THE DØ STATEMENT

As a simple example, suppose the sum of all whole numbers from 1 to 100, $\sum_{i=1}^{100} i$, is to be calculated and stored in NSUM. By using the counters previously described, this could be programmed as per the "counter" in Figure 5-1. Note that five statements are required, three of which are necessary to form the counter.

114

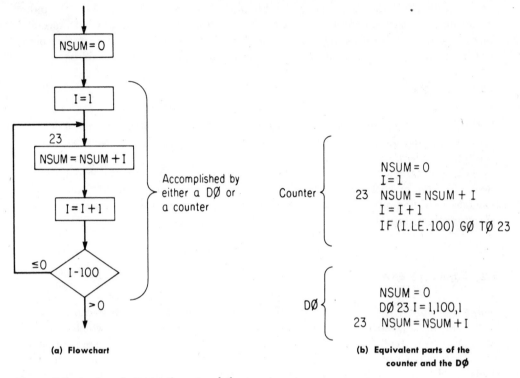

Figure 5-1. Analogy between the DØ and the counter.

This simple example illustrates one case in which the DØ statement is very convenient. By using the DØ, this problem could be programmed as also shown in Figure 5-1. Now only three statements are required.

The analogy between the counter and the DØ can give insight into the operation of the DØ, and is used for that purpose in the ensuing explanation. The general form of the DØ statement is as follows:

$$\text{DØ } n\ i = m_1, m_2, m_3$$

In this statement n is the statement number of the *last statement* under control of the DØ. In the example of the last paragraph n corresponds to 23. It is necessary that n be a statement number; it *cannot* be a variable. The *index i* of the DØ is a *nonsubscripted integer variable*. The index of the DØ in the above example is I, which is also used to form the counter. The value of the index upon initiation of the DØ is given by m_1, which must be a *nonsubscripted* (see Section 5-3) *integer variable* or a *positive integer constant*.‡ In the previous example the index I is initiated at 1, which corresponds to the statement I = 1 in forming the counter. The final value of the index is given by m_2, which also must be either a *nonsubscripted integer variable* or a *positive integer constant*. In the above example m_2 is 100. In the counter the final value is dictated

---

‡ Several recent compilers permit m_1 to be zero; a few even permit negative values.

by the statement IF (I.LE.100) Gø Tø 23. Finally, m_3 is the amount by which the index is incremented between iterations. In the above example m_3 is 1, which is specified for the counter by the statement I = I + 1. If m_3 is not specified in the Dø statement, it is assumed to be 1. Thus the Dø statement for the above example could be

Dø 23 I = 1,100

Nothing else may be omitted. *Note carefully the location of commas.* No comma appears between the statement number and the index of the Dø; but the indexing parameters (m_1, m_2, and m_3) must be separated by commas.

The Dø statement Dø 23 I = 1,100,1 can be read as follows: Do through statement 23 beginning with I equal to one and repeat from the Dø statement, incrementing I by one, until I equals 100. The first time the Dø is executed, I equals one; on the final execution I equals 100.

5-2. COMPLETE EXAMPLE

Before continuing with other details of the Dø, a complete program requiring a Dø statement should clarify a few points. Consider the simple case in which five real variables will be read (each from a separate card), their sum and average computed, and the average printed. The flowchart, the complete program, and possible data cards are shown in Figure 5-2. In this example two statements are in the *range* of the Dø. Thus the range begins with the first statement following the Dø and ends with the one whose statement number is specified by the Dø. The term Dø *loop* denotes all statements in the range of the Dø plus the Dø statement itself. Note that upon completion of the Dø, execution proceeds with the first executable statement following the Dø loop.

As another example, consider the computation of the consumption of a quantity such as electric power. The data are the customer number, the reading of the meter at the beginning of the month, and the reading of the meter at the end of the month. To calculate the kilowatt-hours consumed by each customer, the previous reading is subtracted from the present and added to the running sum. (See Figure 5-3a for flowchart.) As a case in which the previous reading is higher than the present indicates an erroneous condition, the computer upon detecting such a case should print the customer number and the reading. Note the branch within the Dø loop in the flowchart in Figure 5-3a. Furthermore, this entry should be ignored in calculating the total power consumption. Upon completion, the computer prints the total power used by all the customers.

The specific program and a few sample data cards, the first giving the number of customers, are given in Figure 5-3. First, the program reads the number of customers (the value of parameter m_2 in the Dø statement) and then enters the Dø loop. Upon each iteration, the program reads the customer number, the previous reading, and the present reading. If the previous reading is less than the present reading, the difference is added to the sum and the loop repeated. If not, the customer and reading are printed, and the loop repeated.

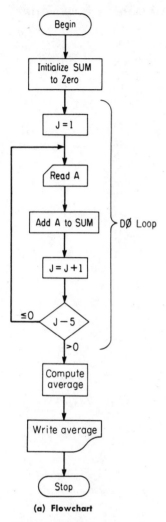

(a) **Flowchart**

Figure 5-2. Calculation of average.

Note the use of the CØNTINUE statement as a dummy statement to end the range of the DØ. The necessity of using the CØNTINUE (or another dummy statement) to end the DØ as in the above example is quite common. After the execution of either alternative, control must be transferred to the end of the range of the DØ. Since the two alternatives have nothing in common, a dummy statement such as CØNTINUE is required.‡ The CØNTINUE statement is considered to be executable; but no machine language instructions are generated from this statement.

---

‡ Many compilers permit free use of the CØNTINUE statement, while others, the IBM 360, for example, require that the CØNTINUE statement have a statement number.

```
      C        INITIALIZE SUM TO ZERO
1              SUM=0.
      C        CONSTRUCT DO LOOP TO READ THE VALUE FOR
      C              A AND ADD TO SUM
2              DO2J=1,5
3              READ,A
4        2     SUM=SUM+A
      C        COMPUTE AVERAGE AND PRINT
5              AVG=SUM/5.
6              PRINT,'AVERAGE IS',AVG
7              STOP
8              END
```
(b)

```
1.
5.
12.2
-3.
.161
```
(c)

```
AVERAGE IS        0.3072199E 01
```
(d)

```
      C        INITIALIZE SUM TO ZERO
1              SUM=0.
      C        CONSTRUCT DO LOOP TO READ THE VALUE FOR
      C              A AND ADD TO SUM
2              DO2J=1,5
3              READ(5,3)A
4        3     FORMAT(F5.0)
5        2     SUM=SUM+A
      C        COMPUTE AVERAGE AND PRINT
6              AVG=SUM/5.
7              WRITE(6,4)AVG
8        4     FORMAT(' AVERAGE IS',F12.4)
9              STOP
10             END
```
(e)

```
1.
5.
12.2
-3.
.161
```
(f)

```
AVERAGE IS        3.0722
```
(g)

Figure 5-2. *Continued.*

118

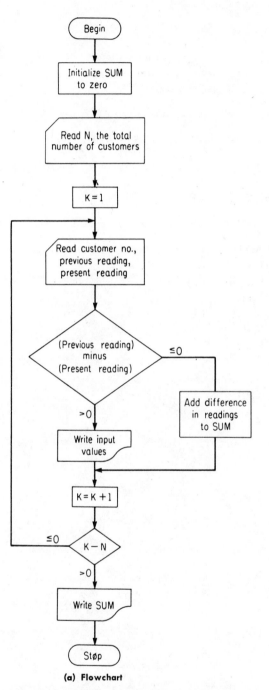

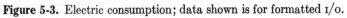

(a) Flowchart

Figure 5-3. Electric consumption; data shown is for formatted I/O.

```
      C         INITIALIZE SUM TO ZERO AND READ N, THE
      C              NUMBER OF CUSTOMERS
1               SUM=0.
2               READ,N
      C         DO LOOP FOR READING INPUT FOR EACH
      C         CUSTOMER AND PROCESSING APPROPRIATELY
3               DO2K=1,N
4               READ,J,PREV,PRES
      C         CHECK IF PREVIOUS READING IS GREATER
      C              THAN PRESENT
5               IF(PREV.GT.PRES)GOTO8
      C         COME HERE IF READING IS VALID.  SUM IS
      C              INCREMENTED.
6               SUM=SUM+(PRES-PREV)
7               GOTO2
      C         COME HERE IF READING IS INVALID.  PRINT
      C              THE INPUT VALUES.
8       8       PRINT,J,PREV,PRES
9       2       CONTINUE
      C         WRITE SUM
10              PRINT,"SUM IS",SUM
11              STOP
12              END
```

(b)

```
4
1,12.1,30.7
2,14.6,26.1
3,27.7,20.1
4,20.0,22.3
```

(c)

```
        3      0.2770000E 02      0.2010001E 02
SUM IS     0.3239999E 02
```

(d)

Figure 5-3. *Continued.*

```
        C       INITIALIZE SUM TO ZERO AND READ N, THE
        C           NUMBER OF CUSTOMERS
 1              SUM=0.
 2              READ(5,1)N
        C       DO LOOP FOR READING INPUT FOR EACH
        C       CUSTOMER AND PROCESSING APPROPRIATELY
 3              DO2K=1,N
 4              READ(5,12)J,PREV,PRES
        C       CHECK IF PREVIOUS READING IS GREATER
        C           THAN PRESENT
 5              IF(PREV.GT.PRES)GOTO8
        C       COME HERE IF READING IS VALID.  SUM IS
        C           INCREMENTED.
 6              SUM=SUM+(PRES-PREV)
 7              GOTO2
        C       COME HERE IF READING IS INVALID.  PRINT
        C           THE INPUT VALUES.
 8      8       WRITE(6,3)J,PREV,PRES
 9      2       CONTINUE
        C       WRITE SUM
10              WRITE(6,4)SUM
11              STOP
        C       FORMAT STATEMENTS
12      1       FORMAT(I5)
13      3       FORMAT(1X,I5,2F12.4)
14      4       FORMAT(' SUM IS',F11.4)
15      12      FORMAT(I5,2F10.0)
16              END
```

(e)

```
4
1       12.1        30.7
2       14.6        26.1
3       27.7        20.1
4       20.0        22.3
```

(f)

```
    3       27.7000         20.1000
SUM IS      32.4000
```

(g)

Figure 5-3. *Continued.*

5-3. FURTHER CLARIFICATION§

The following points regarding Dø loops are worthy of special note:

1. The requirement that the initial, final, and incrementing values (n_1, n_2, n_3) specified by the Dø statement be nonsubscripted integer variables or positive integer constants eliminates the following possibilities:

a. Dø 7 J = 1, N(I). The subscript† is not allowed, but the same result can be obtained with the following two statements:

M = N(I)
Dø 7 J = 1,M

b. Dø 7 J = 1, N + 2. A general rule to remember is that *no numerical calculations may be performed in the Dø statement itself*. The desired result can be obtained by

M = N + 2
Dø 7 J = 1,M

2. Consider the statement Dø 1 I = 1,4,2. On the first pass, I = 1; on the second pass, I = 3; on the third pass, I = 5. Consequently, I never equals four, the value for which the Dø is satisfied. Will the Dø be terminated after I equals three, after I equals five, or will it be terminated at all? The answer is clear after considering the *effective manner* in which the computer executes the Dø. The behavior will be the same as when executing a counter of the following type:

$$
\begin{array}{l}
\quad\; \text{I} = 1 \\
1 \left\{\begin{array}{c} \text{range} \\ \text{of} \\ \text{Dø} \end{array}\right\} \\
\quad\; \text{I} = \text{I} + 2 \\
\quad\; \text{IF (I.LE.4) Gø Tø 1}
\end{array}
$$

From the above counter, it is apparent that I equals three on the last execution of the statements in the range of the Dø, although the value of I is five when leaving the counter.

What will result from the following Dø statement?

Dø 7 I = 4,4

The statements within the range of the Dø will be executed only once. Also, in most

---

§ In this section the idiosyncrasies of various FORTRAN IV compilers lead to some double-talk. FORTRAN IV compilers are available for many different computers, and the differences of opinion of the individuals who wrote the compilers are reflected by certain minor points of the Dø being treated differently by different compilers. In a general manual such as this, the more common or safe variations are given.

† Subscripts themselves are discussed in detail in the next several sections of this chapter.

cases the DØ statement DØ 7 I = 4,3 will be executed once by most FORTRANS and WATFIV (note that a machine executing it according to the counter described in the previous paragraph would execute it once). These situations are sometimes encountered when variables are used as the indexing parameters n_1 and n_2.

3. The index of the DØ may not be altered within the range of the DØ. For example, consider the hypothetical case in which the 10 elements in a column called A are to be summed, except that the third element is to be omitted from the sum. The following statements are proposed:

```
      SUM = 0.
      DØ 7 I = 1,10
      IF (I.EQ.3) I = I + 1
7     SUM = SUM + A(I)
```

However, this series of statements will not be accepted by the compiler, as the IF statement attempts to change the index. Instead, the following procedure is appropriate:

```
      SUM = 0.
      DØ 7 I = 1,10
      IF (I.EQ.3) GØ TØ 7
      SUM = SUM + A(I)
7     CØNTINUE
```

This accomplishes the same result, but does not tamper with the DØ index. *The DØ index is available for calculations within the range of the DØ, but must not be altered by arithmetic statements or by reading a new value of the index within the range of the DØ.*
This same rule applies to the indexing parameters n_1, n_2, and n_3.

4. Control may be transferred outside the range of a DØ by two methods. First, when the execution of the statements in the range of the DØ as specified by the indexing parameters (n_1, n_2 and n_3) is accomplished, the DØ is said to be satisfied and a *normal exit* is achieved. Control is simply transferred to the first executable statement following the DØ loop. All examples cited previously involved normal exits.
However, it is possible to transfer control from within the range of the DØ to a statement outside the range of the DØ. Consider the following statements:

```
      DØ 100 I = 1,20
      X = function (I, other variables)
      IF (X.GT.XLIMIT) GØ TØ 200
      WRITE (6,10) I, X
10    FØRMAT (1X,I10,E20.6)
100   CØNTINUE
200   X = XLIMIT
```

If X never exceeds XLIMIT as I varies from one to twenty, a normal exit is made from the DØ loop. If, however, X exceeds XLIMIT as I varies from one to twenty, control is transferred to statement 200.

In most FORTRANS the index is not available after a normal exit, whereas the index is available after all other exits. This problem can be readily circumvented by setting another variable as equal to the index of the dø loop, for example N = I. The variable N will be retained outside the loop no matter what type of exit is made.

5. Control can be transferred to the statements within the range of a dø *only* by the dø statement: That is, the following sequence is not acceptable in most versions of FORTRAN IV:

```
        I = 5
        Gø Tø 7
          .
          .
          .

        Dø 6 I = 1,12
7       (some valid statement)
          .
          .
          .

6       (Some valid statement)
```

It is, however, possible to re-enter a dø after an exit other than a normal exit, but no rules governing the dø may be violated between exit and re-entry.

6. The last statement in the range of the dø must be executable. The common mistake is the use of a FøRMAT statement to terminate the dø loop.

7. The last statement in the range of the dø must *not* be a Gø Tø, an arithmetic IF, a STøP, or another dø statement. However, these may be used freely elsewhere within the range of the dø.

The use of a logical IF statement as the last statement in the range of the dø is permissible. Consider the following case:

```
        Dø 7 I = 1,5
7       IF (t)s
```

where *t* is a logical expression that is either true or false and *s* is an executable statement. If the logical expression *t* is false, the dø index is incremented without executing *s*. If the logical statement is true, statement *s* is executed and the dø index incremented. However, if *s* were a transfer statement and *t* were true, the transfer is executed.‡

8. The statement *s* used in a logical IF of the type

IF (t)s

may *not* be a dø statement.

---

‡ A few FORTRANS will not accept transfer statements in a logical IF statement when it terminates the range of a dø. Even this uncertainty can be surmounted as follows:

```
        Dø 7 I = 1,5
        IF(t)s
7       CøNTINUE
```

5-4. USEFULNESS OF SUBSCRIPTED VARIABLES

The need for subscripted variables and the motivation for their use may be understood best by means of a simple example. Consider the rather elementary problem in which 40 students take an examination. It is desired to write a computer program to calculate the class average grade and then calculate the ratio of the student's individual grade to this class average grade.

The 40 grade values must be summed in order to calculate the average grade, and this could be accomplished by using the tools that were developed in earlier chapters. Each individual grade could be assigned a separate name, e.g., GRA1, GRA2, . . . , GRA40, and these 40 individual and distinct variables could be read into the computer separately. They each have a separate name, they are stored separately, and they are used separately. In such an approach the average would be calculated with an arithmetic assignment statement; but it should be noted that this arithmetic assignment statement would be quite long since it would involve terms for each of the 40 values of individual student grades. Such an arithmetic assignment statement could be written (using continuation statements); but this overall approach represents a massive "strong arm" approach to a relatively simple problem. In order to calculate the individual grade ratios we could use 40 separate arithmetic assignment statements. This total approach is illustrated in Figure 5-4 where the 45 necessary statements are

```
C FOR COMMENT
STATEMENT NUMBER | Cont. | FORTRAN STATEMENT

      AVERAG =(GRA1 + GRA2 + GRA3 + GRA4 + GRA5 + GRA6 + GRA7 +
     1GRA8 + GRA9 + GRA10 + GRA11 + GRA12 + GRA13 + GRA14 + GRA15 + GRA1
     26 + GRA17 + GRA18 + GRA19 + GRA20 + GRA21 + GRA22 + GRA23 + GRA24
     3+ GRA25 + GRA26 + GRA27 + GRA28 + GRA29 + GRA30 + GRA31 + GRA32 +
     4GRA33 + GRA34 + GRA35 + GRA36 + GRA37 + GRA38 + GRA39 + GRA40)/40.
      RAT1 = GRA1/AVERAG
      RAT2 = GRA2/AVERAG
        .
        .
        .
      RAT39 = GRA39/AVERAG
      RAT40 = GRA40/AVERAG
```

Figure 5-4. Calculation of grade ratio to class average.

shown. The student can also appreciate the massive input/output problems associated with this approach.

The type of problem illustrated above can be handled quite easily and with great facility by the use of subscripted variables, and this will be the solution approach employed. Subscripted variables are not a new concept because people are quite accustomed to working with large arrays of data in which the individual elements of the arrays are indicated by subscripts. It is done in this manner to simplify quite cumbersome problems in notation. We have already tended to do this in the problem mentioned earlier by referring to the individual grades as grade 1, grade 2,..., grade 40.

FORTRAN provides the same possibility for handling subscripted variables with some very minor changes in notation. Instead of writing the grade values as indicated above, FORTRAN subscript notation could be used to write these as GRA(1), GRA(2), GRA(3),..., GRA(I),..., GRA(39), GRA(40).

We have taken grade values and indicated them as being the elements of a one-dimensional array with 40 elements. Observe that the subscript of the individual element of the array is denoted by the use of parentheses immediately following the name of the array, and also observe that this subscript is illustrated as an integer constant and as an integer variable. By introducing the possibility of subscripted variables, the summation indicated earlier and the ratio calculations could be written as shown in Figure 5-5. 12 statements (or six using dø loops) in Figure 5-5 do the same task as the 45 statements indicated in Figure 5-4.

```
C FOR COMMENT
STATEMENT NUMBER          FORTRAN STATEMENT

       SUM = 0.
       I = 1
100    SUM = SUM + GRA(I)              DØ 100 I = 1,40
       I = I + 1                       100 SUM = SUM + GRA(I)
       IF(I.GT.40)GØ TØ 200
       GØ TØ 100
200    AVERAG = SUM/40.
       I = 1
400    RAT(I) = GRA(I)/AVERAG          DØ 400 I = 1,40
       I = I + 1                       400 RAT(I) = GRA(I)/AVERAG
       IF(I.GT.40) GØ TØ 300
       GØ TØ 400
300
```

Figure 5-5. Subscripted variable calculation of grade ratios.

As indicated in subsequent sections of this chapter, the problems associated with the input and output of the array of information used in Figure 5-5 also can be significantly simplified. Referring to Figure 5-5 and noting the relative ease with which the class average has been calculated and the grade ratios formed should be motivation enough to tackle the problem of gaining a clear insight to the use of subscripted variables. The advantage gained if there had been a thousand (or more) data points would be quite obvious since the complexity of the subscripted variable program would not be increased.

In this chapter the terms "subscripted variable," "array element," and "element of an array" will be used interchangeably.

5-5. DEFINITIONS AND SUBSCRIPT ARGUMENTS

Many quantities may be represented with one variable name through the use of subscripts as indicated in the previous section. Only one-dimensional arrays are considered in this chapter, with two and higher dimensional arrays reserved for the next chapter. For convenience in orienting the individual's thinking, the one-dimensional array can be considered (in a geometric sense) as representing points along a line. Alternatively, one may view it as a column or a row of numbers, elements of which can be referenced by their position within the column or row.

An element of a one-dimensional array will be referenced in a FORTRAN program by entries of the following form:

Name (Subscript)

The name of a subscripted variable follows generally the same rules as those for nonsubscripted variables. Furthermore, the variable name must not be identical to that of a FORTRAN function, e.g., SQRT, ABS, etc. It is important to note that all of the elements of any given array must be of the same type. It is possible for a subscripted variable to be integer or real, the type being specified by the first letter in the array name according to the same rules as for nonsubscripted variables. Arrays of other types of variables are possible.

Most Fortran systems allow only integer subscripts; but these may be integer constants, integer variables, or limited forms of integer arithmetic expressions. (Some advanced systems permit unlimited integer expressions and real subscripts.) The usual allowable forms of subscript arguments are restricted on most machines to the following, where I is used to indicate a nonsubscripted integer variable and L and L′ are used to indicate unsigned integer constants.

General Form	Example
I	K2
L	6
I $\pm$ L	J + 6
L * I	6 * K
L * I $\pm$ L′	6 * K − 2

The value of the subscripted variable normally may not be less than one, nor may it be greater than the value dictated at the beginning of the program through the use of the dimensiøn statement (discussed in the next section). fortran IV does not normally allow the variable in the subscript expression to be subscripted; but some advanced forms of automatic programming languages do allow this freedom.

Some examples of invalid subscripts are as follows:

Gøgø(a − 2)	a is not an integer variable
lsd(2 + i)	The variable must normally precede the constant, i.e., i + 2.
td(−i)	The variable may not be signed.
var(i(j))	Not normally allowed to subscript the subscript.
var(i + j)	Variable plus variable addition not normally allowed.

The operation of the fortran compiler is such that every individual element in the array will be associated with a unique memory address, and these addresses for an individual array will be in adjacent storage locations. fortran compilers act to set aside these memory address locations and to maintain a simple system for reference to any individual element of an array. For this reason it is necessary that the fortran compiler knows how many locations to allocate for an individual array, and this leads to the use of the dimensiøn statement which will be discussed in the next section.

For example, consider the following statements in a fortran program:

. . . . .
y(j) = c
. . . . .
. . . . .
a = y(k)
. . . . .

The entries $y(j)$ and $y(k)$ refer to the same array, namely y. Before the statement $y(j) = c$ can be executed, the integer variable j must have been defined previously in the program. Thus, the value of c is stored in the position in array y corresponding to the numerical value of j when this statement is executed. Similarly, the variable k must be defined when the statement $a = y(k)$ is executed.

EXAMPLE 5-1

One rather rough indication of the "expected value" of a person's blood pressure is to add the age in years of the person to 100. Assume that we record the age and blood pressure of 200 men and arrange them in two arrays named press and age. Use them to calculate a third array dif, i.e., the difference between the man's actual blood pressure and the blood pressure given by the crude "rule-of-thumb" given above. The ith element in the dif would be given as:

$$dif(i) = press(i) − (age(i) + 100.)$$

A portion of the computer program necessary to carry out this simple calculation is shown in Figure 5-6.

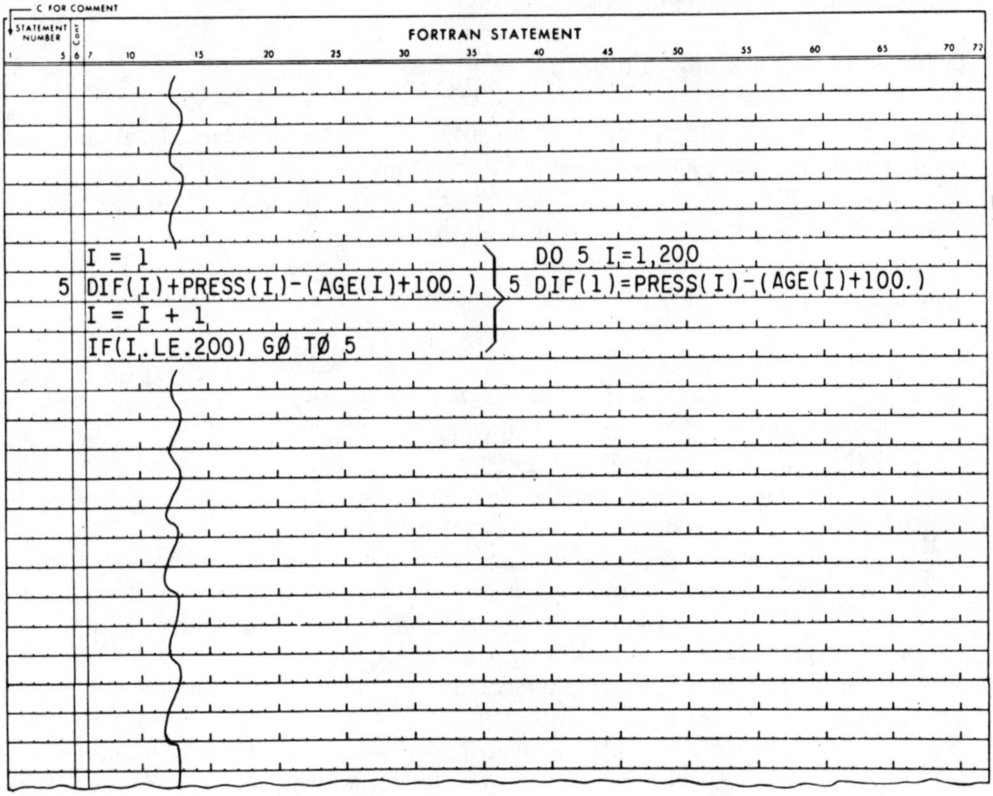

Figure 5-6. Statements for Example 5-1.

5-6. THE DIMENSIØN STATEMENT

The use of subscripted variables in a FORTRAN program necessitates supplying a certain amount of information about the individual subscripted variables to the FORTRAN compiler. This information must include:

1 The names of the variables to be subscripted.

2 The number of subscripts that are to be used for each subscripted variable.

3 The maximum value of each individual subscript for each individual subscripted variable.

Providing this information to the FORTRAN compiler is done by the DIMENSIØN statement which normally appears at the beginning of the FORTRAN program. The DIMENSIØN statements must include every variable that is to be subscripted in the program, and the inclusion of the subscripted variable in a DIMENSIØN statement must take place prior to the first occurrence of the subscripted variable anywhere in the program. The DIMENSIØN statement may mention any number of subscripted variables. It is not necessary, however, that they all have the same number of subscripts. The DIMENSIØN statement is a nonexecutable statement and normally takes the following form for one-dimensional arrays:

DIMENSIØN $name_1$ (d_1), $name_2$ (d_2), . . .

In the above, $name_1$ and $name_2$ stand for array names for subscripted variables appearing in the program, and the d's stand for the dimension of an individual subscript. *The individual d's must be unsigned, nonzero integer constants.* As an actual example of a DIMENSIØN statement, consider the following:

DIMENSIØN I(2), X(15), Y(8)

This DIMENSIØN statement would cause the FORTRAN compiler to assign a total of two storage locations to the I array for storage of the two integer constants which comprise the elements of the array. The compiler will also reserve 15 storage locations for the real constants which comprise the X array, and eight storage locations for the real elements of the Y array. The order of listing arrays in the DIMENSIØN statement is not important, and more than one DIMENSIØN statement may be used.

It is usually not permissible to use zero or negative subscripts. (They are allowed in relatively few FORTRAN compilers.) Neither is it permissible for the program to have any subscript in an executable statement that is larger than the maximum size previously specified in the DIMENSIØN statement. Although subscript values less than one or larger than the maximum size indicated in the DIMENSIØN statement are invalid subscripted-variable references, it is also one of the characteristics of many computers that they do not check subscripts for their individual validity. The net result is that programs incorporating this error may be executed and completely erroneous results obtained.

Even though the DIMENSIØN statement indicates the probable maximum size of subscripted-variable requirements, it is not necessary that the programmer use all of the element address locations that are reserved—i.e., it is permissible to over-dimension arrays in the DIMENSIØN statement. It must be pointed out, however, that overdimensioning of arrays can be expensive in terms of computer running time and memory requirements. (Since most computers only have a limited amount of high-speed access or fast memory, the use of unreasonably large arrays may necessitate the inclusion of a large amount of slow-speed memory in the array address locations that are reserved.) For each individual array the compiler will reserve storage for the number of elements indicated by the subscripts specified in the DIMENSIØN statement.

As some examples of the use of DIMENSIØN statements, the following are appropriate. For the grade average program briefly discussed in Section 5-4, it would be necessary to have a DIMENSIØN statement of the form

DIMENSIØN GRA(40), RAT(40)

For the calculation of the "blood pressure difference" of Figure 5-6, it would be necessary to have a DIMENSIØN statement of the form

DIMENSIØN AGE(200), PRESS(200), DIF(200)

When referring to an array in a DIMENSIØN statement, as opposed to an arithmetic assignment statement, there is an implied difference between the two notations used. In a DIMENSIØN statement the reference to the array is not to one individual element, but gives information on the maximum size of the subscript. In a statement such as an arithmetic assignment statement, a reference such as A(2) would indicate a reference to a specific element in the array.

A common mistake of beginning programmers is to attempt to use the following DIMENSIØN statement for the blood pressure example cited above:

N = 200
DIMENSIØN AGE(N), PRESS(N), DIFF(N)

This is unacceptable because the information in the DIMENSIØN statement is used during *compilation*, whereas N is not actually assigned the value of 200 until the statement is encountered during execution of the program.

Array names may appear in certain nonexecutable specification statements, in

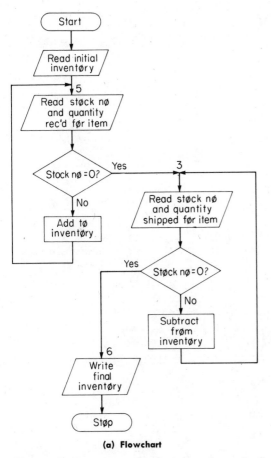

(a) Flowchart

Figure 5-7. Inventory program; data shown for formatted I/O.

```
1                       DIMENSION ISTK(6),IQUAN(6)
          C             READ INITIAL INVENTORY
2                       DO1I=1,6
3         1             READ,ISTK(I),IQUAN(I)
          C             UPDATE INVENTORY FOR STOCK RECEIVED
4         5             READ,NSTK,NQUAN
          C             CHECK FOR ZERO STOCK NUMBER
5                       IF(NSTK.EQ.0)GOTO3
          C             ADD TO INVENTORY
6                       DO4I=1,6
7         4             IF(NSTK.EQ.ISTK(I)) IQUAN(I)=IQUAN(I)+NQUAN
8                       GOTO5
          C             UPDATE INVENTORY FOR STOCK SHIPPED
9         3             READ,NSTK,NQUAN
          C             CHECK FOR ZERO STOCK NUMBER
10                      IF(NSTK.EQ.0)GOTO6
          C             SUBTRACT FROM INVENTORY
11                      DO7I=1,6
12        7             IF(NSTK.EQ.ISTK(I)) IQUAN(I)=IQUAN(I)-NQUAN
13                      GOTO3
          C             WRITE FINAL INVENTORY
14        6             DO8I=1,6
15        8             PRINT,ISTK(I),IQUAN(I)
16                      STOP
17                      END
```

(b)

```
1207,12 ⎤
1049,1  |
0907,5  ⎬  Old Inventory
0412,0  |
1222,7  |
0015,2 ⎦

0412,5 ⎤
0015,3 |
1049,7 ⎬ Received
1222,5 |
0412,5 |
0015,2 ⎦
0,0

1207,2  ⎤
1049,3  |
1222,10 ⎬ Shipped
0015,4  |
0412,7  |
0,0    ⎦
```

(c)

```
1207            10
1049             5
 907             5
 412             3
1222             2
  15             3
```

(d)

Figure 5-7. *Continued.*

```
1              DIMENSION ISTK(6),IQUAN(6)
       C      READ INITIAL INVENTORY
2              DO1I=1,6
3      1       READ(5,2) ISTK(I),IQUAN(I)
4      2       FORMAT(2I5)
       C      UPDATE INVENTORY FOR STOCK RECEIVED
5      5       READ(5,2) NSTK,NQUAN
       C      CHECK FOR ZERO STOCK NUMBER
6              IF(NSTK.EQ.0)GOTO3
       C      ADD TO INVENTORY
7              DO4I=1,6
8      4       IF(NSTK.EQ.ISTK(I)) IQUAN(I)=IQUAN(I)+NQUAN
9              GOTO5
       C      UPDATE INVENTORY FOR STOCK SHIPPED
10     3       READ(5,2) NSTK,NQUAN
       C      CHECK FOR ZERO STOCK NUMBER
11             IF(NSTK.EQ.0)GOTO6
       C      SUBTRACT FROM INVENTORY
12             DO7I=1,6
13     7       IF(NSTK.EQ.ISTK(I)) IQUAN(I)=IQUAN(I)-NQUAN
14             GOTO3
       C      WRITE FINAL INVENTORY
15     6       DO8I=1,6
16     8       WRITE(6,9)ISTK(I),IQUAN(I)
17     9       FORMAT(1X,2I5)
18             STOP
19             END
```

(e)

```
1207      12  ⎫
1049       1  ⎪
0907       5  ⎬ Old Inventory
0412       0  ⎪
1222       7  ⎪
0015       2  ⎭

0412       5  ⎫
0015       3  ⎪
1049       7  ⎬ Received
1222       5  ⎪
0412       5  ⎪
0015       2  ⎭

1207       2  ⎫
1049       3  ⎪
1222      10  ⎬ Shipped
0015       4  ⎪
0412       7  ⎭
```

(f)

```
1207      10
1049       5
 907       5
 412       3
1222       2
  15       3
```

(g)

Figure 5-7. *Continued.*

133

references to subprograms, and in input-output statements without any of the sub-scripts being mentioned, for example:

READ (5, 10)A

Since such reference to an array without any mention of subscripts is permissible, it is obvious that no other variable in the program may have the same name as the array itself. In all cases other than those mentioned above, only array elements may be used. *This is particularly important in arithmetic expressions.*

EXAMPLE 5-2

One current use of a computer is to maintain an up-to-date account of items in inventory. Suppose the status of the inventory at the beginning of the month is punched on cards, the stock number in the first five columns and the quantity in stock in the next five columns. To keep the number of cards reasonable, suppose we write our program to handle only six items in stock. The first section of the program in Figure 5-7 reads cards specifying the initial inventory.

Suppose further that each time a shipment is received, cards are punched for each item giving the stock number in the first five columns and the quantity received in the second five. These cards will be in random order, and depending upon the number of shipments received, there may be zero, one, or several cards for any one item. To allieviate the necessity of counting the cards, a blank card will be the last card in this group. When read, the stock number will be zero, which indicates the end of this set of cards. The second section of the program in Figure 5-7 reads these cards and up-dates the inventory.

Cards analogous to the above are punched for shipments of items. The third section of the program in Figure 5-7 processes these cards. The final section prints the new inventory.

In practice, the old inventory would be stored on a more convenient medium than cards, probably a disk or magnetic tape. The program would read the old inventory from the appropriate source, up-date it, and write the new inventory back on this medium as well as printing it.

5-7. INPUT AND OUTPUT

One of the most straightforward means of providing input and output statements for the elements of an array is to list explicitly every individual element of the array in the input or output statement. As an example, the information for the input of a four element array A and a two element array B might be done by a READ statement as follows:

```
      READ (5, 100) A(1), A(2), A(3), A(4), B(1), B(2)
100   FØRMAT (6F10.2)
```

The four elements of the A array and the two elements of the B array could be written in the READ statement in any sequence whatsoever. The only restriction, of course, would be that the information on the data card would have to be in the corresponding order.

One of the welcomed advantages of subscripted variables is that it is possible to deal with all of the elements of an entire array without having to list them explicitly. As an example, an input or output statement may contain only the name of the array without any reference whatsoever to any subscript, and the entire array will be completely read or written. When this is done it is absolutely necessary to have a complete understanding of the implicit convention regarding the sequence by which the elements must appear on the input or output record. For one-dimensional arrays the elements are taken in an increasing sequence—i.e., first the element with subscript 1, then the element with subscript 2, etc., up to the largest subscript called for in the DIMENSIØN statement (which must have appeared earlier).

This will mean that the previous READ statement could have been written as

    READ (5,100) A,B
100 FØRMAT (6F10.2)

In such a case the elements on the data card *must* be punched in the following sequence:

A(1), A(2), A(3), A(4), B(1), B(2)

This implied sequence always will be assumed to exist.

It is also possible to read in an array using format-free oriented I/Ø, e.g.,

DIMENSIØN HØLD(25)
READ, HØLD

More than one input number may appear on any one data card: The first number read in goes to HØLD(1), etc. These input data numbers are stored in consecutive storage locations until the entire storage set aside for the array by the DIMENSIØN statement has been filled. For the example above, if fewer than 25 numbers are given, an error is diagnosed. These concepts shown may be generalized to other examples, and similar considerations apply to format-free PRINT statements for output.

When an array is called for without explicit reference to subscripts, the entire array will be assumed to exist in the size given in the DIMENSIØN statement, and any overdimensioning of array sizes will present problems because the computer will attempt to read all of the elements of the array whether they exist or not.

FØRMAT statements can have a very important effect on the handling of information associated with arrays. One format field specification is necessary for each individual element in the array. As the elements of the array are read or written, the FØRMAT statement will be scanned from left to right. When the last right parenthesis of the FØRMAT statement is reached (the FØRMAT statement is exhausted) the computer will return to the first left parenthesis *and* go to a new record, e.g., a new line or card, and repeat (scan again) the FØRMAT statement from left to right. As an example of this, assume that we have a one-dimensional array with ten elements called the A array. If we write the statements

        DIMENSIØN A(10)
        READ (5,100) A
100   FØRMAT (F10.2)

the computer will read the 10 values of the 10 elements of A from 10 successive cards or records. This means that the element A(1) will be assumed to appear in the first 10 columns in F10.2 format on the first card or input record; the second element, i.e., A(2), will be expected to appear in the first 10 columns of the second input record or card in F10.2 format, etc. until the 10th element, i.e., A(10) will be expected to appear in the first 10 columns of the tenth record or card in F10.2 format.

As another example, if all five values of an array referred to as the one-dimensional x array were to be found on a single data card, we could read all of these by the following statements:

        DIMENSIØN x(5)
        READ (5,20) x
20   FØRMAT (5F10.4)

This statement would cause the computer to look for x(1) in columns 1–10, x(2) in columns 11–20, etc. through x(5) in columns 41–50.

The individual elements in an array must all be of the same mode, i.e., real or integer; but it is not necessary that they all be read or written in the same format code. As an example, some of the elements in an integer array may be written in I5, some in I7, and some in I15 format.

Sometimes it is desirable to transfer only part of the values into or out of an array via a READ or WRITE statement, and on other occasions it is desirable to have the subscripts in an array vary in some manner other than the sequence normally assumed by the compiler. In such situations it is possible to have as a part of the input or output statement an expression which will dictate the exact order in which the subscripts will vary. The general form of this part, called an implied DØ, of an input or output statement is indicated in Figure 5-8. As a specific example, it might be desirable to read only elements 6 to 10 of a one-dimensional array. The statements for this would appear

        READ (5,10) (v(I), I = 6,10)
10   FØRMAT (5F10.2)

It is also possible to use implied DØ loops with format-free I/Ø, e.g.,

READ, (v(I), I = 6,10)

The statement shown in Figure 5-8 can be extended to handle more than one array. For example we might have statements

        READ (5,10) (A(I), B(I), I = 1,3)
10   FØRMAT (F10.2)

$$\cdots (v(i), \quad i = m_1, m_2, m_3) \cdots$$

where	v	is an array name.
	i	is an integer variable used as an indexed (controlled) subscript.
	m_1	is either an unsigned integer constant or an unsigned integer variable whose value is used as the initial value of i
	m_2	is either an unsigned integer constant or an unsigned integer variable whose value is compared with the current value of i at the completion of reading, or writing, each array element. When the current value of i becomes greater than the value of m_2, the reading or writing operation is terminated.
	m_3	is either an unsigned integer constant or an unsigned integer variable whose value is added to the current value of i after each array element is read or written, but before the comparison between i and m_2 is made. It can be omitted if 1 is to be added to i as the increment.
m_1, m_2, and m_3		must be greater than zero.

Figure 5-8. General form of an indexed or controlled subscripted variable.

These statements would read these two arrays in the following fashion:

A(1)
B(1)
A(2)
B(2)
A(3)
B(3)

The use of input and output statements for arrays and the associated effect of FØRMAT statements on their execution will be shown more vividly in the examples that follow and in the solved examples at the end of this chapter.

EXAMPLE 5-3

As an example of the use of subscripted variables, assume that a student makes 30 measurements of a quantity. These 30 measurements will comprise the elements of a one-dimensional array whose name is DATA. The student also can calculate a value of each of the measurements and therefore have 30 expected or calculated values of these data points. These 30 values comprise a second one-dimensional array named CALC. Assume that these two arrays will be read into the computer, and their differences will be calculated and squared for each point.

As an example, assume that each of the input elements of DATA will appear on a separate card in F10.2 format in the first ten columns of the card. Further assume that the values of CALC will be found on five additional input cards, six values to a card in 6F10.2 format. For the output of this program it is desired to have the record appear with the values of DATA in a vertical column; just to the right of DATA the corresponding values of CALC should appear in a vertical column; and just to the right

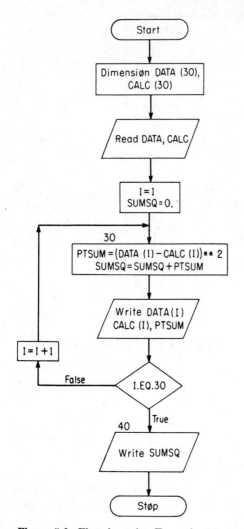

Figure 5-9. Flowchart for Example 5-3 (sum-of-squares calculation).

of CALC the square of the value of the difference (between the DATA element and the CALC element) should appear. These 30 individual point values of the difference squared will be named PTSUM. Below these three vertical columns of DATA, CALC, and PTSUM it is desired to write out the value of the total sum of the squares for all the 30 data points, and this should be written in E20.7 format. The flowchart for a program necessary to make the calculations is shown in Figure 5-9, and the program itself is shown in Figure 5-10.

In the input of the two one-dimensional arrays into the computer the READ statements contain implicit assumptions as to the sequence which the individual elements of the arrays will have on the data cards. Since the values of DATA are each in F10.2 format on a separate card, the input cards must be arranged so that the subscripts on DATA vary from 1 to 30. Since FØRMAT statement number 10 has a single field specification, the computer will read in one input card, look for a single element on that card

```
C     EXAMPLE, CALCULATION OF SUM OF SQUARES
C
C
C     DATA INPUT SECTION
C
      DIMENSION DATA(30),CALC(30)
      READ(5,10)DATA          or    READ, DATA
   10 FORMAT(F10.2)
      READ(5,20)CALC          or    READ, CALC
   20 FORMAT(6F10.2)
C
C     CALCULATION OF SUM OF SQUARES AND ARRAY OUTPUT
C
      DO35I = 1,30
      SUMSQ = 0.
   30 PTSUM = (DATA(I) - CALC(I)) **2
      SUMSQ = SUMSQ + PTSUM
   35 WRITE(6,50)DATA(I),CALC(I),PTSUM  or  PRINT, DATA(I),CALC(I),PTSUM
   50 FORMAT (1X,3F10.2)
C
C     SUM OF SQUARES OUTPUT
C
   40 WRITE(6,60)SUMSQ        or    PRINT, SUMSQ
   60 FORMAT(1X,E20.7)
      STOP
      END
      18.62
      17.79
      17.42
      17.01
      16.89
      16.62
      16.31
      16.09
      15.82
      15.04
      15.11
      14.87
      14.47
      14.26
      14.00
      13.75
      13.53
      13.27
```

```
      13.00
      12.79
      12.56
      12.34
      12.17
      12.03
      11.88
      11.66
      11.47
      11.21
      11.03
      10.69
      18.07    17.62    17.43    17.21    17.00    16.78
      16.45    16.28    15.87    15.61    15.21    15.05
      14.96    14.81    14.62    14.46    14.11    13.75
      14.62    13.42    13.02    12.71    12.46    12.25
      11.98    11.78    11.51    11.36    11.12    11.01
```

Figure 5-10. Program for Example 5-3; data shown for formatted I/O.

in F10.2 format, and then it will go to a new card or new record to look for the next element of the DATA array, etc. In the case of CALC the computer will see the FØRMAT statement 20 which has a repetition number of 6 associated with the field specification. The computer will expect the first six values of the CALC array to be found on the first input card for CALC, and then proceed to a new input card or record for elements 7–12, to a third card for elements 13–18, etc., until five cards have been read for the CALC array. The computer knows there are 30 elements in both DATA and CALC because of the DIMENSIØN statement.

In the calculation of the sum of the squares a dø loop is used to calculate all of the individual differences between DATA and CALC, and in each case the elemental difference at a point is squared. The sum of all of these squares is retained in the computer, but the point value of PTSUM is written out as soon as it is calculated. Since PTSUM is not retained, it is not subscripted, it is not stored, and it is not available for future processing.

The output FØRMAT statement has a 1x to keep the carriage-control column blank on the output record, and a repetition number of 3 is used in the output field specification. A blank, the first element of DATA, the first element of CALC, and PTSUM for the first elements will be written on one output record, and on the second output record the first column also will be blank; followed by the second element of DATA, the second element of CALC, and PTSUM for the second elements (all in F10.2 format). This will continue through the 30 sets of values for the arrays. After all the output arrays have been written, the computer then encounters a new WRITE statement which records the sum of the squares.

For input data appearing in the example the output of the program will appear as shown here and on page 139.

18.62	18.07	0.30
17.79	17.62	0.03
17.42	17.43	0.00
17.01	17.21	0.04
16.89	17.00	0.01
16.62	16.78	0.03
16.31	16.45	0.02
16.09	16.28	0.04
15.82	15.87	0.00
15.04	15.61	0.32
15.11	15.21	0.01
14.87	15.05	0.03
14.47	14.96	0.24
14.26	14.81	0.30
14.00	14.62	0.38
13.75	14.46	0.50
13.53	14.11	0.34
13.27	13.75	0.23
13.00	14.62	2.62
12.79	13.42	0.40
12.56	13.02	0.21
12.34	12.71	0.14

12.17	12.46	0.08
12.03	12.25	0.05
11.88	11.98	0.01
11.66	11.78	0.01
11.47	11.51	0.00
11.21	11.36	0.02
11.03	11.12	0.01
10.69	11.01	0.10
0.6493900E01		

5-8. IN SUMMARY

The combined use of subscripted variables and DØ loops provides one of the most powerful tools available to the FORTRAN programmer. They allow the programmer to handle very large amounts of data with a very minimum of programming effort. Rather long and tedious calculations and quite laborious input and output instructions also can be handled through the use of the subscripted variable notation. The programmer should make every effort to gain facility in the use of subscripted variables and DØ loops. The extension to multidimensional arrays and nested DØ loops (one within another) is treated in the next chapter.

Because of the above reasons, the student should make every effort to work a large number of the problems at the end of this chapter to become very familiar with the use of subscripted variables and DØ loops.

Exercises ‡

5-1 Re-do Exercise 4-44 except enter the number of students on the first data card.

†5-2 A plant whose production rate is P lbs/year produces a product whose value is V \$/lb. The product costs C \$/lb to produce. The gross profit is then $P \cdot (V - C)$. The total tax rate is 52%, so the profit after taxes is .48 times the gross profit. If the plant costs B \$ to build, the pay-out time in years is B divided by the profit after taxes.

Suppose the values of C, B, and P are known to be \$1.50/lb, \$900,000, and 200,000 lbs/yr, respectively. Write a program to calculate the pay-out time for values of V from \$2.75/lb to \$3.25/lb in increments of \$0.05/lb. The listing should be in columnar fashion, with a value of V and a corresponding value of the pay-out time.

5-3 A man invests \$600 per year at 8% interest. How much will he have after ten years?

Write a FORTRAN program to calculate this using a DØ loop. Read the amount invested annually, the interest rate, and how many years from now that the value of his investment is to be calculated.

---

‡ Solutions to Exercises marked with a dagger † are given in Appendix G.

5-4   At an interest rate of 6%, how much must you deposit at the first of each year so that at the end of five years you will have $8000?

Write a program to calculate this. Assume $1.00 is deposited each year and calculate the amount available at the end of five years as per the previous program. The amount to be deposited is $8000 divided by this value. Read the interest rate, how much is to be accrued, and how many years deposits will be made.

5-5   One calculation frequently encountered in financial analysis is the computation of depreciation. One popular technique to do this is the sum-of-the-years-digits method. Suppose $15,000 is to be depreciated over a 5 year period. The sum-of-the-years-digits is $1 + 2 + 3 + 4 + 5 = 15$. According to this method, then 5/15 of $15,000 is depreciated the first year, 4/15 the second, 3/15 the third, etc. Write a program that reads the amount to be depreciated and the number of years over which the depreciation is to be made. The output should be tabulated as follows for the above case:

1	5000.00
2	5000.00
3	3000.00
4	2000.00
5	1000.00

Run this program to calculate the annual depreciation if $50,000 is to be depreciated over ten years.

5-6   Prepare a program to read N and calculate N!. N is always a nonnegative number, but may be zero (0! = 1). The output should be N and N! [N! = 1 × 2 × ··· × (N − 1) × N]. N! is pronounced "N factorial."

†**5-7**   In business applications, a quantity known as the capital-recovery factor is defined as follows:

$$\text{capital-recovery factor} = \frac{i(1 + i)^n}{(1 + i)^n - 1}$$

where i is the interest rate and n is the number of years. Write a program to print a tabulated set of values for $n = 1$ through $n = 25$ for $i = 8\%$. The output should appear as follows:

1	1.08000
2	0.56077
3	0.38804
	etc.

5-8   A man borrows $100.00 at an interest rate of $1\frac{1}{2}\%$ per month. If he pays $10.00 at the end of each month, how much does he owe at the end of 10 months?

Write a program to solve this problem. Read the amount he borrows and the amount he pays each month. To be sure we are in agreement as to how the calculations are to be done, note that the interest for the first month is 0.015 × $100 = $1.50. Since he pays $10 at the end of the month, he owes $100.00 + $1.50 − $10.00 = $91.50. Use a DØ loop to iterate these calculations for each month.

†**5-9** Write a program to calculate the geometric average and the arithmetic average of the following data:

12.2
 7.9
20.2
13.5
49.4
 2.1
 5.8

As output, write only the two averages. The program should read the number of data points from the first card, followed by the data, one value per card. For n data points, the geometric average is the nth root of the product of all the values.

5-10 Evaluate the sum

$$\sum_{n=0}^{20} \frac{1}{a + nb} = \frac{1}{a} + \frac{1}{a + b} + \frac{1}{a + 2b} + \frac{1}{a + 3b} + \cdots + \frac{1}{a + 20b}$$

for $a = 2$ and $b = 0.5$. Read a and b from a data card, and write only the value of the sum.

5-11 Modify Exercise 4-53 by assuming that the data deck contains 25 cards, not counting the final card (the one with the zero value).

5-12 Make the above modification to Exercise 4-54.

5-13 Suppose at time zero a worm is 2 feet away from an apple. At time zero, he moves one half the distance between him and the apple; that is, he moves one foot. Ten minutes later, he moves one-half the remaining distance, or one-half foot. He continues this at regular intervals of 10 minutes, always moving only one-half of the distance between him and the apple at each step. How long does it take him to get to within 0.1 inch of the apple?

†**5-14** Exercise 3-33 gave a formula for computing the sum of an arithmetic progression. Prepare a program to sum the series term by term and compare with the answer given by the formula in Exercise 3-33.

5-15 Exercise 3-34 gave a formula for computing the sum and last term in a geometric progression. Prepare a program to sum the series term by term and to compute the last term. Compare the results with those given by the formulas in Exercise 3-34.

5-16 Exercise 3-35 gave a formula for computing the sum of a combined arithmetic and geometric progression. Prepare a program to sum these series term by term and compare with the answer given by the formula for Exercise 3-35.

5-17 Prepare a program to evaluate a polynomial such as the following:

$$f(x) = a_0 + a_1 x + a_2 x^2 + \cdots + a_n x^n$$

The computations are to proceed as follows:

1 Read a value for x and n.

2 Read a value for a_0 and assign to the initial value of the function.

3 Read a_1, multiply by x, and add to the value of the function.

4 Repeat the previous step for successive values of the coefficients, always multiplying by the appropriate power of x and adding to the value of the function.

5 The program should print the value of $f(x)$.

5-18 Exercise 3-22 described the problem of updating a student's grade-point average. Program this exercise as follows:

1 Read the student's identification number, his old grade-point average, the number of hours to which his old grade-point average applied, and the number of courses taken this semester.

2 Enter the credit hours for one course and the numerical equivalent for the grade, make the necessary updates, and then proceed to the values for the next course.

5-19 Make the modification suggested in the previous exercise to Exercise 4-31 also.

5-20 Suppose we would like to compute the sum of squares of the integer numbers. For the first five integer numbers, the computation is

$$1^2 + 2^2 + 3^2 + 4^2 + 5^2 = 1 + 4 + 9 + 16 + 25 = 55$$

The question is whether or not the result of such a computation is ever a perfect square itself. The answer to this question is yes, since a series of only one term sums to 1, which is a perfect square. But are there any others? Prepare a program to solve this problem, stopping after 200 integers if no perfect square has been found.

5-21 The number 48 has the following interesting characteristics:

1 Addition of 1 produces an exact square ($49 = 7^2$).

2 Addition of 1 to its half produces an exact square ($25 = 5^2$).

Write a computer program that locates the next higher number with this interesting property.

†5-22 Compute the average of the integers between 19 and 127, inclusive.

5-23 Compute the average of the odd integers between 19 and 127 inclusive.

5-24 Compute the average of the integers between -8 and 27 inclusive.

5-25 Compute the product of the even integers between 4 and 12 inclusive.

5-26 The sum of squares of the odd integers between 9 and 13, inclusive, is given by

$$9^2 + 11^2 + 13^2 = 81 + 121 + 169 = 371$$

Compute the sum of squares of the even integers between 4 and 14, inclusive.

5-27 The *reciprocal* of a number is simply the number 1 divided by that number. That is, the reciprocal of 5 is $1/5$. The sum of the reciprocals of the even integers between 2 and 8 is given by

$$\tfrac{1}{2} + \tfrac{1}{4} + \tfrac{1}{6} + \tfrac{1}{8}$$

Compute the sum of the reciprocals of the integers between 12 and 84. *Hint:* Beware of integer arithmetic.

†**5-28** A company currently has 1025 employees. For each employee, a card has been punched with the following information:

Employee's ID-number (all numeric)	columns 1–9
Employee's age	columns 11–13
Number of years with company	columns 15–16
Number of dependents	columns 18–19
Number of days of vacation	columns 21–22
Number of days of sick leave	columns 24–26

Write a program to determine the total number of days vacation and the total number of days sick leave.

5-29 Refer to the above exercise. Write a program to print the ID-number for all employees over 50 years of age and with the company less than five years.

5-30 Refer to Exercise 5-28. Write a program to determine the employee who joined the company at the earliest age. Print his ID number and the age at which he joined the company.

5-31 Five workmen have devoted the following time to a given project:

Workman 1	3 hrs., 19 min.
Workman 2	2 hrs., 45 min.
Workman 3	4 hrs., 7 min.
Workman 4	3 hrs., 55 min.
Workman 5	1 hr., 36 min.

Compute the total time worked on this project and print in hours and minutes. The answer should be adjusted appropriately so that the minutes is less than 60.

5-32 Revise the above exercise to compute the average time worked by the workmen.

†**5-33** Suppose the following table summarized the results of the first ten games of our basketball season:

Game	Opponent	Our Score	Opponent's Score
1	2	82	91
2	5	88	87
3	1	85	76
4	3	89	80
5	1	95	108
6	2	87	83
7	4	76	68
8	6	83	84
9	1	88	87
10	4	92	76

The entries on this table are punched onto cards with the game in columns 1–5, the opponent in columns 6–10, our score in columns 11–15, and the opponent's score in columns 16–21. Prepare a program to determine our average score, our maximum points, and our minimum points.

5-34 Refer to the above exercise. Prepare a program to read these cards and print the following:

Game	Opponent	Result
1	2	Løst by 9.
2	5	Wøn by 1.
3	1	Wøn by 9.

and so on for all 10 games.

5-35 Refer to Exercise 5-33. Write a program to print the results of only those games where either we lost by more than five points or where we scored less than 85 points, but not both. That is, do not print the results of games that we lost by more than five points, but scored less than 85 points.

Note: The following examples are all designed to use subscripted variable concepts.

5-36 Identify the errors, if any, in each of the following subscripts [array A dimensioned A(5)]:

(a) A(B)
(b) A(1 + J)
(c) A(10)
(d) A(J/2)
(e) A(J * 2 + 1)
(f) A(−J)

5-37 A data card contains a list of six numbers each in F10.2 format which we shall consider as a one-dimensional array A. Read in the six numbers, find their sum, and find what fraction each of these numbers is of their sum. The fractions shall be considered as a second one-dimensional array F. Write out A in a single vertical column alongside of which is located the corresponding F elements. Use F10.4 format for the elements in F.

5-38 20 students take an exam on which the marks are from 0 to 100. Write a program to determine how many students make a mark higher than the average. For input data assume one mark per card in F10.1 format. Write out the array of marks and the number (in I10 format) earning a mark higher than the average. Make up some trial data.

5-39 The accounting procedure at the typical computer center consists of assigning a charge number to each user, which he must submit with each job. Suppose at the end of each job, the computer punches a card containing the user's charge number in columns 1–5 and the minutes run in F format in columns 6–15.

Write a program that reads these cards and calculates the total amount of time used by each user on all jobs he ran. The output should be in columnar fashion with user number, total time used, and percent of total. Use a blank card to indicate last card. Input data are shown below:

40709	1.27
80001	2.34
50200	2.11
40709	4.02
40201	3.11
70207	2.06
50200	3.09
80001	1.02
40709	0.79
70207	3.04

†**5-40** Consider preparation of a program to calculate telephone bills. Our booming company has 10 customers, whose identification numbers and base charges are punched on data cards, one card per customer. In addition, we have several cards containing charges for each long distance call made along with the customer number of the calling party. Of course, a given customer may make no calls or several calls. The cards for long distance are neither counted nor ordered. Write a program to compute and print the total charges for each customer. Don't forget to add 10% federal excise tax for long distance calls; but base charges are not taxable. Place the 10 cards with base charges first in the input data, and make up your own data.

5-41 Suppose the sales slips on merchandise sold in a given department contains the amount of the sale and the salesperson's identification number. At the end of the day, these are punched onto cards with the salesperson's identification number in columns 1–3 and the amount of the sale in F format in columns 4–13. We would like to prepare a program to (1) calculate the total sales of each salesperson, (2) calculate the percent of the total, and (3) calculate his or her commission for the day (3% of the sales above $50). These cards are neither counted nor ordered in any way. The program's output should be columns containing the salesperson's identification number, the total amount of his or her sales for the day, the percent of the total, and his or her commission. Make up your own data cards.

5-42 Modify Exercise 5-7 to calculate the capital-recovery factor for interest rates of 2%, 4%, 6%, 8%, and 10% for a given year. The output should be six columns, one column for the year and one column for the capital-recovery factor at each interest rate. The year should be read from a data card, and construct the program to do these calculations for as many cards as in the data deck.

†**5-43** Suppose we are given a set of observations consisting of values of the independent variable x (perhaps the age of a child) and corresponding values of the dependent variable y (perhaps the weight of the child). This data might appear

as follows:

x	y
3	31
5	61
2	27
7	75
9	102

Suppose also that it is anticipated that this data should follow an equation of the type $y = ax + b$, where a and b are constants, specifically 6 and 10, respectively, for this case.

A measure of the "goodness" of the equation is to calculate the sum of squares of the differences between observed and predicted (i.e., by the equation) values of the dependent variable. For example, for the first observation, the predicted value of y is $10 \times 3 + 6 = 36$, the observed value is 31, giving a difference of 5. The sum of squares of these values for each value of x is the quantity desired. Write a program to calculate this value for the above data.

5-44 A one-dimensional array x contains 20 elements which represent experimental measurements. These may be smoothed by calculating:

$$sX_i = \frac{X_{i-1} + X_i + X_{i+1}}{3}$$

for all but the first and 20th elements. Read in x, calculate sx, and write out the two arrays, one above the other.

5-45 Refer to Exercise 4-26. Determine and print the enrollment in each of the 10 sections. The program will be much shorter if an array is used to store the enrollments.

5-46 Modify the above exercise to determine the number of male seniors in each of the 10 sections.

5-47 Refer to Exercise 5-28. Depending upon the number of dependents, suppose the following tax deductions are allowed:

Dependents	Deduction
0	700.
1	1300.
2	1800.
3	2200.
4	2500.
5	2700.
over 5	2800.

Write a program to compute and print the tax deduction allowed for each employee. The program will be shorter if an array is used to store the above deduction table.

†**5-48** Refer to Exercise 5-33. From the 10 data cards, we would like to print the following report:

Opponent	Our Total Points	His Total Points
1	268	270
2	169	174
3	89	80
4	168	144
5	88	87
6	83	84

Write the necessary program.

5-49 Refer to Exercise 5-33. Prepare a program to print the following report:

Opponent	Games		
1	3	5	9
2	1	6	
3	4		
4	7	10	
5	2		
6	8		

5-50 As a conscientious student in basket weaving, Joe Kollage has performed some bursting tests on his products. Since higher mathematics still baffle him, he decides to use the computer.

The experiment consisted of placing weights in each basket until it ruptured. Joe used three different weights—weight one weighing 5 pounds, weight two, 10 pounds, and weight three, 25 pounds. He performed this experiment on four baskets, and he has the number of weights of each type in the basket when it ruptured. The data for each test are entered on a separate card as follows:

	Number of Weight 1	Number of Weight 2	Number of Weight 3
Test 1	12	1	0
Test 2	6	2	1
Test 3	8	1	1
Test 4	0	2	2

Joe is confident he can keep the cards in order, so only the number of weights of each type for each test is entered according to FØRMAT (313). The program should proceed as follows:

a. Read input.

b. Calculate total weight in basket at rupture. This value should be stored in an array.

c. Calculate average weight at rupture.

d. Calculate the difference between individual test value and average test value.

e. Print test number, total weight at rupture, and difference from average for each test.

f. Print average weight at rupture.

†**5-51** The Julian date is the number of days since the beginning of the year. For example, February 19, 1976 would have the Julian date of 50/1976, since it is the 50th day of the year. Write a program to accept the month, the day of the month, and the year, and compute the Julian date. Use an array to store the number of days in each month, or even better, to store the Julian date of the day prior to the beginning of each month.

5-52 Exercise 4-40 treated the computation of the bill for a car rental. Instead of entering the total number of hours the car has been kept, the time and date at which it was rented are entered followed by the time and date that it was returned. For example, an entry might be as follows:

4:54P   8-18-76

The program should then compute the number of hours the car has been rented· For this purpose, the program must use an array containing the number of days in each month as in the previous exercise. The program should also function properly if the car is kept over New Year. Don't worry about leap years unless you are especially ambitious.

5-53 Another modification to Exercise 4-40 would be to keep a table containing the rates on each type of car rented by our company. For each type of car, this table would contain the daily rate and the cents-per-mile charge. Now the clerk only has to enter the type of car, that is, type 1, type 2, etc. A maximum of six types will be used, so the program should check for unrealistic entries.

5-54 Joe Bleaux needs to borrow $1500 for a period of three years. After consulting three loan departments, he has the following possibilities:

a. 8% per year, compounded monthly

b. 9% per year, compounded annually

c. $8\frac{1}{4}$% per year, compounded quarterly

Which one is the most attractive?

Write a FORTRAN program to calculate this. Read i, the annual interest rate, and m, the number of compounding periods annually. The final amount owed is $1500 \cdot (1 + i/m)^{3m}$. The output should be the annual interest rate, the number of compounding periods annually, and the amount owed after three years. The output should be ordered so that the most attractive appears first and the least attractive last. Assume that the data cards are *not* read in this order.

†**5-55** Given a one-dimensional array A containing sixteen elements in F10.2 format. Calculate a new array B whose elements are given as

$$b_i = i \cdot a_i$$

Write out all the A elements in a single vertical column alongside of which is located the corresponding B elements. Use F10.2 format for all output.

5-56 Read in a one-dimensional array A which contains twelve elements in F20.2 format. Calculate a new array B whose elements are given as

$$b_i = (-1)^i (a_i)^{i+1}$$

Write out the A array in F20.2 format on three output records. This should then be followed by the B array in E20.7 format on the next three output records.

5-57 Read in the one-dimensional array A containing 10 elements in F10.2 format. Calculate the following:

SUMNEG = sum of all the negative elements
SUMPOS = sum of all the positive elements
NNEG = number of negative elements
NPOS = number of positive elements

Write out these results in E20.2 or I10 format, as appropriate.

†**5-58** Read in two one-dimensional arrays, A and B, containing five elements each. Assume each input data card contains a single element of A and the single corresponding element of B. Calculate a new array C where

$$c_i = a_i + b_i \quad \text{if} \quad b_i \geq a_i$$
$$c_i = a_i - b_i \quad \text{if} \quad b_i < a_i$$

Write out A, B, and C, in three vertical columns. Use F10.2 format on all input and output.

5-59 Read in two one-dimensional arrays, A and B, containing 10 elements each. Assume the A array is contained on two data cards in F10.2 format and the B array is contained on the next three data cards in E20.7 format. Calculate a new array C where

$$c_i = (a_i + b_i)^2 \quad \text{if} \quad a_i > b_i$$
$$c_i = (a_i - b_i)^2 \quad \text{if} \quad a_i \leq b_i$$

Write out the C array in E20.7 format on three data cards.

5-60 Let **a** be an *n*-dimensional vector (an $n \times 1$ matrix) defined as follows:

$$\mathbf{a} = \begin{bmatrix} a_1 \\ a_2 \\ a_3 \\ \cdot \\ \cdot \\ \cdot \\ a_n \end{bmatrix}$$

Norm $|\mathbf{a}|$ of a vector is defined as follows:

$|\mathbf{a}| = (a_1^2 + a_2^2 + \cdots + a_n^2)^{1/2}$

Prepare a program to read n followed by $a_1, a_2, \ldots, a_n$ (each on a separate card), compute the norm of $\mathbf{a}$ and print the result. The maximum value for n will be 50. For data, let

$$\mathbf{a} = \begin{bmatrix} 2 \\ 1 \\ 0 \\ 3 \end{bmatrix}$$

†**5-61** A normalized vector is one whose norm is unity. Any given vector can be normalized by dividing each of its elements by the norm. Prepare a program to read the elements of a vector as in the previous problem, compute the normalized vector, and print the results (the elements of the normalized vector, one to a line). Use same input as in previous problem.

5-62 Let $\mathbf{a}$, $\mathbf{b}$, and $\mathbf{c}$ be vectors defined as in the previous exercises. If vector $\mathbf{c}$ is to be the sum of $\mathbf{a}$ and $\mathbf{b}$, i.e., $\mathbf{c} = \mathbf{a} + \mathbf{b}$, then c_i, the ith element of $\mathbf{c}$, is the sum of a_i and b_i, i.e., $c_i = a_i + b_i$. Prepare a program to

a. Read n, the order of each of the vectors. The maximum value of n is 50.

b. Read the elements of $\mathbf{a}$, one to a card.

c. Read the elements of $\mathbf{b}$, one to a card.

d. Compute $\mathbf{c}$.

e. Print the elements of $\mathbf{c}$, one to a line.

As input, let

$$\mathbf{a} = \begin{bmatrix} 4 \\ 0 \\ 7 \\ 2 \end{bmatrix} \qquad \mathbf{b} = \begin{bmatrix} -1 \\ 2 \\ 1 \\ -2 \end{bmatrix}$$

MULTIDIMENSIONAL ARRAYS
AND NESTED DØ LOOPS

The previous chapter treated single DØ loops and one-dimensional arrays. The objective of this chapter will be to expand upon this material and, thus, extend the usefulness of subscripted variables and DØ loops to the programmer.

6-1. MULTIDIMENSIONAL ARRAYS

Many quantities may be represented with one variable name through the use of subscripts as indicated in the previous chapter. A subscripted variable in FORTRAN may have one, two, or three subscripts (separated by commas within the parentheses of the subscript), and these in turn represent one-, two-, or three-dimensional arrays. For convenience in orienting the individual's thinking, the one-dimensional array can be considered (in a geometric sense) as representing points along a line, the two-dimensional array as representing points in a plane, and the three-dimensional array as representing points in a three-dimensional space or points in a series of planes stacked one on top of the other.

153

An alternate way of viewing arrays is to consider the one-dimensional array as a column *or* a row of elements; to consider the two-dimensional array as a table of elements, i.e., made up of rows and columns; and to consider the three-dimensional array as a series of tables, i.e., a series of two-dimensional arrays.

The concept of one-, two-, and three-dimensional arrays refers to the number of subscripts for the element and not to the number of elements themselves. For example, a one-dimensional array can have many elements, and it would be possible for a three-dimensional array to only have one element. It might also be pointed out that some versions of FORTRAN allow more than three subscripts (some systems allow as many as seven-dimensional arrays).

A two-dimensional array, in its geometric interpretation, may be thought of as being composed of horizontal *rows* and vertical *columns*. The first subscript of the variable refers to the row number in the array, and it will vary from 1 to the total number of rows. The second subscript refers to the vertical column number, and it will vary from 1 to the number of columns. As an example, two entrants in a beauty contest might have their conventional measurements stored in a 2×3 array which might be shown in mathematical notations as follows:

$$a_{1,1} \qquad a_{1,2} \qquad a_{1,3}$$
$$a_{2,1} \qquad a_{2,2} \qquad a_{2,3}$$

These could be written in Fortran subscript notation as $A(1,1)$, $A(2,1)$, $A(1,2)$, $A(2,2)$, $A(1,3)$, and $A(2,3)$. Note that the subscripts are separated by commas.

In a more general sense, an $n \times m$ array named A might be presented as:

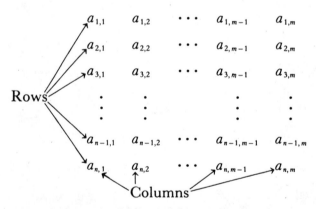

In general, $a_{i,j}$ would be the element in the ith row and the jth column.

In the DIMENSIØN statement, multidimensional arrays must be included in the same manner as for one-dimensional arrays. For example, the statement

DIMENSIØN $A(2,3)$, $K(2,3,4)$

would establish $2 \times 3 = 6$ storage locations for array A and $2 \times 3 \times 4 = 24$ storage

```
┌─ C FOR COMMENT
┌STATEMENT┐
│ NUMBER  │                        FORTRAN STATEMENT
  5  6 7  10    15    20    25    30    35    40    45    50    55    60    65    70  72




     I = 1
     TØTMID = 0.                              TØTMID = 0.
  20 TØTMID = TØTMID + DATA(I,2)              DØ 20I = 1,7
     IF(I.LE.7)GØ TØ 20               20      TØTMID = TØTMID + DATA (I,,2)
     AVGMID = TØTMID/7.                       AVGMID = TØTMID/7




```

Figure 6-1

locations for array κ. As can be seen from Appendix B, most machines allow up to three-dimensional arrays, a few allow up to seven, and one or two permit even more.

The order in which higher-dimensional arrays are stored in memory can be important. The general rule is that storage is arranged as if the first subscript were varied most rapidly and the last subscript varied least rapidly. That is, the storage for an array dimensioned A(2,3) would be in the following order:

A(1,1) A(2,1) A(1,2) A(2,2) A(1,3) A(2,3)

One place where this immediately becomes important is in the reading of arrays. The read statement

READ (5,10) A

would read the elements of array A in the same order as they are stored. If a two-dimensional array is viewed to be a table as suggested previously, then the table is read by columns.

EXAMPLE 6-1

Assume that seven young ladies are entered in a beauty contest. A record is made of their "measurements" and arranged in the usual order in a table (array) as follows:

Contestant Number			
1	34	26	35
2	36	27	37
3	40	26	38
4	35	28	35
5	34	26	34
6	38	26	39
7	37	28	37

These data may be stored in a two-dimensional array named DATA which has 21 elements, i.e., it is a 7 × 3 array. It is desired to calculate the "average" statistics for the entrants in the contest. The statements for computing the average waist measurement are shown in Figure 6-1. The other averages would be calculated similarly.

6-2. NESTED dø's

Consider the table containing five rows and three columns as shown in Figure 6-2a. This table is stored in a two-dimensional array TABLE(I,J), where the first subscript denotes the number of the row and the second subscript denotes the column number. A program is to be prepared to calculate the sum of each column, storing the result in a one-dimensional array SUM.

By using a dø loop, the sum of the first column can be calculated with the following statements:

```
    J = 1
    SUM(J) = 0.
    Dø 3 I = 1,5
3   SUM(J) = SUM(J) + TABLE(I,J)
```

This set of statements is reflected in the inner loop of the flowchart in Figure 6-2b. To calculate the sums for all the columns, these statements must be executed for J = 2 and J = 3. Of course, this is easily accomplished with a dø, and all the sums can be calculated with the following statements:

```
    Dø 4 J = 1,3
    SUM(J) = 0.
    Dø 3 I = 1,5
3   SUM(J) = SUM(J) + TABLE(I,J)
4   CøNTINUE
```

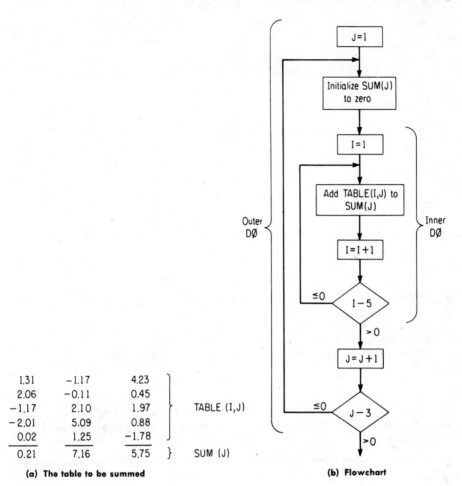

1.31	−1.17	4.23
2.06	−0.11	0.45
−1.17	2.10	1.97
−2.01	5.09	0.88
0.02	1.25	−1.78

TABLE (I,J)

| 0.21 | 7.16 | 5.75 |

SUM (J)

(a) The table to be summed

(b) Flowchart

Figure 6-2. Summing the columns of a table.

This series contains one DØ (the *inner* DØ) within the range of another DØ (the *outer* DØ). DØ statements occurring in this fashion are called *nested* DØ's.

The rules applying to DØ's used in this manner are essentially the same as applicable to single DØ's. The important features of such DØ's are enumerated below:

1 As the index of a DØ cannot be redefined within its range, the index of the inner DØ must *not* be the same as the index of the outer DØ.

2 The range of the inner DØ must not extend beyond the range of the outer DØ. However, this does not prohibit the ranges of nested DØ's from terminating with the same statement. That is, the CØNTINUE statement in the previous example could be eliminated as follows:

```
      DØ 3 J = 1,3
      SUM(J) = 0.
      DØ 3 I = 1,5
3     SUM(J) = SUM(J) + TABLE(I,J)
```

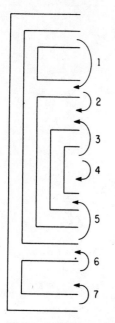

Figure 6-3. Examples of permissible and unpermissible transfers in nested DØ loops. Transfers 1, 3, 4, and 6 are permissible; transfers 2, 5, and 7 are not permissible.

3 The rules applying to transfer are identical for nested and unnested DØ loops. However, transfers within nested DØ's can be somewhat intricate, and several permissible and unpermissible transfers are illustrated in Figure 6-3.

EXAMPLE 6-2

In the preceding paragraphs the DØ loops for calculating the sums of each column in a table were presented. Now consider the preparation of a complete program as given in Figure 6-4 to read into memory the elements of TABLE in Figure 6-2, calculate the sum for each column, and write the results. First, a DØ loop is used to read the table. The statements in the program in Figure 6-4 read each row of the table from a single card. Alternatively, the entries of the table could be arranged one per card, and two DØ's could be used as follows:

```
      DØ 2 I = 1,5
      DØ 2 J = 1,3
   2  READ (5,3) TABLE (I,J)
   3  FØRMAT (F5.0)
```

The data cards would be arranged such that the elements appear in the order TABLE (1,1), TABLE (1,2), TABLE (1,3), TABLE (2,1), TABLE (2,2), etc. Alternatively, the DØ's could be reversed, yielding:

```
      DØ 2 J = 1,3
      DØ 2 I = 1,5
   2  READ (5,3) TABLE (I,J)
   3  FØRMAT (F5.0)
```

```
      DIMENSION SUM(10),TABLE(10,10)
C
C     READ TABLE
C
      DO2I=1,5
2     READ(5,3)TABLE(I,1),TABLE(I,2),TABLE(I,3)
C
C     DO LOOP FOR SUMMING EACH COLUMN
C
      DO5J=1,3
C
C     INITIALIZE SUM TO ZERO
C
      SUM(J)=0.
C
C     DO LOOP FOR ADDING EACH ELEMENT TO SUM
C
      DO4I=1,5
4     SUM(J)=SUM(J)+TABLE(I,J)
C
C     WRITE STATEMENT
C
5     WRITE(6,6)SUM(J)
      STOP
C
C     FORMAT STATEMENTS
C
3     FORMAT(3F5.0)
6     FORMAT(1X,F15.4)
      END
```

(a) **Complete program**

```
 1.31-1.17 4.23
 2.06-0.11 0.45
-1.17 2.10 1.97
-2.01 5.09 0.88
 0.02 1.25-1.78
```

(b) **Input data**

```
     0.2100
     7.1600
     5.7500
```

(c) **Output data**

Figure 6-4. Summation of columns in a table.

The data should now be entered in the order TABLE (1,1), TABLE (2,1), TABLE (3,1), TABLE (4,1), TABLE (5,1), TABLE (1,2), etc.

The statements for calculating the sums are as discussed earlier, except that the WRITE statement is incorporated into the outer DØ loop.

EXAMPLE 6-3

In many problems, it is desired that the output be ordered in some way. For example, consider a program to compute the total price of an invoice. Suppose that for each item ordered the program is provided with a card giving a five-digit stock number

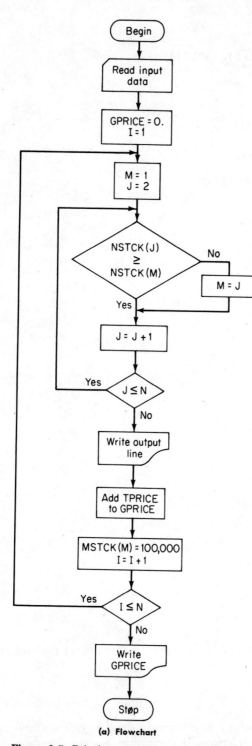

(a) Flowchart

Figure 6-5. Printing output in ascending order.

```
1                    DIMENSION NSTCK(25),JQUAN(25),PRICE(25)
      C
      C              READ INPUT DATA INTO ARRAYS
      C
2                    N=1
3          10        READ(5,1,END=9) NSTCK(N),JQUAN(N),PRICE(N)
4           1        FORMAT(2I5,F10.2)
5                    N=N+1
6                    GOTO10
7           9        N=N-1
      C
      C              WRITE HEADINGS
      C
8                    WRITE(6,19)
9          19        FORMAT('1STOCK-NO   QUANTITY   UNIT PRICE    TOTAL PRICE')
      C
      C              WRITE OUTPUT IN ASCENDING ORDER
      C
10                   GPRICE=0.
11                   DO15I=1,N
12                   M=1
13                   DO20J=2,N
14                   IF(NSTCK(J).GE.NSTCK(M))GOTO20
15                   M=J
16         20        CONTINUE
17                   TPRICE=JQUAN(M)*PRICE(M)
18                   WRITE(6,18) NSTCK(M),JQUAN(M),PRICE(M),TPRICE
19         18        FORMAT(1X,I7,I9,2F14.2)
20                   GPRICE=GPRICE+TPRICE
21         15        NSTCK(M)=100000
      C
      C              WRITE GRAND TOTAL PRICE
      C
22                   WRITE(6,17) GPRICE
23         17        FORMAT(22X,'GRAND TOTAL',F12.2)
24                   STOP
25                   END
```

(b) Program

```
20375      4  147.21
15478     12  29.45
34812      1  457.99
12407      2  45.00
21499      7  99.95
```

(c) Input data

STOCK-NO	QUANTITY	UNIT PRICE	TOTAL PRICE
12407	2	45.00	90.00
15478	12	29.45	353.40
20375	4	147.21	588.84
21499	7	99.95	699.65
34812	1	457.99	457.99
		GRAND TOTAL	2189.88

(d) Output data

Figure 6-5. *Continued.*

of the item, the quantity ordered, and the unit price. The program is to print this data, as well as the total price and to sum the prices to get the grand total for the order. Although the data cards are not ordered in any way, it is desired that the output should be in ascending order of the stock numbers. It may be assumed that no order has more than 25 different items.

Since the output is to be in an order different from the order of the input data, we cannot generate the output as the data is read. Instead, we must first read the input data into arrays in memory. Since it is not known how many data cards are provided, we must provide a "trailer card" or use the END = or equivalent feature to detect the end-of-data. Lines 2–7 of the program in Figure 6-5 reads the input data. The number of input cards is determined by counting and is stored in variable N.

The next problem is to generate the output in ascending order of the stock number. The first line can be generated by simply searching through the output for the smallest stock number. Lines 12–20 locate this stock number, its corresponding sub-script being stored in variable M. In essence, we begin (line 12) by assuming the first element (M = 1) is the smallest element. The do loop in lines 13–16 compares each remaining stock number to the smallest stock number found so far, and if a stock number is found whose value is smaller than any previous stock number, the value of M is changed (line 15) before testing the remaining stock numbers.

While the above procedure will always find the smallest stock number, we must devise some scheme that will first locate the smallest, then the next smallest, and so on. Suppose we use the procedure as given to locate the smallest stock number. From this, the first line of the output can be generated (lines 17 and 18). Since we have printed the output for this stock number, we need to somehow prevent the program from considering this data entry in future searches for the smallest stock number. Since the stock number was specified as having five digits, all stock numbers must be less than 100,000. Suppose we change the stock number for the entry just printed to 100,000 and, then, again use the same search procedure to locate the entry with the smallest stock number. In the arrays as presently defined, the entry with the smallest stock number is the entry with the second smallest stock number in the original arrays.

This process can be repeated for as many entries as in the arrays. On each repeat of the process, the entry with the next smallest stock number will be printed. To repeat this process, we can embed the necessary statements within a do loop, which in the program in Figure 6-5 begins with the do statement in line 11 and ends with line 21 (which changes the value of the stock number just printed to 100000).

In addition to the logic for printing the data in ascending order of the stock numbers, the program in Figure 6-5 also prints headings (line 8), computes the grand total price (lines 10 and 20), and prints the grand total price (line 22).

EXAMPLE 6-4

In many instances it is preferable (if not necessary) for the elements in an array to be in relative numerical (ascending or descending) order. An individual could do this with very little thought for small arrays; but how would you tell a machine to do it?

To more completely define the problem, let A be a one-dimensional array of N elements. The original values of the elements are stored in A, and it is desirable to obtain the rearranged array in A.

A person doing this would probably begin by finding the smallest element and

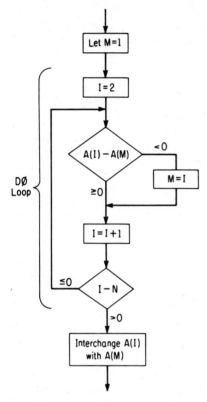

Figure 6-6. Flowchart for locating smallest element in an array and placing in first position.

placing it in A(1), the second smallest in A(2), etc. The computer could proceed in a similar manner by first finding the smallest element in the array and switching with the original A(1). The smallest element could be located by first assuming A(1) is smallest, and comparing with the remaining elements. When a smaller element is found, the assumption is updated. By letting M be the assumed position of the smallest element, it can be located as follows:

```
  M = 1
  DØ 2 I = 2,N
2   IF(A(I).LT.A(M)) M = I
```

See flowchart in Figure 6-6. Upon completion of the DØ, it has been determined that element M is the smallest element in array A.

Now it is necessary to place A(M) in A(1) and A(1) in A(M). By using an intermediate storage position called TEMP, this may be achieved by:

```
TEMP = A(1)
A(1) = A(M)
A(M) = TEMP
```

The elements are thus switched.

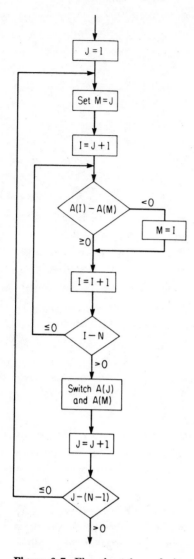

Figure 6-7. Flowchart for ordering elements in an array.

At this point the smallest element is found in A(1); but the remainder of the elements are unordered. In a manner analogous to the above, the elements 2 through N must be searched for their smallest value, and stored in A(2). For this case the statements for locating the smallest element and switching with A(2) are:

```
  M = 2
  DØ 2 I = 3,N
2 IF(A(I).LT.A(M)) M = I
  TEMP = A(2)
  A(2) = A(M)
  A(M) = TEMP
```

As this procedure must be repeated for A(3), A(4),..., A(N − 1), the logic of the flow chart in Figure 6-7 can be used. Coding with the use of DØ loops produces the following statements:

```
   NA = N − 1
   DØ 3 J = 1,NA
   M = J
   MA = J + 1
   DØ 2 I = MA,N
2  IF(A(I).LT.A(M)) M = I
   TEMP = A(J)
   A(J) = A(M)
3  A(M) = TEMP
```

For a specific case, let array A be 1.0, 2.0, 0.5, 4.0, 1.5. In the first iteration, elements 1 and 3 are interchanged, yielding 0.5, 2.0, 1.0, 4.0, 1.5. Elements 2 and 3 are switched on the second iteration, yielding 0.5, 1.0, 2.0, 4.0, 1.5. On the third iteration, elements 3 and 5 are switched to form 0.5, 1.0, 1.5, 4.0, 2.0. Switching elements 4 and 5 on the fourth iteration yields 0.5, 1.0, 1.5, 2.0, 4.0. Thus, the array is successfully ordered after four or N − 1 iterations.

Could the outer DØ in this example be DØ 3 J = 1,N? If so, what would be the value of MA when J = N? This means that the first index for the inner DØ is larger than the second index, which does not seem reasonable (See Item 2, Section 5-3).

6-3. IMPLIED DØ

The implied DØ described in Figure 5-8 can be extended to handle multi-dimensional arrays in a manner analogous to nested DØ loops. For example, to read a two-dimensional array A, the following statement is appropriate:

```
   READ(5,10)((A(I,J),J = 1,4), I = 1,2)
10 FØRMAT(8F10.0)
```

The data must appear in the following order:

A(1,1), A(1,2), A(1,3), A(1,4), A(2,1), A(2,2), A(2,3), A(2,4)

The following combination is also permissible:

```
   WRITE(6,12)((I,A(I,J),J = 1,2),B(I), I = 1,3)
12 FØRMAT(1X,I5,3F10.2)
```

The output would be as follows:

```
1    2.2    3.4    9.1
2    1.7    2.9    0.9
3    0.5    6.3    3.1
```

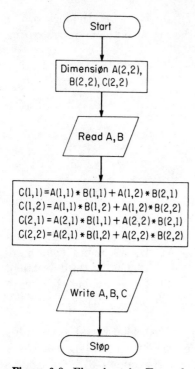

Figure 6-8. Flowchart for Example 6-5 (calculating a two-dimensional array).

This form could *not* be used in a READ statement, since reading I would redefine the index of the implied dø.

Implied dø loops may be used in either format or format-free I/O.

EXAMPLE 6-5

Assume that two arrays are each 2×2. The two arrays are to be read into the computer, and a third two-dimensional array will be calculated. Assume that the input arrays are named A and B and the third array to be calculated is named C. The elements of C may be calculated by the following equations:

$$c_{11} = a_{11}b_{11} + a_{12}b_{21}$$
$$c_{12} = a_{11}b_{12} + a_{12}b_{22}$$
$$c_{21} = a_{21}b_{11} + a_{22}b_{21}$$
$$c_{22} = a_{21}b_{12} + a_{22}b_{22}$$

Those readers who are familiar with matrices will recognize the above relationship as indicating the multiplication of two 2×2 matrices. The flowchart for the program necessary for the indicated multiplication is shown in Figure 6-8 and the program itself is shown in Figure 6-9.

```
———— C FOR COMMENT
• STATEMENT                                    FORTRAN STATEMENT
  NUMBER
  1    5 6 7    10      15      20      25     30      35      40      45      50      55      60      65      70  72
C   EXAMPLE, IN CALCULATING A TWØ-DIMENSIØNAL ARRAY
C
C   INPUT SECTIØN
C
      DIMENSIØN A(2,2),B(2,2),C(2,2)
      READ(5,100)A
100   FØRMAT(4F10.0)
      READ(5,100)B
C
C   CALCULATIØN ØF NEW ARRAY
C
      C(1,1) = A(1,1) * B(1,1) + A(1,2) * B(2,1)
      C(1,2) = A(1,1) * B(1,2) + A(1,2) * B(2,2)
      C(2,1) = A(2,1) * B(1,1) + A(2,2) * B(2,1)
      C(2,2) = A(2,1) * B(1,2) + A(2,2) * B(2,2)
C
C   ØUTPUT SECTIØN
C
      WRITE(6,200)A,B,C
200   FØRMAT(1X,4F10.0)
      STØP
      END
      12.        -6.         27.        -2.
       0.        14.         16.        -2.
```

Figure 6-9. Program for Example 6-5.

Note that in each case the various arrays involved will be written with the (1, 1) element, (2, 1) element, (1, 2) element, and (2, 2) element in this implied sequence. This must be the format of the A and B array on the input cards, and it will be the output order of the A, B, and C arrays with the results as illustrated.

12.	−6.	27.	−2.
0.	14.	16.	−2.
378.	−28.	138.	−92.

6-4. IN SUMMARY

This chapter virtually completes the description of subscripted variables and DØ loops. The utility of both of these cannot be emphasized too highly. The exercises following this chapter are designed to require that they be used.

Exercises‡

6-1 Identify the errors, if any, in each of the following subscripts:

   (a) CØPS(H,I,J)
   (b) RØBBER(I − 2,J ∗ 3 + 2)
   (c) LSU(I + J,K + 2,L − 3)
   (d) GØGØ(I,I(2),NØNØ)
†(e) METWØ(A(I),J,K ∗ 3)
   (f) HØHØ(27,I,NØ,YES)

6-2 Assume that you write a computer program which includes the following statements:

DIMENSIØN EXTRA (5000)
DIMENSIØN BIG (50)
DIMENSIØN BIGGER (4,4,4), SLIM (16)
A = 25.
BIGGER (1,1,1) = 5280
I = 4
J = 5
K = 3

If this is true, then all the following subscripts are invalid. Why?

   (a) EXTRA(40,20)
†(b) BIG(B)
   (c) EXTRA(BIGGER(1,1,1))
   (d) B(I-2)
   (e) SLIM(2 ∗ J-12)
†(f) BIGGER(I,J,K)

†6-3 Five students take four examinations. Their marks are

	Exam 1	Exam 2	Exam 3	Exam 4
Student 1	48.6	30.	62.8	23.4
Student 2	40.1	40.	60.1	29.6
Student 3	63.4	50.	63.7	31.2
Student 4	56.2	60.	58.2	27.3
Student 5	71.0	70.	67.3	26.4

Read their marks as a table (a two-dimensional array) named DATA. Assume one row per input card in F10.1 format. Calculate the average on each test, the average for each student on all four tests, and the average for all students on all tests. Write out these three sets of results in F10.2 format.

---

‡ Solutions to Exercises marked with a dagger † are given in Appendix G.

6-4 Three construction men work a week (five days) and put in the hours shown:

	Day 1	Day 2	Day 3	Day 4	Day 5
Worker 1	8.0	8.5	9.5	8.0	8.5
Worker 2	8.0	8.5	10.0	8.0	9.0
Worker 3	8.0	9.0	9.0	9.0	8.5

Read in their hours as a table (a two-dimensional array) named wørk. Assume one row per input card in f10.1 format. Calculate the total hours worked for each man, and the total hours worked by all men in the week. Write out these results in f10.2 format on a single data card.

6-5 Redo Exercise 6-4 except assume that there are two different projects to which each man can be assigned. In the three-dimensional array below assume the first number applies to Project Number 1 and the second number applies to Project Number 2.

	Day 1	Day 2	Day 3	Day 4	Day 5
Worker 1	5.0, 3.0	5.0, 3.5	4.5, 5.0	5.0, 3.0	4.5, 5.0
Worker 2	5.5, 2.5	5.5, 3.0	5.0, 5.0	4.5, 5.5	5.0, 4.0
Worker 3	6.0, 2.0	4.5, 4.5	4.0, 4.5	4.0, 5.0	6.0, 2.5

Read in this three-dimensional array row by row with one worker's hours on a single input data card. Calculate the total hours worked on Project Number 1 and on Project Number 2. Write these results out in f10.1 format. Now calculate the average hours worked on each project on each day and write these results out in f10.1 format with a single day's totals on a single output card.

6-6 One useful item to a contractor on a construction project is the number of men of each craft required each week. Suppose he will need carpenters, plumbers, and electricians, referred to as crafts 1, 2, and 3, respectively. The contractor usually divides his total effort into various jobs which he then schedules to start on a given week. For each job, he estimates how many weeks are required and how many of each craft are needed. Suppose he punches this information onto cards, the job number in columns 1–2, the starting week in columns 4–5, the weeks required in columns 7–8, and the number of workers in crafts 1, 2, and 3 in columns 11–12, 14–15, and 17–18, respectively.

Assuming the total duration of the contract is 10 weeks, write a program that determines the number of workers in each craft needed each week. The output should be in columnar fashion, with the week number and the number of craftsmen needed in each craft. Use as input the following:

Job	Start	Duration	Craft 1	Craft 2	Craft 3
01	2	4	5	1	2
02	1	2	2	0	0
03	4	1	0	4	0
04	2	2	3	0	1
05	5	5	2	0	0
06	7	1	0	1	0
07	9	1	1	1	1

6-7 What integer number would be stored in each element of the array by the following program (what number would be stored in TEST(1,1), TEST(1,2), etc.)?

```
        DIMENSIØN TEST(3,3)
        K = 1
        DØ 40 J = 1,3
        DØ 40 N = 1,3
        TEST(N,J) = K
40      K = K + 1
```

†6-8 What integer number would be stored in each element of the AGAIN array by the following program?

```
        DIMENSIØN AGAIN(2,2,3)
        K = 2
        DØ 6 J = 1,2
        DØ 6 L = 1,3
        DØ 6 N = 1,2
        AGAIN(J,N,L) = K
6       K = K + 2
```

6-9 Prepare a program to insert either zeros or ones into an array to give the following result for a 4 × 4 array:

$$\begin{bmatrix} 1 & 0 & 0 & 1 \\ 0 & 1 & 1 & 0 \\ 0 & 1 & 1 & 0 \\ 1 & 0 & 0 & 1 \end{bmatrix}$$

That is, place ones on both diagonals and zeros elsewhere. Read the size (≤ 20) of the array from a data card, but do not read values for the elements. Print your final result.

6-10 Revise the inventory program in Example 5-2 to print the final inventory in ascending order of the stock numbers.

†6-11 Read in a one-dimensional array A containing eight elements in F5.1 format on a single data card. Sort the elements into ascending order based on their absolute value. Write out the results on a single data card in F5.1 format.

6-12 Redo Exercise 6-11 for descending order.

6-13 Suppose we have the coordinates of five points in the x,y plane, and would like to find the distance between the two points that lie the farthest apart. The five points are read from five cards punched as follows:

x	y
-0.94	-3.22
-4.02	8.17
7.07	-9.11
5.49	8.76
0.20	4.45

The distance between the first two points is $\sqrt{(x_1 - x_2)^2 + (y_1 - y_2)^2}$; between the first and third is $\sqrt{(x_1 - x_3)^2 + (y_1 - y_3)^2}$; etc. Only the value of the farthest distance is to be printed. Be sure to check all possibilities (a total of 10).

6-14 On large turnpike systems such as the New Jersey Turnpike, automobiles may enter and leave at varying points. Suppose we construct a simple system to audit the collections made by the toll collector at one of the exits. Upon entry to the turnpike system, each motorist is given a card on which his point of entry is punched. Upon exit from the turnpike system, he surrenders this card to the toll collector and pays the toll. At the end of the day, the toll collector counts his money and submits this along with the cards to the accounting department. They then enter the amount collected and the gate at which it was collected on a card. This card followed by the cards on which the entry gate was punched are then processed. Using the table of tolls in the accompanying figure, the amount of fare that should have been collected from each motorist can be computed. These can be summed to give the total amount that should been reported by the toll collector. The program should print this amount along with the amount reported by the toll collector:

Entry gate						
	1	*2*	*3*	*4*	*5*	*6*
1	—	0.45	1.20	1.85	2.45	3.00
2	0.45	—	0.80	1.50	2.15	2.65
3	1.20	0.80	—	0.80	1.50	2.00
4	1.85	1.50	0.80	—	0.75	1.25
5	2.50	2.20	1.50	0.75	—	0.60
6	3.10	2.75	2.00	1.25	0.60	—

EXIT GATE

6-15 30 students take a multiple-choice exam containing 20 questions each with five possible answers. Their answers are punched on data cards containing the student's ID number followed by his 20 answers (a zero is entered for unanswered questions). These 30 cards are preceeded by a card containing a zero in the student number entry followed by the correct answers to the 20 questions. Write a program to determine the number of correct answers given by each of the students. The student number should be printed followed by the number of correct answers.

†6-16 Refer to the above exercise. The instructor would like to know how many students gave answers (correct or incorrect) to all questions, how many students left one question unanswered, how many students left two questions unanswered, and so on to how many students left all 20 questions unanswered. Omit the card with the correct answers from the data deck.

6-17 Refer to Exercise 4-26. Compute and print the number of males in each of the 10 sections *and* the number of females in each of the 10 sections. Use a double-subscripted array.

6-18 Refer to Exercise 4-26. Compute and print the number of females and the number of males of each standing (freshman, sophomore, etc.) in each of the 10 sections. Use a triple-subscripted array.

6-19 The results from the Mayor's race have been reported by each precinct as follows:

Precinct	Candidate 1	Candidate 2	Candidate 3	Candidate 4
1	192	48	206	37
2	147	90	312	21
3	186	12	121	38
4	114	21	408	39
5	267	13	382	29

Write a computer program to do the following:

a. Compute and print the total number of votes received by each candidate and the percent of the total votes cast.

b. If any one candidate received over 50% of the votes, the program should print a message declaring him winner.

c. If no candidate received over 50% of the votes, the program should print a message declaring a run-off between the two candidates receiving the largest number of votes.

†6-20 Suppose you have 12 cards, each of which contains 8 real constants. Write a program to determine the largest value punched on each card. The output from the program should be 12 numbers, all of which are to be printed on the same line.

6-21 Refer to the above exercise. Consider the collection of 12 numbers consisting of the first number punched on each card. Determine the largest of these 12 numbers. Do likewise for the collection of 12 numbers consisting of the second number punched on each card, and so on for each of the 8 numbers. The output should appear on one line.

6-22 Modify Exercise 6-20 to determine the next-to-largest number instead of the largest number in each respective case.

6-23 Make the above modifications to Exercise 6-21.

†6-24 An airline assigns seats to passengers in the coach section of the airplane. This section has 38 rows with six seats on each row with an aisle down the middle. The seats on each row are numbered 1 through 6 as follows:

1—window seat, left side

2—center seat, left side

3—aisle seat, left side

4—aisle seat, right side

5—center seat, right side

6—window seat, right side

The status of the seats is maintained via array ISEAT, which is specified as follows:

DIMENSIØN ISEAT(38,6)

The first subscript of this array designates the row in the aircraft; the second subscript designates the seat on that row. The elements of the array may contain one of the following three values:

+1—seat occupied

0—seat empty

1—seat does not exist on this aircraft

Suppose array ISEAT represents the current status of the seats in the aircraft. Devise appropriate statements to count the number of empty seats on the aircraft.

Should it be desired to write a complete program for this or the ensuing exercises, it may be either assumed that the entries for ISEAT are available on cards or are available from a disk file (see Chapter 7). If any entry in the array is changed, the final array should be either printed or rewritten on the disk file.

6-25 Refer to the above exercise. Suppose rows 1–11 have been designated as the nonsmoking area and the remainder as the smoking area. Write the statements to count the number of empty seats in each area.

6-26 Refer to Exercise 6-24. A passenger has requested an aisle seat as close to the rear of the plane as possible. Write the necessary statements to locate him a seat and fill it.

6-27 Refer to Exercise 6-24. Write the statements to print the percentage of aisle seats that are filled, the percentage of window seats that are filled, and the percentage of center seats that are filled.

6-28 Refer to Exercise 6-24. Three passengers want three seats together if at all possible. Write the code to locate these seats, if available.

6-29 Refer to Exercise 6-24. Write the necessary statements to determine the number of rows that are fully occupied, the number of rows on which five seats are occupied, and so on. The output should appear as follows:

Occupied Seats	Number of Rows
1	3
2	8
3	22
4	3
5	2
6	0

INPUT-OUTPUT OPERATIONS

In the previous chapters, input-output features were introduced only to the extent that enabled the input-output for the programs to be accomplished in a convenient manner. At this point it seems appropriate to devote an entire chapter to the subject of input-output in FORTRAN. Our previous discussion has been fairly complete with regard to most implementations of format-free input-output. We have by no means discussed all of the features of the FØRMAT statement, and we will devote the first two sections of this chapter to this statement. Carriage control will also be described in more detail along with other forms of input-output statements.

Although FORTRAN was designed primarily for the processing of numerical data, the capabilities for processing character data are extensive. Although some other languages are superior to FORTRAN in this respect, the features available in FORTRAN permit some interesting problems involving character data to be undertaken. We shall devote an entire section (Section 7-6) to this subject; but the DATA statement in the previous section (Section 7-5) should be reviewed before undertaking this topic.

The final sections of the chapter describe features such as direct-access input-output and the NAMELIST statement that are powerful, but not in widespread use.

7-1. fØrmat **FIELD SPECIFICATIONS**

Since i, e, and f fields were introduced in Chapter 3, the reader should be familiar with the concept of a field. However, some concepts will be repeated for completeness.

The i *field* is used in input-output operations involving fixed-point or integer variables. Important points are

1 The field specification is rIw, where r is the repetition number and w is the width of the field.

2 On input, any blanks within the i field are interpreted as zeros; hence, the input must be right justified. The computer automatically right justifies any output in the i field.

3 If no sign is provided on input, the number is assumed positive. On output a column must be provided for the sign if the number is negative. Positive numbers are written without a sign.

4 Any nonnumerical character other than the sign that appears in an i field on input is taken to be an indication of error.

5 When the field width on output is insufficient (for example, attempting to write -127 in field i2, a *format overflow* occurs. Some systems simply fill the specified field with asterisks (that is, the output is ** for the aforementioned case), while others write what they can starting from the right (that is, the output for this case is 27 with no indication of a format overflow. Asterisks or other mention that format overflow has occurred is the preferable and more common treatment.

As the i field has been used frequently in previous chapters, further discussion is unnecessary.

The e field is appropriate when a floating-point or real variable on either input or output is to appear with a numerical value accompanied by an exponent. The following points are pertinent:

1 The field specification is $rEw.d$, where r is the repetition number, w is the number of columns in the width of the field, and d is the number of digits following the decimal point.

2 The computer automatically right justifies the output in the e field. Normally, the value appears as $\pm 0.X_1X_2 \cdots X_dE \pm YY$ or minor variations thereof (e.g., $\pm X_0.X_1 \cdots X_dE \pm YY$, where $X_1X_2 \cdots X_d$ are the specified digits and YY is the exponent. Thus, if the value of 9727. is printed under e12.5, the result is b0.97270Eb04 (the b symbolizing a blank column). If the exponent is Eb00, these four characters are omitted by many computers.

3 On output, the minimum width of the e field can be readily obtained by accounting for each character:

Leading sign	1 column
Leading zero	1 column
Decimal point	1 column
d digits	d columns
Character e	1 column
Sign of the exponent	1 column
Exponent digits	2 columns
Total	$d + 7$

Thus the *minimum* value of w in Ew.d must be at least d + 7, or mathematically

$$w \geq d + 7$$

The E field is commonly used when the magnitude of the corresponding variable in the output list cannot be predicted with certainty. If the field width is insufficient, a format overflow occurs with results analogous to the results for the I field discussed previously. *Caution:* if the output specification is E7.0, the output is $\pm 0.\text{E} \pm \text{YY}$. No significant digits are obtained, only the exponent.

4   Although the E field used for output is very regular in appearance, several variations can be conveniently used on input. Useful features include these:

a. If a decimal point is provided, it overrides d in the field specification *Ew.d.* If the decimal is omitted, the d digits preceding the exponent in the field are placed to the right of the decomal. For example, if the value 13848 were entered as 13848E03 right justified in a field with specification E15.3, the number entered would be 13.848E03. If large amounts of data are to be keypunched, this feature saves time.

b. If the exponent is E $\pm$ 00, the exponent can be omitted entirely. Furthermore, if the decimal point is provided, the E field need not be right justified. This applies only to this specific case. In all other cases, the entry in the E field must be right justified.

c. If sufficient, only one digit of the exponent need be punched.

d. Unsigned value or exponent is taken as positive.

e. If the sign is present for both positive and negative exponents, the letter E may be omitted.

f. A decimal point must not appear in the exponent.

As an illustration of these rules, the value 13848. may be entered in field E15.3 by any of the following entries:

```
+13848E+03
      1384E3
   13848+3
      13848.
  13.848E03
  1384.8E01
  13848+05
```

All except the entry 13848. must be right justified.

The *F field* is used whenever a floating-point or real variable without an exponent is to appear in the input or output. This field specification is *rFw.d*, where r is the repetition number, w columns are contained in the width of the field, and d digits appear after the decimal point.

On output, a decimal point is always provided (hence a space must be provided), and a space must be allowed for the sign if the number is negative. The F field must be used carefully on output. For example, the field specification F6.2 provides enough spaces only for numbers in the range −99.99 to 999.99. If the number is less than 1.0, a space must be provided for a zero before the decimal point. Furthermore, if the number 0.00127 is written under the specification F6.2, the output is 0.00 (two digits following decimal point). The F field is always right justified on output, and format overflows are treated in a manner analogous to their treatment for the I field.

On input the use of a decimal point overrides d and also removes the necessity of right justification. If no decimal point is provided, the last d digits in the F field are placed to the right of the decimal point. In this case, the entry must be right justified. For example, the entry 14276 read under F5.2 becomes 142.76 (two digits following decimal point).

A *scale factor* may be incorporated into the field specification whenever E or F fields are used. However, the scale factor does *not* act the same for F fields as for E fields, although the specification is s$PrFw.d$ or s$PrEw.d$ for the respective fields. In each case, s may be a positive or negative integer.

When used with the F field for either input or output, its effect is

$$\text{External value} = \text{internal value} \cdot 10^s$$

For example, if the fraction 0.278 is to be expressed as a percent, a field specification of 2PF10.1 gives the result 27.8. It can also be used on input and output if, for example, the values of certain variables are to be in kilograms on input and output, but grams internally.

When the scale factor is used with the E field, the magnitude of the result is not altered. In fact, scale factors with E fields are ignored entirely on input. On output the fractional part is multiplied by 10^s and the exponent is reduced by s. Thus the magnitude is not affected, but the results are often more readable. For example, the field specification 1PE15.3 for listing 0.00137 yields 1.370E$-$03 instead of 0.137E$-$02. *Caution:* The rule $w \geq d + 7$ for E fields must be modified whenever a scale factor is used.

Another precaution is that a scale factor accompanying an E or F field is automatically applied to succeeding E *and* F field until another scale factor is encountered. Thus if the scale factor is to affect only one field, the next E or F field must be accompanied by scale factor 0P.

The *G field* is a generalized format code that may be used for input-output of either integer or real data. The general form is $rGw.d$, where r is the repetition number, w is the width of the field, and d depends upon the type of the corresponding variable in the I/O list. If this variable is integer, the $.d$ is ignored, and $rGw.d$ is equivalent to rIw. On input of real variables, the data may appear with or without an exponent, and d is the number of digits to the right of the decimal point. On output, d is the number of significant digits to be transmitted. If the number is between .1 and $10 ** d$, the number is printed without an exponent. Otherwise, output is similar to that from the E field. The field width w should be sufficient to allow four spaces for the exponent if it is required.

The G field appears only in a few recent systems; therefore, programmers must check its availability before using it.

The *X field* is used to insert blanks into the output list or to ignore columns on input. The field specification rX on input causes r columns, which may or may not be blank, to be skipped. On output, rX causes r blank columns to be inserted. For example, the statements

```
     READ (5,5)A,B
5    FØRMAT (F6.0,6X,E7.0)
```

read the value of A from columns 1–6, skip columns 7–12, and read the value of B from columns 13–19. Columns 7–12 may or may not be blank. The use of the x field in the FØRMAT statement is not reflected in the input or output variable listing, since no information transfer is associated with the x field.

On output, the x field can be used to provide additional spacing. To illustrate, the statements

WRITE (6,7)A,B
7   FØRMAT (1x,F7.2,4x,E10.3)

yield the output (recall that the first character is used for carriage control, and does not appear in the output)

□□12.70□□□□□0.170E□02

where □ designates a blank character.

The *T code* is a tab code used to specify the column with which the reading or writing for the following format code begins. The general form is Tw, where w is the column number. For example, consider the READ statement

READ (5,4)J,B

Using the FØRMAT statement

4   FØRMAT (T4,I4,T27,F14.6)

The integer variable J is read from columns 4–7 and B is read from columns 27–40. Similarly, the statement

4   FØRMAT (T4,I4,F14.6)

causes the input scan to begin with column 4.

The above manipulations could be obtained using the x field, but the T code is more powerful than this. For example, using the statement

4   FØRMAT (T27,I4,T4,F14.6)

causes J to be read from columns 27–30 and B from columns 4–17. This specification can be used to read two variables from the same positions on the card. For example, using the statements

READ (5,1)J,B
4   FØRMAT (T4,I4,T4,F4.0)

causes the information in columns 4–7 to be stored in integer format in variable J and in real format in variable B.

The *Hollerith* or *H-field* is used in the format statement to insert characters into the output line. In the simplest version of this field specification, the desired characters to be output are simply enclosed in apostrophes.‡ For example, the statements

        A = 1.2
        WRITE (6,18)A
    18 FØRMAT (1x,'A☐ =',F5.1)

generate the following output:

A☐ = ☐☐1.2

where ☐ designates the blank character. As a second example, the statements

        K = 12
        J = 1967
        WRITE (6,2)K,J
    2   FØRMAT (1x,'JUNE',I3,',',I5)

generate the following output:

JUNE☐12,☐1967

Special treatment must be given to apostrophes that occur naturally within the character data. For each apostrophe that appears in the message, an extra apostrophe must be inserted, giving consecutive apostrophes. On output, a single apostrophe is obtained. For example, the statements

        WRITE (6,30)
    30 FØRMAT (1x,'IT''S☐TIME☐TØ☐GØ)

produce the output

IT'S☐TIME☐TO☐GO

The use of apostrophes to designate a Hollerith field did not appear in early versions of FORTRAN, and it is not acceptable on a few current systems (generally small ones). These systems require that the field specification consist of the characters to be printed preceded by the letter H preceded by the number of characters in the message. Using this implementation, the FØRMAT statements presented previously in this section appear as follows:

    18 FØRMAT (1x,3HA = ,F5.1)
    2   FØRMAT (1x,4HJUNE,I3,1H,,I5)
    30 FØRMAT (1x,15HIT'S TIME TØ GØ)

Apostrophes are not repeated in this version.

---

‡ Although apostrophes are used in this text, many systems require quotation marks instead.

The main disadvantage of this version is that the programmer must count the characters in the message. However, this version is universally accepted, even on systems that also recognize the use of apostrophes.

The *A field* permits character data to be read and stored in variables. This field will not be discussed until a subsequent section devoted to character data in this chapter.

7-2. CARRIAGE CONTROL

The carriage on the high-speed printer can be controlled in much the same fashion as the carriage on a typewriter. Essentially all computing systems have adopted the convention of using the first character *in each line* of output for this purpose. This character is never printed, and it causes paper spacing as follows:

Character in Column 1	Printer Action	Resulting Spacing	Field Specifications
Blank	Advance carriage one line and then print.	Single space	1x or 'A' or 1HA
Zero	Advance carriage two lines and then print.	Double space	'0' or 1H0
One	Advance carriage to top of page and then print.	Skip to next next page	'1' or 1H1
Plus	Print without advancing carriage.	Overprint	'+' or 1H+

As all output FØRMAT statements considered in the previous sections began with 1x, single spacing was obtained.

The carriage control can be integrated with other field specifications. For example, the output from the statement

FØRMAT (5x,F12.2)

is five blank columns followed by the floating-point number. The first blank from the x field causes the printer to single space. As a further illustration, consider the following statements:

```
    WRITE (6,2)
2   FØRMAT ('1INPUTbPARAMETERS')
```

The words INPUT PARAMETERS are printed at the top of the next page, as dictated by the 1 in the first column.

Several characters besides the 0, the blank, the 1, or the + can be used to obtain carriage manipulations. These other options are used so infrequently that they will not be discussed here. However, the programmer should pay careful attention to carriage control, as some characters will cause the printer to continuously eject pages of blank paper. For a 600-line per minute printer, this is undesirable.

Another similar situation may arise when using a '1' or 1H1 field for carriage control (skip to a new page) in a statement to be executed repeatedly. Proper use is

```
      WRITE (6,10)
10    FØRMAT ('1')
      DØ 12 J = 1,N
      .
      .
      .
12    WRITE (6,11)ANSWER
11    FØRMAT (1x,F20.6)
```

instead of placing the 1H1 within the DØ loop as follows:

```
      DØ 12 J = 1,N
      .
      .
      .
12    WRITE (6,11)ANSWER
11    FØRMAT ('1',F20.6)
```

The first procedure places the first answer on a new page, subsequent answers appearing on the same page. The second procedure places each answer on a new page.

7-3. FØRMAT OPTIONS

The repetition number used with an individual field can also be used with a group of fields by placing the group of fields within parentheses and placing the repetition number before the parentheses. Thus, the specification 2(F10.2,I6) is equivalent to F10.2,I6,F10.2,I6, but not to 2F10.2,2I6.

Another frequently used option is the slash (/) within the FØRMAT statement, such as

```
      WRITE (6,1)N,A,B
1     FØRMAT (1x,I14/1x,2F14.4)
```

The slash causes one record line to be terminated and another to be begun. In the above case, N appears on the first line, and A and B appear on the second line of the output. Note that carriage control is required for each line of output, and thus the 1x for carriage control follows the slash in the above example. Slashes on input are treated similarly.

Consecutive slashes simply cause consecutive record lines to be terminated. Although treated the same by the computer, slashes in the middle and at the end of the FØRMAT statement appear to give slightly different results. Consider the statement

```
READ (5,4)A,B
```

with the FØRMAT statement

4   FØRMAT (/2F10.2)

Two cards in the input data are read; but the information on the first card is ignored
entirely. On the other hand, if the FØRMAT statement is

4   FØRMAT (F10.2/F10.2)

two cards are still read; but one value is read from each card. To read the value of A
from the first card, skip the next card, and read the value of B from the third card, the
appropriate FØRMAT statement is

4   FØRMAT (F10.2//F10.2)

The first slash terminates the scan of the first card after reading a value for A. The
second slash terminates the scan of the second card without reading any values, which
in effect causes it to be skipped.

To generalize, $n + 1$ slashes at the beginning or end of the FØRMAT statement
cause $n + 1$ records to be skipped on input or $n + 1$ blank records to be written on
output. However, $n + 1$ slashes in the middle of the FØRMAT statement cause only n
records to be skipped on input or n blank records to be written on output.

If the number of variables in an output list is less than the number of field specifications, output continues through Hollerith fields and slashes between the last used
field specification and the next unused one (or the end of the FØRMAT statement if the
number of fields exactly equals the number of variables in the output list). That is, the
output from

WRITE (6,1)RES
1   FØRMAT (1x,F12.4'□ØHMS'/)

appears as (RES = 1.7126)

□□□□□□1.7126□ØHMS

followed by a blank line.

Parentheses within the FØRMAT statement may be used in a manner other than
with a repetition number. Consider the statements

READ (5,2)N,A,B,C,D
2   FØRMAT (I5/(2F10.2))

Note that these parentheses are not preceded by a repetition number. The value of N
is read from the first card, and the slash causes the input scan to proceed to the next
card. The inner parentheses are ignored on the first pass through the FØRMAT specifications, and variables A and B are read from the second card. Now the end of the FØRMAT
has been reached with two variables, C and D, remaining to be read. Control now

reverts back to the *first preceding open parenthesis* (not counting parentheses used with a repetition number) *and the record line is terminated* (equivalent to a slash). Thus C and D are read from the third card according to 2F10.2. Such parentheses are treated analogously on output. Note that if no inner parentheses are present, control reverts back to the beginning of the FØRMAT statement.

The use of commas in FØRMAT statements does not follow stringent rules. Each field within the FØRMAT statement can be separated by commas as in the previous examples, although some may be deleted if desired. For example, consider the following case:

FØRMAT(1x,3F10.5,12x,1HK,2E12.4)

Note that each field is separated by a comma. However, some of these may be omitted according to the following rule: A comma between consecutive fields in a FØRMAT statement may be deleted provided no ambiguity results. For example, consider omission of the first comma, yielding

1x3F10.5

This can only mean fields of 1x and 3F10.5. However, omitting the second comma produces

3F10.512x

This can mean fields of either 3F10.5 and 12x or 3F10.51 and 2x. Thus the comma is necessary here. In fact, all commas in the above example may be omitted except this one, yielding

FØRMAT (1x3F10.5,12x1HK2E12.4)

It is not incorrect to leave these commas, and they are often inserted for clarity.

7-4. OTHER INPUT-OUTPUT STATEMENTS

In the previous cases the input or output statements have followed the form READ (5,i) or WRITE (6,i), where i specified the FØRMAT statement. The more general forms are WRITE (n,i) or READ (n,i), where n denotes the *logical unit* involved. Although the statement number i must be an integer number, n may be either an integer variable or constant. The specific configuration of the logical units depends upon the particular installation, but the total number is usually about 10. Logical unit 5 is the card reader, logical unit 6 is the systems output tape which is subsequently printed, logical unit 7 is the card punch, and the use of the remaining logical units varies so much from one installation to the next that the specific computer center should be consulted for this information. Generally, these units are used for intermediate storage of large amounts of data, and the center can advise as to the best units to use.

When reading cards online, the logical unit may be omitted from the READ statement in some versions of FORTRAN IV to give

READ *i, list*

where *i* is the FORMAT statement number. Note that *i* is not enclosed in parentheses, but it is followed by a comma. Similarly, printing and punching online (as explained previously in Table 3-2) on some machines can be dictated by

PRINT *i, list*
PUNCH *i, list*

In other installations, the statement

PRINT, *i, list*

is equivalent to

WRITE (6,*i*) *list*

in that all output is on logical unit 6, the system output tape.

When transferring large amounts of information to or from logical devices other than 5 or 6, the use of binary (the internal numbering system in the machine) can speed up the process by eliminating the conversion from binary to BCD (binary coded decimal), or vice versa. As this also eliminates the need for a FORMAT statement, the READ and WRITE statements become

READ (*n*)*list*
WRITE (*n*)*list*

To facilitate these intermediate input-output operations, the instructions END FILE *n*, REWIND *n*, and BACKSPACE *n* are used, respectively, to place a mark denoting that the last record has been encountered, to rewind the tape, or to backspace one record (the information corresponding to one card or printed line). Of course, these instructions are not permitted for logical units 5 (the card reader), 6 (the systems output unit), or 7 (the card punch).

Recent versions of FORTRAN IV also permit extension of the READ statement to include transfers upon encounter of an end-of-data and/or an error in the input data. For example, the statement

READ (5,7,END = 19,ERR = 8)A,I,D

would read information from logical unit 5 according to FORMAT statement 7. If an end-of-data is encountered, control is transferred to statement 19. If an error is encountered in the input, control is transferred to statement 8.

To illustrate the use of the END = option, suppose we write a program to compute the arithmetic average of a set of numbers which are punched one per card in the first 10 columns in F10.0 format. It is not known how many numbers are in the set, but we will assume there are too many to be conveniently counted. Using the END = option

```
 1              N=0
 2              SUM=0.
 3        2     READ(5,1,END=4) A
 4        1     FORMAT(F10.0)
 5              SUM=SUM+A
 6              N=N+1
 7              GOTO2
 8        4     AVG=SUM/N
 9              WRITE(6,3)AVG
10        3     FORMAT(' AVERAGE =',F10,3)
11              STOP
12              END
```
(a) Program

```
5.872
15.422
1.245
-2.111
12.55
6.222
```
(b) Input data

```
AVERAGE =        6.533
```
(c) Output data

Figure 7-1. Example of the use of the END = option.

in the READ statement, the program in Figure 7-1 counts the cards, sums the numbers, and computes their average. The END = transfer is made upon encounter of a control card in the input data. The deck arrangement must, therefore, be such that a control card always follows the input data.

Many systems that do not recognize the END = feature as described here provide an alternate mechanism to accomplish the same objective. For example, some systems recognize the following special form of the IF statement:

IF (EØD)n_1, n_2

which must appear immediately following the READ statement. Upon encounter of end-of-data (EØD), control is transferred to statement n_2; otherwise, control is transferred to statement n_1.

7-5. THE DATA STATEMENT

Up to this point, the value 2.7 could be stored in the variable A by either reading the information from a card or by equating with an arithmetic statement such as A = 2.7. If the value of A never changed from one run to the next, reading the value of A would be a nuisance when preparing the data cards. The use of the statement A = 2.7 suffers the disadvantages that, first it is an executable statement and requires time to execute, and second the storage of the associated instructions may consume critically needed storage for large programs. To alleviate these situations, the DATA statement is used to assign the desired values to such variables *before* execution of the program begins. Since this occurs before execution, the DATA statement is not executable.

The general form of the DATA statement is

DATA $list/d_1, n_1 * d_2, \cdots, d_n/, list/d_1, d_2, \cdots d_m/, \cdots/$

The rules governing the list are the same as in READ or WRITE statements. That is, implied DØ's (only with numerical values for n_1, n_2, n_3), use of array names without subscripts, use of subscripted variables (subscript must be given a numerical value unless within an implied DØ, and other options available in READ or WRITE lists are permissible.‡ The list is separated from the values by a slash, and the numerical values are separated by commas. The use of $n_1 * d_2$, where n_1 is an integer constant, denotes that d_2 is repeated n_1 times. The number of variables in the list should equal the number of constants supplied.

As an example, the nonsubscripted variables X,Y,J,B, and A may be assigned values with either of the following DATA statements:

DATA X,Y,J,B,A/12.1,1.7E-2,5,2 * 8./
DATA X,Y/12.1,1.7E-2/,J/5/,B,A/2 * 8./

Several other possibilities may be suggested. The implied DØ can be used to set the first 12 elements of one-dimensional array C equal to 1.0 as follows:

DATA (C(J),J = 1,12)/12 * 1.0/

If C were dimensioned as containing only 12 elements, this could also be accomplished by

DATA C/12 * 1.0/

Recall that the DATA statement is not executable. Thus, these variables are assigned these values at the beginning of execution with the DATA statement. It is permissible to redefine these variables in any way desired; but the DATA statement may not be reexecuted to reassign to them their initial values.

Further examples of the use of the DATA statement will be given in the following section.

7-6. CHARACTER DATA

In all examples presented up to this point, only numerical values were stored in variables. Although FORTRAN's main advantages lie in the realm of numerical computations, FORTRAN permits rather extensive character manipulation.

---

‡ Not all machines will accept implied DØ's or variables written with subscripts in DATA statements. However, all will accept nonsubscripted array names.

As an example of a program that involves the processing of character data, we shall write a program that reads a temperature from columns 1–10 in F10.0 format and reads the scale from column 11, an F representing Fahrenheit and C representing Centigrade. The program should print the temperature in both °F and °C. The appropriate conversions are

$$°F = 1.8 \times °C + 32$$
$$°C = (°F - 32)/1.8$$

In order to solve this problem, we must first discuss the FORMAT features as they apply to character data. The appropriate field specification is the A field whose general form is rAw, where r is the repetition number and w is the width of the field. For example, the statements

    READ (5,8)T,J
8   FØRMAT (F10.0,A1)

read a numerical value from the first 10 columns and store it in variable T and read a character from column 11 and store it in variable J.

In FORTRAN, character data can be stored in either integer or real variables. That is, the above READ statement could be changed to

READ (5,8)T,S

However, in some systems real arithmetic can cause strange things to happen, making the use of integer variables preferable. We shall return to this point later.

The number of characters that can be stored in a single variable depends upon the system, with values commonly ranging from two to ten. Since a number of current systems permit four characters to be stored in a single variable, we shall use four throughout this text. For example, suppose the characters CØMPUTER are punched in the first eight columns of a card, and are to be read and stored in memory. Since the word CØMPUTER consists of eight characters, two storage locations will be required. The following three examples will produce the desired results:

READ (5,4)JA,JB	DIMENSIØN J(2)	DIMENSIØN J(2)
4 FØRMAT (2A4)	READ (5,4)(J(K),K = 1,2)	READ (5,4)J
	4 FØRMAT (2A4)	4 FØRMAT (2A4)

The following example is not correct (K is a simple variable):

    READ (5,4)K
4   FØRMAT (A8)

These statements specify the entry of eight characters of data into a single storage location, which in our system can store only four characters. In these cases, the system will store only the four rightmost characters in the A8 field.

Similarly, the following example is incorrect:

DIMENSIØN J(2)
READ (5,4)(J(K),K = 1,2)
4   FØRMAT (A8)

The FORMAT statement specifies that each card contains one field eight columns in width. The READ statement calls for the entry of the values for two variables. Recall that the contents of each field in the FØRMAT statement are entered into a single variable. Therefore these statements cause the characters in columns 5–8 of the first card to be stored in J(1) and the characters in columns 5–8 of the second card to be stored in J(2).

In the temperature problem described above, an appropriate READ statement is as follows:

READ (5,4)T,J
4   FØRMAT (F10.0,A1)

```
1              DATA ICHC,ICHF/'C','F'/
2      8       READ(5,4)T,J
3      4       FORMAT(F1C.C,A1)
4              IF(J.EQ.ICHF)GOTO2
5              IF(J.EQ.ICHC)GOTO3
6              WRITE(6,6)J
7      6       FORMAT(' INVALID SCALE ',A1)
8              GOTO8
9      2       TF=T
10             TC=(T-32.)/1.8
11     7       WRITE(6,5)TF,TC
12     5       FORMAT(' TEMPERATURE IS',F8.2,' DEG F OR',F8.2,' DEG C')
13             GOTO8
14     3       TC=T
15             TF=1.8*TC+32.
16             GOTO7
17             END
```

(a) Program

```
156.2      F
147.5      D
22.1       C
```

(b) Input data

```
TEMPERATURE IS    156.20 DEG F OR    69.00 DEG C
INVALID SCALE D
TEMPERATURE IS     71.78 DEG F OR    22.10 DEG C
```

(c) Output data

Figure 7-2. Program for temperature conversions.

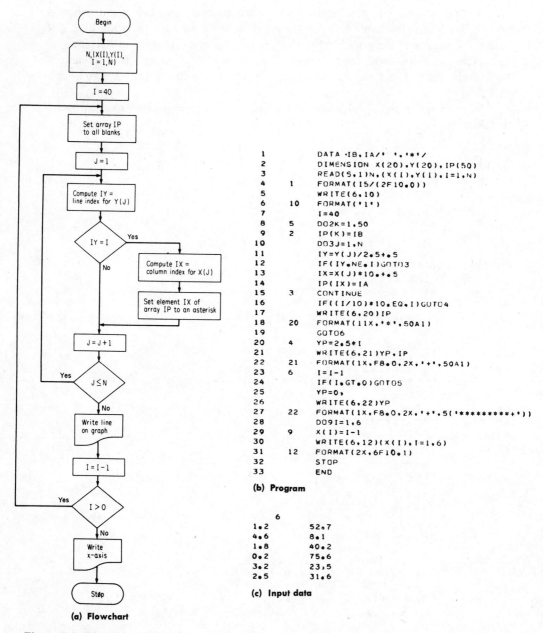

(a) Flowchart

```
1             DATA ·IB,IA/· ·,·*·/
2             DIMENSION X(20),Y(20),IP(50)
3             READ(5,1)N,(X(I),Y(I),I=1,N)
4       1     FORMAT(I5/(2F10.0))
5             WRITE(6,10)
6      10     FORMAT('1')
7             I=40
8       5     DO2K=1,50
9       2     IP(K)=IB
10            DO3J=1,N
11            IY=Y(J)/2.5+.5
12            IF(IY.NE.I)GOTO3
13            IX=X(J)*10.+.5
14            IP(IX)=IA
15      3     CONTINUE
16            IF((I/10)*10.EQ.I)GOTO4
17            WRITE(6,20)IP
18     20     FORMAT(11X,'*',50A1)
19            GOTO6
20      4     YP=2.5*I
21            WRITE(6,21)YP,IP
22     21     FORMAT(1X,F8.0,2X,'+',50A1)
23      6     I=I-1
24            IF(I.GT.0)GOTO5
25            YP=0,
26            WRITE(6,22)YP
27     22     FORMAT(1X,F8.0,2X,'+',5('**********+'))
28            DO9I=1,6
29      9     X(I)=I-1
30            WRITE(6,12)(X(I),I=1,6)
31     12     FORMAT(2X,6F10.1)
32            STOP
33            END
```

(b) Program

```
         6
1.2        52.7
4.6        8.1
1.8        40.2
0.2        75.6
3.2        23,5
2.5        31.6
```

(c) Input data

Figure 7-3. Plotting on the output printer.

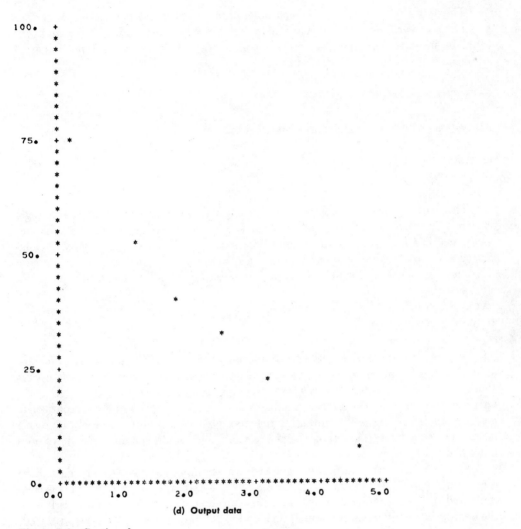

(d) Output data

Figure 7-3. *Continued.*

How do we determine if J contains the character F or the character C? The logical IF may be used to determine equality or inequality, or the arithmetic IF may be used to determine if an expression is zero or nonzero.

A few systems permit the use of alphanumeric constants as in the following statements:

IF (J.EQ.'F')GØ TØ 8
IF (J − 'F')9,8,9

where control is transferred to statement 8 only if J contains the character 'F'. However, most systems do not recognize alphanumeric constants used in this fashion.

The only alternative is to read character data into variables or to initialize character data into variables by the DATA statement. For example, variables ICHF and ICHC could be initialized to the characters F and C, respectively, by the following DATA statement:

DATA ICHF,ICHC/'F','C'/

All systems will now recognize the following statements:

IF (J.EQ.ICHF)GØ TØ 8
IF (J − ICHF)9,8,9

These statements are examples that justify the previous suggestion that integer variables be used to store character data. If real variables are used, the problems mentioned in Chapter 4 regarding comparing real variables for equality apply. Comparing real variables for equality is always a questionable undertaking.

Another problem that may occur is illustrated by the following statements:

DATA CHC,ICHC/'C','C'/
IF (CHC.EQ.ICHC)GØ TØ 20

At first glance, it appears that we are comparing character C to character C, which are surely equal. However, FORTRAN evaluates such comparisons using arithmetic operations. The above IF statement calls for the comparison of an integer variable to a real variable. In such cases, the integer variable is converted to real before the comparison is made. If an integer variable containing the character C is converted to real, the result is not the character C. Therefore, the above statement would conclude that ICHC does not equal CHC.

The complete program for the temperature example posed earlier in this section is given in Figure 7-2. The character in column 11 is read into variable J, and it is then compared to the character F in ICHF and the character C in ICHC. If equality is found, the appropriate conversion is made. If no equality is found, an error message is printed.

To illustrate the flexibility of FORTRAN in character manipulations, suppose we write a program to prepare a plot on the printer. Specifically, we shall plot the following arrays:

x	y
1.2	52.7
4.6	8.1
1.8	40.2
0.2	75.6
3.2	23.5
2.5	31.6

We shall plot x on the horizontal axis (columns) and y on the vertical axis (lines). The plot shall be 50 columns in width and 40 columns in height. The scales are 0 to 5 for x and 0 to 100 for y.

The flowchart, the program, and the resulting plot are given in Figure 7-3. The values of x and y are first read. In preparing the plot, the general approach is to use an array IP of 50 elements to store the 50 characters to be printed on each line of the plot. Since we start plotting at the top, the line index I is set equal to 40 and decremented. Each line of the plot entails the following computations:

1 Each element of array IP is set equal to a blank character.

2 For each value of Y, the line IY on which the point should appear is computed.

3 If IY equals the current value of I, the column IX in which the point should appear is computed, and IP(IX) is set equal to the asterisk character.

4 The line is printed, with every tenth line bearing an annotation for the y axis.

After printing the 40 lines of the graph, the x axis is printed.

Some increase in the efficiency of the program in Figure 7-3 could be obtained by precomputing the line indices for each value of Y and storing them in an array.

As a final example of the processing of character data, we shall prepare a program to code a message, a process known as *enciphering*. In our approach we begin with an original message (called the *clear*) such as the following:

HE HAD A BAD DAY

In performing the enciphering, we will use another message called the keyword. In our example, the keyword will be CØMPUTER

KEYWORD		C	O	M	P	U	T	E	R	C	O	M	P	U	T	E	R
CLEAR			H	E	□	H	A	D	□	A	□	B	A	D	□	D	A	Y
KEYWORD INDEX		3	15	13	16	21	20	5	18	3	15	13	16	21	20	5	18
CLEAR INDEX		8	5	0	8	1	4	0	1	0	2	1	4	0	4	1	25
SUM		11	20	13	24	22	24	5	19	3	17	14	20	21	24	6	43
ADD 10		21	30	23	34	32	34	15	29	13	27	24	30	31	34	16	53
SUBTRACT 27		21	3	23	7	5	7	15	2	13	0	24	3	4	7	16	26
CODED MESSAGE		U	C	W	G	E	G	O	B	M	□	X	C	D	G	P	Z

(a) Enciphering a message

Character	Index	Character	Index	Character	Index
□	0	I	9	R	18
A	1	J	10	S	19
B	2	K	11	T	20
C	3	L	12	U	21
D	4	M	13	V	22
E	5	N	14	W	23
F	6	O	15	X	24
G	7	P	16	Y	25
H	8	Q	17	Z	26

(b) Index table

Figure 7-4. The enciphering process.

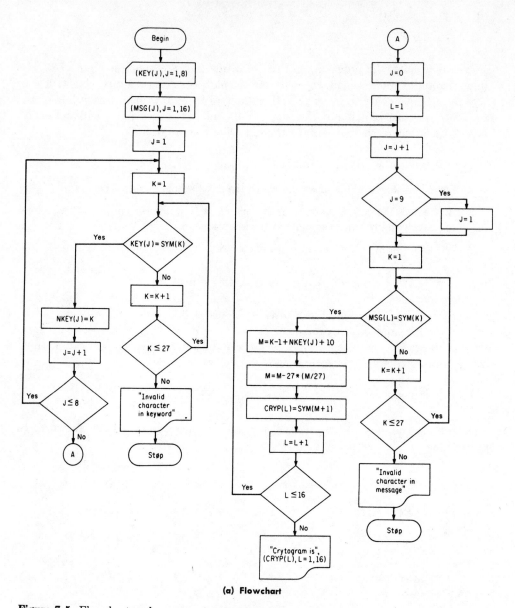

(a) Flowchart

Figure 7-5. Flowchart and program for the enciphering problem.

We begin by writing the keyword, repeated as necessary, over the clear, as illustrated in Figure 7-4. The basic approach is to convert each character in the keyword and the clear according to the index table of Figure 7-4b. The corresponding indices are added; the result is then increased by 10, and then 27 is subtracted whenever necessary in order to obtain a result between 0 and 26. Looking up the corresponding character in the index table gives the coded message.

The flowchart and program for the enciphering process are given in Figure 7-5. The keyword and message are read into arrays KEY and MSG, storing one character per storage location. The next step is to convert each character of the keyword to its index, which is stored in array NKEY. To do this for a given character, it is compared to each

```
 1              INTEGER KEY(8),MSG(16),SYM(27),NKEY(8),CRYP(16)
 2              DATA SYM/' ','A','B','C','D','E','F','G','H','I','J','K',
                1 'L','M','N','O','P','Q','R','S','T','U','V','W','X','Y','Z'/
 3              READ(5,1)KEY,MSG
 4        1     FORMAT(8A1/16A1)
 5              DO2J=1,8
 6              DO3K=1,27
 7              IF(KEY(J).EQ.SYM(K))GOTO2
 8        3     CONTINUE
 9              WRITE(6,4)
10        4     FORMAT(' INVALID CHARACTER IS KEYWORD')
11              STOP
12        2     NKEY(J)=K-1
13              J=0
14              DO5L=1,16
15              J=J+1
16              IF(J.EQ.9)J=1
17              DO6K=1,27
18              IF(MSG(L).EQ.SYM(K))GOTO7
19        6     CONTINUE
20              WRITE(6,8)
21        8     FORMAT(' INVALID CHARACTER IN MESSAGE')
22        7     M=K+NKEY(J)+9
23              M=M-27*(M/27)
24        5     CRYP(L)=SYM(M+1)
25              WRITE(6,9)CRYP
26        9     FORMAT('0CRYPTOGRAM IS ',16A1)
27              STOP
28              END
```
(b) Program

```
*ENTRY
COMPUTER
HE HAD A BAD DAY
```
(c) Input data

```
CRYPTOGRAM IS UCWGEGOBM XCDGPZ
```
(d) Output data

Figure 7-5. *Continued.*

element of array SYM (defined in the DATA statement) until an equality is located. The appropriate index is one less than the index of the element in SYM.

The next section then processes the characters in the message one at a time, converting them to the appropriate character in the cryptogram. Variable J serves as the pointer to the appropriate character in the keyword. It is incremented to eight, and then reset to one. The index of the character in the message is determined by the approach outlined above. The value of the appropriate element in NKEY is added, 10 is added to the result, and units of 27 are removed until the result is between 0 and 26. The easiest approach to accomplish the last step is to compute the remainder obtained by dividing the sum of the indices by 27. The character corresponding to this remainder is readily available from array SYM. The final step is to print the cryptogram.

FORTRAN is somewhat inefficient for problems like this in that only one character is stored in each storage location whereas four or more can actually be stored. This can be accomplished by packing and unpacking; but it is usually not worth the effort. Even so, FORTRAN can be used to introduce students to the processing of nonnumeric data, and several exercises on this topic are available at the end of this chapter.

7-7. EXECUTION-TIME FØRMATs

Consider the case in which a general program has been prepared for use in several applications. Furthermore, assume that there is considerable input according to the read statement

READ (5,8)N,(A(J),B(J),J = 1,N)

Using only previously discussed features of FORTRAN, each user must prepare his data to be consistent with FØRMAT statement number 8.

To surmount this disadvantage, the object-time FØRMAT can be employed. In this case, the READ statement is modified to

READ (5,X)N,(A(J),B(J),J = 1,N)

where X is a one-dimensional array containing the FØRMAT specifications. Specifically, consider the case in which the data are to be entered according to

FØRMAT (I5/(F12.2,E17.3))

The pertinent parts of the program are

```
    DIMENSIØN X(10), A(200), B(200)
    READ (5,6)(X(J),J = 1,10)
6   FØRMAT (10A4)
    READ (5,X) N, (A(J), B(J), J = 1,N)
```

The data card containing the format would contain the following information anywhere in the first forty (dictated by 10A4) columns:

(I5/(F12.2,E17.3))

Note that the word FØRMAT and the statement number are not punched.

The array X in the above example is dimensioned as ten for illustrative purposes only. It may be as large (or small) as necessary, and extremely long FØRMATs may be read from more than one card as necessary. Of course, the field specification A4 varies from machine to machine as discussed in the previous section.

7-8. DIRECT ACCESS INPUT-OUTPUT

Programs for problems requiring the storage of significant amounts of data on peripheral storage devices tend to require input-output capabilities beyond that normally required for most programs. All previous input-output statements involve the reading or writing of records in a sequential fashion. This implies there is no means by which an individual record can be retrieved directly. The direct access I/Ø statements can only be used with direct access storage devices such as a magnetic disc, but these statements allow individual records to be stored and retrieved directly from such devices.

The direct access statements permit the programmer to define files on the peripheral devices, and then under program control to locate a record in these files, to read the contents of this record, or to write new information in this record. The four statements are

DEFINE FILE $j(m,r,f,v)$
FIND $(i'u)$
READ $(i'u,n)$ *list*
WRITE $(i'u,n)$ *list*

Typical examples of each are

DEFINE FILE 2(15,20,E,JFL)
FIND (2'JFL)
READ (2'JFL,7)A
WRITE (2'JFL,8)B

Each of these will be discussed in detail.

The DEFINE FILE is a specification statement used to establish the file on the peripheral device. The various items in the above statement are defined as follows:

j is an unsigned integer number that designates a particular file.

m is an unsigned integer number that specifies the number of records in a particular file.

v is a nonsubscripted integer variable (called an associated variable) that after execution of a READ or WRITE statement contains the designation of the next record in the file.

f must be one of the following letters:

     E   specifies that a FØRMAT statement will be used in conjunction with the READ or WRITE statements. Information is thus stored in the form of characters.

     U   specifies that a FØRMAT statement will not be used. Information is thus stored in binary representation.

     L   specifies that the READ or WRITE statements may be used with or without a FØRMAT statement. Information is thus stored in either binary or character representation.

r is an unsigned integer number that specifies the size of each record in the file. Depending upon f(E,U, or L), r is one of the following:

f	r
E	characters
U	words
L	bytes

The *byte* probably deserves some explanation. On machines like the IBM 360, the fundamental storage unit is the byte, which contains eight bits. Thus, one word contains four bytes. Furthermore, one character may be stored in one byte. Thus, if f equals L and r is 400, then 400 characters or 100 words may be stored in one record on the file.

The WRITE and READ statements are quite similar to the more common statements of this type discussed earlier. The only difference is that the logical unit number is replaced by the file and record designation, $i'u$. The possibilities are

WRITE $(i'u,n)$ *list*
READ $(i'u,n,$ ERR $= d)$ *list*

The individual items in these statements are defined as follows:

i — is an unsigned integer number *or variable* that designates the file to be used. Of course, the file must be specified in a DEFINE FILE statement.

u — is an integer variable *or expression* that designates the particular record in the file that is to be read or written. After execution of the READ or WRITE statement, the value of the associated variable (v in the DEFINE FILE statement) contains the designation of the next subsequent record in the file.

n — is a FØRMAT statement number, if required.

list — is the same as in standard READ and WRITE statements; but it must not contain the associated variable.

The $i'u$ appearing in the FIND statement is defined in the same manner as for the READ or WRITE statements.

Now for a few examples. Suppose two files are defined as follows:

DEFINE FILE 8(50,100,E,IFL8), 33(10,20,U,IFL33)

Thus file 8 contains 50 records of 100 characters each; file 33 contains 10 records of 20 words each. A FØRMAT statement must be used to read or write on file 8, but must not be used for file 33.

Suppose variables A and B are to be written into the fifth record on each file. The statements are

```
   WRITE (8'5,20)A,B
20 FØRMAT (2F10.4)
   WRITE (33'5)A,B
```

After execution of these statements, both IFL8 and IFL33 equal 6. Similarly, these READ statements may be used to retrieve this information

```
K = 8
IFL8 = 5
READ (K'IFL8,20)A,B
J = 3
READ (33'J + 2)A,B
```

If A and B are to be written on successive records in file 8, a slash in the FØRMAT statement or other equivalent measures can be used. For example, the statements

        WRITE (8'10,4)A,B
4   FØRMAT (F10.4/E20.7)

cause A to be stored in record 10 and B in record 11. After execution of this statement, IFL8 equals twelve.

The FIND statement is used to keep the computer's processing unit from being idle during the finite time required for the peripheral device to locate the record. For example, the statements

FIND (8'7)

  .

  .

  .

READ (8'7,20)A,B

allow the record to be located while the computer is also performing the calculations for the statements between the FIND and the READ. However, the FIND in consecutive statements such as

FIND (8'4)
READ (8'4,20)A,B

serves no useful purpose and should be omitted. After execution of a FIND statement, the associated variable contains the location of the record designated in the FIND.

7-9. THE NAMELIST STATEMENT

Many recent versions of FORTRAN IV permit input-output using the NAMELIST feature. A NAMELIST statement such as

NAMELIST/XYZ1/I,J,P,X(2,3)

designates which variables are to be read or printed by input-output statements of the type

READ (5,XYZ1)
WRITE (6,XYZ1)

The NAMELIST statement has the general form

NAMELIST $/x/a,b,\cdots, c/z/d,e,\cdots, f$

where x and z are NAMELIST names and $a,b,\cdots, f$ are variable or array names. Note the use of slashes to enclose the NAMELIST names, and commas to separate the variable or array names.

Subsequent to the appearance of the NAMELIST statement, input-output statements of the form

READ (n,x)
WRITE (n,x)

may be used. The n denotes the logical unit to be used, and x is the appropriate NAMELIST name.

On input, the data must be in a special form in order to be read using the NAMELIST feature. For example, consider the statements

DIMENSIØN I(5)
NAMELIST /ME/A,B,I
READ (5,ME)

An appropriate input card could be (b symbolizes a blank column)

b&MEbI $= 7,3 * 0,14$,A $= 1.76$,B $= -2.01$&END

The rules are

1 The first column *must* be blank.

2 The second column *must* contain the character &.

3 This character is immediately followed by the NZMELIST name with no embedded blanks.

4 The NAMELIST name is followed by a blank.

5 The items in the list *must* be separated by commas.

6 The two types of permissible items are

  a. *Variable name = constant*, where the varaible name may be a subscripted array name.

  b. *Array name = set of constants*, where the array name is *not* subscripted. The constants are separated by commas, and successive occurrences of the same constant are entered in the form $k * constant$ as for the DATA statement. The number of constants *must* be less than or equal to the number of elements in the array.

7 The order is insignificant; but all variable and array names *mus*[3] have appeared in the NAMELIST list.

8 The list of items is terminated with &END, which may or may not be separated from the last item by a comma. Successvie cards are processed until &END is found, thus allowing several cards to be used for entreing the data.

On execution of the READ statement, successive entries in the input data are examined until the entry with the appropriate NAMELIST name is located.

On output, the data written using the NAMELIST list is in a form that can be read using the NAMELIST list. The fields for all entries are appropriately selected such that all significant digits are retained. For example, using the statement

WRITE (6,ME)

with the NAMELIST given above gives the following output:

1st line   &ME
2nd line   A = 1.7600000,   B = −2.0100000,   I = 7,0,0,0,14,
3rd line   &END

The constants in the list may be of any type, including literal.

7-10. IN SUMMARY

Since the ability to communicate with the computer is an important part of program-ming, this chapter should be given due attention. Not all format features are treated in this chapter; but the ones treated are common to essentially all FORTRANS. The follow-ing exercises should elucidate the use of the concepts presented in this chapter.

Exercises‡

7-1 Modify the program for Exercise 4-44 so that the output appears as in the accompanying figure. The heading that gives the specific class should be read from the first data card (use all 80 columns).

```
FINE ARTS 105 - SECTION 4

AVERAGE AGE - 21.250

PER CENT MALES - 58.333

PER CENT FRESHMEN - 16.667

PER CENT SOPHOMORES - 50.000

PER CENT JUNIORS - 16.667

PER CENT SENIORS - 16.667
```
Exercise 7-1

7-2 Modify the inventory program for Exercise 6-10 so that it carries a 20-character description of the item along with the identification number. Appropriately label all columns of output.

†7-3 One use of the high speed printers available with most computers is to print mailing lists. A special form available for this purpose is shown in the accom-panying figure. The form has three gummed labels across the page. Each label can accommodate a four-line address with 32 columns in each line. The first

---

‡ Solutions to Exercises marked with a dagger † are given in Appendix G.

DEPARTMENT HEAD	DEPARTMENT HEAD	DEPARTMENT HEAD
DEPT OF CHEMICAL ENGINEERING	DEPT CF CHEMICAL ENGINEERING	DEPT OF CHEMICAL ENGINEERING
UNIVERSITY CF ARIZONA	UNIVERSITY OF ARKANSAS	CALIFORNIA INSTITUTE OF TECH
TUCSON, ARIZONA 85721	FAYETTEVILLE, ARKANSAS 72701	PASADENA, CALIFORNIA 91109
DEPARTMENT HEAD	DEPARTMENT HEAD	DEPARTMENT HEAD
DEPT OF CHEMICAL ENGINEERING	DEPT OF CHEMICAL ENGINEERING	DEPT OF CHEMICAL ENGINEERING
UNIVERSITY CF CALIFORNIA	UNIVERSITY OF CALIFORNIA	UNIVERSITY OF CALIFORNIA
BERKELEY, CALIFORNIA 94720	DAVIS, CALIFORNIA 95615	LOS ANGELES, CALIFORNIA 90024

Exercise 7-3

character in the first address should begin in column 6, four columns should be left blank (horizontally) between labels, and two lines should be skipped (vertically) between labels. The addresses are to be read from data cards, each card containing one line of an address in the first 32 columns. Prepare a program to read the addresses in a sequential fashion and print as shown in the accompanying figure.

7-4 Modify the program for Exercise 5-39 so that the output contains the user's name along with his charge number. Assume this particular center has only 10 users, whose names and corresponding charge numbers can be obtained from the following cards:

```
JOHN  ANDERSON       70206
FRANK WILSON         40709
JOE EAST             50200
MYRON JOHNSON        40201
JACK EVERS           40710
HENRY WILLIAMSON     70207
JOHN SMITH           80001
MICHAEL SAND         50201
RALPH BLACKWELL      70208
HORACE WHITEHALL     40711
```

By using the time cards given as data for Exercise 5-39, the output of the program should appear as follows:

USER	CHARGE NO	TIME USED	PER CENT
FRANK WILSON	40709	6.08	26.61
JOE EAST	50200	5.20	22.76
MYRON JOHNSON	40201	3.11	13.61
HENRY WILLIAMSON	70207	5.10	22.32
JOHN SMITH	80001	3.36	14.70

Notice that the user's name is not printed if he did not use any time.

7-5 Prepare a program to perform the following:

a. Read the number of students in a class.

b. Read one quiz score for each student along with his name.

c. Arrange the scores in descending order.

d. Compute the average score.

e. Read a "header card" and reproduce as first line of output.

f. Write average grade, the number of students making above average, and the number of students making below average.

COOKIE CUTTING LABORATORY

AVERAGE SCORE   78.2857

NUMBER ABOVE AVERAGE   4

NUMBER BELOW AVERAGE   3

SCORE	NAME	
99.00	ROBERTS	
91.00	STEPHENS	
87.00	KILROY	
82.00	JONES	MEDIAN
71.00	LEVEQUE	
62.00	NO NAME	
56.00	JAMES	

Exercise 7-5

g. List the scores in descending order along with names. Write MEDIAN by median grade.

An example is shown in the accompanying illustration. The maximum number of students is 50, and allow 12 characters for each name.

Note: Machines storing six characters per word will require two words per name; machines storing five alphameric characters per word will require three words per name (field specification 2A5, A2, or 3A4); and similarly for other machines.

7-6 Prepare a program to read a date in the form xx/xx/xx and write in a fashion such as AUGUST 12, 1962. Use only one WRITE and FØRMAT statement for this. Store names of months in an array via a DATA statement. Select and process one date from each month. If the month is greater than 12 or the day is greater than 31, print the words ERRØNEØUS DATE xx/bxx/bxx.

If the DATA statement has not been studied, this can be accomplished by reading the names of the months into the array.

7-7 The following timetable is given for train schedules:

Distance	City	Time, P.M.
0	Chicagø	4:00
93	Niles	6:42
141	Kalamazøø	7:28
164	Battle Creek	7:53
210	Jacksøn	8:39
248	Ann Arbør	9:18
284	Detrøit	10:00

Prepare a program to read the above information, calculate the remaining entries in the table shown in the figure, and print in a similar fashion.

TRAIN SCHEDULE

DISTANCE	CITY	TIME	TIME FROM LAST STOP	ELAPSED TIME
0	CHICAGO	4- 0 P. M.	0 MIN	0 MIN
93	NILES	6- 42	162	162
141	KALAMAZOO	7- 28	46	208
164	BATTLE CREEK	7- 53	25	233
210	JACKSON	8- 39	46	279
248	ANN ARBOR	9- 18	39	318
284	DETROIT	10- 0	42	360

Exercise 7-7

7-8 Consider writing a program to update a student's grade point average. Suppose data cards are available as follows:

1 Student's name in columns 1–20.

2 Number of credit hours taken prior to this semester in columns 21–23 and number of credit hours earned in columns 25–27.

3 Number of quality points earned prior to this semester in columns 29–31.

4 The number of hours for his first class in column 32 and the grade in column 33.

5 The number of hours for his second class in column 35 and the grade in column 36.

6 etc. The student may take up to 10 classes.

A typical set of input cards might appear as follows:

JØE KØLLAGE	65	62	181	3B	3C	1A	4B	5B
KILRØY	71	65	145	3C	5D	3F	3C	
JØE BLEAUX	48	48	159	3A	3B	5A	4B	

Grade point ratios are computed on the 4-point system, i.e., 4 points for A, 3 points for B, 2 points for C, 1 point for D (hours are earned), and 0 points for F (hours are not earned).

Write a computer program that reads these cards and prints the student's name, the number of credit hours taken, the number of credit hours earned, and his quality point ratio at the end of the term. If his quality point ratio is less than 2.0, place an asterisk prior to his name, as illustrated in the accompanying figure for the above input.

NAME	HOURS TAKEN	HOURS EARNED	POINT RATIO
JØE KØLLAGE	81	78	2.802
*KILRØY	86	77	1.907
JØE BLEAUX	63	63	3.365

Exercise 7-8

†**7-9** Wheeler Dealer is the leading automobile dealer in the state. He now spends $2000 a month on advertising, and sells 200 cars a month at about $300 profit

per car. From this, he must subtract another $10,000 as fixed operating costs which are independent of the volume of sales. An advertising agency tells Wheeler that each time he doubles the amount he spends on advertising, he will increase the volume of sales by 20%. Write a program that gives Wheeler the amount spent on advertising, the number of sales he makes, and his net profit. Begin with his current status and successively double the amount of advertising until his net profit "goes over the hump," i.e., begins to decline. The output should appear as follows:

Advertising	Units Søld	Net Prøfit
$2000	200	$48000
$4000	240	$58000
$8000	288	$68400
$16000	346	$77800
$32000	415	$82500
$64000	498	$75400

7-10 Rework the program for Exercise 4-46 so that the status of his debt is shown at the end of each month (after payment is received) as shown in the accompanying figure.

MONTH	INTEREST	PAYMENT	BALANCE
			250.00
1	3.75	10.00	243.75
2	3.66	10.00	237.41
3	3.56	10.00	230.97
4	3.46	10.00	224.43
5	3.37	10.00	217.80
6	3.27	10.00	211.07
7	3.17	10.00	204.23
8	3.06	10.00	197.29
9	2.96	10.00	190.25
10	2.85	10.00	183.11
11	2.75	10.00	175.85
12	2.64	10.00	168.49
13	2.53	10.00	161.02
14	2.42	10.00	153.43
15	2.30	10.00	145.74
16	2.19	10.00	137.92
17	2.07	10.00	129.99
18	1.95	10.00	121.94
19	1.83	10.00	113.77
20	1.71	10.00	105.48
21	1.58	10.00	97.06
22	1.46	10.00	88.51
23	1.33	10.00	79.84
24	1.20	10.00	71.04
25	1.07	10.00	62.11
26	0.93	10.00	53.04
27	0.80	10.00	43.83
28	0.66	10.00	34.49
29	0.52	10.00	25.01
30	0.38	10.00	15.38
31	0.23	10.00	5.61
33	0.08	5.70	0.00

Exercise 7-10

7-11 Modify the program in Exercise 5-3 to print the status of his investment after each year, i.e., after the interest is added, but before the next deposit is made. The output should appear as shown in the accompanying figure.

```
STATUS OF FUND INTO WHICH $  600.00 IS
DEPOSITED ANNUALLY AT AN INTEREST RATE
OF   8.00 PER CENT.
    YEAR        VALUE OF FUND
     1             648.00
     2            1347.84
     3            2103.67
     4            2919.96
     5            3801.56
     6            4753.68
     7            5781.97
     8            6892.52
     9            8091.92
    10            9387.27
```

Exercise 7-11

7-12 Write a program that solves Exercise 5-4 and then prints the status of the investment after each year as shown in the accompanying figure. Note that the final balance is not exactly $8000. This arises from round-off errors, which could be avoided for this case by using the double precision feature discussed in the appendix.

```
TO ACCRUE $   8000.00, ONE MUST DEPOSIT
$   1338.84 AT 6.00 PER CENT INTEREST FOR
    5 YEARS.

STATUS OF INVESTMENT

YEAR      DEPOSIT      INTEREST     BALANCE
  1       1338.84        80.33      1419.17
  2       1338.84       165.48      2923.50
  3       1338.84       255.74      4518.07
  4       1338.84       351.41      6208.32
  5       1338.84       452.83      7999.98
```

Exercise 7-12

7-13 Exercise 5-42 entailed the calculation of the capital-recovery factor for interest rates of 2%, 4%, 6%, 8%, and 10%. Write a program whose output is the table shown in the accompanying figure. Use a DØ loop instead of reading the year from the data cards.

PER CENT		2	4	6	8	10
YEAR		**	**	**	**	**
1	.	1.02002	1.04000	1.06001	1.08000	1.10001
2	.	0.51507	0.53020	0.54544	0.56077	0.57619
3	.	0.34677	0.36035	0.37411	0.38804	0.40212
4	.	0.26263	0.27549	0.28860	0.30192	0.31547
5	.	0.21217	0.22463	0.23740	0.25046	0.26380
6	.	0.17853	0.19076	0.20337	0.21632	0.22961
7	.	0.15452	0.16661	0.17914	0.19207	0.20541
8	.	0.13651	0.14853	0.16104	0.17402	0.18745
9	.	0.12252	0.13449	0.14702	0.16008	0.17364
10	.	0.11133	0.12329	0.13587	0.14903	0.16275
11	.	0.10218	0.11415	0.12679	0.14008	0.15396
12	.	0.09456	0.10655	0.11928	0.13270	0.14676
13	.	0.08812	0.10014	0.11296	0.12652	0.14078
14	.	0.08261	0.09467	0.10759	0.12130	0.13575
15	.	0.07783	0.08994	0.10296	0.11683	0.13147
16	.	0.07365	0.08582	0.09895	0.11298	0.12782
17	.	0.06997	0.08220	0.09545	0.10963	0.12466
18	.	0.06670	0.07899	0.09236	0.10670	0.12193
19	.	0.06378	0.07614	0.08962	0.10413	0.11955
20	.	0.06116	0.07358	0.08719	0.10185	0.11746
21	.	0.05879	0.07128	0.08501	0.09983	0.11562
22	.	0.05663	0.06920	0.08305	0.09803	0.11401
23	.	0.05467	0.06731	0.08128	0.09642	0.11257
24	.	0.05287	0.06559	0.07968	0.09498	0.11130
25	.	0.05122	0.06401	0.07823	0.09368	0.11017

CAPITAL RECOVERY FACTOR

Exercise 7-13

†**7-14** Revise the program for Exercise 5-50 so that the output is appropriately labeled.

†**7-15** Suppose we have an item of equipment worth $1000 which we would like to depreciate over a 5-year lifetime. We propose to do this via one of two ways:

1 Double declining balance method, where the depreciation for the year is $2/n$ times the book value at the beginning of the year ($n =$ number of years over which item is to be depreciated).

2 Straight line method, where the depreciation is $1/n$ times the original value of the equipment.

Write a computer program to calculate the depreciation by each of these methods and print a table, similar to the following:

Year	Double-Declining Balance Depreciation	Beginning Book Value	Straight-Line Depreciation	Beginning Book Value
1	$400.00	$1000.00	$200.00	$1000.00
2	$240.00	$ 600.00	$200.00	$ 800.00
3	$144.00	$ 360.00	$200.00	$ 600.00
4	$ 86.40	$ 216.00	$200.00	$ 400.00
5	$ 51.84	$ 129.60	$200.00	$ 200.00

7-16 As can be seen from the table accompanying the previous problem, the double-declining balance depreciates equipment at a faster initial rate than does the straight line method ($400 vs $200, or twice as fast). However, this method will never reduce the book value to zero, since the depreciation is always a fraction of the present book value. This can be circumvented by using the double-declining balance method during the initial years, and switching to the straight line method at a later date. In fact, the switch should be made whenever the depreciation via the straight line method would exceed that from the double-declining balance method.

Write a program that depreciates a given amount over a given number of years (both read as inputs) via the above method. The output should appear as follows for depreciating $1000 over a five year period:

Year	Depreciation	Beginning Book Value
1	$400.00	$1000.00
2	$240.00	$ 800.00
3	$144.00	$ 360.00
4*	$108.00	$ 216.00
5	$108.00	$ 108.00

*Switched to straight-line method.

7-17 Consider writing a program to print bank statements. The various accounts are stacked one following another, separated by blank cards. The first card for each account contains the customer's name in columns 1–20, the second line of his address in columns 21–40, the third line in columns 41–60, his account number in columns 61–65, and the balance at the beginning of the month in columns 66–75. Each succeeding card contains a transaction, the date being in columns 1–6 (i.e., day in columns 1–2, month in 3–4, and year in 5–6); column 8 containing an asterisk if the transaction is a deposit, a blank if a check; and the amount of the transaction in columns 11–20 (format f10.2).

Write a program to process these cards and print a statement as shown in the accompanying figure. Note that if a check and a deposit are made on the same day, they are written on the same line.

The service charge is computed as follows:

1 No charge if the minimum balance is $400.00 or more.

2 A charge of 60¢ plus 4¢ per check less 20¢ per $100.00 of the minimum balance when under $400.00.

```
                    THE PHANTOM
                    2022 DUNGEON WAY
                    OUT OF THIS WORLD

        ACCOUNT NUMBER  1107

            DATA      WITHDRAWAL        DEPOSIT           BALANCE
        ••••••••••••••••••••••••••••••••••••••••••••••••••••••••••••
                    •               •                •      412.41
            3/ 7/44 •      7.07     •                •      405.34
            3/ 9/44 •     12.41     •                •      392.93
            3/ 9/44 •     45.12     •                •      347.81
            3/15/44 •     57.21     •                •      290.60
            3/19/44 •    107.49     •        32.52   •      215.63
            3/22/44 •               •        12.12   •      227.75
            3/22/44 •               •        47.19   •      274.94
            3/27/44 •     52.12     •                •      222.82
            4/ 5/44 •               •       202.17   •      424.99
                    •      0.57SC   •                •      424.42
```

Exercise 7-17

7-18 In some cases it would be desirable for a program to accept an input such as temperature in either degrees Fahrenheit or degrees centigrade. Suppose the temperature is punched with a decimal point in columns 1–10, and an f or c is punched in column 12 to indicate Fahrenheit or centigrade. Prepare a program to read this card, make any necessary conversions, and print the temperature (appropriately labeled deg f and deg c) in both units. If the entry in column 12 is neither f nor c, print the words errøneøus input. The program should be able to read as many data cards as provided. Degrees f and degrees c are related as follows:

$$°C \ = \ \frac{5}{9}\,(°F \ - \ 32)$$

Double-space the output. Use as input 39°C, 48°F, 137°C, and 122°F.

7-19 The table in the accompanying figure gives the density (specific gravity) of NaOH solutions at various concentrations and temperatures. Write a program that reads the entries in this table from data cards and prints the table as shown.

TEMPERATURE, DEG F

		50	86	122	176	212
	*	*	*	*	*	*
2	*	1.023	1.018	1.010	0.993	0.980
6	*	1.068	1.061	1.052	1.035	1.022
PER 10	*	1.113	1.104	1.094	1.077	1.064
CENT 14	*	1.158	1.148	1.137	1.120	1.107
NAOH 18	*	1.202	1.192	1.181	1.162	1.149
22	*	1.247	1.235	1.224	1.205	1.191

(SOURCE - INT. CRIT. TABLES, VOL. III, PAGE 79)

Exercise 7-19

†**7-20** Same as the previous problem except that the table is entered via a DATA statement.

7-21 Prepare a program to evaluate the factorials of the numbers 1 through 12. The output should be in columnar fashion, the columns labeled NUMBER and FACTØRIAL (see Exercise 5-6 for definition of factorial).

7-22 The binomial coefficients $\binom{n}{j}$ are given by the following expression:

$$\binom{n}{j} = \frac{n!}{j!(n-j)!}, \qquad j = 0, 1, \ldots, n$$

Prepare a program to read a value for n (use $n = 8$ for this case), compute the binomial coefficients, and print the results as in the illustration. Assume n is always greater than 1. The cautious programmer will note that the first term is 1, and each succeeding term is simply $(n - j + 1)/j$, $j = 1, 2, \ldots, n$, times the preceding term. Programming in this manner avoids overflows which may occur if the factorials are evaluated directly. (This is not the case for $n = 8$, and such programming may be used if desired.)

THE BINCMIAL COEFFICIENTS FOR N =   8

N	J	COEFFICIENT
8	0	1
8	1	8
8	2	28
8	3	56
8	4	70
8	5	56
8	6	28
8	7	8
8	8	1

Exercise 7-22

†**7-23** Consider the following experiment:

    a. Fill a vessel of known size and weight with a porous medium, e.g., sand, and weigh.

    b. Fill all voids with water, and weigh again.

    The difference between the weights gives the weight of water, which can be divided by its density (62.4 lb/ft³) to give the volume of water or void volume. The void fraction is the void volume divided by the total volume. The true density is the empty weight minus the weight of the container, divided by the total volume minus the void volume.

    The input to the program is the two weights (in pounds). The container is cylindrical, 0.333 ft in diameter and 0.75 ft in height, weighing 1.04 lb. Enter these and the density of water via a DATA statement. The output should appear as shown.

```
DIMENSIONS OF CONTAINER -
        DIAMETER        0.3330 FT
        HEIGHT          0.7500 FT
        WEIGHT          1.0400 LB


WEIGHT WITHOUT WATER        7.1200

WEIGHT WITH WATER           8.3000

VOID FRACTION           0.2895

DENSITY OF MATERIAL         131.0093 LB/CU FT
```
                  Exercise 7-23

7-24 The roots of the equation $ax^2 + bx + c = 0$ are given by the quadratic formula:

$$r_{1,2} = \frac{-b \pm \sqrt{b^2 - 4ac}}{2a}$$

Note that the roots may be real or complex.

    Prepare a program that reads values of a, b, and c, determines if the roots are real or complex, and calculates their values. The program should accept as many data cards as provided, and the output for the two possible cases should be arranged as shown.

    Determine the roots of the following equations:

$2X^2 - 7X + 9 = 0$
$3X^2 + X + 1 = 0$
$2X^2 - 3X - 7 = 0$
$3X^2 + 1.5X + 0.4 = 0$

```
COEFFICIENTS
        A                 2.00000
        B                -7.00000
        C                 9.00000


    ROOTS ARE COMPLEX
        REAL PART              1.7500
        IMAGINARY PART         1.1990



COEFFICIENTS
        A                 3.00000
        B                 1.00000
        C                 1.00000


    ROOTS ARE COMPLEX
        REAL PART             -0.1667
        IMAGINARY PART         0.5528


COEFFICIENTS
        A                 2.00000
        B                -3.00000
        C                -7.00000


    ROOTS ARE REAL
        ROOT 1                 2.76556
        ROOT 2                -1.26556



COEFFICIENTS
        A                 3.00000
        B                 1.50000
        C                 0.40000


    ROOTS ARE COMPLEX
        REAL PART             -0.2500
        IMAGINARY PART         0.2661
```

Exercise 7-24

7-25 In elementary physics courses, the following experiment is often run in the laboratory:

a. An object is weighed in the atmosphere.

b. The same object is weighed while suspended under water.

The objective is to calculate the specific gravity or density of the material in the object. Of course, this only works for objects whose specific gravity is greater than one.

The calculations are to simply, first, subtract the weight in water from the weight in air to obtain weight of displaced water. Then divide by the density of water (1.0 gm/cc) to obtain the volume of the object. The normal weight of the object divided by its volume is its density (gm/cc) or specific gravity.

Prepare a program to read the respective weights, perform the calculations, and print the results in a fashion similar to that shown.

```
DENSITY DETERMINATION

WEIGHT IN AIR          147.2000

WEIGHT SUBMERGED          134.7000

DENSITY          11.7760 GMS/CC
```

Exercise 7-25

7-26 Modify Exercise 6-15 to make the questions true-false. A T will be entered for questions answered "true," an F for questions answered "false," and a blank is entered for unanswered questions.

†7-27 Make the above modification to Exercise 6-16.

7-28 Refer to Exercise 6-15. If the entry for any question is anything other than a T, an F, or a blank, a keypunch error is assumed to have been made. Print the appropriate student number, print the answers to all 20 questions, and indicate which question corresponds to the invalid entry. Do not compute a grade for that student.

†7-29 Write a program that reads a sentence that contains a maximum of 80 characters (including the period at the end) and counts the total number of characters (excluding blanks and commas) in the sentence. The sentence should be punched on a single card, and the characters should be read into an array as one character per element. Only alphabetic characters, blanks, and commas will appear in the sentence. A comma is always followed by a blank.

```
ORIGINAL SENTENCE
    AN IMPORTANT CHARACTERISTIC OF DIGITAL COMPUTERS IS THEIR INCREDIBLE SPEED,
```

CHAR.	OCCURRENCES		CHAR.	OCCURRENCES
A	5		N	3
B	1		O	3
C	5		P	1
D	3		Q	
E	7		R	6
F	1		S	4
G	1		T	7
H	2		U	1
I	3		V	
J			W	
K			X	
L	2		Y	
M	2		Z	

Exercise 7-29

7-30 Same as Exercise 7-29, except count the number of occurrences of the letter E in the sentence.

7-31 Same as Exercise 7-29, except count the number of occurrences of each letter of the alphabet within the sentence. The output should appear as in the accompanying figure.

7-32 Same as Exercise 7-29, except count the number of occurrences of words containing three letters or less.

7-33 Same as Exercise 7-32, except compute the average length of the words in the sentence. Print the answer to two decimal places.

†7-34 Instead of processing a single sentence, suppose we process a paragraph. The paragraph will be punched on a maximum of 10 cards as illustrated in the accompanying figure. A blank character always follows the decimal point, and no hyphenated words will be used. For this exercise, the paragraph should be read into a single array of 800 elements, one character to each element. Compute the average number of words in the sentences in the paragraph and print the answer to two decimal places.

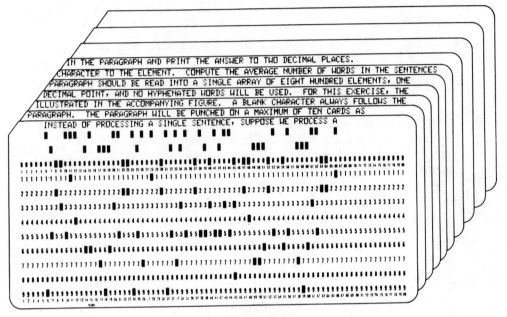

Exercise 7-34

7-35 Same as Exercise 7-34, except print the number of words in each sentence and the average number of characters per word for each sentence.

7-36 Same as Exercise 7-34, except print the distribution of the number of characters in each word as shown in the accompanying figure. Words containing over twelve characters can be considered as containing twelve characters.

WCRD LENGTH DISTRIBUTION

CHS./WCRD	OCCURRENCES
1	5
2	16
3	15
4	6
5	8
6	7
7	13
8	3
9	7
10	2
11	1
12 CR MORE	1

Exercise 7-36

†**7-37** Same as Exercise 7-34, except process the cards one at a time: That is, the array should be defined as containing only 80 characters. A card is read into this area, the computations performed, and then the next card is read into this same area.

7-38 Same as Exercise 7-35, but with the modification suggested in Exercise 7-37.

7-39 Same as Exercise 7-36, but with the modification suggested in Exercise 7-37.

7-40 Same as Exercise 7-37, except that the last word on the card may be hyphenated (using the minus sign) and split onto two cards.

7-41 Same as Exercise 7-38, except that the last word on the card may be hyphenated and split onto two cards.

7-42 Same as Exercise 7-39, except that the last word on the card may be hyphenated and split onto two cards.

†**7-43** Write a FORTRAN program to read a number in integer format from any position on a card *without* using format-free input-output. The card should be read under A format, and the characters stored in an array, one character per element. The number may contain as many digits as desired, and may be preceded by a minus sign, by a plus sign, or no sign at all. The number will not contain any embedded blanks. This number is to be stored in a single integer variable. The program should print the final answer to verify correctness.

7-44 Same as Exercise 7-43, except that a number in real format should be read from any position on the card. The number may contain only the decimal digits, a sign (optional), and a decimal point. The following examples should be acceptable: 127.23, +12.72, −1200., +.02007, and .00030. The number should be stored in a real variable and printed.

7-45 Same as Exercise 7-43, except that the number should be read in exponential format. The number may contain only the decimal digits, an optional sign for the exponent, and a decimal point (in the fraction only). The number should be stored in a real variable and printed.

7-46 A particular hospital maintains on each blood donor a record as follows:

	Cølumn
Dønør's name	1–30
Dønør's age	31–32
Bløød type	33–34

The blood type is either A, B, AB, or ø, and is entered alphabetically. Determine the number of donors for blood of each type. The total number of cards is not known beforehand.

†**7-47** You are not supposed to eat oysters in any month without an *R* in its name. For example, you should not eat oysters in June; but you may eat them in November. Write a program to read a card containing the name of a month

beginning in column 1 and print whether or not you may eàt oysters in that month.

7-48 Write a program to read today's date into variables IDAY, IMØNTH, and IYEAR, then change this date to tomorrow's date, and write the result. The program should work for any day of the year. Using a DATA statement, initialize array month with the number of days in each month. You need not be concerned with leap years.

7-49 Write a FORTRAN program to read a name left justified in the first 10 columns of a card and determine if this name is an acceptable variable name in FORTRAN, and if so, determine whether it is integer or real.

7-50 Refer to Exercise 6-24. Instead of designating the seats on each row by numbers 1–6, suppose they are designated A–F. A passenger might then request seat 37F. Write the necessary statements to read this entry, and determine if this seat is available.

7-51 Refer to Exercise 6-28. The output should designate the three seats by the row and letter designation as described in the previous exercise.

†7-52 Modify Exercise 4-26 by using alphabetic codes for sex and standing, specifically, the following:

    M—Male

     F—Female

    FR—Freshman

    SO—Sophomore

    JR—Junior

    SR—Senior

    GR—Graduate

7-53 Make the above modification to Exercise 4-29.

7-54 Make the above modification to Exercise 5-45.

7-55 Make the above modification to Exercise 6-17.

7-56 Write a program to read a person's full name from a card as follows:

	Cølumns
Last name	1–20
First name	21–30
Middle name	31–40

The program should print initials for both given names. For example, Able Baker Charlie should be printed as A. B. Charlie.

†7-57 Suppose you are working in the Registrar's office at IØU. From the schedule of classes booklet and the student schedule requests, the following could be defined:

DEPT—four-character abbreviation for the department offering the course.

COURSE—four-digit course number

SECT—number of the section

REQ—number of requests for this section

MAX—maximum enrollment permitted in this section

For each section of each course, a card containing these five values is prepared. The entries are ordered only in so far as all sections of the same course appear consecutively and all courses offered by one department also appear consecutively. The total number of sections offered is 1402. Write a program to calculate the average percentage of vacant seats in each course. Assume that the data is available in card image form on unit 9, a disk file.

7-58 Refer to the above exercise. Suppose you have read the entries on all of the cards into arrays. Then read a card containing the departmental abbreviation, course number, and section number of a section to be deleted from the list. Write the program to locate this entry, and delete it by advancing all remaining entries in the arrays. Be sure to consider the case where the section to be deleted is not in the arrays. The program should process as many cards as available, and should write the final arrays on unit 10 in the same format as on unit 9.

7-59 Refer to Exercise 7-57. Write a program to tally the number of sections with 50 or less requests, 51–100 requests, 101–150 requests, 151–200 requests, and more than 200 requests.

7-60 Refer to Exercise 7-57. Assume that the course numbers are four-digit numbers, being assigned as follows:

0000–0999	remedial
1000–1999	Freshman
2000–2999	Sophomore
3000–3999	Junior
4000–4999	Senior
5000–5999	Graduate

Write a program to count the number of *courses* (not sections) offered in these various categories.

7-61 Refer to Exercise 7-57. Write a program to count and print the number of *courses* offered by each department.

7-62 Refer to Exercise 7-57. You are to write a program to process add requests. Cards are punched containing the department, course number, and section number, and student ID number of the student requesting that particular section. The program should take the following action:

a. If space is available, increase the number of requests by 1.

b. If no space is available, print the student's ID number, the course requested, and the sections in which space is available.

Upon completion, write the arrays on unit 10.

7-63 Revise the above exercise assuming that the data is available on a direct access file. Do not read the data into arrays in memory.

7-64 Refer to Exercise 7-57. From this data, a disk file (on unit 15) is to be prepared for which each entry in the file contains the following information:

a. Department offering course.

b. Course number.

c. Total requests for all sections of this course.

d. Total maximum enrollment for all sections.

Write the necessary program.

7-65 Assume that the disk file described in the previous exercise has been created successfully. Write a program that will list the courses for which the number of requests exceeds the maximum number of seats.

FUNCTIONS AND SUBROUTINES

In this chapter we will introduce those features of FORTRAN that are applicable only to functions and subroutines or are generally used only with functions and subroutines. We begin with a fairly general discussion of the concept of a subprogram and the use of arguments. This is followed by a detailed description of the FORTRAN features of statement function, function subprogram, and subroutine. The CØMMØN declaration is then introduced, followed by the EQUIVALENCE declaration. The chapter concludes with a discussion of less commonly used features, including adjustable dimensions, BLØCK DATA, EXTERNAL, and multiple ENTRY and RETURN.

8-1. CONCEPT OF A FUNCTION, A SUBPROGRAM, AND A SUBROUTINE

In Section 2-5, we introduced several functions (for example the square root function, SQRT) available in FORTRAN. In essence, these are pre-programmed or "canned" routines in the computing system available to anyone who writes a FORTRAN program. This frees the programmer from having to write his own routine, and functions such as SQRT are written for widespread use, are completely debugged, programmed in an extremely efficient manner, and always produce the correct answer.

218

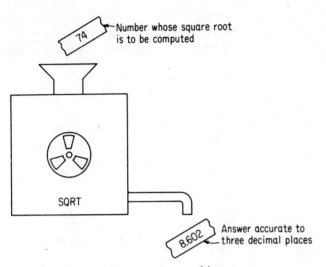

Figure 8-1. Number-processing machine.

The concept of a function is one of unambiguous designation. For any positive value of x, SQRT(x) designates another specific value which can be computed by the library routine. By a mechanism that we shall cover in more detail in a later section, the numerical value of x, the *argument*, is communicated to this library routine, and the value computed by this routine is communicated back, or *returned*, to the point in the program where SQRT appeared.

The use of the SQRT routine is analogous to the use of the "number-processing machine" illustrated in Figure 8-1. The number whose square root is to be taken is fed to the machine, which in turn produces the desired square root. As long as the user is confident that the machine produces the correct answer in an efficient manner, there is little incentive short of plain curiosity to ascertain how the machine works.

In FORTRAN, a programmer may define his own functions in one of two ways. One is the statement function feature which, as we shall see shortly, has its limitations in that the entire function must be defined in a single statement. This statement is defined in, and is a part of, the program in which it appears.

The second approach to defining a function is to prepare a function subprogram. In FORTRAN, a subprogram is very similar to the programs, called main programs, that we have been preparing except that they are executed only when *called* by another program. Subprograms have their own structure, their own specification statements (DIMENSIØN, INTEGER, REAL, etc.) and their own END statement. The compiler treats the subprogram as a separate entity, and the subprogram is compiled separately from the main program and other subprograms.

Communication among the subprogram, the main program and other subprograms is restricted to that which the programmer specifies in terms of arguments (in a later section we shall see that CØMMØN can play a role). Suppose variable K is used in both the main program and in a subprogram. The compiler will always reserve a storage location for K in the main program. If K does not appear in the argument list of the subprogram, the compiler will also reserve a storage location for K in the subprogram.

Since these two storage locations are not the same, there is absolutely no connection between variable K in the main program and variable K in the subprogram.

Being compiled separately from the main program, a transfer statement in the subprogram such as

GØ TØ 56

will always transfer control to statement 56 in the subprogram even though there may be a statement 56 in the main program. Similarly, suppose the following specification statement appears in the main program:

DIMENSIØN A(27)

This statement defines A as an array of 27 elements in the main program but not in the subprogram. In the subprogram, A may be used as a simple variable or may be specified in any manner desired, for example,

INTEGER A(7,9)

Being compiled separately, all specification statements applicable to the subprogram must appear therein.

FORTRAN permits two types of subprograms: a function subprogram and a subroutine. The distinction is basically that the subroutine is called by a special statement (the CALL statement), whereas the function is called by its use within an expression. In addition, the function returns a value, the functional value, that is used in the expression in which the function call appears. For example, in the statement

Y = A + B * SQRT(G)

the functional value ($\sqrt{G}$) is used in computing the value to be assigned to Y. Since subroutines do not appear in expressions, there is no function value.

The programmer benefits from the use of functions and subroutines. Since function subprograms and subroutines are separate programs, they can be written, tested, and debugged separately from the remainder of the program. This enables the programmer to prepare several components of the total program, debug them separately and assemble them into the total program. Several programmers may be assigned portions of large programs to prepare and debug simultaneously.

Another use of functions or subroutines occurs when the same computation is required at different points in the same program. In this case a single routine can be made a function or subroutine, rather than coded at each point in the program where it is needed.

8-2. INTRODUCTION TO FORTRAN FUNCTION AND SUBPROGRAM FEATURES

In this section, an example illustrates the features of statement function, function subprogram, and subroutine. In later sections, we shall examine each of these in detail and present more examples of their use.

```
1           JTME(I,J,K)=I*100+J+1200*K
2           READ(5,20) JHOUR,JMIN,JAMPM
3     20    FORMAT(3I5)
4           MTIME=JTME(JHOUR,JMIN,JAMPM)
5           WRITE(6,30)MTIME
6     30    FORMAT(' TIME IS',I5)
7           STOP
8           END
```

(a) Program

```
4     27     1
```

(b) Input data

```
TIME IS 1627
```

(c) Output data

Figure 8-2. Example of a statement function.

The example used in this section consists of the conversion of civilian time to military time. We shall use the following variables:

JHØUR	Hour in civilian time
JMIN	Minutes in civilian time
JAMPM	Morning-afternoon designator for civilian time (0 = AM; 1 = PM)
MTIME	Military time

Military time is expressed on a 24 hour basis. For example, 8:45 AM in civilian time is 0845 military time; 4:27 PM is 1627. In preparing our programs, we shall make the convenient assumption that JHOUR will never equal 12.

The FORTRAN program in Figure 8-2 illustrates the use of a statement function to convert from civilian time to military time. The first statement in this program defines the statement function JTME. This function is then called from the fourth line. When the function is executed, the value of variable JHØUR is used for I in the function, JMIN for J, and JAMPM for K.

The use of a function subprogram to convert from military to civilian time is illustrated in Figure 8-3. The first statement in the function subprogram is the FUNCTIØN statement (line 8), which should not be confused with the statement function feature described in the previous paragraph. The FUNCTIØN statement defines the name of the function and designates the arguments. This function is called in line 3 in the same manner as the statement function was called in Figure 8-2. In the function JTME in Figure 8-3, the values of JHØUR, JMIN, and JAMPM are communicated to the subprogram by the arguments. The value of military time assigned to variable MTIME in line 3 is the value of variable JTME in the subprogram at the time the RETURN statement is executed. The value returned to the calling program is the value of the variable in the subprogram whose name is identical to the name of the function. In all function subprograms, a value must be returned to the main program in this manner.

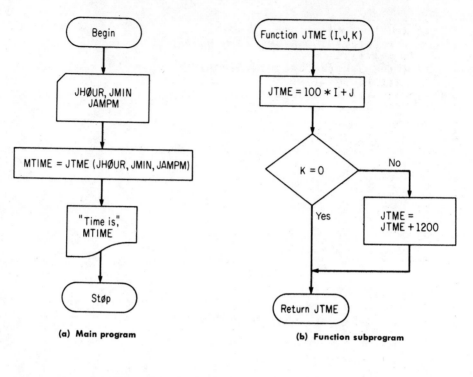

(a) Main program

(b) Function subprogram

```
 1           READ(5,20)JHOUR,JMIN,JAMPM
 2      20   FORMAT(3I5)
 3           MTIME=JTME(JHOUR,JMIN,JAMPM)
 4           WRITE(6,30)MTIME
 5      30   FORMAT(' TIME IS',I5)
 6           STOP
 7           END

 8           FUNCTION JTME(I,J,K)
 9           JTME=100*I+J
10           IF(K)20,20,30
11      30   JTME=JTME+1200
12      20   RETURN
13           END
```

(c) Program

```
4    27    1
```

(d) Input data

```
TIME IS 1627
```

(e) Output data

Figure 8-3. Example of a function subprogram.

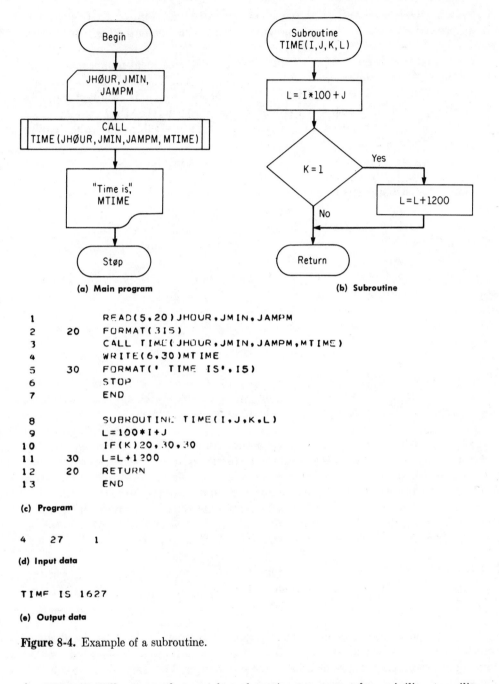

(a) **Main program**   (b) **Subroutine**

```
1            READ(5,20)JHOUR,JMIN,JAMPM
2      20    FORMAT(3I5)
3            CALL TIME(JHOUR,JMIN,JAMPM,MTIME)
4            WRITE(6,30)MTIME
5      30    FORMAT(' TIME IS',I5)
6            STOP
7            END

8            SUBROUTINE TIME(I,J,K,L)
9            L=100*I+J
10           IF(K)20,30,30
11     30    L=L+1200
12     20    RETURN
13           END
```

(c) **Program**

```
4     27     1
```

(d) **Input data**

```
TIME IS 1627
```

(e) **Output data**

Figure 8-4. Example of a subroutine.

Figure 8-4 illustrates the use of a subroutine to convert from civilian to military time. The first statement in the subroutine is the SUBRØUTINE statement which defines the name of the subroutine and designates the arguments. The subroutine is called by the CALL statement in line 3 of the main program. In this case, communication is entirely via the arguments. Values used for variables I, J, and K in the subroutine are the values of variables JHØUR, JMIN, and JAMPM in the main program. The value of MTIME printed in line 4 of the main program is the value computed for L in the subroutine.

Note that in programs in both Figures 8-3 and 8-4, statement numbers 20 and 30 appear both in the main program and in the subprogram. This leads to no confusion whatsoever. The only way to transfer to a function subprogram is by use of the function in an expression. The only way to transfer to a subroutine is by the CALL statement. The only way to transfer from a function subprogram or a subroutine to the calling program is by the RETURN statement.

8-3. ROLE OF ARGUMENTS

In each of the examples in the previous section, arguments are used to communicate information between the main program and the function or subroutine. In this section we examine this aspect in more detail.

Values of variables used as arguments can be communicated to and from subprograms in one of two ways

1 Call by address

2 Call by value

We shall examine each of these using the function subprogram in Figure 8-3 and the subroutine in Figure 8-4 as the basis for our discussion. We shall first explain these two approaches, and then discuss their advantages and disadvantages.

Call by Value. In this approach, the actual numerical value is transferred from the storage location in the main program to a storage location in the subprogram. For the function subprogram in Figure 8-3, storage locations are reserved in the main program for variables JHØUR, JMIN, and JAMPM, and separate storage locations are reserved for variables I, J, and K in the subprogram. At the time the function is called, the current values stored in JHØUR, JMIN, and JAMPM are transfered to the storage locations for I, J, and K. However, upon execution of the RETURN statement, the reverse transfer of values is *not* made. Therefore, if the value of variable I, J, or K is changed in the subprogram, this change is not reflected in the corresponding variable in the main program. Therefore, if call by value is used for the subroutine in Figure 8-4, the value of L is not available in the main program.

Call by Address. In this approach, the address of each of the variables used as arguments in the calling statement is transferred to the subprogram and used for the respective variables in the argument list in the subprogram. For example, in the subroutine in Figure 8-4, the address of the storage location for JHØUR is transferred to the subprogram for use as the address for variable I. The other arguments are treated similarly. Therefore, if the value of variable I is changed in the subprogram, the value of variable JHØUR changes in the main program, since its address is being used for variable I in the subprogram. The subroutine in Figure 8-4 functions properly only if call by address is used.

```
FUNCTION CRF(N,J)
IF(J.EQ.1) N=N/12
K=1.08**N
CRF=0.08*K/(K-1.)
RETURN
END
```

Figure 8-5. Function subprogram to compute capital recovery factor.

Example. As an example of the difference between call by address and call by value, suppose we have written the function subprogram in Figure 8-5 that computes the capital recovery factor for 8% interest:

$$c = .08 * (1.08) ** \text{N}/((1.08) ** \text{N} - 1.)$$

where N is in years. We have written our function so that it accepts N in either months or years. The scale is designated by the second argument J(0 = years; 1 = months). Suppose we use the following statement to call CRF:

$$c = \text{CRF (HOLD,1)}$$

Since the value of the second argument is 1, the value of N is in months. Therefore, when the subprogram is executed, a new value is computed for N in the second statement in the subprogram.

If call by value is used, a separate location is reserved for N in the subprogram, and changing its value in the subprogram in no way changes the value of HOLD in the calling program.

However, if call by address is used, the address of HOLD in the calling program is used as the address for N in the subprogram, and changes to N in the subprogram are changes to HOLD in the main program. In effect, variable N is a dummy: No storage location is reserved for it. After execution of the function subprogram in Figure 8-5, the value of HOLD in the main program is changed from months to years.

Advantages and Disadvantages. Call by address and call by value have the advantages and disadvantages listed:

1 Call by address is meaningless when expressions are used as arguments in the main program. For example, suppose the following statement is used for the function CRF in in Figure 8-5:

$$c = \text{CRF(HOLD} - 2,0)$$

Since the first argument is not a variable, no storage location is reserved in the calling program for this argument in this form. Call by value is best for this argument.

2 Use of call by address is not appropriate when a constant is used as an argument. For example, consider the statement

$$c = \text{CRF(12,1)}$$

This statement evaluates the capital recovery for one year. If call by address is used, the address of the storage location for the constant 12 in the main program is used for variable N in the subprogram. The second statement in the subprogram in Figure 8-5 changes the value from 12 to 1. Since the address for the constant 12 in the main program is used for N, the constant 12 is now 1. If 12 appears in any subsequent statement in the main program, 1 is used instead: The results will be disastrous. Use of call by value avoids this problem.

3   Call by value cannot be used for arguments such as MTIME in the subroutine in Figure 8-4 unless an extra step is taken: transferring values from the locations in the subprogram to the corresponding locations in the main program. However, with the addition of this extra step, call by value has the same disadvantages as call by address in the previous two situations.

4   Call by address is more efficient for arrays. Suppose an entire array A, containing 100 elements is to be available to the subprogram. If call by value is used, 100 storage locations must be reserved in the subprogram in *addition* to the 100 storage locations reserved for A in the calling program. Furthermore, the values of each of the 100 elements must be copied from the storage locations in the calling program to the corresponding storage locations in the subprogram. When call by address is used, *only* the address of the first storage location in the array must be transferred to the subprogram, making call by address attractive for arrays.

Summary. Unfortunately, the choice between call by address and call by value varies from system to system: This prevents us from being explicit here. The choice between call by address and call by value can be summarized as follows:

1   All systems use call by address for arrays.

2   Call by address is used for all arguments of subroutines. Some systems do not accept expressions as arguments in subroutine call statements. In other systems, the compiler creates a storage location for the result of the expressions, and transfers this value to the subprogram. This makes the statement

CALL SUB(X + 2.,Y,Z)

appear to be compiled as

XA = X + 2.
CALL SUB(XA,Y,Z)

If the compiler does not accept expressions as arguments of subroutines, the programmer must insert the extra statement. Better compilers insert these steps when constants are used as arguments, thereby avoidung the pitfall outlined in step 2, above. Unfortunately, not all compilers do this, so many experienced programmers avoid the use of constants as arguments.

3   Some systems use call by address when simple variables are used as arguments of function subprograms; others use call by value. The difference is that if the value of a variable used as an argument in the subprogram is changed within the subprogram, these changes are *not* reflected in the corresponding variable in the calling program when call by value is used, but *are* reflected when call by address is used. In this manual, we assume that call by address is used; but on this point programmers should consult manuals specific to their system.

8-4. THE STATEMENT FUNCTION

Rules regarding the statement function are as follows:

1 The statement function must be defined by a single statement, although the continuation feature can be used as for other statements.

2 The statement function is itself a non-executable statement in that it only defines the function: It is not executed until it is called.

3 The statement function must appear prior to any executable statements in the program.

4 The name of the statement function must conform to the general rules of the naming of variables. That is, the name must consist of from one to six characters, the first of which must be a letter. If the result of the functional evaluation is an integer, the name must begin with one of the letters I through N. For example, the name of the statement function

$$\text{JTME}(\text{I},\text{J},\text{K}) = \text{I} * 100 + \text{J} + 1200 * \text{K}$$

in Figure 8-2 begins with the letter J, which defines the result as an integer. Alternatively, the name can be declared integer in the INTEGER statement as illustrated by the following example:

INTEGER TIME
$$\text{TIME}(\text{I},\text{J},\text{K}) = \text{I} * 100 + \text{J} + \text{K} * 1200$$

Real functions are treated analogously.

5 A statement function must have at least one argument. If it contains more than one argument, arguments are separated by commas.

6 The statement function may include library functions, function subprograms, or other previously defines statement functions.

7 The arguments of the statement function are dummies in that no storage locations are reserved. In fact, variables used as arguments may be subsequently used as variables elsewhere within the program.

8 The statement function may include variables other than those used as arguments. For example, consider the function

$$\text{RES}(\text{T}) = \text{A} + \text{T} * (\text{B} + \text{C} * \text{T})$$

Variable T is a dummy, but variables A, B, and C are not. When this function is called, the current values of variables A, B, and C are used in computing the function.

One example of the use of a statement function is in the following program. Suppose we would like to create a table of values for the function

$$f(X) = \frac{(X + 4.7)^2}{\sqrt{X + X^2 + 1}}$$

```
 1              F(X)=(X+4.7)**2/(SQRT(X)+X**2+1.)
 2              WRITE(6,1)
 3        1     FORMAT(3X,3('X',5X,'F(X)',6X))
 4              DO21=2,20,2
 5              X=I-2
 6              FX=F(X)
 7              Y=X+20.
 8              FY=F(Y)
 9              Z=X+40.
10              FZ=F(Z)
11        2     WRITE(6,3)X,FX,Y,FY,Z,FZ
12        3     FORMAT(1X,3(F4.0,F10.4,2X))
13              STOP
14              END
```

(a) Program

X	F(X)	X	F(X)	X	F(X)
0.	22.0900	20.	1.5046	40.	1.2431
2.	6.9985	22.	1.4558	42.	1.2311
4.	3.9837	24.	1.4155	44.	1.2202
6.	2.9022	26.	1.3817	46.	1.2103
8.	2.3779	28.	1.3530	48.	1.2013
10.	2.0746	30.	1.3283	50.	1.1930
12.	1.8785	32.	1.3068	52.	1.1853
14.	1.7420	34.	1.2860	54.	1.1783
16.	1.6417	36.	1.2713	56.	1.1717
18.	1.5651	38.	1.2564	58.	1.1656

(b) Output data

Figure 8-6. Use of a statement function.

for values of X between zero and fifty-eight in increments of two. The program in Figure 8-6 prints this table in three columns. The statement function is defined in the first line of the program, and it is then called from lines 6, 8, and 10.

8-5. THE FUNCTION SUBPROGRAM

Rules regarding the use of the function subprogram are as follows:

1 The first statement in the function subprogram must be a FUNCTION statement. As illustrated in Figure 8-3, this statement consists of the word FUNCTION followed by the name of the function subprogram followed by the arguments enclosed in parentheses and separated by commas.

2 The function subprogram must have at least one argument.

3 The function subprogram name conforms to the normal rules for the naming of variables. That is, the name consists of from one to six characters, the first of which must be a letter. If the value associated with the function subprogram is integer, the name must begin with one of the letters I through N. If real, the name must begin with any other letter. The use of type declarations to override this convention is illustrated in a subsequent example.

4 The value associated with the function subprogram and used in evaluating the expression in which the function itself appears is the value of the variable in the function

```
1              READ(5,1)N1,N2
2        1     FORMAT(2I5)
3              N=NGCD(N1,N2)
4              WRITE(6,2)N1,N2,N
5        2     FORMAT(' GCD OF',I5,' AND',I5,' IS',I5)
6              STOP
7              END

8              FUNCTION NGCD(N,M)
9              K=N
10             IF(M,LT,K)K=M
11             NGCD=1
12             DO1J=2,K
13             IF((N/J)*J,NE,N)GOTO1
14             IF((M/J)*J,NE,M)GOTO1
15             NGCD=J
16       1     CONTINUE
17             RETURN
18             END
```
(a) **Program**

```
1528 5748
```
(b) **Input data**

```
GCD OF 1528 AND 5748 IS     4
```
(c) **Output data**

Figure 8-7. Use of a function subprogram to determine the greatest common divisor.

```
1              READ(5,1)A,B,TAX
2        1     FORMAT(3F10.0)
3              X=CALC(A,B,TAX,Y)
4              WRITE(6,2)A,B,TAX,X,Y
5        2     FORMAT(1X,3F10.2/1X,2F10.2)
6              STOP
7              END

8              FUNCTION CALC(A,B,C,Y)
9              CALC=A+B-C
10             Z=CALC/30.
11             Y=Z*365.
12             RETURN
13             END
```
(a) **Program**

```
1300.       241.        197.
```
(b) **Input data**

```
1300.00       241.00      197.00
1344.00    16351.99
```
(c) **Output data**

Figure 8-8. Use of a function subprogram.

```
        $JOB             1105.50003
1               DIMENSION Y(12)
2               DATA Y/1.7,1.9,2.2,2.4,3.1,4.2,5.8,7.2,10.5,14.7,19.2,26.5/
3               READ(5.1)X
4       1       FORMAT(F5.0)
5               YX=TER(X,Y)
6               WRITE(6,2)X,YX
7       2       FORMAT(' X =',F8.2,5X,'Y =',F6.2)
8               STOP
9               END

10              FUNCTION TER(X,Y)
11              DIMENSION Y(12)
12              IF(X.LT.45.)GOTO1
13              IF(X.GT.100.) GOTO2
14              F=(X-40.)/5.
15              J=F
16              F=F-FLOAT(J)
17              TER=Y(J)+F*(Y(J+1)-Y(J))
18              RETURN
19      1       WRITE(6,3)X
20      3       FORMAT(' X =',F10.2,' IS BELOW 45')
21              STOP
22      2       WRITE(6,4)X
23      4       FORMAT(' X =',F10.2,' EXCEEDS 100')
24              STOP
25              END
                (a) Program


                67.4
                (b) Input data


                X =    67.40      Y =   3.63
                (c) Output data
```

Figure 8-9. Use of a function subprogram to interpolate.

subprogram that is identical to the name of the function itself. Note the use of variable JTME in function JTME in Figure 8-3.

5   A function subprogram must have at least one RETURN statement. It may have more than one, and it may also include one or more STOP statements.

6   Array names may be used as arguments in the FUNCTION statement, but must not be written with subscripts.

7   The function subprogram may call library functions, other function subprograms, or subroutines.

8   Expressions may be used as arguments of the function subprogram in the calling program.

As an example of a function subprogram, suppose we prepare a subprogram to to find the largest number (called the greatest common divisor) that evenly divides two other numbers. Although there are more efficient approaches, we shall use the approach of trying successive numbers starting with 2 and continuing until the smaller of the two numbers is reached. The function subprogram and a short calling program

```
 1          DIMENSION Y(20)
 2          READ(5,1)N,(Y(I),I=1,N)
 3     1    FORMAT(I5/(F5.0))
 4          A=AVG(Y,N)
 5          WRITE(6,2)A,(I,Y(I),I=1,N)
 6     2    FORMAT(' A =',F10.2/'    I',7X,'Y'/(1X,I3,F10.2))
 7          STOP
 8          END

 9          FUNCTION AVG(X,N)
10          DIMENSION X(20)
11          SUM=0.
12          DO1I=1,N
13     1    SUM=SUM+X(I)
14          AVG=SUM/FLOAT(N)
15          DO2I=1,N
16     2    X(I)=X(I)-AVG
17          RETURN
18          END
```

(a) **Program**

```
      5
19.5
4.8
45.22
13.4
20.11
```

(b) **Input data**

```
A =       20.61
  I          Y
  1       -1.11
  2      -15.81
  3       24.61
  4       -7.21
  5       -0.50
```

(c) **Output data**

Figure 8-10. Function subprogram to compute the average of the elements in an array.

are given in Figure 8-7. Since the value returned by the function subprogram is an integer, a name beginning with N is chosen. Also note the use of NGCD as a variable in the function subprogram.

As a second example, suppose we have a program as illustrated in Figure 8-8a. Using a function subprogram for this problem is complicated by the fact that two values, one for x and one for y, are to be returned. One can be associated with the function name. If the computer system uses call by address for arguments of a function, the function subprogram can be written as in Figure 8-8a. The value of y is transferred back to the main program via the fourth argument. For systems that use call by value for function arguments, this program is not acceptable. Alternatively, cøм-мøn can be used for Y, or a subroutine can be used instead of a function subprogram.

The next example of the use of a function subprogram is in interpolating between a set of data points. Specifically, suppose the following data are available:

x	y
45	1.7
50	1.9
55	2.2
60	2.4
65	3.1
70	4.2
75	5.8
80	7.2
85	10.5
90	14.7
95	19.2
100	26.5

```
 1              INTEGER KEY(8),MSG(16),SYM(27),NKEY(8),CRYP(16)
 2              DATA SYM/' ','A','B','C','D','E','F','G','H','I','J','K',
               1 'L','M','N','O','P','Q','R','S','T','U','V','W','X','Y','Z'/
 3              READ(5,1)KEY,MSG
 4       1      FORMAT(8A1/16A1)
 5              DO2J=1,8
 6       2      NKEY(J)=INDEX(KEY(J))
 7              J=0
 8              DO5L=1,16
 9              J=J+1
10              IF(J.EQ.9)J=1
11              M=INDEX(MSG(L))+NKEY(J)+1C
12              M=M-27*(M/27)
13       5      CRYP(L)=SYM(M+1)
14              WRITE(6,9)CRYP
15       9      FORMAT('0CRYPTOGRAM IS ',16A1)
16              STOP
17              END

18              FUNCTION INDEX(IC)
19              INTEGER SYM(27)
20              DATA SYM/' ','A','B','C','D','E','F','G','H','I','J','K',
               1 'L','M','N','O','P','Q','R','S','T','U','V','W','X','Y','Z'/
21              DO1J=1,27
22              IF(IC.EQ.SYM(J))GOTO2
23       1      CONTINUE
24              WRITE(6,3)
25       3      FORMAT(' INVALID CHARACTER')
26              STOP
27       2      INDEX=J-1
28              RETURN
29              END
```

(a) Program

```
COMPUTER
HE HAD A BAD DAY
```

(b) Input data

```
CRYPTOGRAM IS UCWGEGOHM XCDGPZ
```

(c) Output data

Figure 8-11. Use of a function subprogram in the enciphering problem.

```
1                  INTEGER GCD
2                  READ(5,1)N1,N2
3        1         FORMAT(2I5)
4                  N=GCD(N1,N2)
5                  WRITE(6,2)N1,N2,N
6        2         FORMAT(' GCD OF',I5,' AND',I5,' IS',I5)
7                  STOP
8                  END

9                  INTEGER FUNCTION GCD(N,M)
10                 K=N
11                 IF(M.LT.K)K=M
12                 GCD=1
13                 DO1J=2,K
14                 IF((N/J)*J.NE.N)GOTO1
15                 IF((M/J)*J.NE.M)GOTO1
16                 GCD=J
17       1         CONTINUE
18                 RETURN
19                 END
```

(a) Program

```
1528 5748
```

(b) Input data

```
GCD OF 1528 AND 5748 IS      4
```

(c) Output data

Figure 8-12. Use of specification statements for a function.

For a given value of x, we would like to interpolate between the values of y using a straight-line approximation. The resulting function subprogram is shown in Figure 8-9. Note that the array Y appears in a DIMENSIØN statement in both the main program and the function subprogram. Since the entire array Y is to be available to the function subprogram, the name of the array written without a subscript appears in the calling statement. As we shall see in a subsequent example, an array written with a subscript in the calling statement causes transfer of a single number to the subprogram.

The function subprogram may change elements of an array used as argument. For example, the function subprogram in Figure 8-10 computes the arithmetic average of array Y and then subtracts the average from each of the elements. Since call by address is always used for arrays, the subprogram is actually changing the values in the array in the calling program.

As a final example of the use of a function subprogram, note that in the encipher-ing program in Figure 7-5, a block of code to perform the lookup in the index table appears in two locations: once for the keyword, once for the message. Use of the func-tion subprogram INDEX in Figure 8-11 permits the same block of code to be used for both these lookups. However, the array SYM must be defined by a DATA statement in both the main program and the function subprogram. As we shall see shortly, this can be circumvented by the use of CØMMØN.

At the beginning of this section, we mentioned that type statements could be used to alter the usual integer-real convention for function names. The program in Figure 8-12 is identical to the one in Figure 8-7, except that GCD is used as the function name instead of NGCD. This requires the use of the word INTEGER in the FUNCTIØN statement, defining the function as an integer function and defining variable GCD in the function subprogram as an integer variable. In addition, an INTEGER type statement is required in the calling program to declare the name GCD as integer. Since GCD is used as a function, this defines function GCD as integer in the main program.

8-6. SUBROUTINES

Rules that apply to subroutines are as follows:

1 The first statement in the subroutine is the SUBRØUTINE statement, an example of which is

SUBRØUTINE TIME (I,J,K,L)

The word SUBRØUTINE is followed by the subroutine name which is followed by the arguments enclosed in parentheses.

2 The name of the subroutine is restricted to six characters, the first of which must be alphabetic. Since no value is associated with the subroutine name, there is no integer-real distinction.

```
 1              READ(5,1)A,B,TAX
 2      1       FORMAT(3F10.0)
 3              CALL CALC(A,B,TAX,X,Y)
 4              WRITE(6,2)A,B,TAX,X,Y
 5      2       FORMAT(1X,3F10.2/1X,2F10.2)
 6              STOP
 7              END

 8              SUBROUTINE CALC(A,B,C,X,Y)
 9              X=A+B-C
10              Z=X/30.
11              Y=Z*365.
12              RETURN
13              END
```
(a) Program

```
1300.        241.          197.
```
(b) Input data

```
1300.00        241.00        197.00
1344.00      16351.99
```
(c) Output data

Figure 8-13. Use of a subroutine.

```
1            INTEGER STOCK(20),QUAN(20),STKNO
2            READ(5,1)ITEMS,(STOCK(J),QUAN(J),J=1,ITEMS)
3       1    FORMAT(I5/(2I5))
4       4    READ(5,2)STKNO,NREC
5       2    FORMAT(2I5)
6            IF(NREC.EQ.0)GOTO3
7            CALL UPDATE(STOCK,QUAN,STKNO,ITEMS,NREC)
8            GOTO4
9       3    READ(5,2)STKNO,NSHP
10           IF(NSHP.EQ.0)GOTO6
11           NSHP=-NSHP
12           CALL UPDATE(STOCK,QUAN,STKNO,ITEMS,NSHP)
13           GOTO3
14      6    WRITE(6,5)(STOCK(J),QUAN(J),J=1,ITEMS)
15      5    FORMAT('0FINAL INVENTORY'/'0 ITEM',5X,'QUANTITY'/(1X,I5,I12))
16           STOP
17           END

18           SUBROUTINE UPDATE(STOCK,QUAN,STKNO,ITEMS,N)
19           INTEGER STOCK(20),QUAN(20),STKNO
20           DO1J=1,ITEMS
21           IF(STOCK(J).EQ.STKNO)GOTO2
22      1    CONTINUE
23           WRITE(6,3)STKNO
24      3    FORMAT(' NO ITEM NUMBER',I6)
25           RETURN
26      2    QUAN(J)=QUAN(J)+N
27           RETURN
28           END
```

(a) Program

```
          7
       1519    19
       1206     5
       1317     9
       1802     3
       1988    17
       1012    15
       1303     8
       1802     5
       1012    20
       1206    15
       1802    14
       1012     7
          0     0
       1805     6
       1012     5
       1317     3
       1012     3
       1303     1
       1317     5
          0     0
```

(b) Input data

```
NO ITEM NUMBER   1805

FINAL INVENTORY

 ITEM      QUANTITY
 1519         19
 1206         20
 1317          1
 1802         22
 1988         17
 1012         34
 1303          7
```

(c) Output data

Figure 8-14. Use of a subroutine in the inventory problem.

3 As illustrated by the example in Figure 8-4, the subroutine is called by a CALL statement

CALL TIME(JHØUR,JMIN,JAMPM,MTIME)

The word CALL is followed by the name of the subroutine to be called, which in turn is followed by the arguments. As pointed out in an earlier section, some systems do not permit expressions to be used for arguments in the CALL statement.

```
 1          INTEGER KEY(16),MSG(16),SYM(27),CRYP(16)
 2          DATA SYM/' ','A','B','C','D','E','F','G','H','I','J','K',
          1 'L','M','N','O','P','Q','R','S','T','U','V','W','X','Y','Z'/
 3          READ(5,1)(KEY(J),J=1,8),MSG
 4    1     FORMAT(8A1/16A1)
 5          CALL INDEX(KEY,8)
 6          CALL INDEX(MSG,16)
 7          J=0
 8          DO5L=1,16
 9          J=J+1
10          IF(J.EQ.9)J=1
11          M=MSG(L)+KEY(J)+10
12          M=M-27*(M/27)
13    5     CRYP(L)=SYM(M+1)
14          WRITE(6,9)CRYP
15    9     FORMAT('0CRYPTOGRAM IS ',16A1)
16          STOP
17          END

18          SUBROUTINE INDEX(C,N)
19          INTEGER C(16),SYM(27)
20          DATA SYM/' ','A','B','C','D','E','F','G','H','I','J','K',
          1 'L','M','N','O','P','Q','R','S','T','U','V','W','X','Y','Z'/
21          DO1J=1,N
22          DO2K=1,27
23          IF(SYM(K).EQ.C(J))GOTO1
24    2     CONTINUE
25          WRITE(6,4)
26    4     FORMAT(' INVALID CHARACTER')
27          STOP
28    1     C(J)=K-1
29          RETURN
30          END
```

(a) Program

```
$ENTRY
COMPUTER
HE HAD A BAD DAY
```

(b) Input data

```
CRYPTOGRAM IS UCWGEGOBM XCDGPZ
```

(c) Output data

Figure 8-15. Use of a subroutine in the enciphering problem.

4   The subroutine may have no arguments; this generally occurs only when COMMØN is used.

5   Transfer from the subroutine to the main program is by the RETURN statement. The subroutine may contain more than one RETURN statement, but unlike the function subprogram, it is not necessary that it contain a RETURN statement. STØP statements are permitted in subroutines.

As an example, we shall prepare a program using a subroutine to accomplish the same objective as the program in Figure 8-8. We need only add another argument (x) to the function subprogram in Figure 8-8, replace the function call with a subroutine CALL statement, and change the FUNCTIØN statement to a SUBRØUTINE statement, giving the program in Figure 8-13. All communication between the main program and the subroutine is by the argument list. The values of A, B, and TAX are available to the subroutine since they appear in the argument list. Similarly, the values of x and Y are available to the main program. However, variable z in the subprogram does not appear in the argument list and is not available to the main program.

Although in many cases the use of a function subprogram as opposed to a subroutine or vice versa is purely a matter of personal choice, problems are not suitable for a function subprogram if there is no one value that can be designated as the functional value. An example of this situation occurs if a subroutine is used to perform the inventory update described in Figure 5-7.

If a subroutine to update the inventory is prepared, it can be used for items received and items shipped, provided negative values are used for the latter. In the program in Figure 8-14, array STØCK, array QUAN, variable STKNØ, and variable NREC are available to the subroutine. Its primary objective is to update array QUAN, which appears as an argument. This routine is such that no functional value appears, and thus a subroutine is preferred over a function subprogram.

Another case in which a subroutine is preferred over a function subprogram occurs if an array is computed in the subprogram. Only simple variables, not arrays, can be treated as functional values. As an example of such a situation, suppose we modify our approach in solving the enciphering process by using a subroutine INDEX to replace the alphabetic characters in the vectors for the keyword and the message by their respective indices. The resulting program is given in Figure 8-15. In this way, the vector of numeric indices is the result of the computation in the subprogram. This makes the subroutine a logical choice over the function subprogram.

8-7. THE CØMMØN STATEMENT

In all previous examples in this section, communication between the calling program and the subprogram has been exclusively via arguments. In some cases this leads to long argument lists. Furthermore, as will be pointed out in the next chapter, use of CØMMØN leads to computational efficiency.

The CØMMØN statement causes the system to create a set of storage locations (called the CØMMØN block) that is accessible to all programs and subprograms containing the CØMMØN statement. This is FORTRAN's counterpart to the global declaration of other programming languages. For example, the statement

CØMMØN G,A,K,A4

creates a CØMMØN block consisting of four storage locations.

The CØMMØN statement can be used to define arrays. For example, the statement

CØMMØN A(4,5),J,X,I(7)

creates a CØMMØN block consisting of 29 storage locations. Alternatively, the following two statements can be used:

DIMENSIØN A(5,4),I(7)
CØMMØN A,J,X,I

```
1                   COMMON Y
2                   READ(5,1)A,B,TAX
3          1        FORMAT(3F10.0)
4                   X=CALC(A,B,TAX)
5                   WRITE(6,2)A,B,TAX,X,Y
6          2        FORMAT(1X,3F10.2/1X,2F10.2)
7                   STOP
8                   END

9                   FUNCTION CALC(A,B,C)
10                  COMMON Y
11                  CALC=A+B-C
12                  Z=CALC/30.
13                  Y=Z*365.
14                  RETURN
15                  END
```
(a) Program

```
1300.         241.           197.
```
(b) Input data

```
1300.00       241.00         197.00
1344.00     16351.99
```
(c) Output data

Figure 8-16. Use of CØMMØN declaration.

Either alternative is acceptable; but the same variable must not be declared as an array in both the DIMENSIØN and the CØMMØN statements. REAL and INTEGER can be used similarly. For example, the statements

REAL J(7),IX
CØMMØN G,IX,J,K(8)

are equivalent to the statements

REAL J,IX
CØMMØN G,IX,J(7),K(8)

Either case creates a CØMMØN block consisting of seventeen storage locations.

As an example, we shall use CØMMØN in place of the fourth argument in the subprogram in Figure 8-8. As illustrated in Figure 8-16, we only add the statement

CØMMØN Y

to both the main program and the subprogram, and we delete the fourth argument.

```
 1          COMMON A,B,TAX,X,Y
 2          READ(5,1)A,B,TAX
 3     1    FORMAT(3F10.0)
 4          CALL CALC
 5          WRITE(6,2)A,B,TAX,X,Y
 6     2    FORMAT(1X,3F10.2/1X,2F10.2)
 7          STOP
 8          END

 9          SUBROUTINE CALC
10          COMMON A,B,C,X,Y
11          X=A+B-C
12          Z=X/30.
13          Y=Z*365.
14          RETURN
15          END
```
(a) Program

```
1300.        241.          197.
```
(b) Input data

```
1300.00      241.00     197.00
1344.00    16351.99
```
(c) Output data

Figure 8-17. Use of cØmmØn.

This causes a single location to be created for Y in the cØmmØn block, and this location is available to both the main program and the subprogram.

In the subroutine in Figure 8-13, cØmmØn can be used to remove all the arguments from the argument list as illustrated by the program in Figure 8-17. In the main program the cØmmØn block is defined by the statement

cØmmØn A,B,TAX,X,Y

In the subroutine the cØmmØn block is defined by the statement

cØmmØn A,B,C,X,Y

Each of these statements defines a cØmmØn block of five storage locations. The address of the first storage location is used for variable A both in the main program and in the subroutine. Similarly, the addresses of the second, fourth, and fifth storage locations are used for variables B, X, and Y, respectively, in both main program and subroutine. In the main program the address of the third location is used for variable TAX; but in the subprogram this same storage location is used for variable C. This makes variable TAX in the main program synonymous with variable C in the subprogram.

The CØMMØN statement only defines the addresses of certain variables as being storage locations in the CØMMØN block. In establishing a CØMMØN block, the programmer can select whatever variable names are most convenient. As illustrated in the example in Figure 8-17, the same names do not have to be used in the main program and in the subprogram.

For the sake of illustration, suppose that an array of four elements is most convenient for the main program, but that in the subprogram the use of simple variables for these four storage locations is more convenient. To implement this, the main program should contain the statement

CØMMØN X(4)

and the subprogram should contain the statement

CØMMØN A,G,YA,Z

In this case, the first location in CØMMØN is the first element of array X in the main program and is simple variable A in the subprogram, the second location is the second element of array X in the main program and is simple variable G in the subprogram, etc.

Although it is possible to change the variable names associated with CØMMØN storage locations between the main program and subprogram, it is not permissible to use an integer variable for a storage location in the main program and a real variable in the subprogram for the same storage location, or vice versa. That is, changing variable types is not permissible.

As a final example of CØMMØN, we shall use CØMMØN for array SYM in the program in Figure 8-15. In this program, array SYM is needed in both the main program and the subprogram. In Figure 8-15, separate storage locations are reserved for SYM in the main program and in the subprogram. By use of CØMMØN as illustrated in Figure 8-18, the same storage locations can be used for SYM in both the main program and the subprogram. However, many systems do not permit the DATA statement to assign initial values to storage locations in CØMMØN. In Figure 8-18, the elements of SYM are read into memory. This can be avoided by using the BLØCK DATA subprogram described in Section 8-10.

Most systems permit the length of the CØMMØN block in the calling program to be longer than the CØMMØN block in the subprogram.

Multiple CØMMØN statements may be used. Subsequent CØMMØN statements are treated as continuations of the first CØMMØN statement; together they define a single CØMMØN block. For example, the statements

CØMMØN X(8),J,K(7)
CØMMØN A,B,C(2,4)

are equivalent to the single statement

CØMMØN X(8),J,K(7),A,B,C(2,4)

In programs with several subprograms, the labeled CØMMØN feature can be used to define different CØMMØN blocks. The label, enclosed in slashes, follows the word CØM-

```
 1              INTEGER KEY(16),MSG(16),SYM(27),CRYP(16)
 2              COMMON SYM
 3              READ(5,1)(KEY(J),J=1,8),MSG,SYM
 4       1      FORMAT(8A1/16A1/27A1)
 5              CALL INDEX(KEY,8)
 6              CALL INDEX(MSG,16)
 7              J=0
 8              DO5L=1,16
 9              J=J+1
10              IF(J.EQ,9)J=1
11              M=MSG(L)+KEY(J)+10
12              M=M-27*(M/27)
13       5      CRYP(L)=SYM(M+1)
14              WRITE(6,9)CRYP
15       9      FORMAT('0CRYPTOGRAM IS ',16A1)
16              STOP
17              END

18              SUBROUTINE INDEX(C,N)
19              INTEGER C(16),SYM(27)
20              COMMON SYM
21              DO1J=1,N
22              DO2K=1,27
23              IF(SYM(K).EQ.C(J))GOTO1
24       2      CONTINUE
25              WRITE(6,4)
26       4      FORMAT(' INVALID CHARACTER')
27              STOP
28       1      C(J)=K-1
29              RETURN
30              END
```

(a) Program

```
COMPUTER
HE HAD A BAD DAY
 ABCDEFGHIJKLMNOPQRSTUVWXYZ
```

(b) Input data

```
CRYPTOGRAM IS UCWGEGOBM XCDGPZ
```

(c) Output data

Figure 8-18. Use of CØMMØN for array SYM in the enciphering program.

MØN, as illustrated by the following example:

CØMMØN/JACK/A,G(16)

The name used as a label is generally restricted to six characters, the first of which must be alphabetic. A few systems do not permit the name used as a label in a CØMMØN statement to be used as a variable elsewhere in the program. Unlabeled CØMMØN is referred to as blank CØMMØN.

Labeled CØMMØN enables the programmer to define certain variables as in CØM-MØN between one program or subprogram and another subprogram, while other variables are in CØMMØN between the same program or subprogram and a third subprogram. The same program may contain blank CØMMØN along with one or more labeled CØMMØN blocks. However, the same variable may not appear in more than one CØMMØN block.

8-8. THE EQUIVALENCE STATEMENT

Within a given program or subprogram, a unique variable has been associated with each available storage location in all discussions up to this point. Using CØMMØN, a storage location within the CØMMØN block can be associated with one variable in the main program and another variable in the subprogram. But within the main program this storage location was associated with a single variable name.

Using the EQUIVALENCE statement permits two or more variables to be associated with the same storage location. For example, the statement

EQUIVALENCE (JACK,K)

causes the same storage location to be used for variables JACK and K. In effect, these two variables are identical.

The EQUIVALENCE statement may be used to cause any number of variables to be associated with a given storage location. Furthermore, equivalencing may be accomplished for more than one storage location within the same EQUIVALENCE statement, as illustrated by the following statement:

EQUIVALENCE (JACK,K,LAMP),(X,G)

Elements in an array may also be included in an EQUIVALENCE statement:

EQUIVALENCE (AK,X(4))

This statement causes the fourth storage location within array x to be used for variable AK.

Since arrays are always stored in consecutive storage locations, entire arrays can be equivalenced by equivalencing single elements. For example, the statements

DIMENSIØN G(14),X(9)
EQUIVALENCE (X(1),G(1))

cause the first nine storage locations for array G to be used for array x. In addition to equivalence x(1) and G(1), we have also equivalenced x(2) and G(2), x(3) and G(3), etc.

Equivalencing may be desirable for several reasons:

1 The name used for a variable in one section of the program is changed, erroneously, in another section of the program. The EQUIVALENCE statement corrects this situation without changing the statements.

2 The use of subscripted variables entails more computational overhead than the use of simple variables: The address of the element must be computed from the value of the subscript and the address of the first element reserved for the array. For simple variables, the address is available directly. Therefore, if a specific element of an array, x(4), appears explicitly in several statements within the program, it is more efficient to use

EQUIVALENCE (x(4),x4)

and replace the subscripted variable x(4) with the simple variable x4 throughout the program. Some compilers effectively do this automatically.

3 The EQUIVALENCE statement can be used to conserve storage in large programs. For example, suppose variable A is used only in one section of the program, variable B is used only in another section, and outside these sections these variables are not needed for any purpose. In this case, the statement

EQUIVALENCE (A,B)

reduces the storage requirements by one. Of course, equivalencing arrays produces greater reductions than equivalencing simple variables.

The use of the EQUIVALENCE statement in conjunction with the CØMMØN statement produces interesting results. For example, the statements

DIMENSIØN x(4)
EQUIVALENCE (x(1),A),(x(2),B),(x(3),C),(x(4),D)

equivalences x(1) with A, x(2) with B, x(3) with C, and x(4) with D. This can also be accomplished as follows:

DIMENSIØN x(4)
CØMMØN A,B,C,D
EQUIVALENCE (x(1),A)

The CØMMØN statement defines a CØMMØN block consisting of four storage locations reserved for variables A, B, C, and D. The EQUIVALENCE statement defines the first location in the CØMMØN block as the first element in array x. Since the CØMMØN statement specifies that the storage location reserved for B immediately follows the storage location reserved for A, and since elements in an array are always stored in consecutive storage locations, it follows that these statements have equivalenced x(2) and B, x(3) with C, and x(4) with D.

In the above example, the statement

EQUIVALENCE (x(1),A)

can be replaced by any one of the following statements:

EQUIVALENCE (x(2),B)
EQUIVALENCE (x(3),C)
EQUIVALENCE (x(4),D)

The equivalence statement may also be used to extend the cømmøn block. For example, consider the following statements:

```
DIMENSIØN X(4)
CØMMØN A,B,C,D
EQUIVALENCE (X(1),D)
```

The cømmøn block is defined as consisting of the four storage locations for variables a, b, c, and d. However, the location for d is then defined by the equivalence statement as being the first element of a four-element array. Therefore, the cømmøn block consists of seven storage locations, since three additional consecutive storage locations are reserved for the array in addition to the four locations explicitly reserved by the cømmøn statement.

While it is quite acceptable to extend cømmøn by using the equivalence statement to attach storage locations to the end of the explicitly defined cømmøn block, it is not acceptable to attach locations to the front of the cømmøn block. For example, the statements

```
DIMENSIØN X(4)
CØMMØN A,B,C,D
EQUIVALENCE (X(4),A)
```

equivalence a with the fourth element of array x. For this to be possible, the three storage locations preceding a must be available for array x. fortran does not permit cømmøn blocks to be extended in this manner.

8-9. ADJUSTABLE DIMENSIONS

In the enciphering programs in Figures 8-15 and 8-18, the array key is defined to consist of 16 elements when only eight are used. This is because array c in subroutine index is defined for 16 elements in order to accommodate array msg. In reality, the increase in the size of key is not necessary because no storage locations in the subprogram are reserved for c: It is used as an argument. However, some systems require that consistent array sizes be defined in both the calling program and the subprogram.

On these systems, increasing the sizes of the arrays can be avoided by using the adjustable dimension feature. Since no storage locations are reserved for the subprogram arguments, the compiler need not know how large the array will be, provided it knows that it will be specified when the subprogram is called. A variable may be used in the dimensiøn statement in the subprogram in these cases. The restrictions are as follows:

1   The variable specifying the size of the array in the subprogram appears as an argument. Placing this variable in cømmøn is not acceptable.

2   The name of the array must also be an argument in the subprogram. Arrays not appearing as arguments must be defined as usual in the dimensiøn statement since storage locations must be reserved for them.

```
1            INTEGER KEY(8),MSG(16),SYM(27),CRYP(16)
2            DATA SYM/' ','A','B','C','D','E','F','G','H','I','J','K',
           1 'L','M','N','O','P','Q','R','S','T','U','V','W','X','Y','Z'/
3            READ(5,1)KEY,MSG
4      1     FORMAT(8A1/16A1)
5            CALL INDEX(KEY,8)
6            CALL INDEX(MSG,16)
7            J=0
8            DO5L=1,16
9            J=J+1
10           IF(J.EQ.9)J=1
11           M=MSG(L)+KEY(J)+10
12           M=M-27*(M/27)
13     5     CRYP(L)=SYM(M+1)
14           WRITE(6,9)CRYP
15     9     FORMAT('0CRYPTOGRAM IS ',16A1)
16           STOP
17           END

18           SUBROUTINE INDEX(C,N)
19           INTEGER C(N),SYM(27)
20           DATA SYM/' ','A','B','C','D','E','F','G','H','I','J','K',
           1 'L','M','N','O','P','Q','R','S','T','U','V','W','X','Y','Z'/
21           DO1J=1,N
22           DO2K=1,27
23           IF(SYM(K).EQ.C(J))GOTO1
24     2     CONTINUE
25           WRITE(6,4)
26     4     FORMAT(' INVALID CHARACTER')
27           STOP
28     1     C(J)=K-1
29           RETURN
30           END
```

(a) Program

```
COMPUTER
HE HAD A BAD DAY
```

(b) Input data

```
CRYPTOGRAM IS UCWGEGOBM XCDGPZ
```

(c) Output data

Figure 8-19. Use of adjustable dimensions.

Figure 8-19 presents an example of the use of adjustable dimensions in the enciphering program.

8-10. THE BLØCK DATA STATEMENT

In earlier sections it was pointed out that some systems do not permit DATA statements to assign initial values to variables in CØMMØN. In these cases, a subprogram beginning with the statement

BLØCK DATA

can contain such DATA statements. This subprogram may not contain any executable

```
1              INTEGER KEY(16),MSG(16),SYM(27),CRYP(16)
2              COMMON SYM
3              READ(5,1)(KEY(J),J=1,8),MSG
4        1     FORMAT(8A1/16A1)
5              CALL INDEX(KEY,8)
6              CALL INDEX(MSG,16)
7              J=0
8              DO5L=1,16
9              J=J+1
10             IF(J.EQ.9)J=1
11             M=MSG(L)+KEY(J)+10
12             M=M-27*(M/27)
13       5     CRYP(L)=SYM(M+1)
14             WRITE(6,9)CRYP
15       9     FORMAT('0CRYPTOGRAM IS ',16A1)
16             STOP
17             END

18             SUBROUTINE INDEX(C,N)
19             INTEGER C(16),SYM(27)
20             COMMON SYM
21             DO1J=1,N
22             DO2K=1,27
23             IF(SYM(K).EQ.C(J))GOTO1
24       2     CONTINUE
25             WRITE(6,4)
26       4     FORMAT(' INVALID CHARACTER')
27             STOP
28       1     C(J)=K-1
29             RETURN
30             END

31             BLOCK DATA
32             INTEGER SYM(27)
33             COMMON SYM
34             DATA SYM/' ','A','B','C','D','E','F','G','H','I','J','K',
       1 'L','M','N','O','P','Q','R','S','T','U','V','W','X','Y','Z'/
35             END
```

(a) Program

```
COMPUTER
HE HAD A BAD DAY
```
(b) Input data

```
CRYPTOGRAM IS UCWGEGUBM XCDGPZ
```
(c) Output data

Figure 8-20. Use of BLØCK DATA.

statements; it may only contain the following statements:

1 DIMENSIØN, INTEGER, or REAL statements.

2 CØMMØN statements.

3 EQUIVALENCE statements.

4 DATA statements.

5 An END statement.

An example of the use of the BLØCK DATA subprogram is illustrated in Figure 8-20 for the enciphering program. Although WATFIV and most in-core compilers accept unlabeled CØMMØN statements in the BLØCK DATA subprogram, compilers that produce objects accept only labeled CØMMØN.

8-11. THE EXTERNAL STATEMENT

The names appearing in the EXTERNAL type statement are subprogram names to be used as arguments in a subprogram call. Suppose for one call the subprogram should use ALØG, while for another the subprogram should use ALØG10. The proper statements are

```
C   MAIN PROGRAM
    EXTERNAL ALØG10,ALØG
    .
    .
    .
    CALL SUB(...,ALØG,...)
    .
    .
    .
    CALL SUB(...,ALØG10,...)
    .
    .
    .
    END
    SUBRØUTINE SUB(...,FLØG,...)
    .
    .
    .
    RESULT = FLØG(ARG)
    .
    .
    .
    RETURN
    END
```

8-12. MULTIPLE ENTRY AND RETURN

The normal entry into either a SUBRØUTINE or a FUNCTIØN subprogram occurs when the CALL statement references the subprogram name. Entry into the subprogram is at the first executable statement following the FUNCTIØN or SUBRØUTINE statement. In some cases, this is not always desirable. For example, suppose there is to be some initialization the first time a subprogram is called. Thereafter, this initialization is unnecessary. Thus, all entries except the first can be at some point other than the first executable statement following the FUNCTIØN or SUBRØUTINE statement.

Multiple entry points in the subprograms are created by using the ENTRY statement of the form

ENTRY *name*$(a_1, a_2, \ldots, a_n)$

where *name* is the name of the entry point. Rules for ENTRY names are the same as for FUNCTIØN and SUBRØUTINE names. a_1, $a_2, \ldots$, a_n are arguments analogous to the arguments in a FUNCTIØN or SUBRØUTINE statement.

The ENTRY statement is nonexecutable, and the entry into the subprogram is at the first executable statement following the ENTRY statement. Entry cannot be made within the range of the DØ. Some systems require that the arguments in the ENTRY statement be identical to the arguments in the FUNCTIØN or SUBRØUTINE statement, although others relax this requirement.

As an example, suppose we wish to prepare a function subprogram to calculate the financial return as a function of venture risk from an equation of the form $a + bV + cV^2$. Also suppose that the first time the function subprogram is called, the values of a, b, and c must be read and returned to the calling program. The subprogram can be as follows:

```
      FUNCTIØN FINAN(V)
      READ (5,10)A,B,C
10    FØRMAT (3F10.0)
      ENTRY FIN(V)
      FINAN = A + V * (B + C * V)
      RETURN
      END
```

The value returned at the exit from a function subprogram is the value last assigned to the FUNCTIØN name or any ENTRY name. However, if the last value assigned to an ENTRY name differs in type from the current ENTRY name, the returned value is undefined. That is, it is possible to change types between ENTRY names; but the type of the returned value must be consistent with the type of the current ENTRY name.

A calling sequence for the above subprogram is

```
C    MAIN PRØGRAM
     .
     .
     .
     TNET = FINAN(VENT)
     .
     .
     .
     GRØSS = FIN(VA)
```

The first time the function is called, entry is at the READ statement. Thereafter, it is at the arithmetic statement for calculating FINAN.

Just as it may be desirable to enter a subprogram at different points, it may also be desirable to return to some statement other than the statement following the SUBRØUTINE call (multiple return only applies to SUBRØUTINE subprograms). For example, consider the following sequence:

```
C    MAIN PRØGRAM
     .
     .
     .
     CALL SUB(A,X,Z,&4,Q,&8)
3    B = A * X
     .
     .
     .
4    X = X + A
8    X = X + Q
     .
     .
     .
     END
     SUBRØUTINE SUB(B,C,D,*,Z,*)
     .
     .
     .
     IF (F)8,19,30
8    RETURN 2
19   RETURN
30   RETURN 1
     END
```

Notice that the RETURN statement is of the form

RETURN i

where i is an integer constant or variable whose value denotes the location of the statement number in the argument list at which return to the main program is to be made. Note that statement numbers in the CALL statement are preceded by &, and the corresponding arguments in the SUBRØUTINE statement consist only of an *. In the above example, return is as follows:

F > 0, return to statement 4
F $= 0$, return to statement 3
F < 0, return to statement 8

Perhaps the multiple return illustrated above can be best explained by comparison with the computed Gø Tø. The return is the same as for the following sequence:

```
C   MAIN PRØGRAM
    .
    .
    .
    CALL SUB(A,X,Z,Q,J)
    GØ TØ(3,4,8),J
    .
    .
    .
    END
    SUBRØUTINE SUB(A,X,Z,Q,J)
    .
    .
    .
    IF (F)8,19,30
 8  J = 3
    RETURN
19  J = 1
    RETURN
30  J = 2
    RETURN
    END
```

This could also be accomplished with an assigned Gø Tø.

Exercises‡

8-1 Use a statement function to compute the capital recovery factor on programming Exercise 7-13.

8-2 Use a statement function PØT to calculate the pay-out time from variables B, P, V, and C in the program for Exercise 5-2.

†8-3 For Exercise 5-8 use a statement function UPDATE to up-date the amount owed from one month to the next.

8-4 Use the statement function UPDATE described in the previous exercise in the program for Exercise 7-10.

8-5 Use a statement function for the equation for the final amount owed in Exercise 5-54.

†8-6 Use a statement function for $y = ax + b$ in the program for Exercise 5-43. Let a and b be variables in the statement function, but do not list them in the arguments.

---

‡ Solutions to Exercises marked with a dagger † are given in Appendix G.

8-7 Use a statement function to compute the distance between the two points in a plane for Exercise 6-13.

8-8 Rework the program in Figure 5-2 to use the function subprogram ADD that computes the sum of the elements in an array.

8-9 Prepare a function subprogram CØMM to calculate the commission for the salespeople in Exercise 5-41. Also write the appropriate main program.

†8-10 Prepare and use a function subprogram WEIGHT(N), where N is an array of three elements containing the number of each weight, for the program in Exercise 7-14.

8-11 Write a function subprogram VAL to calculate the value of an investment in which $1.00 is deposited each year at $i\%$ interest for n years. Use this subprogram for Exercise 5-4.

8-12 Prepare a function subprogram similar to ADD in Exercise 8-8 except that the product (instead of sum) and geometric average are computed. Use this subprogram along with ADD to program Exercise 5-9.

8-13 Use a function subprogram IFAC that computes factorials in the program to calculate the binomial coefficients in Exercise 7-22.

8-14 Use the function subprogram ADD in Exercise 8-8 in the program for Exercise 7-5.

8-15 Prepare a FUNCTIØN subprogram to sum the series in Exercise 5-10. Write a main program to compute the sum for $a = 2$ and $b = 0.5$.

8-16 Prepare a FUNCTIØN subprogram to compute the cube root ($\sqrt[3]{x} = |x|^{4/3}/x$) of a number. Prepare a program using this subprogram to compute the cube roots of 5.6 and -7.2.

†8-17 Let $f(x) = a_n x^n + a_{n-1} x^{n-1} + \cdots + a_1 x + a_0$. The coefficients are stored in a one-dimensional array A, a_0 being stored in A(1), a_1 in A(2), etc. Prepare a FUNCTIØN subprogram FUNC (A, N, B) to evaluate $f(b)$. Also prepare a main program to read n, the coefficients of $f(x)$ beginning with a_0, and b; to call FUNC; and to print b and $f(b)$ with appropriate labeling. The maximum value of n is 50. Evaluate $f(x) = x^4 + 1.2x^3 + 1.7x^2 - 1.9x + 0.8$ at $x = 2.2$.

†8-18 Write a subroutine that, given the amount to be depreciated over a given number of years, returns the amount to be depreciated (sum-of-the-years-digits method) each year in a one-dimensional array. Let the maximum number of years be 20. Use this subroutine in the program for Exercise 5-5.

8-19 Prepare a SUBRØUTINE to interchange column I with column J in a table (stored in array A) with n rows and n columns. The CALL statement should transfer I, J, A, N (the order of A), and M (the dimensioned size of A). Prepare a program calling the above SUBRØUTINE to switch columns 2 and 4 in the following table:

```
1  2  1   4
4  1  2   2
0  3  1  -9
7  5  0   2
```

This program should read N, A, I, and J as data, and print the final result in a columnar fashion.

8-20 Suppose we select any positive integer number, say, 116. From this number we generate a new number by summing the squares of the digits, for example,

$$1^2 + 1^2 + 6^2 = 1 + 1 + 36 = 38$$

Suppose we continue this process:

$$3^2 + 8^2 = 9 + 64 = 73$$
$$7^2 + 3^2 = 49 + 9 = 58$$
$$5^2 + 8^2 = 25 + 64 = 89$$
$$8^2 + 9^2 = 64 + 81 = 145$$

If this process is applied to any number and continued, the number 145 will be encountered *unless* the number 1 is encountered in the sequence. Continued application of this procedure generates the repetitive sequence 145, 42, 20, 4, 16, 37, 58, 89, 145.

Suppose we want to write a program that accepts any positive number and is encountered. This program is to use a function that accepts any positive integer number and computes the sum of squares of its digits. Prepare the complete program including the function.

8-21 If the procedure described in the above exercise is applied to the numbers 10 or 100, the sequence converges to 1. Modify the program to determine what numbers if any between 10 and 100 lead to a sequence in which a 1 appears.

8-22 Example 5-4 presented the basic version of a stock-inventory program. In this exercise, we want to make several extensions to this program. The first step is to prepare functions or subroutines to accomplish the following:

1 Arrange array STØCK in ascending order, rearranging array QUAN accordingly.

2 Locate the index of a specific item number in the ordered array stock using the approach in Figure 4-7 and update the corresponding entry in QUAN.

Using these routines, prepare a program that reads an initial inventory in random order, updates this inventory for items received and for items shipped, and then prints the final inventory in ascending order of the stock numbers.

8-23 The greatest common divisor of two numbers is the largest integer number that will divide (with no remainder) each of the two numbers. Although there are more efficient methods, the simplest approach is to assume that 1 is greatest common divisor, and then try 2, 3, 4, etc., until the smaller of the two numbers is reached. To determine the greatest common divisor of three numbers, find the greatest common divisor, say, N, of two of the numbers, and then find the greatest common divisor of N and the third number. Prepare a function subprogram to compute the greatest common divisor of two numbers, and then prepare a main program that uses this function to compute the greatest common divisor of three numbers.

8-24 The number 9 has some interesting properties. For example, suppose we begin with a number that is a multiple of 9, for example, 1953 ($= 217 \times 9$). If we sum the digits of this number, the result will also be a multiple of 9. That is, $1 + 9 + 5 + 3 = 18$ ($= 2 \times 9$). If we then sum the digits of the resulting number, we obtain another number that is a multiple of 9. That is, $1 + 8 = 9$. In fact, if the process is continued long enough the number 9 is obtained.

Prepare a function subprogram that accepts an integer number and sums its digits. Then prepare a program using this function that applies this procedure recursively until the number 9 is obtained, printing the numbers encountered in the process. Note that if the sum of digits is ever less than 9, the original number was not a multiple of 9.

8-25 Suppose we generate a sequence of numbers according to the following rule:

1 Start with any number of your choosing.

2 Halve this number if it is even; triple it and add one if it is odd.

3 Repeat the above step on the resulting number, a process that can be continued indefinitely.

To illustrate, suppose we start with the number 36. The generated sequence is 36, 18, 9, 28, 14, 7, 22, 11, 34, 17, 52, 26, 13, 40, 20, 10, 5, 16, 8, 4, 2, 1, 4, 2, 1,.... Notice that eventually the series begins to repeat the 4, 2, 1 sequence indefinitely. Does this hold for any starting number? No one has proved that it does, nor has a counter-example been found.

Prepare a function subprogram that, given a number in the sequence, computes the next number in the sequence. Then prepare a main program that reads the starting number, generates the sequence, and counts the number of entries required until a 1 is encountered in the sequence.

8-26 Prepare the flowchart for a program to implement the following operations:

1 Begin with any number j of three digits in which the difference between the first and last digits exceeds 1.

2 Form a new number k by reversing the order of the digits in j.

3 Compute the difference $d = j - k$.

4 Form the new number m by reversing the digits in d.

5 Add m and d to obtain the desired result, which is printed.

If performed properly, the result will always be 1089.

In solving this exercise, implement the following routines as functions:

1 Given any integer number, compute and store the individual digits in a single-subscripted array. That is, given the number 347, the first three elements of the array would be given the values 3, 4, and 7.

2 Given the digits of a number in a single-subscripted array, compute the number and store in a simple variable.

8-27 Prepare a subroutine to plot points as does the program in Figure 7-3. The points should be read into arrays x and y by a main program. This program should also read maximum and minimum values for the coordinates of the axes. The number of rows and columns should be fixed at 40 and 50, respectively.

EFFICIENT PROGRAMMING
IN FORTRAN‡

A number of techniques can be used to decrease the running-time and memory-space requirements for FORTRAN programs. The usage of these depends upon the characteristics of a particular compiler and system.

Real mastery of a problem-oriented language implies the ability to describe a job so that it will be done efficiently, i.e. with a minimum of unnecessary extra operations. At present, concern for program efficiency is considered archaic by many people. However, it assumes renewed importance with the advent of the many small computers which can execute problem-oriented languages, in particular FORTRAN. It does not take much of a FORTRAN program to tax the capabilities of these small machines. Therefore, efficiency can make the difference between being able to run such a program in a straightforward manner, or, on the other hand, having to segment the program, resort to machine language, or look for a larger computer—all of which are inconvenient.

The measures that are necessary to improve program efficiency depend upon how optimally each type of FORTRAN statement is handled by a given compiler. In

‡ Charles Erwin Cohn, Argonne National Laboratory, Argonne, Illinois. Reprinted by permission from *Software Age*, Vol. 2, No. 5 (June 1968), pp. 22–31. Work performed under the auspices of the U. S. Atomic Energy Commission.

general, the compilers for the smaller machines do less well in this respect, so that more attention is required from the programmer to obtain optimal code. Therefore, the programmer must know the characteristics of the particular compiler which he uses. Because of the variety of compilers now available and the rate at which new ones are being introduced, it is not practical to give those characteristics here. They can be ascertain by examination of the machine-language output produced by the compiler from some benchmark programs. (Ideally, such information should be provided by the computer manufacturers.)

Normally, the measures discussed in this paper save both running time and memory space. (It is the latter that normally limits the size of problem that can be run on a small computer.) Where a trade-off between the two is involved, that will be noted.

Although the discussion in this paper is in terms of FORTRAN, it applies in general to any problem-oriented language. The points discussed may seem trivial; but it is the author's experience that many "professional" programmers and practically all "amateur" programmers are unaware of them. They are not covered in most texts.

9-1. ARITHMETIC EXPRESSIONS AND REPLACEMENT STATEMENTS

Arithmetic expressions and replacement statements can be optimized by eliminating the repeated calculation of redundant subexpressions. In the statement

$$z = (A * B/C) * \text{SIN}(A * B/C)$$

the redundant subexpression $(A * B/C)$, although appearing twice, should be calculated only once and the result saved until it is needed again. Most compilers will do this automatically if the redundant subexpression is set off by being enclosed in parentheses, as shown here.

If a particularly rudimentary compiler does not optimize this case automatically, the programmer must do it as follows:

```
TEMP1 = A * B/C
Z = TEMP1 * SIN(TEMP1)
```

Practically no compilers, except the most sophisticated, will optimize subexpressions that are redundant between two or more arithmetic replacement statements. These must invariably be optimized by the programmer. For example, the statements

```
X = SIN(A * B/C)
Y = CØS(A * B/C)
```

should instead be written:

```
TEMP1 = A * B/C
X = SIN(TEMP1)
Y = CØS(TEMP1)
```

In both of the above two cases, additional running time and memory space are required for the instructions that store the result of the redundant subexpression in the memory location assigned to the variable TEMP1. This extra time and space is outweighed, however, by the savings resulting from elimination of the instructions required to calculate the subexpression a second time. The net savings become greater, of course, as the subexpression becomes more complicated and as it is used a greater number of times. The saving in time is especially noteworthy, as floating-point operations are unduly time-consuming on small computers that do not have floating-point hardware. The memory space consumed by the temporary-storage variable TEMP1 can be used most efficiently by using the same name wherever temporary storage is required.

If a loop contains an expression whose variables do not change value during the course of the loop, time (but not space) may be saved by evaluating the expression once, outside the loop, and holding the result until needed. For example, the loop

```
      DØ 14 I = 1,N
14    Y(I) = A * B * X(I)/C
```

can be rewritten as

```
      TEMP1 = A * B/C
      DØ 14 I = 1,N
14    Y(I) = TEMP1 * X(I)
```

The latter version may incur a slight space penalty from the extra instructions needed to store and retrieve the result of the expression.

Arithmetic operations on whole numbers are best done in integer mode, with the results converted to real where needed.

9-2. CONSTANTS

Where mixed-mode arithmetic is allowed, it is best to write constants in the dominant mode of the expression to avoid needless conversions. For the expression 2 * A, most compilers will store the 2 as an integer and convert it to real each time the expression is evaluated. With the expression in the form 2. * A (i.e. with the decimal point shown) the constant is stored as real and the conversion is eliminated.

Arithmetic operations on constants should be performed by the programmer before writing an expression. In the expression 4. * A/3. the two constants are stored separately by most compilers and the division is performed each time the expression is evaluated. It should instead be written 1.333333 * A. This and other transcendental constants should be written to as many significant figures as the computer handles in its arithmetic, so that full advantage is taken of the computer's precision. There is no penalty for the additional digits.

Some compilers store constants only as magnitudes. Where a negative constant is used as a subprogram argument, extra instructions to negate the constant are inserted. Where the same negative constant is used in more than one argument list, it is efficient in such a system to assign the value to a variable and use the variable name in the argument lists. For example, instead of

CALL SUBRA(W,X,-3)

$\cdots$

CALL SUBRB(Y,Z,-3)

you would write

M3 = -3

$\cdots$

CALL SUBRA(W,X,M3)

$\cdots$

CALL SUBRB(Y,Z,M3)

9-3. POWERS

In many compilers, the use of the "**" notation calls upon a special subroutine in the library. If only small whole-number powers are to be calculated, the time and space required for this subroutine can be saved by avoiding the "**" notation. Thus, for example, for X ** 2 write X * X, for X ** 3 write X * X * X, and X ** 4 write (X * X) * (X * X) (with the redundant subexpression (X * X) handled as described above).

Where the use of the "**" notation is appropriate, the mode of the exponent can make a difference. That is because many systems use different library subroutines for real or integer exponents of real arguments. If such a program already contains a real exponent, memory space can be saved by making whole-number exponents real, thus eliminating any need for the integer-exponent subroutine. Other systems have a subroutine for real exponents only, and convert all integer exponents to real before calling the subroutine. There, the exponents might as well be shown as real to begin with, thus eliminating the conversion step.

9-4. POLYNOMIALS

Optimization of polynomials is useful for any compiler. For a polynomial of the form

Y = A + B * X + C * X ** 2 + D * X ** 3

calculation requires three additions, three multiplications, and two exponentiations. There is a saving if the polynomial is instead written in *nested* form as

Y = A + X * (B + X * (C + X * D))

which is obviously equivalent. Here, the additions and multiplications remain but the exponentiations have been eliminated. It is straightforward to put any polynomial into this optimal form.

Special treatment is needed when one of the terms carries a minus sign. Since, in the nested form, the minus sign would multiply all subsequent terms, the next term must also carry a minus sign to cancel the effect of the previous minus. Thus, for example, the polynomial

$$Z = A + B * X - C * X ** 2 + D * X ** 3 + E * X ** 4$$

would be written in nested form as

$$Z = A + X * (B - X * (C - X * (D + X * E)))$$

Care must be taken, of course, to close the expression with the correct number of parentheses. The coefficients, shown here as single variables, may be expressions enclosed in parentheses, with any redundancies handled as described above.

9-5. STATEMENT NUMBERS

Ordinarily, there is no penalty for attaching a number to a statement even when not needed for reference by another statement. However, such a penalty can arise under two special circumstances.

First, some small-machine compilers are very limited in the size of program that they can compile because of limited memory space for the assignment tables that keep track of variables, statement numbers, etc. There, elimination of unneeded statement numbers will reduce the burden on the available space.

Secondly, some compilers perform limited optimization on sequences of arithmetic replacement statements. In particular, a variable needed in one statement may not have to be fetched from memory if it is already in a register as the result of a previous statement. This optimization is done only if none of the statements has a number, indicating that the sequence is never entered in the middle. If the last statement in the sequence ends the range of a DØ, its number can be removed and attached to a CØNTINUE statement following. There is never a penalty for the use of a CØNTINUE statement.

9-6. IF STATEMENTS

Where the quantity calculated in the expression imbedded in an IF statement, or any part of it, is also used earlier or later in the program, the unnecessary repeated calculations of that quantity should be avoided as described above for redundant subexpressions. For example, the program segment

```
  X = A * B + E
  IF(A * B - C * D)1,2,2
1 Y = C * D + F
2 ...
```

can be optimized as

```
    TEMP1 = A * B
    TEMP2 = C * D
    X = TEMP1 + E
    IF(TEMP1 − TEMP2) 1,2,2
1   Y = TEMP2 + F
2   ...
```

(Note that here two variables are needed for temporary storage.)

The FORTRAN IV logical IF statement is not handled efficiently by some compilers. These set up an intermediate logical variable according to the results of the relational operations specified, and then test this logical variable to determine the outcome of the IF statement. With such a compiler it is more efficient to replace the logical IF statement with one or more three-branch IF statements as required.

9-7. SUBSCRIPTED VARIABLES

Retrieval or storage of subscripted variables always requires more work than the retrieval or storage of unsubscripted variables. This is because the address of the datum must be calculated from the subscript combination. In more advanced systems, this arithmetic is done through indexing so no additional time or space is required that can readily be eliminated. However, less-advanced compilers insert additional instructions to perform address arithmetic wherever a subscripted variable is referenced. Here, it helps to cut down on such references.

In the statement

$$C(I) = C(I) + X$$

there are two references to the same subscripted variable. A well-designed compiler will perform the necessary address arithmetic only once and save the result until needed. If a compiler is not so optimized, nothing can be done here, because the two references to the subscripted variable are on opposite sides of the equal sign.

In the statement

$$Z = C(I) * SIN(C(I) * D)$$

the compiler should again do the address arithmetic only once for the two references. If that is not the case, the two references can here be treated as redundant subexpressions as explained previously, because they appear on the same side of the equal sign.

Where the same subscripted variable is referenced in two or more statements, these references may be handled as redundant subexpressions, provided that the values of the subscripts do not change through the sequence. The statements

```
    DØ 1 I = 1,M
    IF(INDEX(I,1) − INDEX(I,2))2,1,2
2   JRØW = INDEX(I,1)
    JCØLUM = INDEX(I,2)
1   CØNTINUE
```

may be optimized as

```
    DØ 1 I = 1,M
    ITEMP1 = INDEX(I,1)
    ITEMP2 = INDEX(I,2)
    IF(ITEMP1 − ITEMP2)2,1,2
2   JRØW = ITEMP1
    JCØLUM = ITEMP2
1   CØNTINUE
```

Where the value of a subscripted variable is formed in one statement and used in a subsequent statement, the extra reference may be eliminated similarly. The statements

```
    DØ 4 I = 1,N
    C(I) = A(I) + B(I)
4   WRITE(5,1000)A(I),B(I),C(I)
```

may be changed to

```
    DØ 4 I = 1,N
    TEMP1 = A(I)
    TEMP2 = B(I)
    TEMP3 = TEMP1 + TEMP2
    C(I) = TEMP3
4   WRITE(5,100)TEMP1, TEMP2, TEMP3
```

However, if one of the statements has the subscripted variable on both sides of the equal sign, such a change might not save anything if the compiler would do the address arithmetic only once for the statement in any case.

Subscripted-variable references with constant subscripts need not be handled in this way. Most compilers will perform the address arithmetic during compilation, so that the subscript reference incurs no penalty. For those systems which leave even this address arithmetic until program execution, an unsubscripted variable name may be made equivalent to the element in question and used in all references. Thus the coding

DIMENSIØN B(38)
. . .
B(14) = ...

may be replaced by

DIMENSIØN B(38)
EQUIVALENCE (B14, B(14))
. . .
B14 = ...

Sometimes a two- or three-dimensional array may be handled more efficiently by making it equivalent to a one-dimensional array. The initialization of a matrix to zero is usually written as

DIMENSIØN A(20,10)
. . .
    DØ 3 J = 1,10
    DØ 3 I = 1,20
3   A(I,J) = 0

This may be done more efficiently with any compiler by

DIMENSIØN A(20,10),AA(200)
EQUIVALENCE (A,AA)
. . .
    DØ 3 I = 1,200
3   AA(I) = 0

which saves some address arithmetic as well as the instructions for the inner DØ loop. This approach clearly offers an advantage only in those special cases, such as the one shown, in which computation of the subscript is not necessary.

The use of subscripts with any variable is justified only if the values so saved will actually be needed later in the program. In the DØ loop

    DØ 1 I = 1, N
    . . .
    A(I) = ...
1   WRITE(4,2) I, A(I),...

the variable A should carry subscripts only if the values assigned to it will be needed again after the loop has been completed. If that information will not be needed later, time and space will be saved by dropping the subscripts, handling A as a simple variable.

9-8. INPUT-OUTPUT STATEMENTS

The input or output of an entire array may be specified either by a DØ-implying loop over the array or by mention of the name of the array with no qualification. In many systems, the latter saves space by causing fewer instructions to be compiled, and also saves central-processor time.

In many systems there is a space penalty for specifying additional input-output modes, since each mode requires its own subroutine from the library. For example, consider a program whose primary output is on a line printer. If the programmer decides to include monitor output on the console typewriter for the convenience of the operator, the space penalty incurred may include the typewriter-output subroutine in addition to the coding for the output statements. If memory space is critical, it might be best to forego the monitor output or take it on the line printer.

9-9. SUBPROGRAMS

The use of subprogram organization incurs a time and space penalty because of the linkage instructions. The space penalty is more than made up, however, if the subprogram is called from more than one place in the main program, because the coding to perform the subprogram's functions need then not be repeated at each place it is needed. If, instead, a subprogram is called from only one place in the main program, it is most efficient to eliminate its separate identity as a subprogram and incorporate it directly into the main program. Where a subprogram is a function that can be executed in one replacement statement, it may best be included in the main program as an arithmetic statement function (but see below).

Attention must also be paid to the manner of linking variables between a main program and a subprogram. There are two ways of doing this—through argument lists and through CØMMØN statements—and each has its proper role. There is a time and space penalty associated with the use of argument lists. The subprogram must contain coding that will fetch the address of an argument from the main program and plant that address where it is accessible to those instructions in the subprogram that require it. With CØMMØN linkage, on the other hand, there is no penalty.

Therefore, we may state the following rule: Where a variable in the subprogram always corresponds to the same variable in the main program at every call of the subprogram, then the linkage should be through CØMMØN (or parameters, for an arithmetic statement function). On the other hand, where a variable in the subprogram may correspond to different variables in the main program at different calls of the subprogram, then the linkage should be through the argument list. (Of course, a reference to a FUNCTIØN subprogram must always have at least one argument so that the compiler may distinguish it from a reference to an ordinary variable.)

There is a time penalty and there may be a space penalty associated with each additional reference to an argument within a subprogram. Therefore, if an unsubscripted variable is referenced more than once in a subprogram, it could be worthwhile to use a local variable in its stead. The local variable is made equal to the argument or vice versa at the beginning or end of the subprogram, depending upon whether the argument is an input or output variable. Examples are as follows:

```
FUNCTIØN PØLY(X)
CØMMØN A,B,C,D
XA = X
PØLY = A + XA * (B + XA * (C + XA * D))
RETURN
END
SUBRØUTINE SUM(TØTAL,X,N)
DIMENSIØN X(N)
TEMP = 0.
DØ 1 I = 1,N
1   TEMP = TEMP + X(I)
TØTAL = TEMP
RETURN
END
```

(For an array, this substitution would of course require a DØ loop. It may or may not be worthwhile, depending upon the length of the array and the number of times it is referenced in the subprogram.)

Some compilers handle arithmetic statement functions like open subroutines or macros, repeating the instructions for the function at each place where it is called in the program. This saves a little time (by eliminating linkage) at the cost of much space. (If a program on such a system is space-limited, the arithmetic statement functions should be replaced with function subprograms.

CØMMØN storage has an important use in addition to the linkage of variables. In most systems, variables declared as CØMMØN (blank CØMMØN for FORTRAN-IV) are assigned to the memory area that is occupied by the loader during object-program loading. This space is otherwise unavailable to the FORTRAN programmer. Therefore, a program that taxes memory can obtain some relief by use of CØMMØN storage, even when subprogram linkage is not in question. For best use to be made of this feature, enough arrays and unsubscripted variables should be declared CØMMØN to fill the loader area.

9-10. IN SUMMARY

We have seen how the efficiency of a FORTRAN program can be improved through a number of measures, depending on the properties of the compiler and system. The saving from each of these measures is small individually; but throughout a program their sum total can be quite significant. If applied to all the production programs in a computer installation, a worthwhile reduction could be made in the installation's workload.

TYPES OF VARIABLES

In the main text only real and integer variables and constants have been consdered. FORTRAN IV will also recognize double-precision, complex, and logical variables. Although most programmers find only occasional need for these, their advantages in certain applications make their study worthwhile. For example, problems in electrical engineering are considerably facilitated by using complex variables, and logical variables are used advantageously for problems in Boolean algebra. Double precision is often necessary for matrix inversion, solution of simultaneous equations, etc.

A-1. COMPLEX VARIABLES

A single complex variable is in reality two floating-point (real) variables: one is the real part and the other is the imaginary part of the complex number. To denote which variables are to be treated as complex, the type statement CØMPLEX is used in the following manner:

CØMPLEX A,I,B(20),J(2,3,5)

Note that a complex variable may also be subscripted.

The main advantage in using complex variables in FORTRAN is that the five arithmetic operations of addition, subtraction, multiplication, division and exponentiation (complex variable raised to *integer* exponent only) are defined as usual. The permissible operations with complex variables are shown in Figure A-1. In addition, the complex functions are defined as follows ($i = \sqrt{-1}$):

CABS $(a + ib) = \sqrt{a^2 + b^2}$
CEXP $(a + ib) = e^a (\cos b + i \sin b)$
CLØG $(a + ib) = 1/2 \log (a^2 + b^2) + i \tan^{-1} (b/a)$
CSIN $(a + ib) = \sin (a \cosh b) + i \cos (a \sinh b)$
CCØS $(a + ib) = \cos (a \cosh b) - i \sin (a \sinh b)$
CØNJG $(a + ib) = a - ib$

264

Addition, Subtraction, Multiplication, Division

+ − * /	Real	Integer	Complex	Double-Precision	Logical
Real	Yes	Machine-dependent	Yes	Yes	No
Integer	Machine-dependent	Yes	No	No	No
Complex	Yes	No	Yes	No	No
Double-precision	Yes	No	No	Yes	No
Logical	No	No	No	No	No

Exponentiation

Exponent / Base	Real	Integer	Complex	Double-Precision	Logical
Real	Yes	Yes	No	Yes	No
Integer	No	Yes	No	No	No
Complex	No	Yes	No	No	No
Double-precision	Yes	Yes	No	Yes	No
Logical	No	No	No	No	No

Relational Operators

.GT. .GE. .LT. .LE. .EQ. .NE.	Real	Integer	Complex	Double-Precision	Logical
Real	Yes	No	No	Yes	No
Integer	No	Yes	No	No	No
Complex	No	No	No	No	No
Double-precision	Yes	No	No	Yes	No
Logical	No	No	No	No	No

Figure A-1. Permissible operations for the types of variables.

These complex functions are used in the same manner as the real functions described previously, with the exception that the argument of all must be complex and the result, except for CABS, is also complex. A complete list is given in Appendix C.

The value of a complex variable can be assigned by either a READ statement, an arithmetic statement, or a DATA statement. The arithmetic assignment statement makes use of the CMPLX function as illustrated below

C = CMPLX(A,B)

```
1              COMPLEXA,D,G,CEXP,CMPLX
2              READ(5,2)C,D,G
3       2      FORMAT(F10.0/(2F10.0))
4              A=C*D*CEXP(CMPLX(0.,C))/G-G
5              WRITE(6,3)A
6       3      FCRMAT(14H1REAL PART IS ,F10.3/19H IMAGINARY PART IS ,F10.3)
7              STOP
10             END
```

(a) Program

```
2.1
-1.7        1.2
0.2        -0.7
```

(b) Input data

```
REAL PART IS       5.410
IMAGINARY PART IS     -1.436
```

(c) Output data

Figure A-2. Illustration of the use of complex variables.

where c is a complex variable, and A and B are real variables, constants, or expressions The result is c = A + iB. On input, two real variables, the first being the real part and the second being the imaginary part, are read for each complex variable. For example, if c is a complex variable, the READ and FØRMAT statements are

READ (5,3)c
3   FØRMAT (1x,F10.3,E20.2)

A similar situation exists for output. A complex variable appearing in a DATA statement also requires two constants

DATA c/10. − 1.0/

Arithmetic statements involving complex variables do *not* permit a change of variable type across the equals sign. That is, the results of a complex expression must be stored in a complex variable. However, it is permissible (see Figure A-1) to add, subtract, multiply, and divide complex and real variables, the result being in the complex mode.

To illustrate these points, consider the evaluation of the following expression:

$$a + ib = \frac{c(d + if) \exp(ic)}{g + ih} - (g + ih)$$

The program reads c, $d + if$, and $g + ih$, calculates $a + ib$, and prints the results as shown in Figure A-2. The use of the CØMPLEX type statement‡ in line 1 and the functions CEXP and CMPLX in line 4 should be noted.

---

‡ In some versions of FORTRAN, the functions CEXP and DMPLX must also be included in the type statement.

A-2. DOUBLE PRECISION

On most computers the real variable is accurate to about seven or eight significant figures, depending on the word length of the machine. In some cases these are simply not enough digits for sufficient accuracy. In such cases the double-precision feature of FORTRAN IV is used, at least doubling the number of significant digits. The double-precision variable is designated by the DØUBLE PRECISIØN type statement, an example of which is

DØUBLE PRECISIØN A,J,C(12,12)

Note that a double-precision variable may also be subscripted.

A set of functions have also been developed for double-precision variables, the more common functions being

DABS	absolute value
DSQRT	square root
DSIN	sine
DCØS	cosine
DATAN	arctangent
DEXP	exponentiation
DLØG	natural logarithm

The argument as well as the result of each of these functions is in double precision.

The double-precision variable may be assigned a value by either an arithmetic statement, a READ statement, or a DATA statement. An example of an arithmetic statement is

A = 1.71D2

where the D is the double-precision equivalent of E. On input and output, the FØRMAT field specification corresponding to a double-precision variable is the D field, which is analogous to the E field. For example, a READ statement for A is

    READ (5,5)A
5   FØRMAT (D20.8)

The output is handled in a similar fashion. The DATA statement also follows similarly, an example being

DATA A/1.71D2/

Change of mode across the equals sign in arithmetic statements is permissible. Integer to double precision, double precision to integer, real to double precision, and double precision to real are all legal. Double-precision and real variables may also be

```
1              DOUBLE PRECISION AD(2),BD(2),CD(2),XD,YD
2              READ(5,2)(AD(I),BD(I),CD(I) ,I=1,2)
3      2       FORMAT(3D8.0)
4              YD=(CD(1)*AD(2)-CD(2)*AD(1))/(BD(1)*AD(2)-BD(2)*AD(1))
5              XD=(CD(1)-BD(1)*YD)/AD(1)
6              WRITE(6,4)XD,YD
7      4       FORMAT(25H DOUBLE PRECISION RESULTS/5H X = D30.16/5H Y = D30.16)
10             STOP
11             END
```

(a) Program

```
   1.D00    1.D00    1.D00
1.71D-8 2.78D00 1.45D-4
```

(b) Input data

```
DOUBLE PRECISION RESULTS
X =            0.9999478478773771D 00
Y =            0.5215212262295011D-04
```

(c) Output data

Figure A-3. Illustration of the use of double precision.

mixed in an arithmetic statement. Figure A-1 gives the permissible operations using double-precision variables.

As an example of the use of double precision, consider the solution of the equations

$$x + 2y = 1$$
$$1.0017262x + 1.9991278y = 1$$

These equations can be solved for x and y by double precision. The equations

$$a_1x + b_1y = c_1$$
$$a_2x + b_2y = c_2$$

have solutions

$$y = (c_1a_2 - c_2a_1)/(b_1a_2 - b_2a_1)$$
$$x = (c_1 - b_1y)/a_1$$

The program and the results are shown in Figure A-3. Solution of large sets of simultaneous equations is one application frequently requiring double precision.

A-3. LOGICAL OPERATIONS

In Chapter 4 the use of the logical IF was introduced along with a few logical expressions. Entire logical equations can be programmed so that the computer can solve Boolean algebra or other problems involving logic. The logical variables can assume only the values true or false, and a logical constant is either .TRUE. or FALSE.. A logical variable must be specified in a LØGICAL type statement such as the following:

LØGICAL A,J,K(10)

Again subscripting is permitted.

A logical variable may be assigned values by either a logical assignment statement (analogous to the arithmetic assignment statement), the DATA statement, or the READ statement. An example of the logical assignment statement is

J = .TRUE.

which sets J to be true. Similarly, the DATA statement is used as follows:

DATA J/.TRUE./

The input and output of logical information is by the L field. Consider the following input statements:

```
  READ (5,5) J
5 FØRMAT (L5)
```

Although the width of the L field is five columns, the scan routine looks at only the first nonblank character in the field. If it is a T, J is set true; if an F or if the field is completely blank, J is set false; if neither, a read error occurs. The remaining columns are completely ignored, and may contain anything. On output, a T or an F depending on the value of the logical variable, is inserted in the rightmost column of the L field (right justified).

In Chapter 4 the relational operator .LT., .LE., .EQ., .NE., .GT. and .GE. were defined along with logical operators .AND., .ØR. and .NØT.. Figure A-1 gives the permissible operations using .LT., .LE., .EQ., .NE., .GT. and .GE.. By using these operators, logical assignment statements can be constructed as follows:

J = A.GT.B

If A > B, J is .TRUE.; otherwise, J is .FALSE.. Combinations of logical operators and relational operators to form logical expressions are also permissible, the rules regarding their use being

1 Use of parentheses in a logical expression to control order of execution is analogous to their use in an arithmetic expression.

2 The precedence of execution is

Order of Precedence	Operation
1 (highest)	Any arithmetic operations appearing in the logical expression.
2	The relational operators .GT., .GE., .LT., .LE., .EQ., and .NE.
3	.NØT.
4	.AND.
5 (lowest)	.ØR.

According to these rules, the logical expression

A.LT.B $+$ C.AND..NØT.I.EQ.J.ØR.K.LE.M

is equivalent to

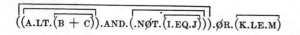

$$((\text{A.LT.}\overline{(\text{B} + \text{C})}).\text{AND.}(.\text{NØT.}\overline{(\text{I.EQ.J})})).\text{ØR.}\overline{(\text{K.LE.M})}$$

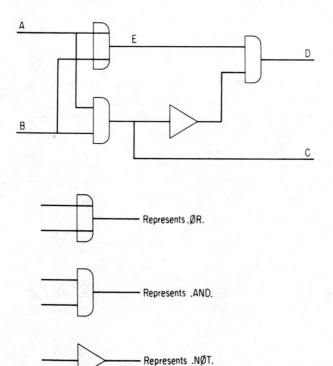

Figure A-4. Binary half-adder.

The use of the logical IF in the following fashion is sometimes advantageous:

```
LØGICAL TEST
TEST = A.GT.B
IF (TEST)C = D + G
IF (.NØT.TEST)C = ALØG10(D)
```

That is, logical variables can be used directly in the logical IF.

To illustrate the use of logical expressions, consider programming the computer to solve the logic circuit corresponding to the binary half-adder in Figure A-4. For all possible combinations of states for A and B (the inputs to the circuit), the states of C and D (the outputs) are to be determined. The results from the program should be as follows:

A	B	C	D
.FALSE.	.FALSE.	.FALSE.	.FALSE.
.FALSE.	.TRUE.	.FALSE.	.TRUE
.TRUE.	.FALSE.	.FALSE.	.TRUE.
.TRUE.	.TRUE.	.TRUE.	.FALSE.

The program reads the values of A and B, computes C and D, and prints the results. The construction of the table with this program is illustrated in Figure A-5.

```
 1              LOGICAL A,B,C,D,E
 2              DO2I=1,4
 3              READ(5,3)A,B
 4      3       FORMAT(2L5)
 5              E=A.OR.B
 6              C=A.AND.B
 7              D=E.AND..NOT.C
10      2       WRITE(6,4)A,B,C,D
11      4       FORMAT(1X,4L5)
12              STOP
13              END
```
(a) **Program**

```
F    F
F    T
T    F
T    T
```
(b) **Input data**

```
F    F    F    F
F    T    F    T
T    F    F    T
T    T    T    F
```
(c) **Output data**

Figure A-5. Illustration of the use of logical variables.

A-4. TYPE STATEMENTS FOR THE IBM SYSTEM 360

On the IBM System 360 and comparable machines of other manufacturers, the standard word length is 32 bits (binary digits). These words are said to consist of four bytes (eight binary digits). The programmer has various options for modifying the standard convention, as shown below:

Variable Type	Standard Length	Optional Length
INTEGER	4 bytes (32 bits)	2 bytes (16 bits)
REAL	4 bytes (32 bits)	8 bytes (64 bits)
CØMPLEX	8 bytes (64 bits)	16 bytes (128 bits)
LØGICAL	4 bytes (32 bits)	1 byte (8 bits)

These types may be selected by either FORTRAN conventions (standard length), by explicit type statements (REAL, CØMPLEX, INTEGER, LØGICAL), or by the IMPLICIT statement. The results of arithmetic operations involving the various modes are given in Figure A-6. Note that mixed mode is permitted.

The REAL statement is essentially the same as described in the previous section except as illustrated in the following examples:

REAL * 4 I,J,C(10)
REAL * 8 A(15)

The number following the asterisk is the number of bytes to be used. The second example is equivalent to the DØUBLE PRECISIØN statement described in Section A-2

+ - * /	INTEGER * 2	INTEGER * 4	REAL * 4	REAL * 8	COMPLEX * 8	COMPLEX * 16
INTEGER * 2	INTEGER * 2	INTEGER * 4	REAL * 4	REAL * 8	COMPLEX * 8	COMPLEX * 16
INTEGER * 4	INTEGER * 4	INTEGER * 4	REAL * 4	REAL * 8	COMPLEX * 8	COMPLEX * 16
REAL * 4	REAL * 4	REAL * 4	REAL * 4	REAL * 8	COMPLEX * 8	COMPLEX * 16
REAL * 8	REAL * 8	REAL * 8	REAL * 8	REAL * 8	COMPLEX * 16	COMPLEX * 16
COMPLEX * 8	COMPLEX * 8	COMPLEX * 8	COMPLEX * 8	COMPLEX * 16	COMPLEX * 16	COMPLEX * 16
COMPLEX * 16	COMPLEX * 16	COMPLEX * 16	COMPLEX * 16	COMPLEX * 16	COMPLEX * 16	COMPLEX * 16

Exponent

** (BASE)	INTEGER * 2	INTEGER * 4	REAL * 4	REAL * 8	COMPLEX * 8	COMPLEX * 16
INTEGER * 2	INTEGER * 2	INTEGER * 4	REAL * 4	REAL * 8	no	no
INTEGER * 4	INTEGER * 4	INTEGER * 4	REAL * 4	REAL * 8	no	no
REAL * 4	REAL * 4	REAL * 4	REAL * 4	REAL * 8	no	no
REAL * 8	REAL * 8	REAL * 8	REAL * 8	REAL * 8	no	no
COMPLEX * 8	COMPLEX * 8	COMPLEX * 8	no	no	no	no
COMPLEX * 16	COMPLEX * 16	COMPLEX * 16	no	no	no	no

Figure A-6. Type of result of arithmetic operations on the IBM System 360.

This convention is directly extendable to the other explicit type statements. One notable feature is that the statement

CØMPLEX * 16 AX(5)

causes the array AX to consist of double-precision complex variables.

It is also worth noting that the DATA statement and the explicit type statement may be combined. For example, the statement

INTEGER B(2)/'INVERSE'/

causes this alphanumeric information to be stored in this array.

All the type statements discussed previously can only change the type of the variables included in the list. The IMPLICIT statement is used to modify the standard FORTRAN convention (i.e., variables beginning with I through N are integer, others real). For example, the statement

IMPLICIT INTEGER * 2(I − N), REAL * 8(Ø − Y), CØMPLEX * 8(C,Z)

causes variables beginning with I through N to be treated as two-byte integer variables, variables beginning with Ø through Y as double-precision real variables, and variables beginning with C and Z as complex variables. All other variables are treated as usual. It is also noteworthy that the statement

IMPLICIT REAL * 8(A − H,Ø − Z,$)

would convert a normal single-precision to a double-precision program. Some compilers in this category would also automatically retype any functions if necessary. The IMPLICIT statement must be the first statement in a main program or the second statement in a subprogram.

VARIOUS SYSTEM CONFIGURATIONS

	ASA Basic	ASA	ASI 6000 Series	Bur-roughs B5500	Computer Control DDP-24, 116, 124,224	CDC 1604 3600 3800	CDC 1700	CDC 6000 Series	PDP-6	EA1 640	EA1 8400	GE 200 Series	GE 400 Series	GE 600 Series
Maximum statement number	9999	99999	99999	99999	99999	99999	99999	99999	99999	99999	32767	32767	32767	99999
Maximum continuation cards	5	19	No limit	9	No limit	No limit	5	No limit	19	19	19	No limit	No limit	19
Specification statements must precede first executable statement	*	*	*		*	*	*	*	*	*		*		*
INTEGER constant, maximum digits			7	11	7	14	5	18	11	5	5	6	7	11
INTEGER maximum magnitude			$2^{23}-1$	$2^{39}-1$	$2^{23}-1$	$2^{47}-1$	$2^{15}-1$	$2^{59}-1$	$2^{35}-1$	$2^{15}-1$	$2^{15}-1$	$2^{19}-1$	$2^{23}-1$	$2^{35}-1$
REAL constant, maximum digits			11	11	7	11	7	15	8	7	7	9	8	9
DØUBLE PRECISIØN constant, digits					14	25		29	16	14	14	18		19
REAL, DØUBLE PRECISIØN magnitude			10^{76}	10^{69}	10^{76}	10^{308}		10^{308}	10^{38}	10^{38}	10^{38}	10^{76}	10^{127}	10^{38}
Variable name maximum characters	5	6	6	6	6	8	6	8	No limit	6	6	12	6	6
Mixed mode arithmetic permitted			*			*		*	*	*	*	*		
Assigned GØ TØ		*	*	*	*	*	*	*	*	*	*	*	*	*
Logical IF, relations		*	*	*	*	*	*	*	*	*	*	*		*
DØUBLE PRECISIØN operations		*			*	*		*	*	*	*	*		*
CØMPLEX operations		*			*	*		*	*	*	*	*		*
LØGICAL operations		*	*	*	*	*	*	*	*	*	*	*		*
Dimension data in type statements		*			*	*		*		*	*	*	*	*
Labeled CØMMØN		*		*	*	*	*	*	*	*	*	*		*
Maximum array dimensions	2	3	3	3	3	3	3	3	3	3	7	63	3	7
Adjustable dimensions		*	*	*	*	*		*	*		*	*		*
Zero and negative subscripts								*			*			
Subscripts may be any expression, with subscripted variables permitted				*		*		*				*		
Subroutine multiple entries and/or nonstandard returns								*						*
DATA statement		*	*	*	*	*	*	*	*	*	*	*	*	*
Object time FØRMAT		*	*		*	*	*	*	*	*	*	*	*	*

Source: D. D. McCracken, *A Guide to Fortran IV Programming*. Wiley, New York, 1965, with updating by authors.

Honey-well 200	Honey-well 800 1800	IBM 1130 1800	IBM 1401 1440 1460	IBM 1410 7010	IBM 7040 7044 (16-32K)	IBM 7090 7094	IBM 360/370 D level E level	IBM 360 H level	NCR Century Series	RCA Spectra 70 Size A	RCA Spectra 70 Size B	SDS Sigma 2	SDS Sigma 5 & 7	Univac 111	Univac 1107
99999	32767	99999	99999	99999	99999	32767	99999	99999	99999	99999	99999	99999	99999	32767	32767
9	19	5	9	9	9	19	19	19	19	19	19	No limit	No limit	9	19
*	*	*		*			*		*	*		*			
20	13	5	20	20	11	11	10	10	10	10	10	5	10	6	11
$2^{119}-1$	$2^{44}-1$	$2^{15}-1$	$10^{20}-1$	$10^{20}-1$	$2^{35}-1$	$2^{35}-1$	$2^{31}-1$	$2^{31}-1$	$2^{31}-1$	$2^{31}-1$	$2^{31}-1$	$2^{15}-1$	$2^{31}-1$	10^6-1	$2^{35}-1$
20	12	7	20	18	9	9	7	7	7	7	7	7	7	10	9
	20				16	16	16	16	16	16	16		16		17
10^{99}	10^{76}		10^{99}	10^{99}	10^{38}	10^{38}	10^{75}	10^{75}	10^{75}	10^{75}	10^{75}		10^{75}	10^{50}	10^{38}
6	6	5	6	6	6	6	6	6	8	6	6	6	No limit	6	6
		*					*	*	*	*	*		*		*
*	*				*	*		*	*		*		*	*	*
*	*		*	*	*	*		*	*		*		*	*	*
	*				*	*	*	*	*	*	*		*		*
	*				*	*		*	*		*		*		*
*	*	*		*	*	*		*	*		*		*		*
*	*	*			*	*	*	*	*	*	*		*	*	*
*	*	1800			*	*		*	*		*		*	*	*
3	3	3	3	3	3	7	3	7	No limit	3	7	3	No limit	3	7
	*		*		*	*		*	*		*		*	*	*
									*						
									*						
					*			*			*				*
															*
*	*	1800	*		*	*		*	*		*	*	*	*	*
*	*		*		*	*		*			*		*	*	*

FORTRAN IV LIBRARY FUNCTIONS

The functions in the following list are common to most FORTRAN IV systems. However, specific installations often add to the basic list as their needs warrant.

Integer functions

Function name	Type of argument	Number of arguments	Examples	Explanation
IABS	Integer	1	I = IABS (J)	Absolute value of argument
INT	Real	1	I = INT (A) ⎫	Convert floating-point to fixed-point
IFIX	Real	1	I = IFIX (A) ⎭	
IDINT	Double-precision	1	I = IDINT (D)	Convert double-precision to fixed-point
MØD	Integer	2	I = MØD (J,K)	Remaindering: arg 1 − [arg 1/arg 2] arg 2, where [X] = integral part of X
MAX0	Integer	≥2	I = MAX0 (J,K,L,...) ⎫	Largest of set of arguments
MAX1	Real	≥2	I = MAX1 (X,Y,Z,...) ⎭	
MIN0	Integer	≥2	I = MIN0 (J,K,L,...) ⎫	Smallest of set of arguments
MIN1	Real	≥2	I = MIN1 (X,Y,Z,...) ⎭	
ISIGN	Integer	2	I = ISIGN (J,K)	Sign of arg 2 × arg 1
IDIM	Integer	2	I = IDIM (J,K)	Positive difference: arg 1 − min (arg 1, arg 2)

Real functions

Function name	Type of argument	Number of arguments	Examples	Explanation
ABS	Real	1	X = ABS (Y)	Absolute value of argument
AINT	Real	1	X = AINT (Y)	Truncation: sign of argument times absolute value of the largest integer in argument
AMØD	Real	2	X = AMØD (Y,Z)	Remaindering: arg 1 − [arg 1/arg 2] arg 2, where $[X]$ = integral part of X
AMAX0	Integer	≥2	X = AMAX0 (I,J,K,..)	Largest value of arguments
AMAX1	Real	≥2	X = AMAX1 (R,S,T,..)	
AMIN0	Integer	≥2	X = AMIN0 (I,J,K,..)	Smallest value of arguments
AMIN1	Real	≥2	X = AMIN1 (R,S,T,..)	
FLØAT	Integer	1	X = FLØAT (I)	Convert fixed point to floating point
SIGN	Real	2	X = SIGN (Y,Z)	Transfer of sign: sign of arg 2 times arg 1
DIM	Real	2	X = DIM (Y,Z)	Positive difference: arg 1 − min (arg 1, arg 2)
SNGL	Double-precision	1	X = SNGL (D)	Convert double precision to single precision
REAL	Complex	1	X = REAL (C)	Obtaining real part of a complex number
AIMAG	Complex	1	X = AIMAG (C)	Obtaining the imaginary part of a complex number
SQRT	Real	1	X = SQRT (Y)	$x = \sqrt{y}$: the square root
EXP	Real	1	X = EXP (Y)	$x = e^y$: the natural antilogarithm of y
ALØG	Real	1	X = ALØG (Y)	$x = \ln y$: the natural logarithm of y
ALØG 10	Real	1	X = ALØG10 (Y)	$x = \log_{10} (y)$: the common logarithm of y
SIN	Real	1	X = SIN (Y)	$x = \sin (y)$: the trigonometric sine
CØS	Real	1	X = CØS (Y)	$x = \cos (y)$: the trigonometric cosine
ATAN	Real	1	X = ATAN (Y)	$x = \tan^{-1} (y)$, the arctangent of y: result is placed in first two quadrants depending upon sign of y

Real functions

Function name	Type of argument	Number of arguments	Examples	Explanation
ATAN2	Real	2	X = ATAN2 (Y,Z)	$x = \tan^{-1} (y/z)$: same as ATAN except that result is placed in proper quadrant
ARSIN	Real	1	X = ARSIN (Y)	$x = \sin^{-1} (y)$: the arcsine of y
ARCØS	Real	1	X = ARCØS (Y)	$x = \cos^{-1} (y)$: the arccos of y
TANH	Real	1	X = TANH (Y)	$x = \tanh (y)$: the hyperbolic tangent
CABS	Complex	1	X = CABS (C)	Magnitude of a complex number: $x = \sqrt{a^2 + b^2}$, where $c = a + ib$

Double-precision functions

Function name	Type of argument	Number of arguments	Examples	Explanation
DABS	Double precision	1	D = DABS (DA)	Absolute value of argument
DMAX1	Double-precision	≥ 2	D = DMAX1 (DA, DB, ...)	Largest of set of arguments
DMIN1	Double-precision	≥ 2	D = DMIN1 (DA, DB, ...)	Smallest of set of arguments
DSIGN	Double-precision	2	D = DSIGN (DA, DB)	Transfer of sign: sign of arg 2 times arg 1
DBLE	Real	1	D = DBLE (X)	Convert single-precision to double-precision
DMØD	Double-precision	2	D = DMØD (DA, DB)	Remaindering: arg 1 − [arg 1/arg 2] arg 2, where $[X]$ = integral part of X
DSQRT	Double-precision	1	D = DSQRT (DA)	Double-precision equivalent of SQRT
DEXP	Double-precision	1	D = DEXP (DA)	Double-precision equivalent of EXP
DLØG	Double-precision	1	D = DLØG (DA)	Double-precision equivalent of ALØG
DLØG10	Double-precision	1	D = DLØG10 (DA)	Double-precision equivalent of ALØG10
DSIN	Double-precision	1	D = DSIN (DA)	Double-precision equivalent of SIN

Double-precision functions

Function name	Type of argument	Number of arguments	Examples	Explanation
DCØS	Double-precision	1	D = DCØS (DA)	Double-precision equivalent of CØS
DATAN	Double-precision	1	D = DATAN (DA)	Double-precision equivalent of ATAN
DATAN2	Double-precision	1	D = DATAN2 (DA)	Double-precision equivalent of ATAN2

Complex functions

Function name	Type of argument	Number of arguments	Examples	Explanation
CMPLX	Real	2	C = CMPLX (X,Y)	Express two arguments in complex form, $C = X + iY$
CØNJG	Complex	1	C = CØNJG (CA)	Obtain complex conjugate of argument
CSQRT	Complex	1	C = CSQRT (CA)	Complex square-root function
CEXP	Complex	1	C = CEXP (CA)	Complex exponential
CLØG	Complex	1	C = CLØG (CA)	Complex natural logarithm
CSIN	Complex	1	C = CSIN (CA)	Complex sine
CCØS	Complex	1	C = CCØS (CA)	Complex cosine

AMERICAN STANDARD FLOWCHART SYMBOLS‡

Any text or notes may be placed inside or beside these symbols:

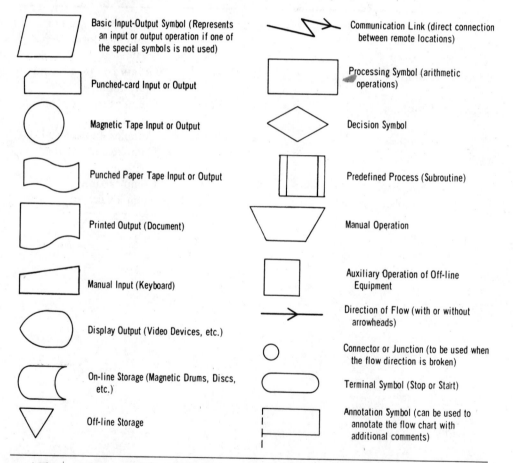

Basic Input-Output Symbol (Represents an input or output operation if one of the special symbols is not used)

Punched-card Input or Output

Magnetic Tape Input or Output

Punched Paper Tape Input or Output

Printed Output (Document)

Manual Input (Keyboard)

Display Output (Video Devices, etc.)

On-line Storage (Magnetic Drums, Discs, etc.)

Off-line Storage

Communication Link (direct connection between remote locations)

Processing Symbol (arithmetic operations)

Decision Symbol

Predefined Process (Subroutine)

Manual Operation

Auxiliary Operation of Off-line Equipment

Direction of Flow (with or without arrowheads)

Connector or Junction (to be used when the flow direction is broken)

Terminal Symbol (Stop or Start)

Annotation Symbol (can be used to annotate the flow chart with additional comments)

‡ These symbols are substantially those recommended by the X6 Committee to the United States of America Standards Institute, New York City.

WATFOR AND WATFIV

Users of computing equipment fall into two categories: expert programmers and poor programmers. Members of the second category are by far the more numerous, encompassing most computer users who view the computer only as a tool to obtain numerical solutions to numerical problems in their field of interest. To best serve their needs, the FORTRAN compilers should possess two characteristics: fast compilation, which means the computer center can potentially give them fast turnarounds (especially for debugging), and excellent error detection capabilities, both during compilation and during execution.

To meet these requirements a compiler named WATFIV, pronounced "what five," has been developed by the Department of Applied Analysis and Computer Science, University of Waterloo. Chronologically, WATFIV is an extension of WATFOR, pronounced "what for," which was developed in 1965 for the IBM 7040 and extended to the IBM 360 in 1967. WATFIV appeared in 1969, and essentially is a more powerful version of WATFOR. WATFIV has now almost completely replaced WATFOR, and WATFIV will receive our prime attention in this appendix. WATFIV is a FORTRAN IV compiler; but a few aspects of the basic language are especially useful. One of these, format-free input-output feature permits the READ, PRINT, and PUNCH statements to be used *without* a FORMAT statement.

This appendix seeks to accomplish three objectives: Describe some aspects of WATFIV, discuss the control cards, and present the error codes for WATFIV.

E-1. SPECIAL ASPECTS

The items to be presented here are only those items which are not covered completely in the regular sequence of this text and which are thought to be most useful to beginning programmers. Except as noted, they apply to both WATFOR and WATFIV. For other facets of these compilers, the student should consult his computer center's reference manuals on these special compilers.

Format-Free Input-Output. Since one of the most perplexing features to the beginning student of FORTRAN is the FØRMAT statement, the format-free input-output feature of the language is very useful. This is first introduced in Chapter 3. The format-free input-output feature permits the READ, PRINT, and PUNCH statements to be used *without* a FØRMAT statement.

First consider the format-free READ statement, which takes the following form:

READ, *variable list*

Note that a comma separates the word READ from the variable list, and no FØRMAT statement number or device number appears, the latter normally assumed to be a card reader. As an example, the statement

READ, A,B,N,C

would cause the reading of values for the variables A, B, N, and C. Execution of this READ statement would cause a card to be read and scanned for these values. The numerical values for these variables should be punched on this card or succeeding cards in the order in which they appear in the READ statement, i.e., the value for A followed by the value for B, etc. The values may be punched anywhere on the card; but successive values should be separated by one or more blanks or by a comma. If the values for all variables in the READ statement are not found on the first card, another card is read and scanned. This process is continued until all values have been read. This permits entry of data with one value per data card, if desired. Floating-point constants may be punched in either decimal or exponential format.

As an example, data for the previous READ statement may appear on one data card in any of the following ways:

1.7	0.0012	5	99.8
1.7,	0.0012,	5,	99.8
1.7,	1.2E–3	5,	9.98E1
1.7	12.E–4	5	99.8

Blank cards are completely ignored, and thus may be placed anywhere in the data deck.

Next, consider use of the format-free PRINT statement, whose general form is

PRINT, *variable list*

Again, only a comma follows the word PRINT. The values of the variables in the output list are printed across the page. Each value is printed to full precision with spaces inserted between values for clarity. Eight values are normally printed across the page; but this varies with computer installations. Real (floating-point) numbers are printed in exponential form with seven significant figures. For example, suppose the variables entered with the above READ statement are printed with the statements

PRINT, N,A
PRINT, B,C

The output would appear as follows:

$$5 \qquad 0.1700000\text{E}01$$
$$0.1200000\text{E}{-}02 \qquad 0.9980000\text{E}02$$

If the PRINT statement contains more values than can be printed on one line, output is continued on the following line.

Rules for the PUNCH statement are analogous to those for the PRINT statement.

Expressions in Output Lists. The WATFOR and WATFIV compilers permit expressions to be used in output lists. Only the results of these expressions are printed. Functions may be freely used in these expressions. For example, the following statement is entirely valid:

PRINT, X,Y,I + J,A/SQRT(B)

Only four values are printed. One restriction must be observed: The expression must not begin with an open parenthesis.‡ That is, the expression $(I + J)/2$ must be written as $+ (I + J)/2$, making the PRINT statement

PRINT, + (I + J)/2

It is also possible for constants to appear in output lists, for example

PRINT, 2

This statement causes the integer 2 to be printed. This feature is helpful in debugging.

WATFIV also permits explanatory messages to be written with format-free input-output statements. For example, the statement

PRINT, 'THE SQUARE RØØT ØF' ,A, 'IS' ,SQRT(A)

gives the ouput

THE SQUARE RØØT ØF 0.4000000E01 IS 0.2000000E01

Extended Assignment Statement. Statements of this type permit more than one variable to be assigned a value in a single FORTRAN statement. Examples are

SUMA = SUM = A = 0.
I = J = 1
A = B = C = D = SQRT(1. − X ** 2)

In the first example, the three variables SUMA, SUM, and A are all assigned the value of zero. The other two statements function analogously.

---

‡ This indicates an implied DØ to the compiler.

When mixed expressions of the type

X = I = Y = 2.4

appear, the manner in which the compiler treats this statement is important. For this example, this statement is equivalent to the three statements

Y = 2.4
I = Y
X = I

Note that x is assigned the value 2.0 rather than 2.4. Precision may also be lost when integers appear in statements of the type

M = A = N = 123456789

When A is in single precision, only about seven of the nine digits are retained.

Multiple Statements per Card. One of the notable extensions of WATFIV over WATFOR and other FORTRAN IV compilers is that several statements may be punched on a single card. For statements without statement numbers, the successive statements are simply separated by semicolons. For example, the program

```
READ, A,B
C = A * SQRT(B)
PRINT, C
STØP
END
```

could be punched on one card as follows:

READ, A,B;C = A * SQRT(B); PRINT, C;STØP;END

Only columns 7–72 are used, although the normal rules for continuation cards still apply.

When statement numbers are used, they must either appear in columns 1–5 as usual or be separated from the FORTRAN statement by a colon. For example, the statements

```
22   SUM = 0.
     DØ 32 J = 2,M
32   SUM = SUM + X(J)
```

could be punched

22   SUM = 0. ;DØ 32 J = 2,M;32:SUM = SUM + X(J)

Statement numbers may not be split onto a continuation card: Nor can FØRMAT statements be punched in this manner.

Comment cards must also be punched in the conventional manner.

E-2. CONTROL CARDS

The program deck when using the WATFOR or WATFIV compiler appears as follows:

$JØB
{FORTRAN *program*}
$ENTRY
{*Data cards*}

The $JØB and $ENTRY cards are known as *control cards*. Both cards must be punched beginning in column 1, with no blank spaces. The $JØB card signifies to the compiler the beginning of the FORTRAN program, and the $ENTRY card signifies that execution is to begin. Both of these cards are usually available prepunched on colored cards from the computer center. WATFIV permits certain options to be obtained with entries in the $JØB card; but again the computer center should be consulted about the use of these.

E-3. ERROR CODES

The WATFOR and WATFIV compilers may generate error messages during either compilation or execution. At compile time, the compiler checks for violations of the rules of FORTRAN. During execution it checks for unreasonable situations that usually mean programming errors. Examples of such situations include undefined variables, value of subscript exceeding dimensioned size of array, etc. Few other compilers detect error of this type.

During compilation, three types of error messages may appear

1 Extension. These messages flag each use (other than format-free input-output) of one of the extensions of these compilers, since it is unlikely that other compilers will accept these statements.

2 Warning. These messages flag situations in which the compiler has encountered ambiguous code, but has taken a predetermined course of action to generate executable code. For example, upon encounter of a variable name with more than six characters, the first six are used as the variable name and a VA-2 warning message is generated.

3 Error. An error message flags code that cannot be interpreted by the compiler. The error message appears with the print-out of the program, designates a particular error code, and in some cases gives other information relating to the source of the error.

The error codes for WATFOR and WATFIV are somewhat different. Since virtually all computer centers now use the WATFIV compiler exclusively (over WATFOR), the WATFIV error codes are reproduced on the following pages for convenience.‡

WATFIV Compiler Error Messages

'ASSEMBLER LANGUAGE SUBPROGRAMMES'
AL-0   'MISSING END CARD ON ASSEMBLY-LANGUAGE OBJECT DECK'
AL-1   'ENTRY-POINT OR CSECT NAME IN AN OBJECT DECK WAS PREVIOUSLY
         DEFINED.FIRST DEFINITION USED'

'BLOCK DATA STATEMENTS'
BD-0   'EXECUTABLE STATEMENTS ARE ILLEGAL IN BLOCK DATA SUBPROGRAMS'
BD-1   'IMPROPER BLOCK DATA STATEMENT'

'CARD FORMAT AND CONTENTS'
CC-0   'COLUMNS 1-5 OF CONTINUATION CARD ARE NOT BLANK.
         PROBABLE CAUSE:STATEMENT PUNCHED TO LEFT OF COLUMN 7'
CC-1   'LIMIT OF 5 CONTINUATION CARDS EXCEEDED'
CC-2   'INVALID CHARACTER IN FORTRAN STATEMENT.
         A '$' WAS INSERTED IN THE SOURCE LISTING'
CC-3   'FIRST CARD OF A PROGRAM IS A CONTINUATION CARD.
         PROBABLE CAUSE:STATEMENT PUNCHED TO LEFT OF COLUMN 7'
CC-4   'STATEMENT TOO LONG TO COMPILE (SCAN-STACK OVERFLOW)'
CC-5   'A BLANK CARD WAS ENCOUNTERED'
CC-6   'KEYPUNCH USED DIFFERS FROM KEYPUNCH SPECIFIED ON JOB CARD'
CC-7   'THE FIRST CHARACTER OF THE STATEMENT WAS NOT ALPHABETIC'
CC-8   'INVALID CHARACTER(S) ARE CONCATENATED WITH THE FORTRAN KEYWORD'
CC-9   'INVALID CHARACTERS IN COLUMNS 1-5.STATEMENT NUMBER IGNORED.
         PROBABLE CAUSE:STATEMENT PLACED TO LEFT OF COLUMN 7'

'COMMON'
CM-0   'THE VARIABLE IS ALREADY IN COMMON'
CM-1   'OTHER COMPILERS MAY NOT ALLOW COMMONED VARIABLES TO BE INITIALIZED IN
         OTHER THAN A BLOCK DATA SUBPROGRAM'
CM-2   'ILLEGAL USE OF A COMMON BLOCK OR NAMELIST NAME'

'FORTRAN TYPE CONSTANTS'
CN-0   'MIXED REAL*4,REAL*8 IN COMPLEX CONSTANT:REAL*8 ASSUMED FOR BOTH'
CN-1   'AN INTEGER CONSTANT MAY NOT BE GREATER THAN 2,147,483,647 (2**31-1)'
CN-2   'THE EXPONENT OF A REAL CONSTANT IS GREATER THAN 99,THE MAXIMUM'
CN-3   'A REAL CONSTANT HAS MORE THAN 16 DIGITS.IT WAS TRUNCATED TO 16'
CN-4   'INVALID HEXADECIMAL CONSTANT'
CN-5   'ILLEGAL USE OF A DECIMAL POINT'
CN-6   'CONSTANT WITH E-TYPE EXPONENT HAS MORE THAN 7 DIGITS. D-TYPE ASSUMED'
CN-7   'CONSTANT OR STATEMENT NUMBER GREATER THAN 99999'
CN-8   'AN EXPONENT OVERFLOW OR UNDERFLOW OCCURRED WHILE CONVERTING A CONSTANT
         IN A SOURCE STATEMENT'

'COMPILER ERRORS'
CP-0   'A COMPILER ERROR WAS DETECTED IN DECK LANDR'
CP-1   'COMPILER ERROR.LIKELY CAUSE:MORE THAN 255 DO STATEMENTS'
CP-2   'A COMPILER ERROR WAS DETECTED IN DECK ARITH'
CP-4   'COMPILER ERROR - INTERRUPT AT COMPILE TIME.RETURN TO SYSTEM'

---

‡ WATFIV error codes have been reproduced by permission from "/360 WATFIV Implementation Guide," Department of Applied Analysis and Computer Science, University of Waterloo, Waterloo, Ontario, September 1969.

WATFIV **Compiler Error Messages (continued)**

'CHARACTER VARIABLE'
CV-0   'A CHARACTER VARIABLE IS USED WITH A RELATIONAL OPERATOR'
CV-1   'LENGTH OF A CHARACTER VALUE ON RIGHT OF EQUAL SIGN EXCEEDS THAT ON
        LEFT. TRUNCATION WILL OCCUR'

'DATA STATEMENT'
DA-0   'REPLICATION FACTOR IS ZERO OR GREATER THAN 32767.
        IT IS ASSUMED TO BE 32767'
DA-1   'MORE VARIABLES THAN CONSTANTS'
DA-2   'ATTEMPT TO INITIALIZE A SUBPROGRAM PARAMETER IN A DATA STATEMENT'
DA-3   'OTHER COMPILERS MAY NOT ALLOW NON-CONSTANT SUBSCRIPTS IN DATA
        STATEMENTS'
DA-4   'NON-AGREEMENT BETWEEN TYPE OF VARIABLE AND CONSTANT'
DA-5   'MORE CONSTANTS THAN VARIABLES'
DA-6   'A VARIABLE WAS PREVIOUSLY INITIALIZED.THE LATEST VALUE IS USED.
        CHECK COMMONED AND EQUIVALENCED VARIABLES'
DA-7   'OTHER COMPILERS MAY NOT ALLOW INITIALIZATION OF BLANK COMMON'
DA-8   'A LITERAL CONSTANT HAS BEEN TRUNCATED'
DA-9   'OTHER COMPILERS MAY NOT ALLOW IMPLIED DO-LOOPS IN DATA STATEMENTS'

'DEFINE FILE STATEMENTS'
DF-0   'THE UNIT NUMBER IS MISSING'
DF-1   'INVALID FORMAT TYPE'
DF-2   'THE ASSOCIATED VARIABLE IS NOT A SIMPLE INTEGER VARIABLE'

'DIMENSION STATEMENTS'
DM-0   'NO DIMENSIONS ARE SPECIFIED FOR A VARIABLE IN A DIMENSION STATEMENT'
DM-1   'THE VARIABLE HAS ALREADY BEEN DIMENSIONED'
DM-2   'CALL-BY-LOCATION PARAMETERS MAY NOT BE DIMENSIONED'
DM-3   'THE DECLARED SIZE OF ARRAY EXCEEDS SPACE PROVIDED BY CALLING ARGUMENT'

'DO LOOPS'
DO-0   'THIS STATEMENT CANNOT BE THE OBJECT OF A DO-LOOP'
DO-1   'ILLEGAL TRANSFER INTO THE RANGE OF A DO-LOOP'
DO-2   'THE OBJECT OF THIS DO-LOOP HAS ALREADY APPEARED'
DO-3   'IMPROPERLY NESTED DO-LOOPS'
DO-4   'ATTEMPT TO REDEFINE A DO-LOOP PARAMETER WITHIN THE RANGE OF THE LOOP'
DO-5   'INVALID DO-LOOP PARAMETER'
DO-6   'ILLEGAL TRANSFER TO A STATEMENT WHICH IS INSIDE THE RANGE OF A DO-LOOP'
DO-7   'A DO-LOOP PARAMETER IS UNDEFINED OR OUT OF RANGE'
DO-8   'BECAUSE OF ONE OF THE PARAMETERS,THIS DO-LOOP WILL TERMINATE AFTER THE
        FIRST TIME THROUGH'
DO-9   'A DO-LOOP PARAMETER MAY NOT BE REDEFINED IN AN INPUT LIST'
DO-A   'OTHER COMPILERS MAY NOT ALLOW THIS STATEMENT TO END A DO-LOOP'

'EQUIVALENCE AND/OR COMMON'
EC-0   'EQUIVALENCED VARIABLE APPEARS IN A COMMON STATEMENT'
EC-1   'A COMMON BLOCK HAS A DIFFERENT LENGTH THAN IN A PREVIOUS
        SUBPROGRAM:GREATER LENGTH USED'
EC-2   'COMMON AND/OR EQUIVALENCE CAUSES INVALID ALIGNMENT.
        EXECUTION SLOWED.REMEDY:ORDER VARIABLES BY DECREASING LENGTH'
EC-3   'EQUIVALENCE EXTENDS COMMON DOWNWARDS'
EC-4   'A SUBPROGRAM PARAMETER APPEARS IN A COMMON OR EQUIVALENCE STATEMENT'
EC-5   'A VARIABLE WAS USED WITH SUBSCRIPTS IN AN EQUIVALENCE STATEMENT BUT HAS
        NOT BEEN PROPERLY DIMENSIONED'

'END STATEMENTS'
EN-0   'MISSING END STATEMENT:END STATEMENT GENERATED'
EN-1   'AN END STATEMENT WAS USED TO TERMINATE EXECUTION'

Watfiv Compiler Error Messages (continued)

'EQUAL SIGNS'
EQ-0   'ILLEGAL QUANTITY ON LEFT OF EQUALS SIGN'
EQ-1   'ILLEGAL USE OF EQUAL SIGN'
EQ-2   'OTHER COMPILERS MAY NOT ALLOW MULTIPLE ASSIGNMENT STATEMENTS'
EQ-3   'MULTIPLE ASSIGNMENT IS NOT IMPLEMENTED FOR CHARACTER VARIABLES'

'EQUIVALENCE STATEMENTS'
EV-0   'ATTEMPT TO EQUIVALENCE A VARIABLE TO ITSELF'
EV-2   'A MULTI-SUBSCRIPTED EQUIVALENCED VARIABLE HAS BEEN INCORRECTLY
        RE-EQUIVALENCED.REMEDY:DIMENSION THE VARIABLE FIRST'

'POWERS AND EXPONENTIATION'
EX-0   'ILLEGAL COMPLEX EXPONENTIATION'
EX-1   'I**J WHERE I=J=0'
EX-2   'I**J WHERE I=0, J.LT.0'
EX-3   '0.0**Y WHERE Y.LE.0.0'
EX-4   'C.0**J WHERE J=0'
EX-5   'C.0**J WHERE J.LT.0'
EX-6   'X**Y WHERE X.LT.0.0, Y.NE.0.0'

'ENTRY STATEMENT'
EY-0   'ENTRY-POINT NAME WAS PREVIOUSLY DEFINED'
EY-1   'PREVIOUS DEFINITION OF FUNCTION NAME IN AN ENTRY IS INCORRECT'
EY-2   'THE USAGE OF A SUBPROGRAM PARAMETER IS INCONSISTENT WITH A PREVIOUS
        ENTRY-POINT'
EY-3   'A PARAMETER HAS APPEARED IN A EXECUTABLE STATEMENT BUT IS NOT A
        SUBPROGRAM PARAMETER'
EY-4   'ENTRY STATEMENTS ARE INVALID IN THE MAIN PROGRAM'
EY-5   'ENTRY STATEMENT INVALID INSIDE A DO-LOOP'

'FORMAT'
    SOME FORMAT ERROR MESSAGES GIVE CHARACTERS IN WHICH ERROR WAS DETECTED
FM-0   'IMPROPER CHARACTER SEQUENCE OR INVALID CHARACTER IN INPUT DATA'
FM-1   'NO STATEMENT NUMBER ON A FORMAT STATEMENT'
FM-2   'FORMAT CODE AND DATA TYPE DO NOT MATCH'
FM-4   'FORMAT PROVIDES NO CONVERSION SPECIFICATION FOR A VALUE IN I/O LIST'
FM-5   'AN INTEGER IN THE INPUT DATA IS TOO LARGE.
        (MAXIMUM=2,147,483,647=2**31-1)'
FM-6   'A REAL NUMBER IN THE INPUT DATA IS OUT OF MACHINE RANGE (1.E-78,1.E+75)'
FT-0   'FIRST CHARACTER OF VARIABLE FORMAT IS NOT A LEFT PARENTHESIS'
FT-1   'INVALID CHARACTER ENCOUNTERED IN FORMAT'
FT-2   'INVALID FORM FOLLOWING A FORMAT CODE'
FT-3   'INVALID FIELD OR GROUP COUNT'
FT-4   'A FIELD OR GROUP COUNT GREATER THAN 255'
FT-5   'NO CLOSING PARENTHESIS ON VARIABLE FORMAT'
FT-6   'NO CLOSING QUOTE IN A HOLLERITH FIELD'
FT-7   'INVALID USE OF COMMA'
FT-8   'FORMAT STATEMENT TOO LONG TO COMPILE (SCAN-STACK OVERFLOW)'
FT-9   'INVALID USE OF P FORMAT CODE'
FT-A   'INVALID USE OF PERIOD(.)'
FT-B   'MORE THAN THREE LEVELS OF PARENTHESES'
FT-C   'INVALID CHARACTER BEFORE A RIGHT PARENTHESIS'
FT-D   'MISSING OR ZERO LENGTH HOLLERITH ENCOUNTERED'
FT-E   'NO CLOSING RIGHT PARENTHESIS'
FT-F   'CHARACTERS FOLLOW CLOSING RIGHT PARENTHESIS'
FT-G   'WRONG QUOTE USED FOR KEY-PUNCH SPECIFIED'
FT-H   'LENGTH OF HOLLERITH EXCEEDS 255'

'FUNCTIONS AND SUBROUTINES'
FN-1   'A PARAMETER APPEARS MORE THAN ONCE IN A SUBPROGRAM OR STATEMENT
        FUNCTION DEFINITION'

WATFIV **Compiler Error Messages (continued)**

```
FN-2    'SUBSCRIPTS ON RIGHT-HAND SIDE OF STATEMENT FUNCTION.
        PROBABLE CAUSE:VARIABLE TO LEFT OF EQUAL SIGN NOT DIMENSIONED'
FN-3    'MULTIPLE RETURNS ARE INVALID IN FUNCTION SUBPROGRAMS'
FN-4    'ILLEGAL LENGTH MODIFIER'
FN-5    'INVALID PARAMETER'
FN-6    'A PARAMETER HAS THE SAME NAME AS THE SUBPROGRAM'

'GO TO STATEMENTS'
GO-0    'THIS STATEMENT COULD TRANSFER TO ITSELF'
GO-1    'THIS STATEMENT TRANSFERS TO A NON-EXECUTABLE STATEMENT'
GO-2    'ATTEMPT TO DEFINE ASSIGNED GOTO INDEX IN AN ARITHMETIC STATEMENT'
GO-3    'ASSIGNED GOTO INDEX MAY BE USED ONLY IN ASSIGNED GOTO AND ASSIGN
        STATEMENTS'
GO-4    'THE INDEX OF AN ASSIGNED GOTO IS UNDEFINED OR OUT OF RANGE,OR INDEX OF
        COMPUTED GOTO IS UNDEFINED'
GO-5    'ASSIGNED GOTO INDEX MAY NOT BE AN INTEGER*2 VARIABLE'

'HOLLERITH CONSTANTS'
HO-0    'ZERO LENGTH SPECIFIED FOR H-TYPE HOLLERITH'
HO-1    'ZERO LENGTH QUOTE-TYPE HOLLERITH'
HO-2    'NO CLOSING QUOTE OR NEXT CARD NOT A CONTINUATION CARD'
HO-3    'UNEXPECTED HOLLERITH OR STATEMENT NUMBER CONSTANT'

'IF STATEMENTS (ARITHMETIC AND LOGICAL)'
IF-0    'AN INVALID STATEMENT FOLLOWS THE LOGICAL IF'
IF-1    'ARITHMETIC OR INVALID EXPRESSION IN LOGICAL IF'
IF-2    'LOGICAL,COMPLEX OR INVALID EXPRESSION IN ARITHMETIC IF'

'IMPLICIT STATEMENT'
IM-0    'INVALID DATA TYPE'
IM-1    'INVALID OPTIONAL LENGTH'
IM-3    'IMPROPER ALPHABETIC SEQUENCE IN CHARACTER RANGE'
IM-4    'A SPECIFICATION IS NOT A SINGLE CHARACTER.THE FIRST CHARACTER IS USED'
IM-5    'IMPLICIT STATEMENT DOES NOT PRECEDE OTHER SPECIFICATION STATEMENTS'
IM-6    'ATTEMPT TO DECLARE THE TYPE OF A CHARACTER MORE THAN ONCE'
IM-7    'ONLY ONE IMPLICIT STATEMENT PER PROGRAM SEGMENT ALLOWED. THIS ONE
        IGNORED'

'INPUT/OUTPUT'
IO-0    'I/O STATEMENT REFERENCES A STATEMENT WHICH IS NOT A FORMAT STATEMENT'
IO-1    'A VARIABLE FORMAT MUST BE AN ARRAY NAME'
IO-2    'INVALID ELEMENT IN INPUT LIST OR DATA LIST'
IO-3    'OTHER COMPILERS MAY NOT ALLOW EXPRESSIONS IN OUTPUT LISTS'
IO-4    'ILLEGAL USE OF END= OR ERR= PARAMETERS'
IO-5    'INVALID UNIT NUMBER'
IO-6    'INVALID FORMAT'
IO-7    'ONLY CONSTANTS,SIMPLE INTEGER*4 VARIABLES,AND CHARACTER VARIABLES ARE
        ALLOWED AS UNIT'

'JOB CONTROL CARDS'
JB-0    'CONTROL CARD ENCOUNTERED DURING COMPILATION:
        PROBABLE CAUSE:MISSING $ENTRY CARD'
JB-1    'MIS-PUNCHED JOB OPTION'

'JOB TERMINATION'
KO-0    'SOURCE ERROR ENCOUNTERED WHILE EXECUTING WITH RUN=FREE'
KO-1    'LIMIT EXCEEDED FOR FIXED-POINT DIVISION BY ZERO'
KO-2    'LIMIT EXCEEDED FOR FLOATING-POINT DIVISION BY ZERO'
KO-3    'EXPONENT OVERFLOW LIMIT EXCEEDED'
KO-4    'EXPONENT UNDERFLOW LIMIT EXCEEDED'
KO-5    'FIXED-POINT OVERFLOW LIMIT EXCEEDED'
```

WATFIV Compiler Error Messages (continued)

```
KO-6    'JOB-TIME EXCEEDED'
KO-7    'COMPILER ERROR - EXECUTION TIME:RETURN TO SYSTEM'
KO-8    'TRACEBACK ERROR. TRACEBACK TERMINATED'

'LOGICAL OPERATIONS'
LG-0    '.NOT. WAS USED AS A BINARY OPERATOR'

'LIBRARY ROUTINES'
LI-0    'ARGUMENT OUT OF RANGE DGAMMA OR GAMMA. (1.382E-76 .LT. X .LT. 57.57)'
LI-1    'ABSOLUTE VALUE OF ARGUMENT .GT. 174.673, SINH,COSH,DSINH,DCOSH'
LI-2    'SENSE LIGHT OTHER THAN 0,1,2,3,4 FOR SLITE OR 1,2,3,4 FOR SLITET'
LI-3    'REAL PORTION OF ARGUMENT .GT. 174.673, CEXP OR CDEXP'
LI-4    'ABS(AIMAG(Z)) .GT. 174.673 FOR CSIN, CCOS, CDSIN OR CDCOS OF Z'
LI-5    'ABS(REAL(Z)) .GE. 3.537E15 FOR CSIN, CCOS, CDSIN OR CDCOS OF Z'
LI-6    'ABS(AIMAG(Z)) .GE. 3.537E15 FOR CEXP OR CDEXP OF Z'
LI-7    'ARGUMENT .GT. 174.673, EXP OR DEXP'
LI-8    'ARGUMENT IS ZERO, CLOG, CLOG10, CDLOG OR CDLOG10'
LI-9    'ARGUMENT IS NEGATIVE OR ZERO, ALOG, ALOG10, DLOG OR DLOG10'
LI-A    'ABS(X) .GE. 3.537E15 FOR SIN, COS, DSIN OR DCOS OF X'
LI-B    'ABSOLUTE VALUE OF ARGUMENT .GT. 1, FOR ARSIN, ARCOS, DARSIN OR DARCOS'
LI-C    'ARGUMENT IS NEGATIVE, SQRT OR CSQRT'
LI-D    'BOTH ARGUMENTS OF DATAN2 OR ATAN2 ARE ZERO'
LI-E    'ARGUMENT TOO CLOSE TO A SINGULARITY, TAN, COTAN, DTAN OR DCOTAN'
LI-F    'ARGUMENT OUT OF RANGE DLGAMA OR ALGAMA. (0.0 .LT. X .LT. 4.29E73)'
LI-G    'ABSOLUTE VALUE OF ARGUMENT .GE. 3.537E15, TAN, COTAN, DTAN, DCOTAN'
LI-H    'LESS THAN TWO ARGUMENTS FOR ONE OF MIN0,MIN1,AMIN0,ETC.'

'MIXED MODE'
MD-0    'RELATIONAL OPERATOR HAS LOGICAL OPERAND'
MD-1    'RELATIONAL OPERATOR HAS COMPLEX OPERAND'
MD-2    'MIXED MODE - LOGICAL OR CHARACTER WITH ARITHMETIC'
MD-3    'OTHER COMPILERS MAY NOT ALLOW SUBSCRIPTS OF TYPE COMPLEX,LOGICAL OR
        CHARACTER'

'MEMORY OVERFLOW'
MO-0    'INSUFFICIENT MEMORY TO COMPILE THIS PROGRAM.REMAINDER WILL BE ERROR
        CHECKED ONLY'
MO-1    'INSUFFICIENT MEMORY TO ASSIGN ARRAY STORAGE. JOB ABANDONED'
MO-2    'SYMBOL TABLE EXCEEDS AVAILABLE SPACE,JOB ABANDONED'
MO-3    'DATA AREA OF SUBPROGRAM EXCEEDS 24K -- SEGMENT SUBPROGRAM'
MO-4    'INSUFFICIENT MEMORY TO ALLOCATE COMPILER WORK AREA OR WATLIB BUFFER'

'NAMELIST STATEMENTS'
NL-0    'NAMELIST ENTRY MUST BE A VARIABLE,NOT A SUBPROGRAM PARAMETER'
NL-1    'NAMELIST NAME PREVIOUSLY DEFINED'
NL-2    'VARIABLE NAME TOO LONG'
NL-3    'VARIABLE NAME NOT FOUND IN NAMELIST'
NL-4    'INVALID SYNTAX IN NAMELIST INPUT'
NL-6    'VARIABLE INCORRECTLY SUBSCRIPTED'
NL-7    'SUBSCRIPT OUT OF RANGE'

'PARENTHESES'
PC-0    'UNMATCHED PARENTHESIS'
PC-1    'INVALID PARENTHESIS NESTING IN I/O LIST'

'PAUSE, STOP STATEMENTS'
PS-0    'OPERATOR MESSAGES NOT ALLOWED:SIMPLE STOP ASSUMED FOR STOP,
        CONTINUE ASSUMED FOR PAUSE'
```

WATFIV **Compiler Error Messages (continued)**

'RETURN STATEMENT'
RE-1   'RETURN I, WHERE I IS OUT OF RANGE OR UNDEFINED'
RE-2   'MULTIPLE RETURN NOT VALID IN FUNCTION SUBPROGRAM'
RE-3   'VARIABLE IS NOT A SIMPLE INTEGER'
RE-4   'A MULTIPLE RETURN IS NOT VALID IN THE MAIN PROGRAM'

'ARITHMETIC AND LOGICAL STATEMENT FUNCTIONS'
        PROBABLE CAUSE OF SF ERRORS - VARIABLE ON LEFT OF = WAS NOT DIMENSIONED
SF-1   'A PREVIOUSLY REFERENCED STATEMENT NUMBER APPEARS ON A STATEMENT
        FUNCTION DEFINITION'
SF-2   'STATEMENT FUNCTION IS THE OBJECT OF A LOGICAL IF STATEMENT'
SF-3   'RECURSIVE STATEMENT FUNCTION DEFINITION:NAME APPEARS ON BOTH SIDES OF
        EQUAL SIGN.LIKELY CAUSE:VARIABLE NOT DIMENSIONED'
SF-4   'A STATEMENT FUNCTION DEFINITION APPEARS AFTER THE FIRST EXECUTABLE
        STATEMENT'
SF-5   'ILLEGAL USE OF A STATEMENT FUNCTION NAME'

'SUBPROGRAMS'
SR-0   'MISSING SUBPROGRAM'
SR-1   'SUBPROGRAM REDEFINES A CONSTANT,EXPRESSION,DO-PARAMETER OR ASSIGNED
        GOTO INDEX'
SR-2   'THE SUBPROGRAM WAS ASSIGNED DIFFERENT TYPES IN DIFFERENT PROGRAM
        SEGMENTS'
SR-3   'ATTEMPT TO USE A SUBPROGRAM RECURSIVELY'
SR-4   'INVALID TYPE OF ARGUMENT IN REFERENCE TO A SUBPROGRAM'
SR-5   'WRONG NUMBER OF ARGUMENTS IN A REFERENCE TO A SUBPROGRAM'
SR-6   'A SUBPROGRAM WAS PREVIOUSLY DEFINED. THE FIRST DEFINITION IS USED'
SR-7   'NO MAIN PROGRAM'
SR-8   'ILLEGAL OR MISSING SUBPROGRAM NAME'
SR-9   'LIBRARY PROGRAM WAS NOT ASSIGNED THE CORRECT TYPE'
SR-A   'METHOD FOR ENTERING SUBPROGRAM PRODUCES UNDEFINED VALUE FOR
        CALL-BY-LOCATION PARAMETER'

'SUBSCRIPTS'
SS-0   'ZERO SUBSCRIPT OR DIMENSION NOT ALLOWED'
SS-1   'YOU ALREADY HAVE THE MESSAGE'
SS-2   'INVALID SUBSCRIPT FORM'
SS-3   'SUBSCRIPT IS OUT OF RANGE'

'STATEMENTS AND STATEMENT NUMBERS'
ST-0   'MISSING STATEMENT NUMBER'
ST-1   'STATEMENT NUMBER GREATER THAN 99999'
ST-2   'STATEMENT NUMBER HAS ALREADY BEEN DEFINED'
ST-3   'UNDECODEABLE STATEMENT'
ST-4   'THIS STATEMENT SHOULD HAVE A STATEMENT NUMBER'
ST-5   'STATEMENT NUMBER IN A TRANSFER IS A NON-EXECUTABLE STATEMENT'
ST-6   'ONLY CALL STATEMENTS MAY CONTAIN STATEMENT NUMBER ARGUMENTS'
ST-7   'STATEMENT SPECIFIED IN A TRANSFER STATEMENT IS A FORMAT STATEMENT'
ST-8   'MISSING FORMAT STATEMENT'
ST-9   'SPECIFICATION STATEMENT DOES NOT PRECEDE STATEMENT FUNCTION DEFINITIONS
        OR EXECUTABLE STATEMENTS'

'SUBSCRIPTED VARIABLES'
SV-0   'THE WRONG NUMBER OF SUBSCRIPTS WERE SPECIFIED FOR A VARIABLE'

SV-1   'AN ARRAY OR SUBPROGRAM NAME IS USED INCORRECTLY WITHOUT A LIST'
SV-2   'MORE THAN 7 DIMENSIONS ARE NOT ALLOWED'
SV-3   'DIMENSION OR SUBSCRIPT IS TOO LARGE (MAXIMUM 10**-1)'
SV-4   'A VARIABLE USED WITH VARIABLE DIMENSIONS IS NOT A SUBPROGRAM PARAMETER'
SV-5   'A VARIABLE DIMENSION IS NOT ONE OF:SIMPLE INTEGER VARIABLE,SUBPROGRAM
        PARAMETER,IN COMMON'

WATFIV Compiler Error Messages (continued)

```
'SYNTAX ERRORS'
SX-0    'MISSING OPERATOR'
SX-1    'EXPECTING OPERATOR'
SX-2    'EXPECTING SYMBOL'
SX-3    'EXPECTING SYMBOL OR OPERATOR'
SX-4    'EXPECTING CONSTANT'
SX-5    'EXPECTING SYMBOL OR CONSTANT'
SX-6    'EXPECTING STATEMENT NUMBER'
SX-7    'EXPECTING SIMPLE INTEGER VARIABLE'
SX-8    'EXPECTING SIMPLE INTEGER VARIABLE OR CONSTANT'
SX-9    'ILLEGAL SEQUENCE OF OPERATORS IN EXPRESSION'
SX-A    'EXPECTING END-OF-STATEMENT'

'TYPE STATEMENTS'
TY-0    'THE VARIABLE HAS ALREADY BEEN EXPLICITLY TYPED'
TY-1    'THE LENGTH OF THE EQUIVALENCED VARIABLE MAY NOT BE CHANGED.
        REMEDY: INTERCHANGE TYPE AND EQUIVALENCE STATEMENTS'

'I/O OPERATIONS'
UN-0    'CONTROL CARD ENCOUNTERED ON UNIT 5 AT EXECUTION.
        PROBABLE CAUSE:MISSING DATA OR INCORRECT FORMAT'
UN-1    'END OF FILE ENCOUNTERED (IBM CODE IHC217)'
UN-2    'I/O ERROR (IBM CODE IHC218)'
UN-3    'NO DD STATEMENT WAS SUPPLIED (IBM CODE IHC219)'
UN-4    'REWIND,ENDFILE,BACKSPACE REFERENCES UNIT 5, 6 OR 7'
UN-5    'ATTEMPT TO READ ON UNIT 5 AFTER IT HAS HAD END-OF-FILE'
UN-6    'AN INVALID VARIABLE UNIT NUMBER WAS DETECTED (IBM CODE IHC220)'
UN-7    'PAGE-LIMIT EXCEEDED'
UN-8    'MISSING DEFINE FILE STATEMENT OR ATTEMPT TO DO SEQUENTIAL I/O ON A
        DIRECT ACCESS FILE (IBM CODE IHC231)'
UN-9    'WRITE REFERENCES 5 OR READ REFERENCES 6 OR 7'
UN-A    'ATTEMPT TO DO DIRECT ACCESS I/O ON A SEQUENTIAL FILE (IBM CODE IHC235)'
UN-B    'RECORD SIZE IN DEFINE FILE STATEMENT IS TOO LARGE(MAX=32768),OR EXCEEDS
        DD STATEMENT SPECIFICATION (IBM CODE IHC233,IHC237)'
UN-C    'FOR DIRECT ACCESS I/O THE RELATIVE RECORD POSITION IS NEGATIVE,ZERO,OR
        TOO LARGE (IBM CODE IHC232)'
UN-D    'AN ATTEMPT WAS MADE TO READ MORE INFORMATION THAN LOGICAL RECORD
        CONTAINS (IBM CODE IHC236)'
UN-E    'FORMATTED LINE EXCEEDS BUFFER LENGHT'
UN-F    'I/O ERROR - SEARCHING LIBRARY DIRECTORY'
UN-G    'I/O ERROR - READING LIBRARY'
UN-H    'ATTEMPT TO DEFINE THE OBJECT ERROR FILE AS A DIRECT ACCESS FILE
        (IBM CODE IHC234)'
UN-I    'RECFM OTHER THAN V(B) IS SPECIFIED FOR I/O WITHOUT FORMAT CONTROL
        (IBM CODE IHC214)'
UN-J    'MISSING DD CARD FOR WATLIB.NO LIBRARY ASSUMED'
UN-K    'ATTEMPT TO READ OR WRITE PAST THE END OF CHARACTER VARIABLE BUFFER'

'UNDEFINED VARIABLES'
UV-0    'VARIABLE IS UNDEFINED'
UV-3    'SUBSCRIPT IS UNDEFINED'
UV-4    'SUBPROGRAM IS UNDEFINED'
UV-5    'ARGUMENT IS UNDEFINED'
UV-6    'UNDECODABLE CHARACTERS IN VARIABLE FORMAT'

'VARIABLE NAMES'
VA-0    'A NAME IS TOO LONG.IT HAS BEEN TRUNCATED TO SIX CHARACTERS'
VA-1    'ATTEMPT TO USE AN ASSIGNED OR INITIALIZED VARIABLE OR DO-PARAMETER IN A
        SPECIFICATION STATEMENT'
VA-2    'ILLEGAL USE OF A SUBROUTINE NAME'
VA-3    'ILLEGAL USE OF A VARIABLE NAME'
```

WATFIV Compiler Error Messages (continued)

VA-4 'ATTEMPT TO USE THE PREVIOUSLY DEFINED NAME AS A FUNCTION OR AN ARRAY'
VA-5 'ATTEMPT TO USE A PREVIOUSLY DEFINED NAME AS A SUBROUTINE'
VA-6 'ATTEMPT TO USE A PREVIOUSLY DEFINED NAME AS A SUBPROGRAM'
VA-7 'ATTEMPT TO USE A PREVIOUSLY DEFINED NAME AS A COMMON BLOCK'
VA-8 'ATTEMPT TO USE A FUNCTION NAME AS A VARIABLE'
VA-9 'ATTEMPT TO USE A PREVIOUSLY DEFINED NAME AS A VARIABLE'
VA-A 'ILLEGAL USE OF A PREVIOUSLY DEFINED NAME'

'EXTERNAL STATEMENT'
XT-0 'A VARIABLE HAS ALREADY APPEARED IN AN EXTERNAL STATEMENT'

Appendix F

USE OF THE KEYPUNCH MACHINE

Many beginning students of FORTRAN submit programs to the computer via punched cards. Characters are punched onto these cards using a special machine known as a keypunch machine. Consequently, students using punched cards must learn how to use the keypunch machine. The objective is only to be able to punch a few (usually 25 or less) cards in a reasonable length of time. Special courses are available for those who plan to make keypunching a career, and such courses will encompass several features of the machine that we shall omit. Students of FORTRAN need not achieve such a high degree of proficiency.

In this appendix, we shall limit our discussion to the IBM 029 keypunch machine, which is the most commonly used machine for student work.

F-1. GENERAL DESCRIPTION

An overall view of the keypunch machine is shown in Figure F-1. Blank cards are fed from the card hopper at the upper right of the machine into the punch station just above and to the right of the keyboard. After being punched, the card advances to the read station at the center of the machine, and then on to the card stacker.

Below the keyboard and to the right is the power switch for turning the machine on and off. Most centers request students to turn the machine off after use.

F-2. THE KEYBOARD

Figure F-2 shows the keyboard of the IBM 029 keypunch machine. The position of the alphabetic characters is identical to their position on the typewriter keyboard. As on the typewriter, the space bar is at the bottom of the keyboard. However, the locations of the digits and the special symbols are different.

294

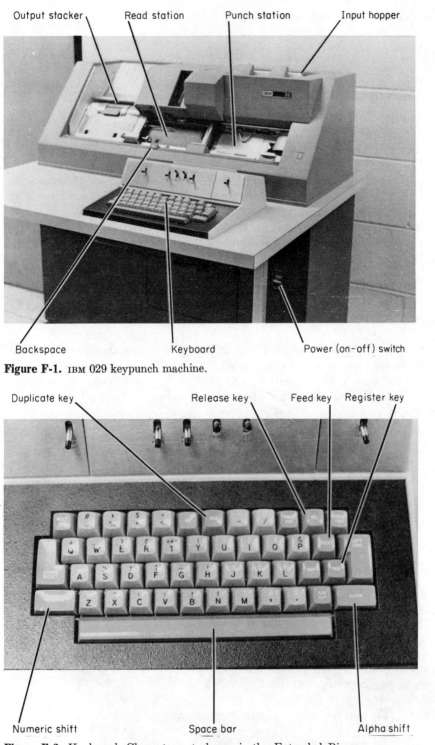

Figure F-1. ɪʙᴍ 029 keypunch machine.

Figure F-2. Keyboard. Character set shown is the Extended Binary Coded Decimal Interchange Code or ᴇʙᴄᴅɪᴄ character set; some centers use the Binary Coded Decimal or ʙᴄᴅ character set which provides different special characters and for which the location of some special characters, notably the t, =, (, and), is different.

The light or cream colored keys are for punching the characters. The dark or blue colored keys are for special purposes such as feeding cards or shift selection. For brevity, we shall explain only those keys of general use to the beginning programmer.

All but two of the keys exhibit two symbols. The symbol punched when the key is depressed depends upon the status of the shift. The two possible states are the ALPHA shift and the NUMERIC shift. The ALPHA shift key is on the lower right of the keyboard, and the NUMERIC shift key is on the lower left. As normally configured for student use, the machine is in the ALPHA shift state unless the NUMERIC shift key is depressed. If the machine is in the ALPHA shift position when a key is depressed, the lower character on the key is punched onto the card. If the machine is in the NUMERIC shift position, the upper character is punched.

Just below the center (read) station is located the backspace button (refer to Figure F-1). Depressing this button causes the card to be moved backwards. This feature has limited utility since backspacing does not, of course, fill up any holes in the card.

F-3. PROGRAM CONTROL

The program control feature permits the machine to be automatically skipped to certain positions, for the ALPHA or NUMERIC shift to be selected as appropriate, and other similar functions to be selected automatically. To use this feature requires punching a special program card. This effort can be justified only if a large number of cards are being punched, and thus students in beginning courses need not learn how to use this feature, but must learn how to turn it off.

Program control lever   Read station

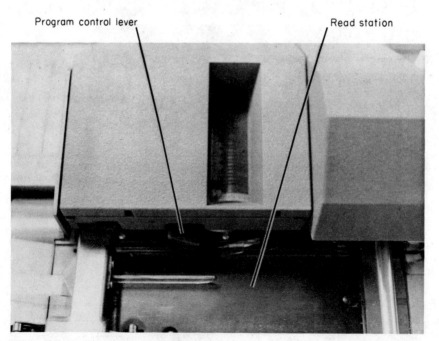

Figure F-3. Program control feature.

The program control feature is engaged via the program control lever near the center of the machine and just above the read (center) station. Depressing this switch to the right as illustrated in Figure F-3 disengages the program control feature.

F-4. SWITCH POSITIONS

Immediately above the keyboard are six switches (illustrated in Figure F-4) that serve various functions. From the left, these switches and their functions are as follows:

AUTO SKIP DUP (auto skip/duplicate) switch is used in conjunction with the program control feature. Since this feature offers no advantage to beginning students, this switch should be set OFF (down).

PROG SEL (program select) switch is also used in conjunction with the program control feature. If the program control lever is set so as to disengage the program control feature, the setting of the PROG SEL switch is immaterial.

AUTO FEED (automatic feed) switch provides for the automatic feeding of cards. This feature will be explained in a subsequent section; but until that time this switch should be set OFF (down).

PRINT switch causes the characters to be printed across the top of the card. This switch should be set ON (up).

LZ PRINT (left-zero print) should also be set ON (up).

CLEAR switch is spring loaded so that it automatically returns to the down position when released. Its use will be explained subsequently.

The switch positions illustrated in Figure F-4 are those recommended for use by the beginning programmer.

Figure F-4. Switches.

F-5. LOADING CARDS

Some centers provide cards for use by students, while others expect the students to provide their own. In either case, the student must know how to load the cards into the card hopper.

A spring loaded pressure plate is provided in the guide to force the cards to the front of the card hopper. If this plate is pushed to the rear of the hopper, a catch retains it in the position shown in Figure F-5. The cards are then readily inserted as illustrated. Care should be taken that they are straight, and the cards should be moved to the front of the hopper before the spring-loaded pressure plate is released (by a lever on the back of the pressure plate). Should the cards fail to feed, it usually means that they were not correctly inserted or that the front card is bent.

Pressure plate

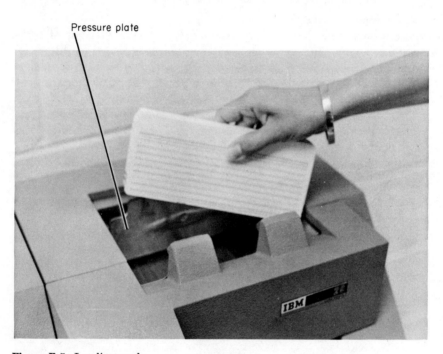

Figure F-5. Loading cards.

F-6. FEEDING CARDS

Before a card can be punched, it must be moved from the card hopper to the proper position in the punch station.

Starting with the machine free of cards at both the punch station and the read station,‡ the first step is to depress the FEED key on the right-hand side of the keyboard.

---

‡If the machine is not free of cards, momentarily raise the CLEAR switch and the machine should automatically clear both read and punch station of any cards.

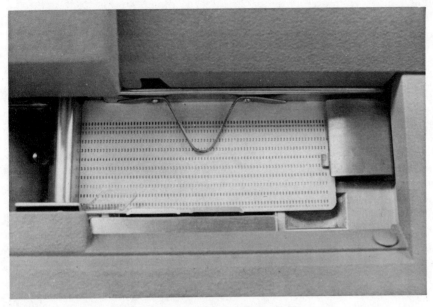

Figure F-6. Card in preregistered position in punch station.

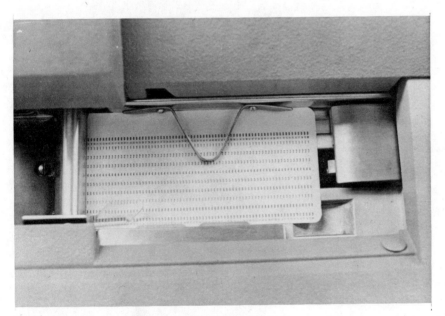

Figure F-7. Card in registered position at punch station.

A card should move from the card hopper into the punch station as illustrated in Figure F-6. At this point, the card is said to be in the preregistered position and is not yet in the proper position for punching.

The next step is to depress the REG (register) key immediately below the FEED key. This causes the card to be placed in the proper position for punching, as illustrated in Figure F-7.

F-7. PUNCHING

In FORTRAN, the location of the characters on the card is important. For example, the FORTRAN statement should begin in column 7. After depressing the REG key, the card is positioned at column 1. Thus, we can advance the card to column 7 by skipping the first six columns, which is accomplished by depressing the space bar six times.

Naturally, it is impractical to mentally keep track of the current position of the card. Above the program control lever is a window through which can be seen a red pointer and a dial indicating the current position of the card. As illustrated in Figure F-8, the card is now positioned at column 7. We can now proceed to punch the FORTRAN statement.

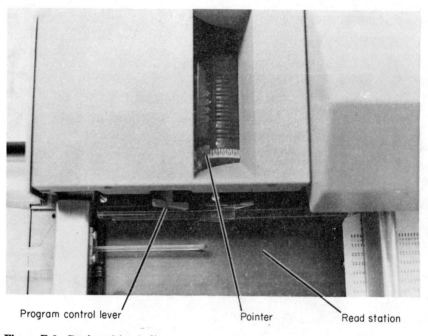

Program control lever   Pointer   Read station

Figure F-8. Card position indicator.

F-8. RELEASING THE CARD

Upon completion of punching the FORTRAN statement, the card remains positioned in the punch station as indicated in Figure F-9. One approach to removing the card is to momentarily raise the CLEAR switch to the ON position. This causes any card or cards in the punch and/or read stations to be cleared from the machine.

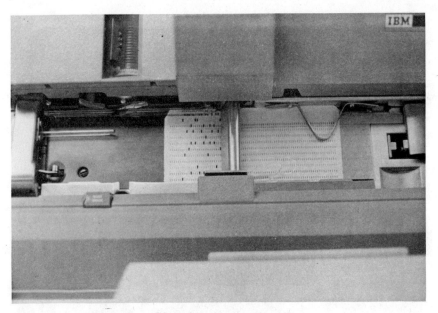

Figure F-9. Card after punching of FORTRAN statement.

Figure F-10. Card at preregistered position at read station.

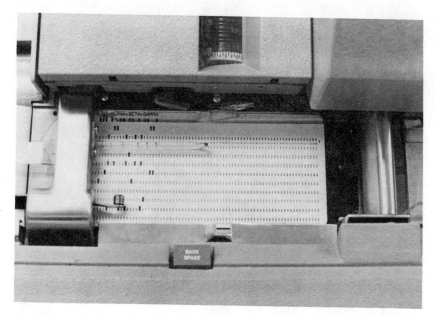

Figure F-11. Card at registered position at read station.

Figure F-12. Card at preposition in output stacker.

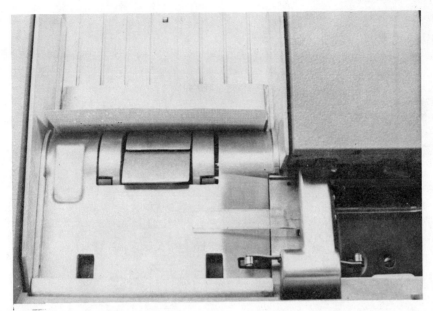

Figure F-13. Card in output stacker.

An alternate approach is to use the REL (release) key located on the keyboard immediately above the FEED key. Depressing this key causes the card to be moved from the punch station (as in Figure F-9) to a preregistered position in the read station as illustrated in Figure F-10. Depressing the REG key moves the card to the registered position in the read station (Figure F-11). Depressing the REL key again causes the card to be advanced to a pre-position in the output stacker as illustrated in Figure F-12. Depressing the REG key a second time advances the card to the output stacker (Figure F-13).

In using the REL key, it should be noted that the card must be in the registered position before it may be released. That is, a card in the preregistered position is not affected by depressing the REL key.

F-9. PUNCHING SUCCESSIVE CARDS

After punching a card, it is not necessary to completely clear it to the output stacker before commencing the punching of the next card. Instead, it need only be released from the punch station by depressing the REL key. At that point, the FEED key may be depressed, which causes a card to be fed from the card hopper to the preregistered position in the punch station. Incidental to this operation, the card in the read station is moved to the registered position. Depressing the REG key causes the card in the punch station to also be moved to the registered position. The result is that the card previously punched is at the registered position in the read station and a blank card is at the registered position at the punch station, as illustrated in Figure F-14. Punching of the blank card may now commence.

Figure F-14. Cards at registered position at read and at punch stations.

F-10. CORRECTION OF ERRORS

Even the most proficient keypunch operators make errors, so a very convenient mechanism has been provided for correcting errors. To illustrate the procedure, suppose
you are punching a FORTRAN statement and realize that you have made an error, say
in column 17, while the card is still in the punch station. To correct the error, the first
step is to depress the REL key to release the card from the punch station. This is followed by depressing the FEED key followed by the REG key, which results in the card
containing the error being in the registered position at the read station and a new
card being in the registered position at the punch station.

Since the error is in column 17, the first step is to copy the contents of columns
1 through 16 from the old card onto the new card. This is accomplished by depressing
the DUP (duplicate) key at the upper center of the keyboard. While this key is depressed, it is necessary to watch the column position pointer, releasing the key when
column 17 is approached. Briefly depressing the DUP key will cause the contents of a
single column to be copied onto the new card. When column 17 is reached, the appropriate character is entered. Thereafter, the DUP key can be used to copy the remainder
of the old card onto the new card, or one may continue to enter characters from the
keyboard.

In some cases, it is not realized that an error has occurred until the card has
been completely removed from the machine. However, it can be inserted directly into
the read station. After clearing the machine, the first step is to depress the FEED key
to advance a card to the preregistered position at the punch station. Then the card
containing the error is inserted into the special guides at the read station as illustrated
in Figure F-15. Depressing the REG key causes both of these cards to advance to the

Guides

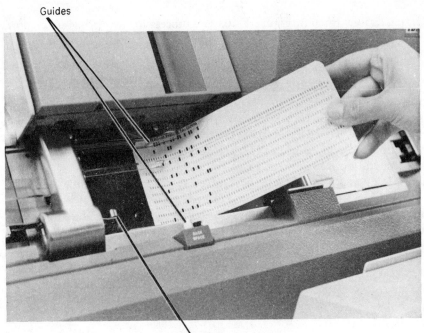

Insert card until
end of card is
beneath roller

Figure F-15. Inserting card into read station.

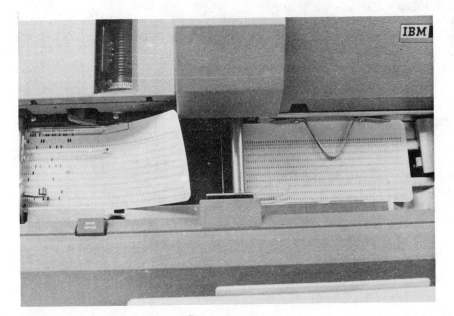

Figure F-16. Card in position for duplication.

registered position as illustrated in Figure F-16. The process for correcting errors now proceeds as before.

F-11. USE OF AUTOMATIC FEED

Setting the AUTO FEED switch in the ON (up) position causes the release operation to be immediately followed by a feed operation. That is, depressing the REL key causes the release operation to occur as usual; but the operation is then automatically followed by a FEED operation just as if the FEED key were depressed.

To set the machine up for automatic feed, first clear the read and punch stations of all cards (this is most conveniently accomplished with the CLEAR switch). Then depress the FEED key twice, which results in one card being in the registered position in the punch station and a second card being in the preregistered position in the punch station. The first card is now ready for punching. Depressing the REL key advances the first card to the registered position in the read station, advances the second card to the registered position in the punch station, and advances a card from the card hopper to the preregistered position at the punch station. The position of the cards is illustrated in Figure F-17.

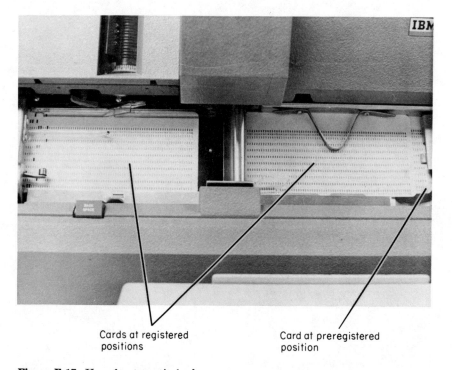

Cards at registered
positions

Card at preregistered
position

Figure F-17. Use of automatic feed.

SOLUTIONS TO SELECTED EXERCISES

CHAPTER 2

Exercise 2-1

(C) -16 (D)86487

Exercise 2-3

(E)8.2E-6

Exercise 2-4

(A)-27281.0

Exercise 2-5

(C)EXPONENTIAL PRESENT AND NORMALLY TOO LARGE

Exercise 2-6

(C)IMBEDDED COMMA

Exercise 2-7

(B)NORMALLY TOO LARGE

Exercise 2-8

(C)IMBEDDED COMMA AND NO DECIMAL

Exercise 2-9

(B)REAL (E)UNACCEPTABLE (I)REAL

Exercise 2-10

(B)UNACCEPTABLE (E)UNACCEPTABLE (J)INTEGER

Exercise 2-11

(D)A*B/(C+10.0)

Exercise 2-12

(B)(A+B)/(C+D/E) (E)A/B+C*D/(E*F%G)

Exercise 2-13

(D)(P*R/S)**(T-1.0)

Exercise 2-14

(A)3 (E)0

Exercise 2-15

(B)0.0   (F)4.3333333

Exercise 2-16

(C)TWO ADJACENT ARITHMETIC OPERATIONS
(F)MIXED MODE. 3 IS AN INTEGER AND Y IS REAL.   SHOULD READ
(Y+3.0)**2

Exercise 2-17

(C)INVALID VARIABLE NAME ON LEFT OF EQUATION. MULTIPLICATION
SIGN CANNOT BE USED IN VARIABLE NAME.
(F)MIXED MODE.

Exercise 2-21

```
JQ=43/9
JR=43-9*JQ
```

CHAPTER 3

Exercise 3-1(c)

```
    READ(5,25)X,J,YES
 25 FORMAT(F10.2,I10,F10.2)
```

or

```
 READ,X,J,YES
```

Exercise 3-2(d)

```
    READ(5,101)CONST,OUKID,A,J
101 FORMAT(3F10.2,I10)
```

or

```
 READ,CONST,CUKID,A,J
```

Exercise 3-5(a)

```
   WRITE(6,13)A,B,CAT,CO,ANS
13 FORMAT(1X,5(E20.7,3X))
```

Exercise 3-5(b)

```
   WRITE(6,51)I,J,KID,ANS
51 FORMAT(1X,3(I10,3X),E20.7)
```

Exercise 3-5(c)

```
    WRITE(6,130)X,J,YES,ANS
130 FORMAT(1X,E20.7,3X,I10,3X,E20.7,3X,E20.7)
```

Exercise 3-5(d)

```
   WRITE(6,33)A,SIMPLE,GO,I,ANS
33 FORMAT(1X,3(E20.7,3X),I10,3X,E20.7)
```

Exercise 3-8, Format-Free

Program

```
1          READ,A,B,C,S
2          T=A*SQRT(S)+B*S+C*S*S
3          PRINT,A,B,C,S,T
4          STOP
5          END
```

Input

```
5.0,6.92,1.73,1.0472
```

0.5000000E 01   0.6920000E 01   0.1730000E 01   0.1047200E 01   0.1426043E 02

Exercise 3-8, Format

Program

```
1        READ(5,1)A,B,C,S
2        T=A*SQRT(S)+B*S+C*S*S
3        WRITE(6,2)A,B,C,S,T
4        STOP
5    1   FCRMAT(4F10.2)
6    2   FORMAT(1X,4F10.2,E20.7)
7        ENC
```

Input

5.0   6.92   1.73   1.0472

Output

5.00   6.92   1.73   1.05   0.1426043E 02

Exercise 3-12, Format-Free

Program

```
1        READ, A, B, C
C
C        CALCULATE A1
C
2        DUM1=1.0+A*B*C
3        DUM2=1.0+(A**2/(B*C))**0.3333333
4        A1=1.0/(1.0-DUM1/DUM2)
C
C        CALCULATE A2
C
5        A2=(A1+3.)/(A1-5.)
6        PRINT,A,B,C,A1,A2
7        STCP
8        ENC
```

309

Input

3.0,5.0,0.33333

Output

0.3000000E 01   0.5000000E 01   0.3333300E 00   -0.8486789E 00   -0.3678302E 00

Exercise 3-12, Format

Program

```
1        READ(5,1)A,B,C
C
C        CALCULATE A1
C
2        DUM1=1.0+A*B*C
3        DUM2=1.0+(A**2/(B*C))**0.3333333
4        A1=1.0/(1.0-DUM1/DUM2)
C
C        CALCULATE A2
C
5        A2=(A1+3.)/(A1-5.)
6        WRITE(6,2)A,B,C,A1,A2
7        STOP
8    1   FORMAT(3F10.2)
9    2   FCRMAT(1X,3F10.2,2E20.7)
10       END
```

Input

3.0   5.0   0.33333

Output

3.00   5.00   0.33   -0.8486789E 00   -0.3678302E 00

Exercise 3-15, Format-Free

Program

```
1          READ,X,Y,Z
2          A1=X**3+X**2+X+1.
3          A2=Y**3+Y**2+Y+1.+A1
4          A3=Z**3+Z**2+Z+1.+A2
5          PRINT,X,Y,Z
6          PRINT,A1,A2,A3
7          STOP
8          END
```

Input

```
-17.5,8.0,3.
```

Output

```
-0.1750000E 02      0.8000000E 01      0.3000000E 01
-0.5069625E 04     -0.4484625E 04     -0.4444625E 04
```

Exercise 3-15, Format

Program

```
 1          READ(5,1)X,Y,Z
 2          A1=X**3+X**2+X+1.
 3          A2=Y**3+Y**2+Y+1.+A1
 4          A3=Z**3+Z**2+Z+1.+A2
 5          WRITE(6,2)X,Y,Z
 6          WRITE(6,3)A1,A2,A3
 7          STOP
 8     1    FORMAT(3F10.2)
 9     2    FORMAT(1X,3F10.2)
10     3    FORMAT(1X,3E20.7)
11          END
```

Input

```
-17.5       8.0        3.
```

Output

```
-17.50        8.00    3.00
   -0.5069625E 04     -0.4484625E 04    -0.4444625E 04
```

Exercise 3-18, Format-Free

Program

```
 1          READ,R,S,T,U,X,Y
 2          UP=R-S+T-U+X-Y
 3          DOWN=R+S+T+U+X+Y
 4          FIRST=R+T+X
 5          SEC=S+U+Y
 6          FINAL=UP**2+SQRT(DOWN)+1./FIRST
 7          PRINT,R,S,T,U,X,Y
 8          PRINT,UP,DOWN,FIRST
 9          PRINT,SEC,'                    ',FINAL
10          STOP
11          END
```

```
10..9.
 8..7.
 6..5.
```

Output

```
0.1000000E 02 0.9000000E 01 0.8CCCCCOE 01 0.7CCOOO0E 01 0.6000000E 01 0.5000000E 01
0.3000000E 01 0.4500000E 02 0.24CC000E C2
0.2100000E 02                0.1574987E 02
```

Exercise 3-18, Format

Program

```
1           READ(5,1)R,S,T,U,X,Y
2           UP=R-S+T-U+X-Y
3           DOWN=R+S+T+U+X+Y
4           FIRST=R+T+X
5           SEC=S+U+Y
6           FINAL=UP**2+SQRT(DOWN)+1./FIRST
7           WRITE(6,2)R,S,T,U,S,Y
8           WRITE(6,3)UP,DOWN,FIRST
9           WRITE(6,4)SEC,FINAL
10          STCP
11   1      FORMAT(2F10.2)
12   2      FORMAT(1X,6F10.2)
13   3      FORMAT(1X,3E20.7)
14   4      FORMAT(1X,E20.7,30X,E20.7)
15          ENC
```

Input

```
10.
 8.
 6.
```

```
9.
7.
5.
```

```
10.00      9.00      8.00      7.00      9.00      5.00
  0.3000000E 01    0.4500000E 02    0.2400000E 02
  0.2100000E 02                              0.1574987E 02
```

Exercise 3-22, Format-Free

Program

```
 1        READ, ID, OGPA, OHRS
 2        READ, JH1, JG1, JH2, JG2, JH3, JG3, JH4, JG4, JH5, JG5
 3        HRS=OHRS+(JH1+JH2+JH3+JH4+JH5)
 4        QPTS=OGPA*OHRS+(JH1*JG1+JH2*JG2+JH3*JG3+JH4*JG4+JH5*JG5)
 5        GFA=QPTS/HRS
 6        PRINT,'ID =',ID
 7        PRINT,'HOURS =',HRS
 8        PRINT,'GRADE POINT AVERAGE =',GPA
 9        STOP
10        END
```

Input

```
10708,2.76,82.
3.3
5.2
3.3
3.4
1.3
```

Output

```
ID =      10708
HOURS =   0.9700000E 02
GRADE POINT AVERAGE =    0.2776492E 01
```

313

Exercise 3-22, Format

Program

```
 1          REAC(5,1) ID,OGPA,OHRS
 2          REAC(5,2)JH1,JG1,JH2,JG2,JH3,JG3,JH4,JG4,JH5,JG5
 3          HRS=OHRS+(JH1+JH2+JH3+JH4+JH5)
 4          QPTS=OGPA*OHRS+(JH1*JG1+JH2*JG2+JH3*JG3+JH4*JG4+JH5*JG5)
 5          GPA=QPTS/HRS
 6          WRITE(6,3)ID
 7          WRITE(6,4)HRS
 8          WRITE(6,5)GPA
 9          STOP
10   1      FORMAT(I5,2F10.0)
11   2      FORMAT(2I3)
12   3      FORMAT(' ID =',I5)
13   4      FCRMAT(' HOURS =',F6.1)
14   5      FORMAT(' GRADE POINT AVERAGE =',F5.2)
15          END
```

Input

```
10708 2.76      82.0
   3  3
   5  2
   3  3
   3  4
   1  3
```

Output

```
ID =10708
HOURS =   97.0
GRADE FCINT AVERAGE = 2.78
```

314

Exercise 3-26, Format-Free

Program

```
 1              READ,CUFT
 2              GAL=7.48*CUFT
 3              XLIT=28.316*CUFT
 4              CUYDS=CUFT/27.
 5              BUSH=0.8036*CUFT
 6              BLS=GAL/31.5
 7              PRINT,CUFT,' CUBIC FEET'
 8              PRINT,GAL,' GALLONS'
 9              PRINT,XLIT,' LITERS'
10              PRINT,CUYDS,' CUBIC YARDS'
11              PRINT,BUSH,' BUSHELS'
12              PRINT,BLS,' BARRELS'
13              STOP
14              END
```

Input

```
10.
```

Output

```
0.1000000E 02    CUBIC FEET
0.7479999E 02    GALLONS
0.2831599E 03    LITERS
0.3703703E 00    CUBIC YARDS
0.8035999E 01    BUSHELS
0.2374602E 01    BARRELS
```

Exercise 3-26, Format

Program

```
 1              READ(5,1)CUFT
 2              GAL=7.48*CUFT
 3              XLIT=28.316*CUFT
 4              CUYDS=CUFT/27.
 5              BUSH=0.8036*CUFT
 6              BLS=GAL/31.5
 7              WRITE(6,2)CUFT
 8              WRITE(6,3)GAL
 9              WRITE(6,4)XLIT
10              WRITE(6,5)CUYDS
11              WRITE(6,6)BUSH
12              WRITE(6,7)BLS
13              STOP
14        1     FORMAT(F10.0)
15        2     FORMAT(1X,F10.4,' CUBIC FEET')
16        3     FORMAT(1X,F10.4,' GALLONS')
17        4     FORMAT(1X,F10.4,' LITERS')
18        5     FORMAT(1X,F10.4,' CUBIC YARDS')
19        6     FORMAT(1X,F10.4,' BUSHELS')
```

```
20      7      FORMAT(1X,F10.4,' BARRELS')
21             END
```

Input

```
10.
```

Output

```
 10.0000 CUBIC FEET
 74.8000 GALLONS
283.1599 LITERS
  0.3704 CUBIC YARDS
  8.0360 BUSHELS
  2.3746 BARRELS
```

Exercise 3-29, Format-Free

Program

```
1              READ,NUM
2              K=NUM/10
3              JD3=NUM-K*10
4              JD1=K/10
5              JD2=K-10*JD1
6              NUMR=100*JD3+10*JD2+JD1
7              PRINT,'OLD NUMBER',NUM
8              PRINT,'NEW NUMBER',NUMR
9              STOP
10             END
```

Input

```
829
```

Output

```
OLD NUMBER           829
NEW NUMBER           928
```

Exercise 3-29, Format

Program

```
1              READ(5,1)NUM
2              K=NUM/10
3              JD3=NUM-K*10
4              JD1=K/10
5              JD2=K-10*JD1
6              NUMR=100*JD3+10*JD2+JD1
7              WRITE(6,2)NUM
8              WRITE(6,3)NUMR
9              STOP
10      1      FORMAT(I3)
11      2      FORMAT(' OLD NUMBER',I4)
12      3      FORMAT(' NEW NUMBER',I4)
13             END
```

Input

```
829
```

Output

```
OLD NUMBER 829
NEW NUMBER 928
```

Exercise 3-33, Format-Free

Program

```
1       READ,N,A,D
2       S=N*(2.*A+(N-1)*D)/2.
3       PRINT,'N=',N,'    A=',A,'    D=',D,'    S=',S
4       STOP
5       END
```

Input

```
20,1.5,2.
```

Output

```
N=    20    A=  0.1500000E 01    D=  0.2000000E 01    S=  0.4100000E 03
```

Exercise 3-33, Format

Program

```
1       READ(5,1)N,A,D
2       S=N*(2.*A+(N-1)*D)/2.
3       WRITE(6,2)N,A,D,S
4       STOP
5   1   FORMAT(I5,2F10.0)
6   2   FORMAT(' N=',I5,5X,'A=',F6.2,5X,'D=',F6.2,5X,'S=',F10.4)
7       END
```

Input

```
20 1.5   2.
```

Output

```
N=    20    A=  1.50    D=  2.00    S=  410.0000
```

317

CHAPTER 4

Exercise 4-1(c) Format-Free

Program

```
1      10      READ,X,Y,Z
2              A1=X**3+X**2+X+1.
3              A2=Y**3+Y**2+Y+1.+A1
4              A3=Z**3+Z**2+Z+1.+A2
5              PRINT,X,Y,Z
6              PRINT,A1,A2,A3
7              PRINT,' '
8              GCTO10
9              END
```

Input

```
-17.5,8.0,3.
 15.0,8.0,3.0
 15.0,9.,3.
 17.5,9.,3.00
```

Output

```
-0.1750000E 02        0.8000000E 01        0.3000000E 01
-0.5069625E 04       -0.4484625E 04       -0.4444625E 04

 0.1500000E 02        0.8000000E 01        0.3000000E 01
 0.3616000E 04        0.4201000E 04        0.4241000E 04

 0.1500000E 02        0.9000000E 01        0.3000000E 01
 0.3616000E 04        0.4436000E 04        0.4476000E 04

 0.1750000E 02        0.9000000E 01        0.3000000E 01
 0.5684125E 04        0.6504125E 04        0.6544125E 04
```

Exercise 4-1(c) Format

Program

```
1      10      READ(5,1)X,Y,Z
2              A1=X**3+X**2+X+1.
3              A2=Y**3+Y**2+Y+1.+A1
4              A3=Z**3+Z**2+Z+1.+A2
5              WRITE(6,2)X,Y,Z
6              WRITE(6,3)A1,A2,A3
7              GCTO10
8      1       FORMAT(3F10.2)
9      2       FORMAT(1X,3F10.2)
10     3       FORMAT(1X,3E20.7)
11             END
```

Input

```
-17.5      8.0       3.
 15.0      8.0       3.0
 15.0      9.        3.
 17.5      9.        3.00
```

Output

```
-17.50          8.00       3.00
   -0.5069625E 04      -0.4484625E 04       -0.4444625E 04
 15.00          8.00       3.00
    0.3616000E 04       0.4201000E 04        0.4241000E 04
 15.00          9.00       3.00
    0.3616000E 04       0.4436000E 04        0.4476000E 04
 17.50          9.00       3.00
    0.5684125E 04       0.6504125E 04        0.6544125E 04
```

Exercise 4-3, Flowchart

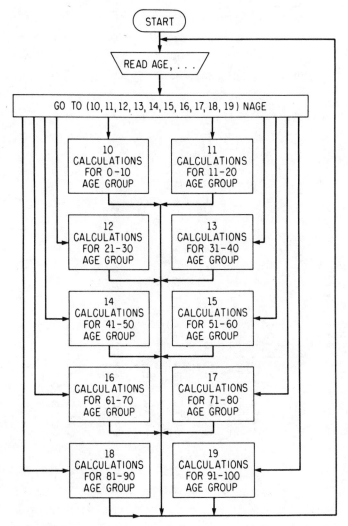

Exercise 4-3

```
C        CALCULATION OF CALORIC INTAKE REQUIREMENTS
C        DEPENDENT ON AGE
C
```

```
C*****FORMAT FREE INPUT STATEMENT
C
100   READ,AGE.....
C
C*****FORMATTED INPUT STATEMENTS
C
100   READ(5,1)AGE.....
1     FORMAT(F10.1.....)
C
C     ASSIGN INTEGER VALUES TO REPRESENT THE AGE GROUPS
C
      AGE=AGE-0.001
      NAGE=AGE/10.
      NAGE=NAGE+1
C
C     COMPUTED GO TO FOR BRANCH SELECTION
C
      GOTO(10,11,12,13,14,15,16,17,18,19),NAGE
C
C     BRANCHES
C
10    CALCULATIONS FOR 0-10 AGE GROUP AND OUTPUT OF RESULTS
      GOTO100
C
11    CALCULATIONS FOR 11-20 AGE GROUP AND OUTPUT OF RESULTS
      GOTO100
C
12    CALCULATIONS FOR 21-30 AGE GROUP AND OUTPUT OF RESULTS
      GOTO100
```

```
C
13    CALCULATIONS FOR 31-40 AGE GROUP AND OUTPUT OF RESULTS
      GCTC100
C
14    CALCULATIONS FCR 41-50 AGE GROUP AND OUTPUT OF RESULTS
      GOTO100
C
15    CALCULATIONS FOR 51-60 AGE GROUP AND OUTPUT OF RESULTS
      GCTO100
C
16    CALCULATIONS FOR 61-70 AGE GROUP AND OUTPUT OF RESULTS
      GCTO100
C
17    CALCULATIONS FOR 71-80 AGE GROUP AND OUTPUT OF RESULTS
      GCTO100
C
18    CALCULATIONS FOR 81-90 AGE GROUP AND OUTPUT OF RESULTS
      GOTO100
C
19    CALCULATIONS FOR 91-100 AGE GROUP AND OUTPUT OF RESULTS
      GCTO100
      END
```

Exercise 4-6, Format-Free

Program

```
1     101   READ.Y1,Y2,Y3
      C
      C         ARITHMETIC IF TO CHECK FOR LOCAL MAXIMUM AND TRANSFER
      C         CCNTROL TO INPUT IF NONE EXISTS IN PRESENT SET OF DATA
      C
```

```
2            IF(Y1-Y2)110,101,101
3      110  IF(Y3-Y2)120,101,101
  C
  C         IF LOCAL MAX EXISTS, WRITE THE THREE VALUES
  C
4      120  PRINT,Y1,Y2,Y3
5            GOTO101
6            END
```

Input

```
0.,3.,9.
3.,9.,12.
9.,12.,7.
12.,7.,5.
7.,5.,10.
5.,10.,6.
10.,6.,0.
6.,0.,0.
0.,0.,8.
0.,8.,3.
```

Output

```
0.9000000E 01    0.1200000E 02    0.700CCC0E 01
0.5000000E 01    0.1000000E 02    0.60CCC00E 01
0.0000000E 00    0.8000000E 01    0.3000000E 01
```

Exercise 4-6, Flowchart

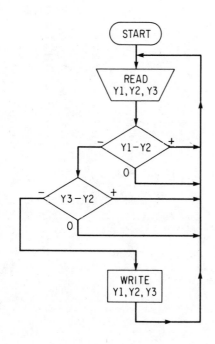

Exercise 4-6, Format

Program

```
1    101   READ(5,112)Y1,Y2,Y3
           C
           C     ARITHMETIC IF TO CHECK FOR LOCAL MAX9MUM 1N4 TR1NSF5R
           C     CONTRCL TO INPUT IF NONE EXISTS IN PRESENT SET OF DATA
           C
2          IF(Y1-Y2)110,101,101
3    110   IF(Y3-Y2)120,101,101
           C
           C     IF LOCAL MAX EXISTS, WRITE THE THREE VALUES
           C
4    120   WRITE(6,102)Y1,Y2,Y3
5          GOTO101
6    112   FORMAT(3F10.2)
7    102   FORMAT(3F10.2)
8          END
```

Input

```
0.      3.       9.
3.      9.      12.
9.     12.       7.
12.     7.       5.
7.      5.      10.
5.     10.       6.
10.     6.       0.
6.      0.       0.
0.      0.       8.
0.      8.       3.
```

Output

```
9.00   12.00    7.00
5.00   10.00    6.00
0.00    8.00    3.00
```

323

Exercise 4-12, Flowchart

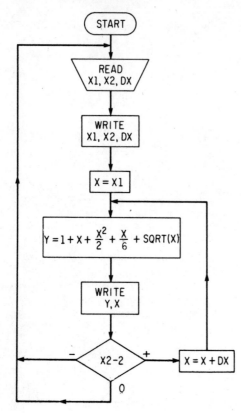

Exercise 4-12, Format-Free

Program

```
1       1       READ,X1,X2,DX
2               PRINT,'X1=',X1,'      X2=',X2,'      DX=',DX
3               X=X1
        C
        C       CALCULATE AND WRITE Y
4       10      Y=1.+X+X**2/2.+X**3/6.+SQRT(X)
5               PRINT,'      X=',X,'      Y=',Y
        C
        C       INCREMENT AND TEST X
        C
6               X=X+DX
7               IF(X.LE.X2)GOTO10
8               GOTO1
9               END
```

Input

```
1..15..1.5
2..10..2.
75..500..25.
```

Output

X1= 0.1000000E 01   X2= 0.1500000E 02   DX= 0.1500000E 01

X= 0.1000000E 01   Y= 0.3666666E 01
X= 0.2500000E 01   Y= 0.1081030E 02
X= 0.4000000E 01   Y= 0.2566666E 02
X= 0.5500000E 01   Y= 0.5169936E 02
X= 0.7000000E 01   Y= 0.9231239E 02
X= 0.8500000E 01   Y= 0.1508946E 03
X= 0.1000000E 02   Y= 0.2308289E 03
X= 0.1150000E 02   Y= 0.3354551E 03
X= 0.1300000E 02   Y= 0.4682720E 03
X= 0.1450000E 02   Y= 0.6325369E 03

X1= 0.2000000E 01   X2= 0.1000000E 02   DX= 0.2000000E 01

X= 0.2000000E 01   Y= 0.7747546E 01
X= 0.4000000E 01   Y= 0.2566666E 02
X= 0.6000000E 01   Y= 0.6344948E 02
X= 0.8000000E 01   Y= 0.1291617E 03
X= 0.1000000E 02   Y= 0.2308289E 03

X1= 0.7500000E 02   X2= 0.5000000E 03   DX= 0.2500000E 02

X= 0.7500000E 02   Y= 0.7320963E 05
X= 0.1000000E 03   Y= 0.1717776E 06
X= 0.1250000E 03   Y= 0.3334704E 06
X= 0.1500000E 03   Y= 0.5739132E 06
X= 0.1750000E 03   Y= 0.9087308E 06
X= 0.2000000E 03   Y= 0.1353548E 07
X= 0.2250000E 03   Y= 0.1923990E 07
X= 0.2500000E 03   Y= 0.2635682E 07
X= 0.2750000E 03   Y= 0.3504248E 07
X= 0.3000000E 03   Y= 0.4545318E 07
X= 0.3250000E 03   Y= 0.5774508E 07
X= 0.3500000E 03   Y= 0.7207451E 07

```
X=    0.3750000E 07      Y=    0.8859768E 07
X=    0.4000000E 03      Y=    0.1074709E 08
X=    0.4250000E 03      Y=    0.1288503E 08
X=    0.4500000E 03      Y=    0.1528922E 08
X=    0.4750000E 03      Y=    0.1797526E 08
X=    0.5000000E 03      Y=    0.2095883E 08
```

Exercise 4-12, Format

Program

```
 1       1      READ(5,2)X1,X2,DX
 2              WRITE(6,3)X1,X2,DX
 3              X=X1
         C
         C      CALCULATE AND WRITE Y
 4      10      Y=1.+X+X**2/2.+X**3/6.+SQRT(X)
 5              WRITE(6,4)X,Y
         C
         C      INCREMENT AND TEST X
         C
 6              X=X+DX
 7              IF(X.LE.X2)GOTO10
 8              GOTO1
 9       2      FORMAT(3F10.2)
10       3      FORMAT(' X1=',F10.2,5X,'X2=',F10.2,5X,'DX=',F10.2)
11       4      FORMAT(6X,'X=',F10.2,5X,'Y=',E15.5)
12              END
```

Input

```
 1.      15.      1.5
 2.      10.      2.
75.     500.     25.
```

Output

X1 = 1.00   X2 = 1.00   DX = 15.00   1.50

X= 1.00   Y= 0.36667E 01
X= 2.50   Y= 0.10810E 02
X= 4.00   Y= 0.25667E 02
X= 5.50   Y= 0.51699E 02
X= 7.00   Y= 0.92312E 02
X= 8.50   Y= 0.15089E 03
X= 10.00 Y= 0.23083E 03
X= 11.50 Y= 0.33550E 03
X= 13.00 Y= 0.46827E 03
X= 14.50 Y= 0.63254E 03

X1 = 2.00   X2 = 2.00   DX = 10.00   2.00

X= 2.00   Y= 0.77475E 01
X= 4.00   Y= 0.25667E 02
X= 6.00   Y= 0.63449E 02
X= 8.00   Y= 0.12916E 03
X= 10.00 Y= 0.23083E 03

X1 = 75.00   X2 = 500.00 DX = 25.00

X= 75.00   Y= 0.73210E 05
X= 100.00 Y= 0.17178E 06
X= 125.00 Y= 0.33347E 06
X= 150.00 Y= 0.57391E 06
X= 175.00 Y= 0.90873E 06
X= 200.00 Y= 0.13535E 07
X= 225.00 Y= 0.19240E 07
X= 250.00 Y= 0.26357E 07
X= 275.00 Y= 0.35042E 07
X= 300.00 Y= 0.45453E 07
X= 325.00 Y= 0.57745E 07
X= 350.00 Y= 0.72075E 07

```
X =   375.00      Y =    0.88598E 07
X =   400.00      Y =    0.10747E 08
X =   425.00      Y =    0.12885E 08
X =   450.00      Y =    0.15289E 08
X =   475.00      Y =    0.17975E 08
X =   500.00      Y =    0.20959E 08
```

Exercise 4-15, Format-Free

Program

```
      C        USE VARIABLE K AS THE COUNTER
      C
1              K=1
2  , 101       READ,Y1,Y2,Y3
      C
      C        ARITHMETIC IF TO CHECK FOR LOCAL MAXIMUM AND TRANSFER
      C        CONTROL TO COUNTER INCREMENT IF NONE EXISTS IN PRESENT DATA SET
      C
3              IF(Y1-Y2)110,104,104
4    110       IF(Y3-Y2)120,104,104
5    120       PRINT,Y1,Y2,Y3
      C
      C        INCREMENT AND TEST COUNTER
6    104       K=K+1
7              IF(K-7)101,101,11
8    11        STOP
9              END
```

Input

```
3.,9.,12.
9.,12.,7.
12.,7.,5.
7.,5.,10.
5.,10.,6.
10.,6.,0.
6.,0.,0.
```

```
0.9000000E 01        0.1200000E 02        0.7000000E 01
0.5000000E 01        0.1000000E 02        0.6000000E 01
```

Exercise 4-15, Format

Program

```
      C         USE VARIABLE K AS THE COUNTER
      C
    1           K=1
    2     101   READ(5,112)Y1,Y2,Y3
      C
      C         ARITHMETIC IF TO CHECK FOR LOCAL MAXIMUM AND TRANSFER
      C         CONTROL TO COUNTER INCREMENT IF NONE EXISTS IN PRESENT DATA SET
    3           IF(Y1-Y2)110,104,104
    4     110   IF(Y3-Y2)120,104,104
    5     120   WRITE(6,102)Y1,Y2,Y3
      C
      C         INCREMENT AND TEST COUNTER
    6     104   K=K+1
    7           IF(K-7)101,101,11
    8     11    STOP
    9     102   FORMAT(1X,3F10.2)
   10     112   FORMAT(3F10.2)
   11           END
```

Input

```
    3.        9.       12.
    9.       12.        7.
   12.        7.        5.
    7.        5.       10.
    5.       10.        6.
   10.        6.        0.
    6.        0.        0.
```

Output

```
0.9000000E 01          0.1200000E 02          0.7000000E 01
0.5000000E 01          0.1000000E 02          0.6000000E 01
0.0000000E 00          0.8000000E 01          0.3000000E 01
```

Exercise 4-19, Format-Free

Program

```
1     101    READ,Y1,Y2,Y3,N
      C
      C      ARITHMETIC IF TC CHECK FOR LOCAL MAXIMUM AND TRANSFER
      C      CONTROL IF NONE EXISTS IN PRESENT SET OF DATA
      C
2            IF(Y1-Y2)110,101,101
3     110    IF(Y3-Y2)120,101,101
      C
      C      IF LOCAL MAX EXISTS WRITE THE THREE VALUES
      C
4     120    PRINT,Y1,Y2,Y3
      C
      C      CHECK FOR END OF DATA
      C
5            IF(N)150,101,150
6     150    STCP
7            END
```

Input

```
0.,3.,9.,0
3.,9.,12.,0
9.,12.,7.,0
12.,7.,5.,0
7.,5.,10.,0
5.,10.,6.,0
10.,6.,0.,0
```

330

Output

```
9.00    12.00    7.00
5.00    10.00    6.00
```

Exercise 4-19, Format

Program

```
1    101    READ(5,112)Y1,Y2,Y3,N
     C
     C      ARITHMETIC IF TO CHECK FOR LOCAL MAXIMUM AND TRANSFER
     C      CONTROL IF NONE EXISTS IN PRESENT SET OF DATA
     C
2           IF(Y1-Y2)110,101,101
3    110    IF(Y3-Y2)120,101,101
     C
     C      IF LOCAL MAX EXISTS WRITE THE THREE VALUES
     C
4    120    WRITE(6,102)Y1,Y2,Y3
     C
     C      CHECK FOR END OF DATA
     C
5           IF(N)150,101,150
6    150    STOP
7    112    FORMAT(3F10.2,I5)
8    102    FORMAT(1X,3F10.2)
9           END
```

Input

```
0.    3.    9.
3.    9.    12.
9.    12.   7.
```

```
   12.            7.            5.
    7.            5.           10.
    5.           10.            6.
   10.            6.            0.
    6.            0.            0.
    0.            0.            8.
    0.            8.            3.
```

Output
```
    9.00          12.00         7.C0
    5.00          10.00         6.00
    0.00           8.00         3.00
```

Exercise 4-26, Format-Free

Program
```
    1               N=0
    2       3       READ, ISEC, ISEX, ISTND
    3               IF(ISEC.EQ.0)GOTO9
    4               IF(ISEC.EQ.8)N=N+1
    5               ·GCTO3
    6       9       PRINT,N,'STUDENTS  IN SECTION 8'
    7               STOP
    8               END
```

Input
```
    1,1,2
    3,1,4
    8,2,2
    3,2,3
    8,2,2
    8,1,4
    1,2,2
    2,1,1
    1,1,3
    8,1,2
    1,2,2
    0,0,0
```

Output
```
    4 STUDENTS  IN SECTICN 8
```

Exercise 4-26, Format

Program
```
    1               N=0
    2       3       READ(5,1)ISEC,ISEX,ISTND
    3               IF(ISEC.EQ.0)GOTO9
    4               IF(ISEC.EQ.8)N=N+1
    5               GCTO3
    6       9       WRITE(6,2) N
    7               STOP
    8       1       FORMAT(3I2)
```

```
    9        2       FORMAT(1X,I5,' STUDENTS IN SECTION 8')
   10                END
```

Input

```
   1  1  2
   3  1  4
   8  2  2
   3  2  3
   8  2  2
   8  1  4
   1  2  2
   2  1  1
   1  1  3
   8  1  2
   1  2  2
   0
```

Output

```
   4 STUDENTS IN SECTION 8
```

Exercise 4-33, Format-Free

Program

```
    1                READ,JTIME
    2                JHR=JTIME/100
    3                JMIN=JTIME-100*JHR
    4                IF(JTIME.EQ.2400)GOTO15
    5                IF(JHR.GE.24.OR.JMIN.GE.60)GOTO30
    6                IF(JHR.EQ.0)GOTO15
    7                IF(JHR.LT.12)GOTO10
    8                IF(JHR.EQ.12)GOTO20
    9                JHR=JHR-12
   10        20      PRINT,JHR,'-',JMIN,' PM'
   11                STOP
   12        15      JHR=12
   13        10      PRINT,JHR,'-',JMIN,' AM'
   14                STOP
   15        30      PRINT,'ERRONECUS TIME ENTERED',JTIME
   16                STOP
   17                END
```

Input

```
   1420
```

Output

```
   2                20   PM
```

Exercise 4-33, Format

Program

```
    1                READ(5,1)JTIME
    2                JHR=JTIME/100
    3                JMIN=JTIME-100*JHR
    4                IF(JTIME.EQ.2400)GOTO15
    5                IF(JHR.GE.24.OR.JMIN.GE.60)GOTO30
```

```
 6            IF(JHR.EQ.0)GOTO15
 7            IF(JHR.LT.12)GOTO10
 8            IF(JHR.EQ.12)GOTO20
 9            JHR=JHR-12
10      20    WRITE(6,2)JHR,JMIN
11            STOP
12      15    JHR=12
13      10    WRITE(6,3)JHR,JMIN
14            STOP
15      30    WRITE(6,4) JTIME
16            STOP
17       1    FORMAT(I4)
18       2    FORMAT(1X,I2,'-',I2,' PM')
19       3    FORMAT(1X,I2,'-',I2,' AM')
20       4    FORMAT(' ERRONEOUS TIME ENTERED',I5)
21            END
```

Input

```
1420
```

Output

```
2-20 PM
```

Exercise 4-38, Format-Free

Program

```
 1            READ,NUNITS,PRICE
 2            IF(NUNITS.LE.12)GOTO10
 3            IF(NUNITS.LE.100)GOTO20
 4            TOTAL=PRICE*(12.+0.9*88.+0.7*(NUNITS-100)
 5            GOTO30
 6      10    TOTAL =NUNITS*PRICE
 7            GOTO30
 8      20    TOTAL=PRICE*(12.+0.9*(NUNITS-12))
 9      30    AVG=TOTAL/NUNITS
10            PRINT,'TOTAL PRICE',TOTAL
11            PRINT,'AVERAGE PRICE',AVG
12            STOP
13            END
```

Input

```
200,10.
```

Output

```
TOTAL PRICE        0.1612000E 04
AVERAGE PRICE      0.8059999E 01
```

Exercise 4-38, Format

Program

```
 1            READ(5,1)NUNITS,PRICE
 2            IF(NUNITS.LE.12)GOTO10
 3            IF(NUNITS.LE.100)GOTO20
 4            TOTAL=PRICE*(12.+0.9*88.+0.7*(NUNITS-100))
```

```
5               GOTO30
6       10      TOTAL =NUNITS*PRICE
7               GOTO30
8       20      TOTAL=PRICE*(12.+0.9*(NUNITS-12))
9       30      AVG=TOTAL/NUNITS
10              WRITE(6,2)TOTAL
11              WRITE(6,3)AVG
12              STOP
13      1       FORMAT(I5,F10.0)
14      2       FORMAT(' TOTAL PRICE',F10.2)
15      3       FORMAT(' AVERAGE PRICE',F8.2)
16              END
```

Input

```
200 10.
```

Output

```
TOTAL PRICE     1612.00
AVERAGE PRICE      8.06
```

Exercise 4-41, Format-Free

Program

```
1               READ,JX
2               PRINT,'YEAR ',JX
     C*****STEP 1
3               JQ=JX/19
4               JA=JX-19*JQ
     C*****STEP 2
5               JB=JX/100
6               JC=JX-100*JB
     C*****STEP 3
7               JD=JB/4
8               JE=JB-4*JD
     C*****STEP 4
9               JG=(8*JE+13)/25
     C*****STEP 5
10              J=19*JA+JB-JD-JG+15
11              JQ=J/30
12              JH=J-30*JQ
     C*****STEP 6
13              MU=(JA+11*JH)/319
     C*****STEP 7
14              I=JC/4
15              K=JC-4*I
     C*****STEP 8
16              J=2*JE+2*I-K-JH+MU+32
17              JR=J/7
18              LAMBDA=J-JR*7
     C*****STEP 9
19              N=(JH-MU+LAMBDA+90)/25
```

```
            C*****STEP 10
20                  J=JH-MU+LAMBDA+N+19
21                  JR=J/32
22                  JP=J-32*JR
23                  PRINT,'MONTH',N
24                  PRINT,'DAY  ',JP
25                  STOP
26                  END
```

Input

```
 1972
```

Output

```
YEAR              1972
MONTH                4
DAY                  2
```

Exercise 4-41, Format

Program

```
1                   READ(5,1)JX
2                   WRITE(6,2)JX
            C*****STEP 1
3                   JG=JX/19
4                   JA=JX-19*JQ
            C*****STEP 2
5                   JB=JX/100
6                   JC=JX-100*JB
            C*****STEP 3
7                   JD=JB/4
8                   JE=JB-4*JD
            C*****STEP 4
9                   JG=(8*JB+13)/25
            C*****STEP 5
10                  J=19*JA+JB-JD-JG+15
11                  JG=J/30
12                  JH=J-30*JQ
            C*****STEP 6
13                  MU=(JA+11*JH)/319
            C*****STEP 7
14                  I=JC/4
15                  K=JC-4*I
            C*****STEP 8
16                  J=2*JE+2*I-K-JH+MU+32
17                  JR=J/7
18                  LAMBDA=J-JR*7
            C*****STEP 9
19                  N=(JH-MU+LAMBDA+90)/25
            C*****STEP 10
20                  J=JH-MU+LAMBDA+N+19
21                  JR=J/32
```

```
22              JP=J-32*JR
23              WRITE(6,3)N
24              WRITE(6,4)JP
25              STOP
26       1      FORMAT(I4)
27       2      FORMAT(' YEAR',I6)
28       3      FORMAT(' MONTH',I5)
29       4      FORMAT(' DAY',I7)
30              END
```

Input

```
1972
```

Output

```
YEAR    1972
MONTH      4
DAY        2
```

Exercise 4-48, Format-Free

Program

```
        C*****USE VARIABLE N TO COUNT DATA POINTS
        C*****USE VARIABLE SUM TO COMPUTE TOTAL
1              N=0
2              SUM=0.
3       20     READ,X
4              IF(X.EQ.0.)GOTO10
5              N=N+1
6              SUM=SUM+ABS(X)
7              GOTO20
8       10     AVG=SUM/N
9              PRINT,N,' VALUES, AVERAGE =',AVG
10             STOP
11             END
```

Input

```
0.7
1.9
-2.2
7.1
17.0
-4.2
7.9
-5.1
0.
```

Output

```
8  VALUES, AVERAGE =      0.5762497E 01
```

Exercise 4-48, Format

Program

```
        C*****USE VARIABLE N TO COUNT DATA POINTS
        C*****USE VARIABLE SUM TO COMPUTE TOTAL
1              N=0
```

```
2              SUM=0.
3       20     READ(5,1)X
4              IF(X.EQ.0.)GOTO10
5              N=N+1
6              SUM=SUM+ABS(X)
7              GOTO20
8       10     AVG=SUM/N
9              WRITE(6,2)N,AVG
10             STOP
11      1      FORMAT(F10.0)
12      2      FORMAT(1X,I5,' VALUES, AVERAGE =',F14.4)
13             END
```

Input

```
0.7
1.9
-2.2
7.1
17.0
-4.2
7.9
-5.1
0.
```

Output

```
8 VALUES, AVERAGE =          5.7625
```

Exercise 4-51, Format-Free

Program

```
        C*****USE VARIABLE K TO COUNT DIGITS
1              K=1
2              NUM=1
3       10     NUM=NUM*10
4              IDIG=NUM/7
5              NUM=NUM-IDIG*7
6              PRINT,IDIG
7              K=K+1
8              IF(K.LE.20)GOTO10
9              STOP
10             END
```

Input   None

Output

```
1
4
2
8
5
7
1
4
```

2
8
5
7
1
4
2
8
5
7
1
4

Exercise 4-51, Format

Program

```
      C*****USE VARIABLE K TO COUNT DIGITS
   1          K=1
   2          NUM=1
   3     10   NUM=NUM*10
   4          IDIG=NUM/7
   5          NUM=NUM-IDIG*7
   6          WRITE(6,1)IDIG
   7          K=K+1
   8          IF(K.LE.20)GOTO10
   9          STOP
  10      1   FORMAT(1X,I5)
  11          END
```

Input   None

Output

1
4
2
8
5
7
1
4
2
8
5
7
1
4
2
8
5
7
1
4

Exercise 4-58, Format-Free

Program

```
1          REAC,A1,B1,C1,A2,B2,C2
2          D=B2*A1-B1*A2
3          IF(D.LT.1.E-10)GOTO10
4          X=(C1*B2-C2*B1)/D
5          Y=(A1*C2-A2*C1)/D
6          PRINT,'X=',X,'        Y=',Y
7          STOP
8     10   PRINT,'NO SOLUTION'
9          STCP
10         ENC
```

Input

```
1.,4.,2.7,3.8
-3.8,1.1,3.4
```

Output

```
X=  -0.4237285E 00      Y=      0.1627118E 01
```

Exercise 4-58, Format

Program

```
1          REAC(5,1)A1,B1,C1,A2,B2,C2
2          D=B2*A1-B1*A2
3          IF(D.LT.1.E-10)GOTO10
4          X=(C1*B2-C2*B1)/D
5          Y=(A1*C2-A2*C1)/D
6          WRITE(6,2)X,Y
7          STOP
8     10   WRITE(6,3)
9          STOP
10    1    FORMAT(3F10.0)
11    2    FCRMAT(' X=',F10.4,5X,'Y=',F10.4)
```

340

```
12      3    FORMAT(' NO SOLUTION')
13           END
```

```
1.4      2.7      3.8
-3.8     1.1      3.4
```

Output

```
X=   -0.4237    Y=    1.6271
```

CHAPTER 5

Exercise 5-2, Format-Free

Program

```
C           DEFINE PRODUCT COST, PLANT COST, AND PRODUCTION RATE
1           C=1.50
2           B=900000.
3           P=200000.
C           WRITE HEADINGS
4           PRINT,'     PRODUCT VALUE     PAYOUT TIME '
C           ITERATE ON VALUES OF PRODUCT VALUE
5           DO10I=275,325,5
6           V=I/100.
7           PNET=P*(V-C)
8           PROF=0.48*PNET
9           TIME=B/PROF
10    10    PRINT,V,TIME
11          STOP
12          END
```

Input   None

Output

```
PRODUCT VALUE       PAYOUT TIME
0.2750000E 01       0.7500000E 01
```

341

```
0.2799999E 01    0.7211545E 01
0.2849999E 01    0.6944448E 01
0.2900000E 01    0.66964311E 01
0.2950000E 01    0.6465520E 01
0.3000000E 01    0.6250000E 01
0.3049999E 01    0.6048391E 01
0.3099999E 01    0.5859377E 01
0.3150000E 01    0.5681820E 01
0.3200000E 01    0.5514708E 01
0.3250000E 01    0.5357142E 01
```

Exercise 5-2, Format

Program

```
    C      DEFINE PRODUCT COST, PLANT COST, AND PRODUCTION RATE
 1         C=1.50
 2         B=900000.
 3         P=200000.
    C      WRITE HEADINGS
 4         WRITE(6,1)
 5   1     FORMAT(' PRODUCT VALUE     PAYOUT TIME')
    C      ITERATE ON VALUES OF PRODUCT VALUE
 6         DO10I=275,325,5
 7         V=I/100.
 8         PNET=P*(V-C)
 9         PROF=0.48*PNET
10         TIME=B/PROF
11  10     WRITE(6,2)V,TIME
12   2     FORMAT(1X,F9.2,F17.2)
13         STOP
14         END
```

Input   None

Output

PRODUCT VALUE	PAYOUT TIME
2.75	7.50
2.80	7.21
2.85	6.94
2.90	6.70
2.95	6.47
3.00	6.25
3.05	6.05
3.10	5.86
3.15	5.68
3.20	5.51
3.25	5.36 .

Exercise 5-7, Format-Free

Program

```
      C          WRITE HEADINGS
1                PRINT,'           YEAR           CRF'
      C          DO FOR 25 YEARS
2                DO10N=1,25
3                X=1.08**N
4                CRF=.08*X/(X-1.)
5          10    PRINT,N,CRF
6                STOP
7                END
```

Input   None

Output

YEAR	CRF
1	0.1080000E 01
2	0.5607716E 00
3	0.3880342E 00
4	0.3019212E 00
5	0.2504567E 00
6	0.2163156E 00
7	0.1920725E 00
8	0.1740149E 00
9	0.1600798E 00
10	0.1490295E 00
11	0.1400763E 00
12	0.1326950E 00
13	0.1265218E 00
14	0.1212968E 00
15	0.1168295E 00
16	0.1129768E 00
17	0.1096294E 00
18	0.1067021E 00
19	0.1041276E 00
20	0.1018522E 00

21	0.9983224E-01
22	0.9803206E-01
23	0.9642214E-01
24	0.9497792E-01
25	0.9367877E-01

Exercise 5-7, Format

Program

```
      C       WRITE HEADINGS
1             WRITE(6,1)
2     1       FORMAT('    YEAR     CRF')
      C       DO FOR 25 YEARS
3             DO10N=1,25
4             X=1.08**N
5             CRF=.08*X/(X-1.)
6     10      WRITE(6,2)N,CRF
7     2       FORMAT(1X,I5,F10.5)
8             STOP
9             END
```

Input   None

Output

YEAR	CRF
1	1.08000
2	0.56077
3	0.38803
4	0.30192
5	0.25046
6	0.21632
7	0.19207
8	0.17401
9	0.16008
10	0.14903
11	0.14008
12	0.13270
13	0.12652
14	0.12130
15	0.11683
16	0.11298
17	0.10963
18	0.10670
19	0.10413
20	0.10185
21	0.09983
22	0.09803
23	0.09642
24	0.09498
25	0.09368

Exercise 5-9, Format-Free

Program

```
        C           INITIALIZE SUM TO ZERO AND PRODUCT TO 1.0
   1                SUM=0.
   2                PROD=1.
        C           READ NUMBER OF DATA POINTS
   3                READ,N
        C           READ DATA AND COMPUTE SUM AND PRODUCT
   4                DO3I=1,N
   5                READ,VALUE
   6                PROD=PROD*VALUE
   7        3       SUM=SUM+VALUE
        C           COMPUTE MEANS
   8                AMEAN=SUM/N
   9                GMEAN=PROD**(1./N)
  10                PRINT,'ARITHMETIC MEAN =',AMEAN
  11                PRINT,'GEOMETRIC MEAN =',GMEAN
  12                STOP
  13                END
```

Input

```
      7
 12.2
 7.9
 20.2
 13.5
 49.4
 2.1
 5.8
```

Output

```
 ARITHMETIC MEAN =       0.1587142E 02
 GEOMETRIC MEAN =        0.1067665E 02
```

Exercise 5-9, Format

Program

```
        C           INITIALIZE SUM TO ZERO AND PRODUCT TO 1.0
   1                SUM=0.
   2                PROD=1.
        C           READ NUMBER OF DATA POINTS
   3                READ(5,1)N
   4        1       FORMAT(I5)
        C           READ DATA AND COMPUTE SUM AND PRODUCT
   5                DO3I=1,N
   6                READ(5,2)VALUE
   7        2       FORMAT(F5.1)
   8                PROD=PROD*VALUE
   9        3       SUM=SUM+VALUE
        C           COMPUTE MEANS
```

```
10          AMEAN=SUM/N
11          GMEAN=PROD**(1./N)
12          WRITE(6,5) AMEAN,GMEAN
13      5   FORMAT(' ARITHMETIC MEAN =',F6.1,5X,'GEOMETRIC MEAN =',F6.1)
14          STOP
15          END
```

Input

```
7
12.2
7.9
20.2
13.5
49.4
2.1
5.8
```

Output

```
ARITHMETIC MEAN =   15.9      GEOMETRIC MEAN =   10.7
```

Exercise 5-14, Format-Free

Program

```
1           READ,N,A,D
2           PRINT,'N=',N,'   A=',A,'   D=',D
    C       COMPUTE SUM TERM BY TERM
3           SUM=0.
4           TERM=A
5           DO7 I=1,N
6           SUM=SUM+TERM
7       7   TERM=TERM+D
    C       COMPUTE SUM BY FORMULA
8           SUMA=N*(2.*A+(N-1)*D)/2.
9           PRINT,'SUM COMPUTED TERM BY TERM =',SUM
```

```
10        PRINT,'SUM COMPUTED BY FORMULA =',SUMA
11        STOP
12        END
```

Input

20,1.5.2.

Output

```
N=        20     A=    0.1500000E 01      D=      0.2000000E 01
SUM COMPUTED TERM BY TERM =       0.4100000E 03
SUM COMPUTED BY FORMULA =        0.4100000E 03
```

Exercise 5-14, Format

Program

```
 1        READ(5,1)N,A,C
 2   1    FORMAT(I5,2F10.0)
 3        WRITE(6,2)N,A,D
 4   2    FORMAT(' N=',I5,5X,'A=',F10.2,5X,'D=',F10.2)
 C        COMPUTE SUM TERM BY TERM
 5        SUM=0.
 6        TERM=A
 7        DO7I=1,N
 8        SUM=SUM+TERM
 9   7    TERM=TERM+D
 C        COMPUTE SUM BY FORMULA
10        SUMA=N*(2.*A+(N-1)*D)/2.
11        WRITE(6,3)SUM
12   3    FORMAT(' SUM COMPUTED TERM BY TERM =',F10.4)
13        WRITE(6,4)SUMA
14   4    FORMAT(' SUM COMPUTED BY FORMULA =',F10.4)
15        STOP
16        END
```

Input

20 1.5   2.

347

Output

```
N=      20        A=        1.50       D=        2.00
SUM COMPUTED TERM BY TERM =   410.0000
SUM COMPUTED BY FORMULA =   410.0000
```

Exercise 5-22, Format-Free

Program

```
1               ISUM=0
2               DO10J=19,127
3        10     ISUM=ISUM+J
4               AVG=ISUM/109.
5               PRINT,' AVERAGE =',AVG
6               STOP
7               END
```

Input   None

Output

```
AVERAGE =       0.7300000E 02
```

Exercise 5-22, Format

Program

```
1               ISUM=0
2               DO10J=19,127
3        10     ISUM=ISUM+J
4               AVG=ISUM/109.
5               WRITE(6,1) AVG
6        1      FORMAT(' AVERAGE =',F12.4)
7               STOP
8               END
```

Input   None

Output

```
AVERAGE =       73.0000
```

Exercise 5-28, Format-Free

Program

```
1               KVAC=0
2               KSL=0
3               DO10I=1,1025
4               READ,ID,IAGE,NYRS,NDEP,NDVAC,NDSL
5               KVAC=KVAC+NDVAC
6        10     KSL=KSL+NDSL
7               PRINT,'TOTAL DAYS VACATION IS',KVAC
8               PRINT,'TOTAL DAYS SICK LEAVE IS',KSL
9               STOP
10              END
```

Exercise 5-28, Format

Program

```
1               KVAC=0
2               KSL=0
3               DO10I=1,1025
```

```
 4              READ(5,1)ID,IAGE,NYRS,NDEP,NDVAC,NDSL
 5              KVAC=KVAC+NDVAC
 6        10    KSL=KSL+NDSL
 7              WRITE(6,2)KVAC
 8              WRITE(6,3)KSL
 9              STOP
10        1     FORMAT(I9,1X,I3,1X,I2,1X,I2,1X,I2,1X,I3)
11        2     FORMAT(' TOTAL DAYS VACATION IS',I8)
12        3     FORMAT('TOTAL DAYS SICK LEAVE IS',I8)
13              END
```

Exercise 5-33, Format-Free

Program

```
 1              MAXPTS=0
 2              MINPTS=100000
 3              KSCORE=0
 4              DO8I=1,10
 5              READ,JGAME,JOPP,JSC,JOSC
 6              IF(JSC.GT.MAXPTS)MAXPTS=JSC
 7              IF(JSC.LT.MINPTS)MINPTS=JSC
 8        8     KSCORE=KSCORE+JSC
 9              AVG=KSCORE/10.
10              PRINT,'OUR AVERAGE SCORE WAS',AVG
11              PRINT,'OUR MAXIMUM POINTS WAS',MAXPTS
12              PRINT,'OUR MINIMUM POINTS WAS',MINPTS
13              STOP
14              END
```

Input

```
 1     2     82      91
 2     5     88      87
 3     1     85      76
 4     3     89      80
 5     1     95     108
 6     2     87      83
 7     4     76      68
 8     6     83      84
 9     1     88      87
10     4     92      76
```

Output

```
OUR AVERAGE SCORE WAS        0.8650000E 02
OUR MAXIMUM POINTS WAS               95
OUR MINIMUM POINTS WAS               76
```

Exercise 5-33, Format

Program

```
 1              MAXPTS=0
 2              MINPTS=100000
 3              KSCORE=0
 4              DO8I=1,10
```

```
 5              READ(5,1)JGAME,JOPP,JSC,JOSC
 6      1       FORMAT(4I5)
 7              IF(JSC.GT.MAXPTS)MAXPTS=JSC
 8              IF(JSC.LT.MINPTS)MINPTS=JSC
 9      8       KSCORE=KSCORE+JSC
10              AVG=KSCORE/10.
11              WRITE(6,2)AVG
12      2       FORMAT(' OUR AVERAGE SCORE WAS',F8.2)
13              WRITE(6,3)MAXPTS
14      3       FORMAT(' OUR MAXIMUM POINTS WAS',I5)
15              WRITE(6,4)MINPTS
16      4       FORMAT(' OUR MINIMUM POINTS WAS',I5)
17              STOP
18              END
```

Input

```
 1    2    82     91
 2    5    88     87
 3    1    85     76
 4    3    89     80
 5    1    95    108
 6    2    87     83
 7    4    76     68
 8    6    83     84
 9    1    88     87
10    4    92     76
```

Output

```
OUR AVERAGE SCORE WAS     86.50
OUR MAXIMUM POINTS WAS       95
OUR MINIMUM POINTS WAS       76
```

Exercise 5-40, Format-Free

Program

```
 1              DIMENSION NO(50),BILL(50)
        C       READ BASE CHARGES
 2              DO1I=1,10
 3      1       READ,NO(I),BILL(I)
        C       READ LONG DISTANCE CHARGES
 4      77      READ,NUMBER,CHARGE
        C       CHECK FOR TRAILER CARD
 5              IF(NUMBER.EQ.0)GOTO6
        C       ADD TO APPROPRIATE BILL
 6              DO4I=1,10
 7      4       IF(NUMBER.EQ.NO(I))BILL(I)=BILL(I)+1.1*CHARGE
 8              GOTO77
        C       WRITE FINAL BILLS
 9      6       PRINT,'        CUSTOMER      BILL'
10              DO7I=1,10
11      7       PRINT,NO(I),BILL(I)
```

```
12              STOP
13              END
```

Input

```
 1      1.50
 2      1.29
 3      1.75
 4      1.75
 5      2.00
 6      1.10
 7      1.75
 8      1.75
 9      2.00
10      1.75
 8      6.00
 7      3.12
 1      1.75
 4      5.60
 8      1.50
10      4.20
 0      0.00
```

Output

```
CUSTOMER        BILL
     1      0.3425000E 01
     2      0.1290000E 01
     3      0.1750000E 01
     4      0.7910002E 01
     5      0.2000000E 01
     6      0.1100000E 01
     7      0.5182000E 01
     8      0.1000000E 02
     9      0.2000000E 01
    10      0.6370001E 01
```

Exercise 5-40, Format

Program

```
1              DIMENSION NO(50),BILL(50)
    C          READ BASE CHARGES
2              DO1I=1,10
3     1        READ(5,2)NO(I),BILL(I)
    C          READ LONG DISTANCE CHARGES
4    77        READ(5,2)NUMBER,CHARGE
5     2        FORMAT(I3,F6.2)
    C          IS CARD BLANK
6              IF(NUMBER.EQ.0)GOTO6
    C          ADD TO APPROPRIATE BILL
7              DO4I=1,10
8     4        IF(NUMBER.EQ.NO(I))BILL(I)=BILL(I)+1.1*CHARGE
9              GOTO77
```

```
       C        WRITE FINAL BILLS
10     6        WRITE(6,10)
11     10       FORMAT('1CUSTOMER    BILL')
12              DO7I=1,10
13     7        WRITE(6,8)NO(I),BILL(I)
14     8        FORMAT(1X,I5,F10.2)
15              STOP
16              END
```

Input

```
 1    1.50
 2    1.29
 3    1.75
 4    1.75
 5    2.00
 6    1.10
 7    1.75
 8    1.75
 9    2.00
10    1.75
 8    6.00
 7    3.12
 1    1.75
 4    5.60
 8    1.50
10    4.20
```

Output

```
CUSTOMER     BILL
   1         3.43
   2         1.29
   3         1.75
   4         7.91
   5         2.00
   6         1.10
   7         5.18
   8        10.00
   9         2.00
  10         6.37
```

Exercise 5-43, Format-Free

Program

```
1              SUM=0.
2              DO7I=1,5
3              READ,X,Y
4              YH=10.*X+6.
5     7        SUM=SUM+(YH-Y)**2
6              PRINT,'SUM OF SQUARES =',SUM
7              STOP
8              END
```

Input

```
3..31.
5..61.
2..27.
7..75.
9..102.
```

Output

```
SUM OF SQUARES =     0.8800000E 02
```

Exercise 5-43, Format

Program

```
 1              SUM=0.
 2              DO7 I=1,5
 3              READ(5,1)X,Y
 4     1        FORMAT(2F5.0)
 5              YH=10.*X+6.
 6     7        SUM=SUM+(YH-Y)**2
 7              WRITE(6,2)SUM
 8     2        FORMAT(' SUM OF SQUARES =',F10.2)
 9              STOP
10              END
```

Input

```
3.     31.
5.     61.
2.     27.
7.     75.
9.     102.
```

Output

```
SUM OF SQUARES =       88.00
```

Exercise 5-48, Format-Free

Program

```
 1              DIMENSION JOUR(6),JHIS(6)
       C        ZERO ARRAYS
 2              DO10 I=1,6
 3              JCUR(I)=0
 4     10       JHIS(I)=0
       C        READ SCORES
 5              DO11 I=1,10
 6              READ,JGAME,JOPP,JSC,JOSC
 7              JOUR(JOPP)=JOUR(JOPP)+JSC
 8     11       JHIS(JOPP)=JHIS(JOPP)+JOSC
       C        WRITE OUTPUT
 9              PRINT,'  OPPONENT  OUR TOTAL   HIS TOTAL'
10              PRINT,'               POINTS      POINTS'
11              DO7 I=1,6
12     7        PRINT,I,JOUR(I),JHIS(I)
13              STOP
14              END
```

Input

1	2	82	91
2	5	88	87
3	1	85	76
4	3	89	80
5	1	95	108
6	2	87	83
7	4	76	68
8	6	83	84
9	1	88	87
10	4	92	76

Output

OPPONENT	OUR TOTAL POINTS	HIS TOTAL POINTS
1	268	271
2	169	174
3	89	80
4	168	144
5	88	87
6	83	84

Exercise 5-48, Format

Program

```
 1              DIMENSION JOUR(6),JHIS(6)
        C       ZERO ARRAYS
 2              DO10I=1,6
 3              JOUR(I)=0
 4       10     JHIS(I)=0
        C       READ SCORES
 5              DO11I=1,10
 6              READ(5,1)JGAME,JOPP,JSC,JOSC
 7        1     FORMAT(4I5)
 8              JOUR(JOPP)=JOUR(JOPP)+JSC
 9       11     JHIS(JOPP)=JHIS(JOPP)+JOSC
        C       WRITE OUTPUT
10              WRITE(6,2)
11        2     FORMAT('OPPONENT  OUR TOTAL  HIS TOTAL'/
               1 13X,'POINTS        POINTS')
12              DO7I=1,6
13        7     WRITE(6,3)I,JOUR(I),JHIS(I)
14        3     FORMAT(I5,2I12)
15              STOP
16              END
```

Input

1	2	82	91
2	5	88	87
3	1	85	76
4	3	89	80

5	1	95	108
6	2	87	83
7	4	76	68
8	6	83	84
9	1	88	87
10	4	92	76

Output

OPPONENT	OUR TOTAL POINTS	HIS TOTAL POINTS
1	268	271
2	169	174
3	89	80
4	168	144
5	88	87
6	83	84

Exercise 5-51, Format-Free

Program

```
1        DIMENSION JD(12)
2        READ,JD
3        READ,MONTH,JDAY,JYEAR
4        JDATE=JD(MONTH)+JDAY
C        CHECK FOR LEAP YEAR
5        IF(MONTH.GT.2.AND.(JYEAR/4)*4.EQ.JYEAR)JDATE=JDATE+1
6        PRINT,' JULIAN DATE IS',JDATE
7        STOP
8        END
```

Input

```
0  31  59  90  120  151  181  212  243  273  3C4  334
3  19  72
```

Output

```
JULIAN DATE IS          79
```

355

Exercise 5-51, Format

Program

```
      1          DIMENSION JD(12)
      2          READ(5,1)JD
      3          READ(5,1)MONTH,JDAY,JYEAR
      4    1     FORMAT(12I4)
      5          JDATE=JD(MONTH)+JDAY
             C   CHECK FOR LEAP YEAR
      6          IF(MONTH.GT.2.AND.(JYEAR/4)*4.EQ.JYEAR)JDATE=JDATE+1
      7          WRITE(6,2)JDATE
      8    2     FORMAT(' JULIAN DATE IS',I5)
      9          STOP
     10          END
```

Input

```
   0  31  59  90 120 151 181 212 243 273 304 334
   3  19  72
```

Output

```
JULIAN DATE IS    79
```

Exercise 5-55, Format-Free

Program

```
      1          DIMENSION A(16),B(16)
      2          READ,(A(I),I=1,16)
      3          DO12I=1,16
      4   12     B(I)=I*A(I)
      5          PRINT,'               A                    B'
      6          DO15I=1,16
      7   15     PRINT,A(I),B(I)
      8          STOP
      9          END
```

Input

1.	2.	3.	4.
5.	6.	7.	8.
9.	1.	2.	3.
4.	5.	6.	7.

Output

A	B
0.1000000E 01	0.1000000E 01
0.2000000E 01	0.4000000E 01
0.3000000E 01	0.9000000E 01
0.4000000E 01	0.1600000E 02
0.5000000E 01	0.2500000E 02
0.6000000E 01	0.3600000E 02
0.7000000E 01	0.4900000E 02
0.8000000E 01	0.6400000E 02
0.9000000E 01	0.8100000E 02
0.1000000E 01	0.1000000E 02
0.2000000E 01	0.2200000E 02
0.3000000E 01	0.3600000E 02
0.4000000E 01	0.5200000E 02
0.5000000E 01	0.7000000E 02
0.6000000E 01	0.9000000E 02
0.7000000E 01	0.1120000E 03

Exercise 5-55, Format

Program

```
 1              DIMENSION A(16),B(16)
 2              READ(5,11)(A(I),I=1,16)
 3       11     FORMAT(4F10.2)
 4              DO12I=1,16
 5       12     B(I)=I*A(I)
 6              WRITE(6,3)
 7        3     FORMAT(8X,'A',9X,'B')
 8              DO15I=1,16
 9       15     WRITE(6,5)A(I),B(I)
10        5     FORMAT(1X,2F10.2)
11              STOP
12              END
```

Input

1.	2.	3.	4.
5.	6.	7.	8.
9.	1.	2.	3.
4.	5.	6.	7.

Output

A	B
1.00	1.00
2.00	4.00
3.00	9.00

4.00	16.00
5.00	25.00
6.00	36.00
7.00	49.00
8.00	64.00
9.00	81.00
1.00	10.00
2.00	22.00
3.00	36.00
4.00	52.00
5.00	70.00
6.00	90.00
7.00	112.00

Exercise 5-58, Format-Free

Program

```
1             DIMENSION A(5),B(5),C(5)
2             READ,(A(I),B(I),I=1,5)
3             DO20I=1,5
4             IF(B(I).GE.A(I))GOTO50
5             C(I)=A(I)-B(I)
6             GOTO20
7        50   C(I)=A(I)+B(I)
8        20   CONTINUE
9             PRINT,'          A           B           C'
10            DO30I=1,5
11       30   PRINT,A(I),B(I),C(I)
12            STOP
13            END
```

Input

0.	5.
10.	7.
6.	6.
7281.00	82.
0.111	0.112

Output

A	B	C
0.0000000E 00	0.5000000E 01	0.5000000E 01
0.1000000E 02	0.7000000E 01	0.3000000E 01
0.6000000E 01	0.6000000E 01	0.1200000E 02
0.7281000E 04	0.8200000E 02	0.7199000E 04
0.1110000E 00	0.1120000E 00	0.2230000E 00

Exercise 5-58, Format

Program

```
1             DIMENSION A(5),B(5),C(5)
2             READ(5,11)(A(I),B(I),I=1,5)
3        11   FORMAT(2F10.2)
4             DO20I=1,5
```

```
 5              IF(B(I).GE.A(I))GOTO50
 6              C(I)=A(I)-B(I)
 7              GOTO20
 8      50      C(I)=A(I)+B(I)
 9      20      CONTINUE
10              WRITE(6,3)
11       3      FORMAT(8X,'A',9X,'B',9X,'C')
12              DO30I=1,5
13      30      WRITE(6,4)A(I),B(I),C(I)
14       4      FORMAT(1X,3F10.2)
15              STOP
16              END
```

Input

```
0.              5.
10.             7.
6.              6.
7281.00         82.
0.111           0.112
```

Output

A	B	C
0.00	5.00	5.00
10.00	7.00	3.00
6.00	6.00	12.00
7281.00	82.00	7199.00
0.11	0.11	0.22

Exercise 5-61, Format-Free

Program

```
 1              DIMENSION A(50)
 2              READ,N
    C           READ ELEMENTS OF VECTOR AND COMPUTE NORM
 3              SUM=0.
 4              DO2I=1,N
 5              READ,A(I)
 6       2      SUM=SUM+A(I)**2
 7              SUM=SQRT(SUM)
    C           DIVIDE EACH ELEMENT BY NORM AND PRINT
 8              DO4I=1,N
 9              A(I)=A(I)/SUM
10       4      PRINT,A(I)
11              STOP
12              END
```

Input

```
   4
2.
1.
0.
3.
```

Output

```
0.5345225E 00
0.2672612E 00
0.0000000E 00
0.8017837E 00
```

Exercise 5-61, Format

Program

```
 1                DIMENSION A(50)
 2                READ(5,1)N
 3        1       FORMAT(I3)
         C        READ ELEMENTS OF VECTOR AND COMPUTE NORM
 4                SUM=0.
 5                DO2I=1,N
 6                READ(5,3)A(I)
 7        3       FORMAT(F10.0)
 8        2       SUM=SUM+A(I)**2
 9                SUM=SQRT(SUM)
         C        DIVIDE EACH ELEMENT BY NORM AND PRINT
10                DO4I=1,N
11                A(I)=A(I)/SUM
12        4       WRITE(6,5)A(I)
13        5       FORMAT(1X,F12.4)
14                STOP
15                END
```

Input

```
   4
2.
1.
0.
3.
```

Output

```
0.5345
0.2673
0.0000
0.8018
```

CHAPTER 6

Exercise 6-1(e)

Subscript must be an integer variable; Subscript must not be a subscripted variable; $K * 3$ should be $3 * K$.

Exercise 6-2(b)

Subscript must be an integer.

Exercise 6-2(f)

As $J = 5$, subscript exceeds size specified in dimension statement.

Exercise 6-3

Program

```
 1        DIMENSION DATA(5,4),TAVG(4),SAVG(5)
   C      READ INPUT DATA
 2        READ(5,1)((DATA(I,J),J=1,4),I=1,5)
 3   1    FORMAT(4F10.1)
   C      COMPUTE TEST AVERAGES
 4        DO2I=1,4
 5        SUM=0.
 6        DO3J=1,5
 7   3    SUM=SUM+DATA(J,I)
 8   2    TAVG(I)=SUM/5.
   C      COMPUTE STUDENT AVERAGES
 9        SUMA=0.
10        DO4I=1,5
11        SUM=0.
12        DO5J=1,4
13   5    SUM=SUM+DATA(I,J)
14        SAVG(I)=SUM/4.
15   4    SUMA=SAVG(I)+SUMA
16        AVG=SUMA/5.
   C      WRITE RESULTS
17        WRITE(6,6)TAVG,SAVG,AVG
18   6    FORMAT('0TEST AVERAGES'/1X,4F10.2/'0STUDENT AVERAGES'/1X,5F10.2/
     1 '0OVERALL AVERAGE'/1X,F10.2)
19        STOP
20        END
```

Input

```
48.6      30.0      62.8      23.4
40.1      40.0      60.1      29.6
63.4      50.0      63.7      31.2
```

```
56.2    60.0    58.2    27.3
71.0    70.0    67.3    26.4
```

Output

```
TEST AVERAGES
   55.86    50.00    62.42    27.58

STUDENT AVERAGES
   41.20    42.45    52.07    50.42    58.67

OVERALL AVERAGE
   48.96
```

Exercise 6-11

Program

```
 1        DIMENSION A(10)
 2        READ(5,11) (A(J),J=1,8)
 3    11  FCRMAT(8F5.1)
 4        DO75I=1,7
 5        DO75J=1,7
 6        K=J+1
 7        IF(ABS(A(J)).LE.ABS(A(K)))GOTO75
 8        DA=A(J)
 9        A(J)=A(K)
10        A(K)=DA
11    75  CONTINUE
12        WRITE(6,101) (A(J),J=1,8)
13   101  FORMAT(1X,8F6.1)
14        STOP
15        END
```

Input

```
50  -250  -130  -975  131  430  74
```

Output

0.0   5.0   7.4 -13.0   13.1 -25.0   43.0 -97.5

Exercise 6-16

Program

```
      C        NANS(1) IS NUMBER OF STUDENTS THAT ANSWERED ALL QUESTIONS
      C        NANS(2) IS NUMBER OF STUDENTS THAT LEFT 1 QUESTION UNANSWERED
      C        NANS(3) IS NUMBER OF STUDENTS THAT LEFT 2 QUESTION UNANSWERED
      C        ETC.
      C        STUDENT'S ANSWERS ARE READ INTO ARRAY JANS
    1          DIMENSION NANS(21),JANS(20)
      C        ZERO ARRAY NANS
    2          DO15I=1,21
    3       15 NANS(I)=0
      C        PROCESS DATA FOR EACH STUDENT
    4          DO16K=1,30
    5          READ(5,1)JANS
    6        1 FORMAT(20I1)
      C        COUNT UNANSWERED QUESTIONS
    7          NUNANS=0
    8          DO17J=1,20
    9       17 IF(JANS(J).EQ.0)NUNANS=NUNANS+1
   10          L=NUNANS+1
   11       16 NANS(L)=NANS(L)+1
   12          WRITE(6,2)
   13        2 FORMAT(' NU-ANSWERS        STUDENTS')
   14          DO20J=1,21
   15          L=J-1
   16       20 WRITE(6,21)L,NANS(J)
   17       21 FORMAT(1X,I7,I13)
   18          STOP
   19          END
```

363

Input

```
4144323432121212234223
4143323433312112342 3
41422324311111
4142323433121212233223
41442231   1212
4144323422121212234223
4144123311121121234222
3144224331121222342
41443 343212122234222
4143323132121212234222
11443234331222234
4144423432121212244333
42443234221222 3
414222343
    44 23   1   2
41443234321212234222
41422132322222234
4144323432221212234223
414422313 12122234222
41343234 21211   3
21422133
4144223422221212234221
3244223432122222234333
4124323   12222234222
414 32343 12122234
41443234321212234222
41443234321
34  22 133 1224
4244323422121212234422
4144323421121212234223
```

Output

NO-ANSWERS	STUDENTS
0	13
1	3
2	1
3	3
4	0
5	2
6	1
7	1
8	1
9	2
10	0
11	1
12	1
13	0

14 1
15 0
16 0
17 0
18 0
19 0
20 0

Exercise 6-20

Program

```
 1        DIMENSICN ALARG(12),DATA(8)
 2        DO7 I=1,12
 3        READ(5,1)DATA
 4      1 FORMAT(8F5.0)
 5        AMX=DATA(1)
 6        DO8 J=2,8
 7      8 IF(DATA(J).GT.AMX)AMX=DATA(J)
 8      7 ALARG(I)=AMX
 9        WRITE(6,2) ALARG
10      2 FORMAT(1X,12F6.2)
11        STOP
12        END
```

Input

1.2	5.3	2.1	4.6	2.7	8.1	9.1	1.4
5.1	4.2	7.4	1.2	3.1	5.2	4.0	1.1
2.1	1.2	2.0	1.7	0.1	1.5	0.4	1.4
5.1	4.1	2.1	3.1	6.5	4.8	2.0	0.2
1.1	2.4	5.1	1.2	3.0	2.3	3.9	1.8
8.9	5.6	2.1	9.9	5.4	2.0	1.7	1.0
1.2	3.2	5.4	6.7	8.3	5.1	0.9	2.1
2.5	4.1	3.0	2.7	2.6	0.9	2.8	1.0
2.1	4.1	5.9	6.4	5.7	3.2	1.0	2.9

```
1.2   4.5   3.1   7.4   1.2   5.9   6.3   1.7
2.4   5.1   6.4   2.0   3.1   4.2   1.9   0.1
2.0   1.4   5.3   1.2   6.4   5.1   7.9   2.4
```

Output

```
9.10   7.40   2.10   6.50   5.10   9.90   8.30   4.10   6.40   7.40   6.40   7.90
```

Exercise 6-24

Program

```
1          DIMENSION ISEAT(38,6)
2          READ(5,1) ((ISEAT(I,J),J=1,6),I=1,38)
3    1     FORMAT(6I2)
4          NEMPTY=0
5          DO10I=1,38
6          DO10J=1,6
7    10    IF(ISEAT(I,J).EQ.0)NEMPTY=NEMPTY+1
8          WRITE(6,2)NEMPTY
9    2     FORMAT(1X,I5," EMPTY SEATS")
10         STOP
11         END
```

Input

```
1 0 1 1 0 1
1 0 1 1 0 1
1 1 0 1 1 1
1 1 1 1 1 1
1 0 1 0 1 1
1 0 1 0 1 1
1 1 0 1 1 1
1 0 0 1 0 1
1 1 0 0 0 1
1 0 0 0 0 1
1 0 0 1 0 0
```

```
1  0  1  0   0  1
1  0  0  1   1  1
1  0  1  1   0  1
0  0  0  1   1  1
1  0  1  0   1  1
1  1  0  0   0  1
1  1  0  0   0  1
1  1  0  0   0  1
1  1  0  1   1  1
1  0  1  0   1  1
1  0  0  0   0  0
1  1  0  0   0  1
1  1  0  1   1  1
1  0  0  1   0  1
1  0  0  1   1  1
1  1  0  0   0  1
1  1  0  0   0  1
1  0  1  0   1  1
1  0  1  1   0  1
1  0  1  1   0  1
1  0  0  1   0  1
1  0  0  1   0  1
1  0  1  1   0  1
1  0  1  0   1  1
1  0  1  0   1  1
1  0  1 -1  -1 -1
1  1  0 -1  -1 -1
```

Output

```
88 EMPTY SEATS
```

CHAPTER 7

Exercise 7-3

Program

```
 1          DIMENSION LOCATE(12,8)
     C      READ THREE ADDRESSES
 2    3     READ(5,2) ((LOCATE(I,J),J=1,8),I=1,12)
 3    2     FORMAT(8A4)
     C      WRITE THREE ADDRESSES
 4          DO4I=1,3
 5          M=I+8
 6    4     WRITE(6,5)((LOCATE(K,J),J=1,8),K=I,M,4)
 7    5     FORMAT(2X,3(4X,8A4))
 8          WRITE(6,6)
 9    6     FORMAT('0')
10          GOTO3
11          END
```

Input

```
JOHN ADAMS
503 CARDINAL STREET
PORT ALLEN, LOUISIANA
```

TAR ZAN
701 VINE STREET
JUNGLE, ARKANSAS

TING A LING
DING DONG STREET
PLENTYBELLS, IDAHO

SKIP HAPPY
5000712 SHORT STREET
INNSVILLE, CALIFORNIA

RONALD MATHEWS
1717 CRANBERRY LANE
LUKEFALLS, NEBRASKA

SUSAN STUDKUP
9010 COLLAR AVE.
RICHVILLE, VIRGINIA

Output

JOHN ADAMS
503 CARDINAL STREET
PORT ALLEN, LOUISIANA

SKIP HAPPY
5000712 SHORT STREET
INNSVILLE, CALIFORNIA

TAR ZAN
701 VINE STREET
JUNGLE, ARKANSAS

RONALD MATHEWS
1717 CRANBERRY LANE
LUKEFALLS, NEBRASKA

TING A LING
DING DONG STREET
PLENTYBELLS, IDAHO

SUSAN STUDKUP
9010 COLLAR AVE.
RICHVILLE, VIRGINIA

Exercise 7-9

Program

```
1       DATA MONYAD.NUMSA.KPROFO/2000.200.0/
C       WRITE HEADINGS
```

```
2        WRITE(6,1)
3    1   FORMAT(6X,'ADVERTISING',10X,'UNITS SOLD',10X,'NET PROFIT')
     C   COMPUTE PROFIT AND WRITE RESULTS
4        KPROF=300*NUMSA-MONYAD-10000
5        WRITE(6,2)MONYAD,NUMSA,KPROF
6    2   FORMAT(9X,'$',I5,I19,14X,'$',I5)
     C   STOP IF PROFIT DECREASES
7        IF(KPROF.LT.KPROFO)STOP
     C   UPDATE PARAMETERS TO NEW LEVEL
8        NUMSA=(12*NUMSA+5)/10
9        MONYAD=2*MONYAD
10       KPROFO=KPROF
11       GOTO3
12       END
```

Input   None

Output

ADVERTISING	UNITS SOLD	NET PROFIT
$ 2000	200	$48000
$ 4000	240	$58000
$ 8000	288	$68400
$16000	346	$77800
$32000	415	$82500
$64000	498	$75400

Exercise 7-14

Program

```
1    C   DIMENSION WT(10)
         READ INPUT AND CALCULATE TOTAL WEIGHT AND SUM
2        SUM=0.
3        DO1I=1,4
4        READ(5,2)N1,N2,N3
```

369

```
5       WT(I)=N1*5+N2*10+N3*25
6 1     SUM=SUM+WT(I)
7       AVG=SUM/4.
  C     CALCULATE DIFFERENCE AND PRINT
8       WRITE(6,6)
9       DO3I=1,4
10      DIFF=WT(I)-AVG
11 3    WRITE(6,4)I,WT(I),DIFF
12      WRITE(6,5) AVG
13      STOP
14 2    FORMAT(3I3)
15 4    FORMAT(1X,I3,F9.2,F16.2)
16 5    FORMAT('0AVERAGE =',F10.2)
17 6    FORMAT(' TEST   WEIGHT       DIFF. FROM AVG.')
18      END
```

Input

```
12  1  0
 6  2  1
 8  1  1
 0  2  2
```

Output

TEST	WEIGHT	DIFF. FROM AVG.
1	70.00	-2.50
2	75.00	2.50
3	75.00	2.50
4	70.00	-2.50

AVERAGE =   72.50

Exercise 7-15

Program

```
1       DATA BVALUE,AVALUE/1000.,1000./
  C     WRITE HEADINGS
```

```
2          WRITE(6,1)
3    1      FORMAT('  YEAR        DOUBLE DECLINING        BEGINNING        STRAIGHT-L
     1INE    BEGINNING'/10X,'BALANCE DEPRECIATION    BOOK  VALUE        DEPR
     2ECIATION    BOOK  VALUE')
4          DEPSL=BVALUE/5.
     C     DO FOR FIVE YEARS
5          DO2I=1,5
     C     COMPUTE DEPRECIATIONS AND WRITE RESULTS
6          DEPCD=0.4*AVALUE
7          WRITE(6,3)I,DEPDD,AVALUE,DEPSL,BVALUE
8    3      FORMAT(2X,I2,12X,'$',F6.2,11X,'$',F7.2,9X,'$',F6.2,8X,'$',F7.2)
9          BVALUE=BVALUE-DEPSL
10   2      AVALUE=AVALUE-DEPDD
11         STOP
12         END
```

Input None

Output

YEAR	DOUBLE DECLINING BALANCE DEPRECIATION	BEGINNING BOOK VALUE	STRAIGHT-LINE DEPRECIATION	BEGINNING BOOK VALUE
1	$400.00	$1000.00	$200.00	$1000.00
2	$240.00	$ 600.00	$200.00	$ 800.00
3	$144.00	$ 360.00	$200.00	$ 600.00
4	$ 86.40	$ 216.00	$200.00	$ 400.00
5	$ 51.84	$ 129.60	$200.00	$ 200.00

Exercise 7-20

Program

```
1          DIMENSION T(6,5)
2          DATA T/1.023,1.068,1.113,1.158,1.202,1.247,
     *       1.018,1.061,1.104,1.148,1.192,1.235,
     *       1.010,1.052,1.094,1.137,1.181,1.224,
     *       0.993,1.035,1.077,1.120,1.162,1.205,
```

371

```
*      0.980,1.022,1.064,1.107,1.149,1.191/
3      WRITE(6,2) ((T(I,J),J=1,5),I=1,6)
4   2  FORMAT(24X,'TEMPERATURE, DEG F'//16X,'50',6X,'86',5X,'122',
      *5X,'176',5X,'212'//11X,'*',4X,5('*',7X)//8X,'2 *',F7.3,4F8.3//
      *8X,'6 *',F7.3,4F8.3//' PER'/7X,'10 *',F7.3,4F8.3/' CENT'/
      *7X,'14 *',F7.3,4F8.3//' NAOH'/7X,'18 *',F7.3,4F8.3//7X,'22 *',
      *F7.3,4F8.3//13X,'(SOURCE - INT. CRIT. TABLES, VOL. III,'/
      *16X,'PAGE 79)')
5      STOP
6      END
Input   None
Output
```

TEMPERATURE, DEG F

	50	86	122	176	212
*	*	*	*	*	*
2 *	1.023	1.018	1.010	0.993	0.980
6 *	1.068	1.061	1.052	1.035	1.022
PER					
10 *	1.113	1.104	1.094	1.077	1.064
CENT					
14 *	1.158	1.148	1.137	1.120	1.107
NAOH					
18 *	1.202	1.192	1.181	1.162	1.145
22 *	1.247	1.235	1.224	1.205	1.191

(SOURCE - INT. CRIT. TABLES, VOL. III, PAGE 79)

Exercise 7-23

Program

```
 1          DATA DENSW,HT,DIA,WTCON,WTDRY,WTWET/62.4,0.75,0.333,1.04/
 2          READ(5,1)WTDRY,WTWET
 3          VOID=(WTWET-WTDRY)/DENSW
 4          VOL=3.1416*HT*(0.5*DIA)**2
 5          VOIDFR=VOID/VOL
 6          DENS=(WTDRY-WTCON)/(VOL-VOID)
 7          WRITE(6,2)DIA,HT,WTCON,WTDRY,WTWET,VOIDFR,DENS
 8          STOP
 9    1     FORMAT(2F10.0)
10    2     FORMAT('1DIMENSIONS OF CONTAINER -'/6X,'DIAMETER',F15.4,' FT'/
     *   6X,'HEIGHT',F15.4,' FT'/6X,'WEIGHT',F15.4,' LB'/
     *   ' WEIGHT WITHOUT WATER',F15.4/' WEIGHT WITH WATER',F15.4/
     *   ' VOID FRACTION',F15.4/' DENSITY OF MATERIAL',F15.4/
     *   ' LBS/CU. FT.')
11          END
```

Input

```
7.12      8.30
```

Output

```
DIMENSIONS OF CONTAINER -
      DIAMETER          0.3330 FT
      HEIGHT            0.7500 FT
      WEIGHT            1.0400 LB
 WEIGHT WITHOUT WATER       7.1200
 WEIGHT WITH WATER          8.3000
 VOID FRACTION              0.2895
 DENSITY OF MATERIAL      131.0096 LBS/CU. FT.
```

Exercise 7-27

Program

```
C     NANS(1) IS NUMBER OF STUDENTS THAT ANSWERED ALL QUESTIONS
C     NANS(2) IS NUMBER OF STUDENTS THAT LEFT 1 QUESTION UNANSWERED
C     NANS(3) IS NUMBER OF STUDENTS THAT LEFT 2 QUESTION UNANSWERED
```

```
        C       ETC.
        C       STUDENT'S ANSWERS ARE READ INTO ARRAY JANS
 1              DIMENSION NANS(21),JANS(20)
 2              DATA IBLK/' '/
        C       ZERO ARRAY NANS
 3              DO15I=1,21
 4      15      NANS(I)=0
        C       PROCESS DATA FOR EACH STUDENT
 5              DO16K=1,30
 6              READ(5,1)JANS
 7      1       FORMAT(20A1)
        C       COUNT UNANSWERED QUESTIONS
 8              NUNANS=0
 9              DO17J=1,20
10      17      IF(JANS(J).EQ.IBLK)NUNANS=NUNANS+1
11              L=NUNANS+1
12      16      NANS(L)=NANS(L)+1
13              WRITE(6,2)
14      2       FORMAT(' NO-ANSWERS      STUDENTS')
15              DO20J=1,21
16              L=J-1
17      20      WRITE(6,21)L,NANS(J)
18      21      FORMAT(1X,I7,I13)
19              STOP
20              END
```

Input

```
TTTTTFFTTTTTFFFFFFFF
TTT  FFTFFTTFF FFFFT
TTTFF FF  TT  F    T
TTTTTFFTTFTTFFTFFFFF
TTT TTTFTTFFFFFFFFFF
FTTFTFFTTFTTFFTFFFTF
TTTTFFFTTTTTFFFFFFFF
TTFTTFFTTFFFTTTF
FTFFTTFTFTFFFFFFFTTFF
TTFTTF TTTFTFFFTFFFF
TTTTTFFTTFTTFFFT
TT  F TFF
TTTFTFFTTFTTTFTFFFFF
TTFTTTTTTTTTFFFFFTTF
FTTTTF
FTTFFTTFFFFFFFFFFFFF
FFFFFFFFFFFFFFFFFFFF
TTFTT FTTFTTFFFFFFFF
TFFTFFFTFFTTFFTFFTFF
TFFFTFFTTTFFFFFFFFFF
TTTTTFFTT TTFFFTFFFF
```

```
TTFTTFFTTTFFFFFFFFFF
TT   FFTFFTTFF
TTFFT FTTT TFFFFFFF
TTF    TTTTTFFFFFFFFF
TTTT FFTTTFFFFFFFFFFF
TTTTTFFTTTTTFFFFF
TTTTTFFFTTFTFFFFFFFFF
TTTTTFFT FFFFFFFFFFF
TTTTTFFT TFFFFFFFFFF
TTTFTFFTFTTFFFFTFFFF
```

Output

NO-ANSWERS	STUDENTS
0	13
1	7
2	0
3	3
4	3
5	0
6	0
7	0
8	0
9	2
10	0
11	0
12	0
13	0
14	2
15	0
16	0
17	0
18	0
19	0
20	0

Exercise 7-29

Program

```
1         DIMENSION IA(80)
2         DATA ICOM,IPER,IBLK/',','.',' '/
3         READ(5,1)IA
4    1    FORMAT(80A1)
5         N=0
6         DO2I=1,80
7         IF(IA(I).EQ.IPER)GOTO3
8         IF(IA(I).EQ.ICOM.OR.IA(I).EQ.IBLK)GOTO2
9         N=N+1
10   2    CONTINUE
11   3    WRITE(6,4)N
```

```
12    4    FORMAT(' SENTENCE CONTAINS',I3,' CHARACTERS')
13         STOP
14         END
```

Input

```
AN IMPORTANT CHARACTERISTIC OF DIGITAL COMPUTERS IS THEIR INCREDIBLE SPEED.
```

Output

```
SENTENCE CONTAINS 65 CHARACTERS
```

Exercise 7-34

Program

```
1          DIMENSION IA(800),N(12)
2          DATA N/12*0/
3          DATA IBLK,IPER,ICOM/' ','.',','/
4          READ(5,1)IA
5     1    FORMAT(80A1)
6          I=1
7     3    IF(I.GT.800)GOTO4
8          IF(IA(I).NE.IBLK)GOTO2
9          I=I+1
10         GOTO3
11    2    NC=1
12    6    I=I+1
13         IF(IA(I).EQ.IBLK)GOTO5
14         IF(IA(I).EQ.IPER)GOTO5
15         IF(IA(I).EQ.ICOM)GOTO5
16         NC=NC+1
17         GOTO6
18    5    IF(NC.GT.12)NC=12
19         N(NC)=N(NC)+1
20         I=I+1
21         GOTO3
```

```
22    4    WRITE(6,7)(I,N(I),I=1,12)
23    7    FORMAT('1WORD LENGTH DISTRIBUTION',''0CHS./WORD    OCCURRENCES'/
           $ 11(1X,I5,I16/),1X,I5,' OR MORE',I8)
24         STCP
25         END
```

Input

INSTEAD CF PROCESSING A SINGLE SENTENCE, SUPPOSE WE PROCESS A PARAGRAPH. THE PARAGRAPH WILL BE PUNCHED ON A MAXIMUM OF TEN CARDS AS ILLUSTRATED IN THE ACCOMPANYING FIGURE. A BLANK CHARACTER ALWAYS FOLLOWS THE DECIMAL POINT, AND NO HYPHENATED WORDS WILL BE USED. FOR THIS EXERCISE, THE PARAGRAPH SHOULC BE READ INTO A SINGLE ARRAY OF EIGHT HUNDRED ELEMENTS. ONE CHARACTER TO THE ELEMENT. COMPUTE THE AVERAGE NUMBER OF WORDS IN THE SENTENCES IN THE PARAGRAPH ANC PRINT THE ANSWER TO TWO DECIMAL PLACES.

Output

WORD LENGTH DISTRIBUTION

CHS./WCRD	OCCURRENCES
1	5
2	16
3	15
4	6
5	8
6	8
7	12
8	3
9	7
10	2
11	1
12 CR MORE	1

Exercise 7-37

Program

```
 1        DIMENSION IA(80)
 2        DATA IBLK,IPER/' ','.'/
 3        NWCS=0
 4        NSEN=0
 5        DO7I=1,10
 6        READ(5,1)IA
 7   1    FORMAT(80A1)
 8        JW=0
 9        J=1
10   5    IF(IA(J).NE.IPER)GOTO2
11        IF(JW.NE.0)NWDS=NWDS+1
12        NSEN=NSEN+1
13        GOTO3
14   2    IF(IA(J).EQ.IBLK)GOTO4
15        JW=1
16        GOTO3
17   4    IF(JW.EQ.1)NWCS=NWDS+1
18        JW=0
19   3    J=J+1
20        IF(J.LE.80)GOTO5
21   7    IF(JW.EQ.1)NWCS=NWDS+1
22        AVG=FLOAT(NWDS)/FLOAT(NSEN)
23        WRITE(6,6) AVG
24   6    FORMAT('0AVERAGE WORDS PER SENTENCE =',F10.2)
25        STOP
26        END
```

Input

INSTEAD OF PROCESSING A SINGLE SENTENCE, SUPPOSE WE PROCESS A
PARAGRAPH. THE PARAGRAPH WILL BE PUNCHED ON A MAXIMUM OF TEN CARDS AS

378

ILLUSTRATED IN THE ACCOMPANYING FIGURE. A BLANK CHARACTER ALWAYS FOLLOWS THE
DECIMAL POINT, AND NO HYPHENATED WORDS WILL BE USED. FOR THIS EXERCISE, THE
PARAGRAPH SHOULD BE READ INTO A SINGLE ARRAY OF EIGHT HUNDRED ELEMENTS, ONE
CHARACTER TO THE ELEMENT. COMPUTE THE AVERAGE NUMBER OF WORDS IN THE SENTENCES
IN THE PARAGRAPH AND PRINT THE ANSWER TO TWO DECIMAL PLACES.

Output

```
AVERAGE WORDS PER SENTENCE =     17.80
```

Exercise 7-43

Program

```
 1          DIMENSION IDIG(10),IA(80)
 2          DATA IBLK,IDIG,IPLS,IMIN/' ','.','+',',','-','0','1','2','3','4','5','6','7','8',
           1 '9','+','.','-'/
 3          READ(5,1)IA
 4        1 FORMAT(80A1)
 5          IDG=0
 6          NUM=0
 7          J=0
 8        3 J=J+1
 9          IF(J.GT.80)GOTO2
10          IF(IA(J).EQ.IBLK)GOTO3
11          IS=+1
12          IF(IA(J).NE.IMIN)GOTO4
13          IF=-1
14          J=J+1
15          GOTO5
16        4 IF(IA(J).EQ.IPLS)J=J+1
17        5 IF(J.GT.80)GOTO6
18          DO7I=1,10
19          IF(IA(J).EQ.IDIG(I))GOTO8
20        7 CONTINUE
21          IF(IA(J).NE.IBLK)GOTO9
```

```
22        IF(IDG.EQ.0)GOTO9
23   12   NUM=NUM*IS
24        WRITE(6,10)NUM
25   10   FORMAT('0VALUE =',I10)
26        STOP
27    2   WRITE(6,11)
28   11   FORMAT('0BLANK CARD')
29        STOP
30    6   IF(IDG.NE.0)GOTO12
31    9   WRITE(6,13)IA,J
32   13   FORMAT(6X,80A1/6X,'INVALID CHARACTER NEAR COLUMN',I3)
33        STOP
34    8   NUM=NUM*10+I-1
35        IDG=1
36        J=J+1
37        GOTO5
38        END
```

Input

+154678

Output

VALUE =   154678

Exercise 7-47

Program

```
1    DIMENSION IA(9)
2    DATA JR/'R'/
3    READ(5,1)IA
4  1  FORMAT(9A1)
5    DO7I=1,9
6    IF(IA(I).EQ.JR)GOTO10
7  7  CONTINUE
8    WRITE(6,20)IA
```

```
 9       20      FORMAT('YOU SHOULD NOT EAT OYSTERS IN ',9A1)
10               STOP
11       10      WRITE(6,21)IA
12       21      FORMAT(' YOU MAY EAT OYSTERS IN ',9A1)
13               STOP
14               END
```

Input

```
SEPTEMBER
```

Output

```
YOU MAY EAT OYSTERS IN SEPTEMBER
```

Exercise 7-52

Program

```
 1               N=0
 2        3      READ(5,1)ISEC,ISEX,ISTND
 3               IF(ISEC.EQ.0)GOTO9
 4               IF(ISEC.EQ.8)N=N+1
 5               GOTO3
 6        9      WRITE(6,2)N
 7               STOP
 8        1      FORMAT(I2,2A2)
 9        2      FORMAT(1X,I5,' STUDENTS IN SECTION 8')
10               END
```

Input

```
1  MSO
1  MSO
8  FSO
3  FJR
8  FSO
8  MSR
1  FSO
2  MFR
1  MJR
8  MSO
1  FSO
```

Output

```
4 STUDENTS IN SECTION 8
```

Exercise 7-57

Program

```
 1               INTEGER DEPT,COURSE,SECT,REQ,DEPTO,COURSO
 2               ISTOP=0
 3               READ(5,1)DEPT,COURSE,SECT,REQ,MAX
 4        1      FORMAT(A4,I4,I2,2I3)
 5       20      DEPTO=DEPT
 6               COURSO=COURSE
 7               NSECT=1
 8               SPCT=FLOAT(REQ)/FLOAT(MAX)
```

```
 9      10      READ(5,1,END=99)DEPT,COURSE,SECT,REQ,MAX
10              IF(DEPTO.NE.DEPT)GOTO5
11              IF(COURSE.NE.COURSO)GOTO5
12              SPCT=SPCT+FLOAT(REQ)/FLOAT(MAX)
13              NSECT=NSECT+1
14              GOTO10
15      99      ISTOP=1
16      5       AVG=100.*SPCT/NSECT
17              WRITE(6,2)DEPTO,COURSO,AVG
18      2       FORMAT(1X,A4,1X,A4,F10.2)
19              IF(ISTOP.EQ.1)STOP
20              GOTO20
21              END
```

CHAPTER 8

Exercise 8-3

Program

```
 1              UPDATE(X)=1.1015*X-PAYMNT
 2              READ(5,1)PRIN,PAYMNT
 3              DO2I=1,10
 4      2       PRIN=UPDATE(PRIN)
 5              WRITE(6,3)PRIN
 6              STOP
 7      1       FORMAT(2F10.2)
 8      3       FORMAT(1X,F10.2)
 9              END
```

Input

```
100.        10.
```

Output

```
102.41
```

Exercise 8-6

```
 1              YH(X)=10.*X+6.
 2              SUMSQ=0.
 3              DO1I=1,5
 4              READ(5,2)X,Y
 5      2       FORMAT(2F5.2)
 6      1       SUMSQ=SUMSQ+(YH(X)-Y)**2
 7              WRITE(6,3)SUMSQ
 8      3       FORMAT(' SUM OF SQUARES =',F10.2)
 9              STOP
10              END
```

Input

```
3.      31.
5.      61.
2.      27.
7.      75.
9.      102.
```

Output

```
 SUM OF SQUARES =        88.00
```

Exercise 8-10

Program

```
  1              DIMENSION WT(10),N(3)
      C          READ WEIGHTS AND COMPUTE TOTAL WEIGHT
  2              SUM=0.
  3              DO1 I=1,4
  4              READ(5,2) N
  5              WT(I)=WEIGHT(N)
  6       1      SUM=SUM+WT(I)
  7              AVG=SUM/4.
      C          COMPUTE DIFFERENCES AND WRITE
  8              WRITE(6,6)
  9              DO3I=1,4
 10              DIFF=WT(I)-AVG
 11       3      WRITE(6,4)I,WT(I),DIFF
 12              WRITE(6,5)AVG
 13              STOP
 14       2      FORMAT(3I3)
 15       4      FORMAT(1X,I3,F9.2,F16.2)
 16       5      FORMAT('0AVERAGE =',F10.2)
 17       6      FORMAT('TEST   WEIGHT   DIFF. FROM AVG.')
 18              END

 19              FUNCTION WEIGHT(N)
 20              DIMENSION N(3)
 21              WEIGHT=5*N(1)+10*N(2)+25*N(3)
 22              RETURN
 23              END
```

Input

```
 12    1    0
  6    2    1
  8    1    1
  0    2    2
```

Output

```
 TEST     WEIGHT        DIFF. FROM AVG.
   1      70.00            -2.50
   2      75.00             2.50
   3      75.00             2.50
   4      70.00            -2.50

 AVERAGE =        72.50
```

Exercise 8-17

Program

```
  1              DIMENSION A(51)
  2              READ(5,1)N,(A(I),I=1,N),A(N+1),B
  3       1      FORMAT(I5/(F10.0))
```

```
4               R=FUNC(A,N,B)
5               WRITE(6,2)B,R
6         2     FORMAT('0F(',F10.4,') =',F15.4)
7               STOP
8               END


9               FUNCTION FUNC(A,N,B)
10              DIMENSION A(51)
11              FUNC=A(1)
12              DO1I=1,N
13        1     FUNC=FUNC+A(I+1)*B**I
14              RETURN
15              END
```

Input

```
      4
1.
1.2
1.7
1.9
0.8
2.2
```

Output

```
 F( 2.2000) =    50.8396
```

Exercise 8-18

Program

```
1               DIMENSION D(20)
2               READ(5,9)AMT,NYEARS
3               CALL DEP(AMT,NYEARS,D)
4               WRITE(6,4) (I,D(I),I=1,NYEARS)
5               STOP
6         4     FORMAT('1 YEAR DEPRECIATION'/(1X,I5,F14.3))
7         9     FORMAT(F10.2,I4)
8               END


9               SUBROUTINE DEP(AMT,N,D)
10              DIMENSION D(20)
     C          COMPUTE SUM OF THE YEARS DIGITS
11              K=0
12              DO1I=1,N
13        1     K=K+1
14              S=K
     C          COMPUTE YEARLY DEPRECIATION
15              DO2J=1,N
16              T=N+1-J
17        2     D(J)=AMT*T/S
18              RETURN
19              END
```

Input

50000. 10

Output

YEAR	DEPRECIATION
1	50000.000
2	45000.000
3	40000.000
4	35000.000
5	30000.000
6	25000.000
7	20000.000
8	15000.000
9	10000.000
10	5000.000

INDEX